A PROBLEM-SOLVING
APPROACH
TO
PENSION FUNDING
AND
VALUATION

Second Edition

William H. Aitken, FSA, FCIA, EA
Professor Emeritus
University of Waterloo

ACTEX Publications
Winsted, Connecticut

Requests for permission should be addressed to
ACTEX Publications
P.O. Box 974
Winsted, CT 06098

Manufactured in the United States of America

10 9 8 7 6 5 4 3

Cover Design by MUF

The ankh was the ancient Egyptian symbol for life.
Its use on the cover of this text symbolizes the payment of
pension income for life.

Library of Congress Cataloging-in-Publication Data

Aitken, William H., 1927-
        A problem-solving approach to pension funding and
valuation / William H. Aitken.
            p.   cm.
        Includes bibliographical references and index.
        ISBN 1-56698-200-6
        1.   Pensions--Costs--Mathematics.   2.   Pensions--
Valuation-Mathematics.   I. Title.
HD7105.A37   1994
331.25'2'0151--dc20   94-9260
                                                          CIP

ISBN: 1-56698-200-6

Contents

Preface

Over the past twenty-five years, several efforts have been made to produce a high-quality introductory textbook covering the mathematics of pension funding and valuation. Although all of the resulting texts have had considerable merit, it does not appear that any one of them has been seen as totally satisfactory.

This work, first published in 1994, has been guided by the principle that many students, particularly at an introductory level, learn best by doing. The defining characteristic of this text is a large number of worked examples. Each unit is introduced with enough explanatory material to allow the reader to move quickly to problem solving. It is this basic feature that gives the text its name. The first mention of each technical term is indicated in bold type.

In addition to the explanatory material and worked examples, the text contains non-numerical discussion questions intended to provoke further thinking about the material. Finally, each major section contains several exercises for the reader to use as reinforcement of the learning attained in that section. Numerical answers to the exercises are given in the text. A separate solutions manual, containing answers to the discussion questions and detailed solutions to the exercises, is also available.

The text presumes a knowledge of basic actuarial mathematics, as contained in such textbooks as Parmenter [9], Jordan [6], or Bowers, *et al.* [5]. In particular, the reader is presumed to understand multiple-decrement theory, multiple life functions (including joint and last-survivor functions), and concepts of reserving.

The text is organized into eight chapters. The first chapter introduces the reader to pension plans themselves, and gives an overview of the remaining topics. Chapters 2-4 cover the standard cost methods (individual methods in Chapters 2 and 3, and aggregate methods in Chapter 4). Chapters 5-7 cover, respectively, gain and loss analysis, plan changes and ancillary benefits, and options and assets. Chapter 8 presents an analysis and summary of the earlier material intended to enhance understanding on a more conceptual level. The text concludes with answers to the exercises, a bibliography, an index to notation (giving the page on which each symbol first appears), and a subject index.

Many people have contributed to the completion of this project, and their assistance is gratefully acknowledged. Excellent contributions were made by Mary Weiler, Nandanee Basdeo, Hoque Sharif, and Ali Zaker-Shahrak. Credit and appreciation for the improved typesetting reflected in the second edition go to Marilyn Baleshiski, at ACTEX Publications.

Early drafts of the first edition were made available to candidates for the EA-1B exam of the Joint Board for the Enrolment of Actuaries in May 1993 and May 1994, and to candidates for the Course 210 exam of the Society of Actuaries in November 1993. We received many valuable comments from this exposure, and we wish to thank these candidates for their help.

The first edition was reviewed by an industry task force consisting of Harold Brownlee, FSA, Richard Daskais, FSA, Ralph Garfield, ASA, Ph.D., and Terry Vaughan, Ph.D., and chaired by Geoffrey Crofts, FSA, then of the University of Hartford. Additional review was provided by Professor Kelley McKeating, ASA, of the University of Iowa, and Professor Srinivasa Ramanujam, ASA, EA, Ph.D., of the College of Insurance.

Special thanks goes to Richard J. Barney, FSA, EA, of Mutual of New York, who reviewed the text on behalf of the Society of Actuaries. His insights and suggestions over the past three years have strengthened the text in many ways.

Numerous improvements have been made in the second edition, with many of them arising from suggestions made by students and other readers. Several symbols have been changed to improve clarity, and certain unnecessary symbols were deleted altogether. Some practical observations, historical notes, summaries (*e.g.*, Section 4.6), and alternate solutions to examples have been added. There are also additional discussion questions and exercises. Thanks to Leslie N. Taylor, FCIA, FIA, for much of the improvement in Chapter 8.

Notwithstanding the review the text has received, there are no doubt some errors and inadequacies remaining. The author and publisher would appreciate hearing from readers in this regard.

We hope that you the reader will find this text of great value in your pursuit of an understanding of the world of pension mathematics.

Waterloo, Ontario, Canada
April, 1996

William H. Aitken, FSA, FCIA, EA

To my wife, Lillian

Chapter 1

Pension Benefits

For a retired person, the prospect of no money coming in each month is not at all attractive. However, a *continuation* of the same financial standard of living after retirement as before represents an attractive and important objective. Attaining this objective requires planning, assumptions, funding, and continuous monitoring. Falling short of this objective suggests a decline in the standard of living of the retired person, whereas exceeding this objective suggests overly generous employer contributions and tax assistance.

1.1 Introduction

The rapid growth in pension plans since 1940 has resulted in pensions being a significant factor in the financial markets, where billions of dollars of pension assets are invested, and in personal financial security where, for many, the pension will become the largest asset. This rapid growth can be attributed to several factors, including the following:

growth of pensions can be attributed to

- Employer participation
- Union demands
- A strong post-war economy
- Government legislation
- Tax assistance

Moreover, the need for personal retirement savings has increased due to factors such as the decline of the extended family, the change in attitude toward older workers, and increased competition for employees. Today we enter the work force at a later age. We leave earlier. We live longer. Therefore, we must accrue more retirement funds over a shorter period of time.

For most retirees there are three sources of retirement income, which include (a) retirement income from government sources, (b) individual income from individual savings, and (c) income from pension plans, generally employer sponsored. In turn, employer plans can be categorized as (a) single employer, (b) multiple employer, and (c) multi-employer.

source of retirement income

The most common arrangement is the single employer plan. One employer creates, administers, and contributes to the operation of the plan for the employees. Multiple employer plans generally result when employers have small numbers of employees. Since a minimum administration cost is unavoidable, a small number of employees will result in an administration cost per participant which is unmanageably large; the cost per participant can be reduced by employers banding together to share expenses. Multi-employer plans are usually negotiated by unions. This arrangement is effective for mobile employees who can move from job to job within an industry, without the concern of losing pension rights.

1.2 Design of Pension Plans

There are two basic types of pension plans, which are (a) defined contribution plans, and (b) defined benefit plans. The fundamental difference, as the names suggest, is the defined parameter.

Defined contribution plans define in advance what participants and plan sponsors will contribute each year. The benefit received by a participant at retirement is a function of the contributions made to his account and the fund's investment return during, and at the end of, the accrual period. The participant in a defined contribution plan bears the investment risk, for better or for worse.

Defined benefit plans use a formula to determine in advance the amount of the retirement benefit, although this may not be accurately known until retirement. Again, the participant's contributions, if any, are clearly defined. The plan sponsor's contributions vary with actual experience in order to accrue the amount of the defined benefit at retirement.

1.2.1 Defined Benefits   _Design type_

A common benefit is a **unit benefit per year of service**. One example of a ①
retirement benefit would be $40 per month at retirement for each year of
service. This design is very popular with unions, due to ease of understanding the benefit and negotiating benefit improvements. When a union
is bargaining, an improvement in the pension benefit can be effected by
merely changing the unit amount from $40 to, say, $45 per month. This
type of benefit improvement is usually retroactive, thereby providing protection to workers from preretirement inflation. Another example would be
a pension benefit of 1.5% of compensation (or salary) for each year of
service, where the compensation can be career average compensation or the
average compensation over the last few years of service. Compensation
generally increases with time due to merit and inflation. The closer the
averaging period is to retirement, the more is the protection from preretirement inflation.

These several ways to define the pension benefit are illustrated in the
following example.

EXAMPLE 1.1

Suppose a participant has 30 years of service, career average compensation
of $40,000, and final average compensation of $100,000. Let B_r denote
the annual pension benefit, payable monthly, from retirement age r. Find
B_r if the defined pension benefit is (a) $50 per month for each year of
service, (b) 1.5% of career average compensation for each year of service,
and (c) 1.5% of final average compensation for each year of service.

SOLUTION

(a) The annual pension benefit is $B_r = 50 \times 12 \times 30 = \$18,000$.
(b) Here the benefit is $B_r = .015 \times 40,000 \times 30 = \$18,000$.
(c) This time we have $B_r = .015 \times 100,000 \times 30 = \$45,000$.   □

Two other basic types of defined benefit are flat and fixed. The **flat** ②
benefit type is a function of compensation but not of service, such as 60%
of compensation at retirement. The **fixed benefit** type is not a function of ③
compensation *or* service, but rather a specified amount at retirement such
as $40,000 per year. Since these designs have an arbitrary accrual of bene-
fit, they are often not acceptable to government or industry except for providing a minimum guaranteed benefit contingent on a minimum service
period. This is illustrated in the following two examples.

EXAMPLE 1.2

Using the data from Example 1.1, find B_r if the annual pension benefit is to be $10,000 or 1.5% of final average compensation for each year of service, whichever is greater.

SOLUTION   The benefit is $10,000 or, if greater,

$$(.015)(100,000)(30) = \$45,000.$$

In this case $B_r = \$45,000$.   □

EXAMPLE 1.3

Rework Example 1.2 assuming the participant has only 5 years of service.

SOLUTION   The benefit is $10,000 or, if greater,

$$(.015)(100,000)(5) = \$7500.$$

In this case $B_r = \$10,000$.   □

1.2.2 Defined Contributions and Defined Benefits

Plan designs differ slightly between Canada and the United States. In Canada, most pension plans are defined contribution plans, although they include only about 10% of the plan participants. Large pension plans, those with more than one thousand participants, are generally defined benefit plans. In the U.S., much more than 10% of plan participants are in defined contribution plans.

   In a defined contribution plan an individual account is maintained for each plan participant. The amount in this account, including investment income, is then used to provide benefits at retirement. The employer makes a prearranged contribution to the account. No investment risk is borne by the employer.

   Like defined benefit plans, defined contribution plans have different types of designs. The most significant structures in the marketplace are (a) money purchase plans, and (b) profit sharing plans. In Canada, about 95% of defined contribution plans are money purchase. Money purchase plans utilize a formula to predefine required employer contributions; the formula is either a function of the salary or the contributions made by the employee.

[handwritten annotations: "45% money purch.", "money purchase", "Canada < 50% profit sharing"]

For example, the employer may contribute 6% of participant salaries or may match the employee contributions. Contributions may be reduced by any forfeitures on account of terminated participants with short periods of service. This design is popular with multi-employer plans.

Profit sharing plans comprise the remaining 5% of defined contribution plans. The contributions can vary within an allowable range and will be less in bad financial years and more in good years. As an example, the employer may contribute 10% of company profit before income tax to the pension plan, prorated by the salaries of the participants.

Canadian government legislation stipulates a minimum employer contribution of 1% of the earnings of plan participants. This requirement helps to protect participants from receiving very little pension upon retirement.

[handwritten annotation: "401(k)"]

In the U.S., 401(k) plans, also referred to as cash-or-deferred arrangements, or salary reduction plans, allow a participant to contribute a portion of compensation to the plan on a before-tax basis. The voluntary employee salary reduction contributions are not classified as income in the year of contribution, and the entire payout, including interest, is taxable income in the years in which the benefits are received. The employer may or may not make matching contributions. These plans are named after the section of the Internal Revenue Code under which they are regulated. More than half of all U.S. employees in defined contribution plans are in 401(k) plans. Their widespread acceptance is due mostly to allowing employees to make contributions on a before-tax basis. Tax treatment has a significant effect on the accumulation of pension funds, and 401(k) plans, along with Section 403(b) and Section 457 plans, are the principal private plans which allow employees to defer a portion of their salary on a before-tax basis. A typical 401(k) thrift savings plan might allow a participant to contribute up to 15% of compensation to the plan. The employer, in turn, might agree to make a matching contribution, but no more than 3% of compensation. Profit sharing plans are more common in the U.S. than in Canada.

The maximum dollar amount which may be deferred by an individual employee under a 401(k) plan is $8994 for 1993 and cost-of-living adjusted amounts for each subsequent year.

Defined pension benefits and contributions are often based on compensation as defined in the plan document. The measure of compensation may be either salary or wages and may or may not include overtime and bonuses. In this text we will use C to denote contribution and S to denote salary or compensation.

Pension plans always contain pension benefits and usually contain additional related benefits called ancillary benefits, payable in the event of total disability before retirement, death before retirement, or death after retirement.

Defined contribution arrangements inherently emphasize termination benefits over retirement benefits, whereas typical defined benefit plans emphasize retirement benefits over termination benefits. An employer wishing to attract younger, more mobile employees may feel that defined benefit plans should be abandoned in favor of money purchase plans. For certain employee groups this may indeed be a satisfactory approach. It may seem strange to adopt improved termination benefits as a hiring inducement, but to an employee assessing the merits of a particular plan, that may be a very significant factor and may outweigh the disadvantage of a less attractive retirement benefit that usually comes with a change to a defined contribution plan.

There are other alternatives to a pure defined contribution plan which retain the defined benefit concept and its inherent advantages in retirement and personnel planning, but at the same time incorporate some of the desirable features of defined contribution plans. According to The Mercer Bulletin [8], some of them are the following:

(1) A combination plan consists of a defined benefit base plan, typically non-contributory and with a low benefit level, in conjunction with a supplementary defined contribution plan. This type of arrangement can have significantly enhanced termination benefits if the supplementary portion requires employer contributions.

(2) A hybrid plan provides benefits based on the greater of a defined benefit formula and a defined contribution formula. In effect, such plans provide, on termination, money purchase benefits for employees terminating prior to a certain age and defined benefit pensions thereafter.

(3) A flexible pension plan consists of a non-contributory basic defined benefit pension plan supplemented by employee contributions which are notionally credited to the plan and used later at the employee's option to purchase ancillary benefits.

(4) Perhaps the simplest concept is to retain the basic defined benefit pension plan and then *enhance the commuted values paid on termination.* This can be done either by providing for assumed future salary increases up to normal retirement age, or by including the value of ancillary benefits, such as early retirement enhancements, which are now commonly excluded unless an employee meets minimum age and/or service requirements. Alternatively, deferred pensions could be indexed for inflation that may occur before their commencement date.

1.3 Plan Cost

In a defined benefit plan, an actuary is required to determine what contributions need to be made. The employer's year-to-year costs vary with the actuary's assumptions for investment income, mortality, terminations, and salary increases; the actual experience of the plan can also have a significant effect on costs. For an employer with a low profit margin this uncertainty may be undesirable. Pension benefit guarantees and funding standards exist, and actuarial reports must be completed periodically. Defined benefit plans are more complicated, leading to higher actuarial expenditures which are usually borne by the employer. Fortunately, there has been a substantial improvement in pension plan administration software and hardware.

In a defined contribution plan, contributions are set by a formula and, for the most part, are known, but legislation changes in the United States have made the filing requirements for defined contribution plans almost as complicated as for defined benefit plans. Furthermore, the advent of nondiscrimination, daily record-keeping, and Section 404(c) rules may make defined contribution plans nearly as expensive to administer as well.

Section 8.3 contains further comments on cost, contributions, and expenses.

1.3.1 Replacement Ratio

The replacement ratio is the ratio of retirement income just after retirement to compensation just before retirement. It is commonly felt that a ratio of 70% will, in most cases, maintain a satisfactory standard of living after retirement.

To be more sophisticated, we could assume mortgage payments and child-care expenses are spread over the preretirement period, we could recognize work-related expenses and pension contributions, and we could calculate preretirement and (lower) postretirement income taxes. Last but not least, we could estimate Social Security income. Then we could calculate a net replacement ratio taking these factors into account. A net ratio of 80% would represent a 20% drop in standard of living. With good forward planning it would be possible to achieve a net ratio of 100% and no financial diminution of the standard of living.

The defined benefit design, combined with Social Security, is more closely attuned to a satisfactory net replacement ratio than is the defined contribution design. With good investment performance, the defined contribution design could easily give a net ratio of over 130% and perhaps, in such a case, the tax relief on the pension fund investment income is excessive. With poor investment performance the defined contribution design could easily give a net ratio of under 70% and the pensioner would suffer.

1.3.2 The Effects of Age and Plan Design

Younger employees may be better served by a defined contribution plan. Generally they are more mobile and therefore need a pension plan which can move with them with no significant loss. In a defined benefit plan, the pension benefit is a usually a function of final average salary. If the participant changes jobs, the defined benefit reflects the present salary, not the salary at retirement age, and the participant usually suffers from the effects of inflation between termination and retirement.

In calculating the cost of a defined benefit, there is more discounting if the participant is young and less discounting for a participant near retirement; a participant close to retirement tends to receive a more expensive benefit from a defined benefit plan than from a defined contribution plan.

People closer to retirement are more security conscious and more protected in a defined benefit plan compared to a defined contribution plan. Another difference is investment risk; a fund manager for a large defined benefit plan may take a long-term view with more risk and reward; a small defined contribution fund is often more conservatively invested.

1.3.3 Anticipating Inflation

When performing an actuarial valuation for a pension plan, the actuary must choose an approximation to the future unknown rates of interest and salary increase. Either an explicit or implicit inflation component is normally included in future interest rate and salary increase assumptions. A simple assumption for the interest rate might be 6%, of which 3% represents inflation and 3% represents the real interest rate. Similarly, a salary scale might include 3% for inflation and 2% for expected average annual merit increases, or 3% of current salary for inflation and 4% of the starting salary for the participant's salary class for average annual merit increases. Salary assumptions are discussed in Section 6.5.

The actuary will review the last ten or fifteen years, and will use this review of the past to assist in making assumptions for the future, recognizing current trends and being conservatively realistic without unwarranted complications. The assumptions should be understandable and exhibit common sense.

The mathematics of gains and losses will arise when actual experience is different from what was expected. If the expected inflation rate is lower than the actual inflation rate, there will often be experience losses from salary and experience gains from investment return. These gains and losses will partially offset each other; however, they must be quantified, disclosed, explained and amortized in each actuarial valuation. The mathematics of gains and losses and the concepts involved in developing actuarial assumptions are discussed in Sections 5.1, 5.5, 6.4 and 8.3.

1.3.4 Recognizing Inflation

The first two paragraphs of this section comment on the problem of protecting the participant's pension from inflation before retirement, and the remainder of this section deals with postretirement inflation protection.

Many flat dollar plans are issued to members of unions and are subject to renegotiation every three years. This may provide partial, full, or even more than full protection to the worker if the increase in the pension benefit is greater than the increase in the Consumer Price Index. For example, the benefit may change from $40 per month per year of service to $45 per month per year of service, an increase of 12.5%, while inflation may be only, say, 9% for the three-year period.

Final average compensation plans give reasonable protection against inflation occurring before retirement; career average compensation plans do not. This is because the compensation used to determine the benefit in a final average plan is a recent figure and presumably reflects past inflation, whereas that used in a career average plan can be many years old (perhaps fifteen years old for an employee with thirty years of service).

Participants begin receiving retirement benefits upon reaching retirement age, usually on the first day of each month. If these benefits are not indexed to inflation, then participants will receive the same amount of monthly pension throughout their entire retired lifetimes, but the purchasing power of the pension will decrease each year. As an example, inflation of 6% per year would leave pensioners with half of their original purchasing power after only 12 years.

Some plans provide *ad hoc* adjustments in which the plan sponsor decides each year, without prior commitment, if the benefit for the upcoming year will be increased. Other plans may provide partial indexing or even full indexing.

For a defined contribution plan participant to receive postretirement benefit increases, the participant may purchase an increasing annuity; the increases may or may not match inflation, and the initial income will be lower.

1.3.5 Benefit Payments

Pension payments are often made from the pension fund or from a retired life section of the pension fund. This is the usual case when pension payments are indexed for inflation.

On the other hand, pension payments are often purchased from a life insurance company at the date of retirement, and the purchase price may be less than or more than the liability for the participant which was held just before the date of retirement. The benefits are usually guaranteed for life by the insurance company, and the retired life usually does not receive indexation.

The payment of pension benefits in a lump sum at retirement is a feature of many pension plans. This feature gives flexibility and control to the participant; on the other hand, monthly pension benefits give the retired participant security and peace of mind, and the arbitrariness of actuarial equivalence is avoided. The actuarial mathematics of retirement is developed in Sections 5.4, 6.2, 7.1, and 7.2.

In addition to the payment of pension benefits, many pension plans also provide for the payment of death benefits and withdrawal benefits.

1.3.6 Surplus

Before 1975, many pension funds were in a deficit position because of initial unfunded liabilities and low investment returns. Since then, many of the initial unfunded liabilities have been paid off and many pension plans have experienced favorable investment returns. As a result, surpluses have emerged in many defined benefit plans and have grown to such significant levels that unions, employers, employees, and government have been actively debating the question of who owns them.

Recent trends in the industry have been toward stating ownership rights in the plan document, using part of this surplus for reductions in employer contributions, and introducing partial indexation. Indexation can be an enormous expenditure, and in some cases these surpluses have been replaced by unfunded liabilities. When plan improvements are introduced to a pension plan (such as partial indexation) and unfunded liabilities result, legislation places maximum time restrictions on the amortization of the new liability. In the United States, the maximum time frame is sometimes 30 years and often less; in Canada, the maximum is often 15 years and often 5 years, depending on the type of liability being amortized. The concepts, but not the regulations, are discussed in Section 3.5.

| DISCUSSION QUESTIONS |

1-1 Using any reasonable assumptions, what is the ratio of a career average pension to a final average pension for a typical participant?

1-2 Describe in detail whether or not defined contribution plans provide full inflation protection before and after retirement.

1-3 Explain the differences between anticipating inflation and protecting against inflation.

1.4 Plan Documents and Funding

A pension plan can include various documents. The most important one is the **plan document** which describes (a) who gets a benefit, (b) under what circumstances it becomes payable, (c) how much it is to be, and (d) what are the terms of payment. A trust agreement or an insurance or annuity contract may be used as a vehicle to hold and protect the funds contributed to the plan, and the investment income thereon, until they are paid to the beneficiaries. Other agreements may be used to provide services such as investment advice, investment analysis, and administration.

The main content of this text is a description of the common **actuarial cost methods** for the funding of defined benefit pension plans, with accompanying examples (with solutions) and exercises. These cost methods have the common goal of the orderly build-up of the necessary funds over the working lifetimes of the participants (but only while the pension plan is operating) and the full (or almost full) funding by retirement of appropriate pension benefits.

The primary reason for the goal described above is *participant security*. Suppose a pension plan has been in force for seven years, and the funds or invested assets amount to 60 million dollars. Let us measure the participant security. Based on the commitments given in the plan document, it would be possible to measure the liability incurred for each participant; the total liability for all participants might amount to, say, 100 million dollars. In this case the participant security could be described as 60%. After another seven years the funds might have grown to, say, 270 million dollars, and the total liability to 300 million dollars; then the participant security would be 90% of full funding, and the unfunded portion would be 10% of the total liability. After another seven years, the funds might be 840 million dollars and the total liability 800 million dollars, in which case there would be full funding and, in addition, a surplus of 5% of the total liability. The plan document may give more security to pensioners than to active participants; in the example describing 60% security to all participants, the plan could provide 100% security to pensioners and hence less than 60% to active participants.

The funds arise from the contributions to the pension fund and the investment earnings on the pension fund assets (including capital gains), less benefit payments. The contributions are often equal to, but sometimes more or less than, the **normal cost**, which is a measure of suggested funding based on the actuarial cost method which has been adopted. All the cost methods are rational methods of funding, but some are faster (with larger funds) than average and some are slower (with smaller funds). The **actuarial liabilities**, as we shall see, are related to the normal costs, and both are based on the cost method. In general, however, the actuarial liability (for each participant separately and for all participants combined) grows from zero at entry to an amount which makes provision for all pension plan benefits at and after retirement. The reader familiar with life insurance terminology should note that normal costs and actuarial liabilities are the pension terms analogous to the insurance terms premiums and actuarial reserves.

A subtle but important point is that the actuarial liability based on the cost method and the actuarial liability for the benefits promised in the plan document are not necessarily the same. The former relates to the desired pace of funding, whereas the latter relates to the accrued legal entitlement of the participants.

A second reason for funding is to relate pension costs to the *working years* rather than the *retirement years.* Salaries are clearly a cost of production, and many actuaries consider pension costs to be a cost of production as well. Often pension costs are expressed as a percentage of payroll, and the funding proceeds at this pace; for example, the actuary may express pension costs as 13% of payroll, and the employer may remit 13% of payroll to the pension fund each month.

Pay-as-you-go funding, where the pension costs are charged to the retirement years as benefits are paid out, is not usually acceptable because, if adopted, the production costs would be understated in the working years and overstated in the retirement years, and participant security would be entirely insufficient. Terminal funding, where all the funding is done in the year of retirement, is usually not acceptable for the same reasons.

A third reason for funding is to achieve lower costs and lower taxes. In order to encourage the funding of pensions, the government, within reasonable limits, allows tax relief on the investment income earned on the tens of billions of dollars in pension funds. The result of this tax policy is huge pools of savings invested in equities, bonds, mortgages, and real estate, millions of pension accounts, and fewer retired lives dependent on the state. The government allows a choice of funding or cost methods; the faster the funding, the greater the tax relief.

Comments on matters related to funding are found in Chapter 8.

1.5 Actuarial Valuations

Actuarial valuations are performed periodically to inform those interested of the current condition of the pension plan. Valuations of pension plans are required every three years (or more frequently) in the United States and in Canada.

The normal cost (NC) for a year is the actuarial value of the part of the total pension benefit assigned to the year following the valuation date, assuming valuation at the beginning of the year.

The actuarial liability (AL) for a participant will vary among different cost methods and will increase with age. For individual cost methods the total actuarial liability is the sum of the individual actuarial liabilities. The actuarial liability may be determined by either of the following approaches:

(1) The **prospective approach**, whereby AL is the present value of future benefits (pvB) minus the present value of future normal costs ($pvNC$).

(2) The **retrospective approach**, in which AL is the accumulation of normal costs, with adjustments due to interest and benefit payments.

Pension plans have trust funds into which contributions are deposited and from which benefits are withdrawn. The amount in the **pension fund**, denoted by F, consists of the contributions made and the investment income earned, less benefit withdrawals and expenses if paid from the fund. At retirement, the accumulated value of the assets is approximately equal to the actuarial liability required for the payment of the pension benefits. Any excess of the actuarial liability over the fund is called the **unfunded actuarial liability** (UAL). The breakdown of the plan can be shown using a valuation balance sheet as follows:

Assets	Liabilities
F	AL
UAL	
Total	Total

In the balance sheet, AL is the estimated amount *owed* by the pension fund to the participants, F is the value of the invested assets *owned* by the fund (usually with a dampening of market value fluctuations), and UAL is the balancing item. Note, however, that UAL is often converted by the method of Section 3.5 into an amount owed to the fund by the plan sponsor. Assets are dicussed briefly in Section 7.3. If F exceeds AL, the excess, called the **surplus**, is shown on the right side of the balance sheet and there is no UAL. AL is also called the **accrued liability**, or simply the **liability**. It can always be expressed by the prospective approach. The retrospective approach is normally equivalent. For simplicity, we refer to the date of valuation as time 0 and one year later as time 1. Then at time 0, the balance sheet equation is normally $F_0 + UAL_0 = AL_0$.

In addition to calculating AL and UAL at time 0, the actuary will calculate the **expected unfunded actuarial liability** ($^{\text{exp}}UAL$) at time 1. If the **actual unfunded actuarial liability** ($^{\text{act}}UAL$) at time 1 turns out to be less than $^{\text{exp}}UAL$, then a gain will result. This is called the **total experience gain,** and it will be broken down in the valuation report into gains (or losses) due to mortality, investment earnings, termination, compensation, and early (or late) retirement.

Chapters 2, 3, and 4 discuss the various cost methods usually under the assumption that actual experience is the same as expected experience, so that no gain or loss results, and Chapter 5 discusses the gains and losses resulting from actual experience being different from expected experience under the various cost methods.

In addition to what has already been discussed, an actuarial valuation should also include a summary of the plan provisions, the actuarial assumptions, the components of the fund, and the actual experience. Actuarial valuations are discussed further in Section 8.2.

DISCUSSION QUESTIONS

1-4 Is investment income earned on normal costs, actuarial liabilities, funds, or assets?

1-5 The retrospective actuarial liability is normally the accumulation of past normal costs. Are there pitfalls in using the retrospective method?

1.6 Notation and Terminology

This text assumes that the reader is familiar with standard actuarial notation. (Those in need of a review of this notation should consult a standard actuarial text, such as Parmenter [9], Jordan [6], or Bowers, *et al.* [5].) Since pension calculations are generally made from a multiple-decrement service table, the formulas in this text will use standard multiple-decrement notation. (See Section 7.6 of Parmenter [9], Chapters 14 and 16 of Jordan [6], or Chapter 10 of Bowers, *et al.* [5].)

On occasion the pension actuary might assume that there are no preretirement decrements other than death. This means that the calculations can be made from a single-decrement table for mortality only. For notational consistency in this text, however, we will use multiple-decrement notation (such as $\ell_x^{(\tau)}$, $p_x^{(\tau)}$, $q_x^{(d)}$, and so on), rather than the corresponding single-decrement notation (ℓ_x, p_x, q_x, and so on). In effect we are simply assuming that the service table entries of $d_x^{(i)}$ (and hence of $q_x^{(i)}$) are equal to zero for all decrements i other than death.

Going one step further, some pension actuarial calculations may be made assuming no preretirement decrements at all, which means that $q_x^{(d)} = 0$ for all ages prior to retirement. The effect of this simplifying assumption is that the present value calculations are done at interest only. The assumptions in this, and the previous, paragraph appear in many of the examples and exercises in this text.

1.6.1 Dates and Ages

For convenience, most of the dates used in this text are January 1; all dates are stated in the form month/day/year.

There are four key ages that arise in pension calculations.

(1) **Age e.** This is the age at entry to a pension plan, or the age from which benefits accrue. The actuarial liability at age e is usually 0.

(2) **Age a.** This is the age of a participant at plan inception, if the plan inception occurs later than the beginning of benefit accrual. This would occur if the plan is installed after an employee begins service, and benefit credit is given for the past service. Note that necessarily $a > e$. The actuarial liability at age a is based on the benefits, if any, which accrue from age e to age a.

(3) **Age x.** This is the age at which an actuarial valuation is performed.

(4) **Age r.** This is the age at normal retirement as specified in the plan document; it is commonly age 65.

To illustrate these four ages, consider a pension plan that was introduced on 1/1/80. At 1/1/93 there are two participants in the plan, and an actuarial valuation is being performed. Participant A was born on 1/1/40 and was hired on 1/1/70. Participant B was born on 1/1/50 and was hired on 1/1/85. The following is a time diagram for this plan.

	1970	1980	1985	1993	1994	2005	2015
Age of A	$e = 30$	$a = 40$		53	54	$r = 65$	
Age of B			$e = 35$	43	44		$r = 65$

Date (1/1)	1970	1980	1985	1993	1994	2005	2015
Time				0	1		
Age				x	$x+1$		

1.6.2 Definitions

The following terms are used frequently in this text:

- **Participant**. A person belonging to a pension plan (also called member or employee in some cases).
- **Deferred Vested**. A former participant who has terminated employment but has acquired a right to a future benefit. (See Example 2.6.)
- **Plan Sponsor**. The party establishing the pension plan (also called employer in some cases).

1.6.3 Pension Notation Specific to This Text

The symbol B_r was introduced in Section 1.2.1. It is the expected annual pension benefit, payable monthly, commencing at retirement. B_r accrues over the years from age e to age r. The *portion* of B_r that accrues or is attributed to the period from age e to age x is denoted B_x. The *present value* of B_r and of B_x will be needed, sometimes at age e and sometimes at age x. Thus we need to specify both the age at which the present value is taken and the age to which the benefit has accrued. We will use the symbols pv_eB_r, pv_eB_x, pv_xB_r, and pv_xB_x for these four different present values. Note that the *expected* final salary and the *expected* B_r may change on each actuarial valuation date!

The concept of benefit payments was introduced in Section 1.3.5. We will often have occasion to quantify, for the year under consideration, both the benefits actually paid out and those expected to be paid out. The notation we will use includes *BEN* (for benefits in general), made up of *DBEN* (death benefits), *WBEN* (withdrawal benefits), *RBEN* (refund benefits on contributory plans), and *PBEN* (pension benefits, either monthly, annual or lump sum).

If the benefit is being accounted for at the end of the year (EOY), including interest to EOY, we will use the notation ^iBEN, ^iDBEN, and so on, where i is the interest *assumption* being used by the actuary in the pension valuation, not the actual earned rate. For example, if BEN is a value at EOY, then $^iBEN = BEN$, but if BEN is payable at the beginning of the year (BOY), then $^iBEN = BEN(1+i)$. Benefit payments are included in a few examples in Chapters 3 and 4, and in many examples in Chapters 5 and 6.

Additional notation is defined for presenting the subject matter of this text, such as the symbols NC, AL, ^{exp}UAL, and so on, already defined in Section 1.5. These symbols will be subscripted by age (*e.g.*, NC_x or AL_x) when there is only one participant or one entry age, or by time (*e.g.*, NC_0 or AL_1) when there are several different ages involved. Each example of such special notation will be carefully defined when first introduced. This notation, and the page of first mention, is listed in the Index of Notation beginning on page 397.

1.7 Cost Methods

The next three chapters describe the common cost methods; they are generally acceptable to the supervisory authorities for funding purposes.

Chapters 2 and 3 describe **individual methods**, wherein the total actuarial liability is equal to the sum of the individual actuarial liabilities. Chapter 2 describes two cost methods which are based on the pension benefits accrued to the date of valuation, as opposed to the total pension benefits that accrue to the date of retirement. The costs are low at the low ages with these methods, due to discounting from retirement back to these ages, but the costs usually *increase* with age. Chapter 3 describes four individual methods based on the pension benefits accrued to the date of retirement; the normal costs are *level* with age. The notation TNC and TAL will be used to distinguish the total normal cost and total actuarial liability, respectively, for the entire group from the corresponding values for a single participant.

Chapter 4 describes four **aggregate methods**, wherein the TNC value under each method is increased to the extent that there are liabilities for retired lives and decreased to the extent that there are funds on hand. Here too the TNC values are level with age.

Cost methods are discussed in Chapter 8 on a more conceptual basis.

Chapter 2

Increasing Cost
Individual Cost Methods

In this chapter we learn how to calculate the cost *each year* of a piece of pension benefit. Younger participants have low costs because we discount at interest for many years. Older participants have higher costs because we discount for fewer years. (In the following two chapters we calculate the *levelized* annual cost of the expected pension.)

2.1 Traditional Unit Credit

Traditional Unit Credit (TUC) is the first actuarial cost method we will study. The TUC actuarial liability is the value, at the valuation date, of the pension benefit accrued from the date of entry into the plan to the date of valuation. This method is also called the **Unit Credit Cost Method** by other ERISA and by Anderson [2], and the **Accrued Benefit Cost Method** by names McGill and Grubbs [7]. A salary scale assumption for salaries in all future no scale years is *not* made with this method; with other methods, a salary scale scale assumption is often made. assumpt.

If a participant is to retire at age r with an expected annual pension of B_r, with one-twelfth of B_r payable at the beginning of each month, then $B_r \cdot \ddot{a}_r^{(12)}$ is sufficient to fund this pension at age r. B_r denotes the benefit accrued (or earned) during the participant's active years of service, from age e to age r.

Let us consider a pension fund valuation at time 0 for a participant who is age x at time 0. The annual pension benefit which has accrued from age e to age x is usually a certain number of dollars per month for each year of service. The annual benefit that has accrued to age x is denoted by B_x. For example, if the pension benefit is \$30 per month for each of 20 years of service, then $B_x = 30 \times 12 \times 20 = \$7200$. The actuarial liability at age x is the value of the pension benefit accrued from age e to age x. It is given by

includes
mort.
w/disability
disability
discharge

$$ AL_x = B_x \cdot \frac{D_r^{(\tau)}}{D_x^{(\tau)}} \cdot \ddot{a}_r^{(12)}, $$

where $D_r^{(\tau)}/D_x^{(\tau)}$ is computed from a service table. The calculation includes interest and decrements such as mortality, withdrawal, disability, and discharge. Under the Unit Credit method, we obtain the total actuarial liability (TAL) at time 0 for all active participants in a pension plan by summing the individual liabilities for each active participant, obtaining

$$ TAL_0 = \sum AL_x = \sum B_x \cdot \frac{D_r^{(\tau)}}{D_x^{(\tau)}} \cdot \ddot{a}_r^{(12)}. $$

The liability for each participant increases with age. It follows that, if no participants leave the group and no new participants enter the group, the total liability will increase with time.

when
used
The TUC cost method is most often used with pension plans that provide a flat pension benefit, such as \$30 per month for each year of service. If the entry age is 35 and the retirement age is 65, the annual pension benefit commencing at retirement will be $30 \times 30 \times 12 = \$10,800$. At age 45, after ten years of service, the accrued pension benefit will be $B_{45} = 30 \times 10 \times 12 = \$3600$.

b_x denotes the piece of the total pension benefit that is earned in the year following age x. The simplest case is the one in which the same benefit is earned each year, so that

assume same
benefit earned
each year

$$ b_x = \frac{B_r}{r - e}. $$

This case will be assumed to apply unless otherwise stated. Therefore in our example of a benefit of $30 per month for each year of service, we have $b_x = 30 \times 12 = \$360$.

The normal cost at the beginning of each year is the cost of the pension benefit that is earned (accrues) in that year. It is given by

$$NC_x = b_x \cdot \frac{D_r^{(\tau)}}{D_x^{(\tau)}} \cdot \ddot{a}_r^{(12)}.$$

The normal cost for younger participants is lower due to the greater effect of discounting in the $D_r^{(\tau)}/D_x^{(\tau)}$ term. The total normal cost for the plan each year is the sum of the normal costs for all participants receiving benefit accruals. The total normal cost in future years will be affected by aging, the size of the unit benefit, withdrawals, retirements, deaths, and new entrants.

In single-decrement situations, we will often use the simple variations

single decrement.

$$NC_x = b_x \cdot \frac{N_r^{(12)}}{D_x} = b_x \cdot v^t \, {}_tp_x \cdot \ddot{a}_r^{(12)},$$

where $t = r - x$, and

$$AL_x = NC_x(x-e).$$

DISCUSSION QUESTIONS

2-1 Write an expression for NC_{44}, where the benefit is $35 per month for each year of service.

2-2 Write an expression for the total actuarial liability for all active, terminated, and retired participants.

2-3 What is the normal cost for a retired or terminated participant?

EXAMPLE 2.1

Plan effective date: 1/1/84
Normal retirement benefit: $30 per month for each year of service
All employees were hired at age 25.

Retired or terminated vested participants: None
Preretirement terminations other than by death: None
Selected annuity value: $\ddot{a}_{65}^{(12)} = 10$
Census data on 1/1/94, and commutation functions:

Age x	Participants	D_x
25	8	16
35	0	8
45	2	4
55	0	2
65	0	1

What is the TUC actuarial liability and normal cost as of 1/1/94?

SOLUTION Let 1/1/94 be time 0. The participants who are age 25 have just been hired, so $B_{25} = 0$ since no benefit has yet accrued. For each of the two participants who are attained age 45, we have a benefit accrual of $B_{45} = 30 \times 12 \times 20 = 7200$. Then

$$AL_{45} = 7200 \cdot \frac{D_{65}}{D_{45}} \cdot \ddot{a}_{65}^{(12)} = 18{,}000$$

and the total liability is

$$TAL_0 = 2 \cdot AL_{45} = \$36{,}000.$$

The normal cost for the plan is the sum of the several NC_x, so

$$TNC_0 = \sum b_x \cdot \frac{D_r}{D_x} \cdot \ddot{a}_r^{(12)},$$

where $b_x = 30 \times 12 = 360$. Thus we have

$$TNC_0 = 8 \left[3600 \cdot \frac{D_{65}}{D_{25}} \cdot \ddot{a}_{65}^{(12)} \right] + 2 \left[360 \cdot \frac{D_{65}}{D_{45}} \cdot \ddot{a}_{65}^{(12)} \right]$$

$$= 360 \ddot{a}_{65}^{(12)} [8(1/16) + 2(1/4)] = \$3600. \qquad \square$$

Note that because there are no decrements other than death, we can use an appropriate single-decrement table (mortality only). This explains the use of D_x rather than $D_x^{(\tau)}$.

EXAMPLE 2.2

Normal retirement benefit: $10 per month for each year of service
Actuarial cost method: Unit Credit
Actuarial assumptions:
    Interest: 6%
    Preretirement terminations other than deaths: None
    Retirement age: 65
Participants as of 1/1/93: 100 active employees, all age 60
Normal cost for 1993 as of 1/1/93: $100,000
Selected mortality value: $q_{60} = .04$

Calculate the normal cost for 1994 as of 1/1/94 (a) per survivor, (b) for the total group if 92 participants are alive at 1/1/94, (c) if 96 participants are alive, and (d) if all participants are alive.

SOLUTION The normal cost per participant at age 60 is

$$NC_{60} = (10 \times 12)v^5 \, {}_5p_{60} \, \ddot{a}_{65}^{(12)},$$

and the normal cost per survivor at age 61 is

$$NC_{61} = (10 \times 12)v^4 \, {}_4p_{61} \, \ddot{a}_{65}^{(12)}.$$

Note that $\dfrac{NC_{60}}{NC_{61}} = vp_{60}$. Then we have the following results.

(a) $NC_{61} = \dfrac{NC_{60}}{vp_{60}} = \dfrac{100,000/100}{.96/1.06} = \dfrac{1060}{.96} = \$1104.17.$

(b) $TNC_{61} = 92\left(\dfrac{1060}{.96}\right) = \$101,583.$

(c) $TNC_{61} = 96\left(\dfrac{1060}{.96}\right) = \$106,000.$

(d) $TNC_{61} = 100\left(\dfrac{1060}{.96}\right) = \$110,417.$

Note that in (a) the normal cost per survivor does not depend on the actual mortality experience; in (b) more than expected die so there is a gain from mortality (see Chapter 5); in (c) the expected mortality is exactly realized, so the *TNC* at 1/1/94 is $100,000(1+i)$; in (d) there is a loss from mortality. □

If F_0 is the amount of the pension fund at time 0 and TAL_0 represents the plan's total actuarial liability for all active, retired and terminated vested participants at time 0, then the surplus at that time is $F_0 - TAL_0$. Traditionally, most plans had, and many plans still have, a *negative* surplus, called the unfunded actuarial liability, where

$$UAL_0 = TAL_0 - F_0.$$

The disposition of an unfunded actuarial liability is an important actuarial matter; it is discussed in Section 3.6.

| EXAMPLE 2.3 |

Refer to the data given in Example 2.1. Under the Unit Credit cost method, what is the unfunded actuarial liability as of 1/1/94 if the plan assets amount to $5000 at that time?

| SOLUTION | We need the total actuarial liability for the plan since the unfunded liability at time 0 is

$$UAL_0 = TAL_0 - F_0.$$

From Example 2.1 we have $TAL_0 = \$36,000$, so

$$UAL_0 = 36,000 - 5,000 = \$31,000. \qquad □$$

The fund balance at the beginning of the year (BOY), which we have denoted by F_0, will increase during the year by actual investment income and contributions to the fund. It will be diminished by amounts withdrawn from the fund as benefits. At time 0, we can calculate what we *expect* the unfunded actuarial liability to be at time 1 as

$$^{\exp}UAL_1 = (UAL_0 + NC_0)(1+i) - {}^iC,$$

where ^{i}C is the contribution plus the interest earned during the year on the contribution using the actuarial interest assumption. If the contribution is made at the end of the year (EOY), then $^{i}C = C$, and if it is made at BOY, then $^{i}C = C(1+i)$. A total experience gain, ^{tot}G, will result if the *actual* unfunded actuarial liability (^{act}UAL) is less than ^{exp}UAL. In other words

$$^{tot}G_1 = {}^{exp}UAL_1 - {}^{act}UAL_1.$$

A negative gain is called a loss. The relationship between UAL_0 and UAL_1 is developed, and the subject of gains and losses is discussed, in Chapter 5.

EXAMPLE 2.4

Actuarial cost method: Unit Credit
Assumed interest rate: 6%
Valuation results as of 1/1/93:

Actuarial liability	$100,000
Actuarial value of assets	50,000
Normal cost as of 12/31/93	10,000

Valuation results as of 1/1/94:

Actuarial liability	$115,000
Actuarial value of assets	70,000

Contributions:
$13,910 at 12/31/93
$15,587 at 12/31/94

What is the experience gain for 1993?

SOLUTION   Let 1/1/93 be time 0 and 1/1/94 be time 1. There is a gain when the actual unfunded liability turns out to be less than the expected. Since the normal cost is at 12/31/93 and $^{i}C = C$, then the expected unfunded liability at time 1 is

$$^{exp}UAL_1 = UAL_0(1+i) + NC - C$$

$$= (100,000-50,000)(1.06) + 10,000 - 13,910$$

$$= 49,090.$$

The actual unfunded liability at time 1 is the difference between AL_1 and F_1, so

$$^{\text{act}}UAL_1 \;=\; 115{,}000 - 70{,}000 \;=\; 45{,}000.$$

Then

$$^{\text{tot}}G \;=\; {}^{\text{exp}}UAL - {}^{\text{act}}UAL$$

$$=\; 49{,}090 - 45{,}000 \;=\; \$4{,}090. \qquad \square$$

Note that the normal cost is usually at BOY but occasionally, as in Example 2.4, it is at EOY; the contribution is usually at EOY but occasionally it is at BOY or mid-year.

EXAMPLE 2.5

Which of the following statements concerning the Unit Credit cost method are true?

I.   Under this method, the assumption must be made that each participant will remain in the plan until retirement or prior death.

II.   If the benefit accrual in each year is constant for any given participant, the normal cost for that participant will also remain constant, provided actual experience is in accordance with actuarial assumptions.

III.   The actuarial liability of a newly established plan is equal to the present value of the benefits attributable to credited service prior to the effective date of the plan.

SOLUTION

I.   Not true. We could use other decrements such as withdrawal or disability.

II.   Not true. The effect of mortality and interest discount is reducing with age.

III.   True. $\qquad \square$

EXAMPLE 2.6

Normal retirement benefit: $10 per month for each year of service
Vesting eligibility: 100% after 5 years of service
Preretirement death benefit: None
Actuarial cost method: Unit Credit
Actuarial assumptions:

Interest rate: 7% per year

Preretirement terminations other than deaths: EOY

$$q_x^{(d)} = q_x^{\prime(d)}$$

$$q_x^{(\tau)} = q_x^{(d)} + q_x^{(w)}$$

Retirement age: 65

Selected annuity value: $\ddot{a}_{65}^{(12)} = 8.736$

Data for sole participant:

Date of birth	1/1/31
Date of hire	1/1/89
Status as of 1/1/94	Active

Selected probabilities:

x	$q_x^{(\tau)}$	$q_x^{(d)}$
63	.069	.019
64	.081	.021
65	.023	.023

What is the normal cost for 1994 as of 1/1/94?

SOLUTION The participant is 63 years old on 1/1/94. Then

$$NC_{63} = 120 \times 8.736 \times v^2 \,_2p_{63}^{(\tau)}$$

$$= 1048.32 \times v^2(1-.019)(1-.021) = \$879.38.$$

- In this defined benefit plan with no participant contributions, 100% **vesting** means that the *participant* is entitled to 100% of the retirement benefit accrued to the date of withdrawal. If withdrawal occurs before five years of service, no retirement benefit is payable because there is no vesting. 60%

vesting, for example, would mean that the participant is entitled to 60% of the accrued benefit.

- Since deaths occur at EOY, $q_x^{(d)} = q_x^{\prime(d)}$, and we discount for mortality because the death benefit is zero. If, alternatively, the terminal reserve were paid out on death, we would not discount for mortality. Similarly, we do not discount for withdrawal because vesting is 100%, and the unit credit liability is not released. The student may wish to review these important aspects of contingency theory. (See, for example, Chapter 9 of Bowers, *et al.* [5].) $\square$

Plan experience and changes in plan benefits will affect plan liabilities and costs. These are discussed in Section 3.5 and Chapters 5 and 6. If death and withdrawal benefits are not stated, they are assumed to be zero; they are discussed in more detail in Chapter 5.

2.2 Benefits with a Salary Scale

The benefit formulas in Section 2.1 did not make use of projected future salary, but those of Section 2.3 will. This section will introduce the idea of salary scales themselves.

If a salary scale is not being used in the benefit projection, it would appear that the actuary is assuming that salaries are not expected to increase. The effect of such an assumption is normally to shift a portion of the costs from the present to the future. This is often not appropriate.

If the actuary does use a salary scale, it may be a scale independent of age, such as 5% per year, or it may be a more sophisticated scale that depends on age. In any event, it will make due allowance for inflation, actual past salaries, and expected future salaries which are also discussed in Sections 3.2 and 3.3.

We will illustrate the use of a 5% scale by calculating the pension benefits for (a) a 2% final salary plan, (b) a 2% final three-year average plan, and (c) a 2% career average plan.

(a) For a person currently age x with a salary of S_x, the expected (or projected) final salary, at age $r - 1$, is

$$S_{r-1} = (1.05)^{r-1-x} S_x,$$

and the pension benefit accrued to age x is

$$B_x = .02(1.05)^{r-1-x} S_x \cdot (x-e).$$

(b) The expected final three-year average salary is

$$FAS = \frac{1}{3} \left[S_{r-3} + S_{r-2} + S_{r-1} \right]$$

$$= \frac{1}{3} \left[(1.05)^{r-3-x} + (1.05)^{r-2-x} + (1.05)^{r-1-x} \right] S_x$$

$$= \frac{1}{3} (1.05)^{r-1-x} S_x \cdot \ddot{a}_{\overline{3}|.05} ,$$

and the accrued pension benefit is

$$B_x = .02 \, FAS (x-e).$$

(c) The expected career average salary is

$$\frac{1}{r-e} \left[S_e + \cdots + S_x + S_{x+1} + \cdots + S_{r-1} \right]$$

$$= \frac{1}{r-e} \left[S_e + \cdots + S_x + 1.05 S_x + \cdots + (1.05)^{r-1-x} S_x \right],$$

where salaries before age x are historical and salaries after age x are projected. If historical salaries have followed the projection (as is the case in many problems), then the accrued benefit is

$$B_x = \frac{.02}{r-e} \left[(1.05)^{e-x} S_x \cdot s_{\overline{r-e}|.05} \right] (x-e).$$

Often a salary study will reveal larger percentage increases at young ages and smaller percentage increases at older ages. For plans with many participants, instead of using a simple salary scale s, the actuary may wish to use a salary scale dependent on age, such as s_{r-1}/s_x instead of $(1+s)^{r-1-x}$. In this case the expected final salary is $\frac{s_{r-1}}{s_x} \cdot S_x$, and the accrued benefit is

$$B_x = .02 \cdot \frac{s_{r-1}}{s_x} \cdot S_x \cdot (x-e).$$

The expected final three-year average salary is

$$FAS = \frac{s_{r-1} + s_{r-2} + s_{r-3}}{3 \cdot s_x} \cdot S_x,$$

and the accrued benefit is

$$B_x = .02FAS(x-e).$$

DISCUSSION QUESTIONS

2-4   What is B_x when the actuary uses a salary scale dependent on age for a career average plan?

2-5   At the next valuation the actuary will introduce a salary scale. Will the salary scale assumption increase or decrease the normal cost and actuarial liability for each participant?

2-6   At the next valuation the actuary will increase the interest rate assumption and will introduce mortality and termination assumptions. Will the normal cost and actuarial liability for each participant be increased or decreased?

2.3 Projected Unit Credit

The **Projected Unit Credit** (PUC) cost method adds the use of a salary scale to the Traditional Unit Credit cost method. The current salary is projected to the date of retirement using a salary scale, and the projected retirement benefit is distributed evenly over the participant's career if the unit benefit is *the same* for each year of service. Example 2.8 shows how to handle a unit benefit which is *not the same* for each year of service.

Assume a participant's actual salary at age x is S_x with increases of 5% each year, and the plan provides a retirement benefit of 2% of final salary for each year of service. Final salary is the salary in the year preceding retirement; if the normal retirement age is r, the final salary is projected to be S_{r-1}. The projected retirement pension benefit can then be expressed as

$$B_r = .02S_{r-1}(r-e)$$

$$= .02(s_{r-1}/s_x) S_x(r-e)$$

$$= .02(1.05)^{r-1-x} S_x(r-e),$$

where s_{r-1}/s_x is the salary scale dependent on age which, in this example, is $(1.05)^{r-1-x}$. It is normal to use a simple salary scale or an age-dependent one, but not both.

This projected benefit can be prorated in direct proportion to service, so the amount of pension benefit allocated to prior years of service by the PUC cost method is

$$B_x = .02\, S_{r-1}(x-e)$$

$$= .02(s_{r-1}/s_x)S_x(x-e)$$

$$= .02(1.05)^{r-1-x}S_x(x-e).$$

The pension benefit which accrues in the year following age x is

$$b_x = \frac{.02(s_{r-1}/s_x)S_x(r-e)}{r-e} = .02S_{r-1}.$$

The PUC actuarial liability for a participant age x is

$$AL_x = .02(s_{r-1}/s_x)\, S_x(x-e)\, \frac{D_r^{(\tau)}}{D_x^{(\tau)}}\, \ddot{a}_r^{(12)}$$

$$= .02(1.05)^{r-1-x}S_x(x-e)\, \frac{D_r^{(\tau)}}{D_x^{(\tau)}}\, \ddot{a}_r^{(12)},$$

and the PUC normal cost is

$$NC_x = .02(s_{r-1}/s_x)\, S_x\, \frac{D_r^{(\tau)}}{D_x^{(\tau)}}\, \ddot{a}_r^{(12)}$$

$$= .02(1.05)^{r-1-x}\, S_x\, \frac{D_r^{(\tau)}}{D_x^{(\tau)}}\, \ddot{a}_r^{(12)}.$$

The concept of *the portion of the projected pension benefit accrued to age x, B_x,* is needed for (a) PUC calculations, (b) TUC calculations, and (c) plan document calculations.

(a) In a 2% final average plan,

$$AL_x = B_x \frac{D_r^{(\tau)}}{D_x^{(\tau)}} \ddot{a}_r^{(12)},$$

where $B_x = .02FAS(x-e)$.

(b) In a 2% plan, using TUC,

$$AL_x = B_x \frac{D_r^{(\tau)}}{D_x^{(\tau)}} \ddot{a}_r^{(12)},$$

where $B_x = .02S_x(x-e)$. If the participant remains active, the liability will increase rapidly from a comparatively low AL_x to AL_r. $^{TUC}AL_x$ is based on S_x. $^{PUC}AL_x$ is based on FAS.

(c) If the participant is vested and terminates at age x, the plan document may specify a payout on termination of

$$AL_x = B_x \frac{D_r^{(\tau)}}{D_x^{(\tau)}} \ddot{a}_r^{(12)},$$

where $B_x = .02S_x(x-e)$, or a deferred pension of B_x.

B_x in (b) is customarily referred to as the accrued benefit. B_x in (a) can be referred to as the amount of benefit allocated to prior years of service. The method in this section is called Projected Unit Credit by Anderson [2], and the Projected Accrued Benefit Cost Method by McGill and Grubbs [7]. Other factors affecting the three liabilities are mentioned in Section 8.2.3.

DISCUSSION QUESTIONS

2-7　Will the PUC actuarial liability always be higher than the TUC actuarial liability? Is the method more conservative? Will the percent increase in liability be higher at the younger ages or older ages?

2-8 Will the PUC normal cost be higher than the TUC normal cost at the younger ages? at the older ages?

The following four examples provide practice and greater understanding of the concepts of normal cost and actuarial liability.

| EXAMPLE 2.7 |

Normal retirement benefit: 1% of final salary per year of service
Actuarial cost method: Projected Unit Credit
Actuarial assumptions:
    Interest: 8%
    Salary increases: 6% per year
    Preretirement deaths and terminations: None
    Retirement age: 65
    Selected annuity value: $\ddot{a}_{65}^{(12)} = 8.33$

Participant data as of 1/1/94:

	Date of Birth	Date of Hire	Salary for 1994
Smith	1/1/34	1/1/74	$72,000
Brown	1/1/34	1/1/67	24,000

What is the normal cost for 1994 as of 1/1/94?

| SOLUTION | Let 1/1/94 be time 0. The total normal cost of the plan is given by

$$NC_0 = \sum b_x (1+i)^{-(r-x)} \,_{r-x}p_x \, \ddot{a}_r^{(12)},$$

where $\,_{r-x}p_x = 1$ because the preretirement probabilities of death are assumed to be zero. The pension benefit which accrues in the year following time 0 is

$$b_x = .01(s_{r-1}/s_x)\, \dot{S}_x$$

$$= .01(1.06)^{r-1-x}\, S_x,$$

since the salary scale is 6% for all ages. Then

$$NC_0 = [.01(1.06)^4 \, 72{,}000] \, (1.08)^{-5}(8.33)$$
$$+ \; [.01(1.06)^4 \, 24{,}000](1.08)^{-5}(8.33)$$

$$= \$6871. \qquad\qquad \square$$

| EXAMPLE 2.8 |
Plan effective date: 1/1/94
Monthly normal retirement benefit: 1% of average monthly salary for each
  of the first 10 years of service, plus 1.25% of average monthly salary
  for each year of service in excess of 10 years; average monthly salary
  is determined over the year immediately preceding retirement
Actuarial cost method: Projected Unit Credit
Actuarial assumptions:
  Interest: 6%
  Salary increases: 5% per year
  Retirement age: 65
  Selected annuity value: $\ddot{a}_{65}^{(12)} = 10$
  Preretirement mortality and terminations: None
Participant data as of 1/1/94:

Current Age	Hire Age	1994 Annual Salary
40	30	$10,000
50	35	20,000

Calculate the normal cost and the actuarial liability as of 1/1/94.

| SOLUTION | Let 1/1/94 be time 0. From the data given,

$$NC_0 = [(1.05)^{64-40} S_{40}(1.06)^{-(65-40)}$$

$$+ (1.05)^{64-50} S_{50}(1.06)^{-(65-50)}] \, .0125 \times 10$$

$$= \left[10{,}000\left(\frac{1.05}{1.06}\right)^{25} + 20{,}000\left(\frac{1.05}{1.06}\right)^{15}\right] .125 \div 1.05 = \$3005.$$

$$AL_0 = \sum (1.05)^{64-x} S_x[1\% \text{ (first 10 years)}$$
$$+ 1.25\% \text{ (service after 10 years)}] (1+i)^{-(65-x)} \ddot{a}_{65}^{(12)}$$

$$= (1.05)^{24} 10,000 [1\% (10) + 0] (1.06)^{-25} (10)$$
$$+ (1.05)^{14} 20,000[1\% (10) + 1.25\% (5)] (1.06)^{-15} (10)$$

$$= 7,514 + 26,850 = \$34,364. \qquad \square$$

- Example 2.8 is a **back-loaded plan,** and the normal costs in the first ten years are based on the 1% unit.

- With a **front-loaded plan**, such as 2% in the first ten years, 1.5% in the next ten, and nothing thereafter, the normal costs are based on the 2% unit in the first ten years, 1.5% in the next ten, and nothing thereafter.

EXAMPLE 2.9

Normal retirement benefit: 1% of final 3-year average salary for each year of service
Actuarial cost method: Projected Unit Credit
Actuarial assumptions:
    Interest rate: 7% per year
    Compensation increases: 5% per year
    Preretirement terminations other than deaths: None
    Retirement age: 65
    Selected mortality value: $q_{55} = .009$
Data for sole plan participant:
    Date of birth   1/1/38
    Status as of 1/1/93 and 1/1/94   Active
The sole participant received an 8% increase from 1993 to 1994.

What is the percentage increase in the normal cost for 1994 as of 1/1/94 over the normal cost for 1993 as of 1/1/93?

| **SOLUTION** | At 1/1/93 the participant is age 55. To find the percentage increase in normal cost, simply divide NC_{56} by NC_{55}. The benefit which accrues in 1993 is

$$b_{55} = .01 S_{55} \frac{(1.05)^9 + (1.05)^8 + (1.05)^7}{3},$$

and the normal cost is

$$NC_{55} = b_{55} \, v^{10} \, \frac{\ell_{65}}{\ell_{55}} \, \ddot{a}_{65}.$$

If the actual salary increase in 1993 were as expected, then b_{56} would be the same as b_{55}; but the salary increased by 8%, so

$$b_{56} = .01(1.08) \, S_{55} \frac{(1.05)^8 + (1.05)^7 + (1.05)^6}{3} = b_{55} \left(\frac{1.08}{1.05} \right),$$

and the normal cost is

$$NC_{56} = \left(b_{55} \frac{1.08}{1.05} \right) v^9 \, \frac{\ell_{65}}{\ell_{56}} \, \ddot{a}_{65}.$$

Now we find

$$\frac{NC_{56}}{NC_{55}} = \frac{1.08}{1.05}(1.07) \frac{\ell_{55}}{\ell_{56}} = 1.111,$$

which is an increase of 11.1% of NC_{55}. $\qquad\qquad\qquad\qquad\square$

ALTERNATE SOLUTION   If the actual compensation increase were 5%, then $\dfrac{NC_{56}}{NC_{55}}$ would be $\dfrac{1}{vp_{55}}$. But the actual compensation increase is 8%, so $\dfrac{NC_{56}}{NC_{55}}$ is $\dfrac{1.08}{1.05} \cdot \dfrac{1}{vp_{55}} = 1.111$. $\qquad\qquad\square$

Some plans allow for early retirement, with the benefit normally reduced since it is paid for a longer period of time. The following is an example of a change in an actuarial assumption, where the actuary has decided that an assumption of retirement at age 62 is more realistic than an assumption of retirement at age 65. (Note that it is the retirement age assumption, not the actual plan, that has changed. Actual plan changes are discussed in Chapter 6.)

EXAMPLE 2.10

Normal retirement benefit: 2% of final 3-year average salary for each year of service

Early retirement eligibility: Age 60

Early retirement benefit: Accrued benefit, reduced by 1/15 for each year by which the benefit commencement date precedes the normal retirement date

Actuarial cost method: Projected Unit Credit

Actuarial assumptions:

    Interest rate: 7% per year

    Compensation increases: 5% per year

    Preretirement deaths and terminations: None

    Retirement age:

        Before 1994: 65

        After 1993: 62

    Selected annuity values: $\ddot{a}_{62}^{(12)} = 9.40$; $\ddot{a}_{65}^{(12)} = 8.75$

Data for sole participant:

Date of birth	1/1/54
Date of hire	1/1/92
1994 compensation	$21,000

age 40

=> age 65

What is the change in the actuarial liability as of 1/1/94 due to the change in the assumed retirement age?

SOLUTION The participant is age 40 and has 2 years of service. Assuming retirement at 65, the accrued benefit at time 0 is

$$B_{40} = .02(21,000) \frac{(1.05)^{24} + (1.05)^{23} + (1.05)^{22}}{3} (2) = 2582,$$

and the actuarial liability is

$$AL_{40} = 2582(1.07)^{-25}(8.75) = 4163.$$

(Note the present value calculation is at interest only, since we assume no preretirement decrements.) Assuming retirement at 62, the accrued benefit at time 0 is

$$B'_{40} = .02(21,000) \frac{(1.05)^{21} + (1.05)^{20} + (1.05)^{19}}{3} (2) = 2231,$$

and the actuarial liability is

$$AL'_{40} = 2231(1.07)^{-22}(9.40)\left(\frac{12}{15}\right) = 3786.$$

The change in the actuarial liability is a decrease of

$$4163 - 3786 = \$377. \qquad \square$$

The following example is designed to show how a loss from salary experience can arise. For simplicity, we will assume no expected or actual deaths. Let the parameter values be $e = 30$, $x = 40$, and $r = 65$.

Suppose the salary at age 40 is \$10,000 and the benefit formula is 3% of salary for each year of service. Then the benefit at age 40 is 300 per year at retirement for each year of service, and the expected accrued benefit at age 41 is $300(41-30)$. Suppose there is a benefit improvement, such that the actual benefit at age 41 becomes 324 annually per year of service, or $324(41-30)$.

Using TUC, we have

$$^{\exp}AL_{41} = 300(41-30)v^{65-41} \cdot \ddot{a}^{(12)}_{65}$$

and

$$^{\rm act}AL_{41} = 324(41-30)v^{65-41} \cdot \ddot{a}^{(12)}_{65},$$

for a loss of

$$^{\rm act}AL_{41} - {}^{\exp}AL_{41} = 24(41-30)v^{65-41} \cdot \ddot{a}^{(12)}_{65}.$$

Using PUC with a 4% benefit improvement assumption, we have

$$^{\exp}AL_{41} = 1.04 \times 300(41-30)v^{65-41} \cdot \ddot{a}^{(12)}_{65}$$

and

$$^{\rm act}AL_{41} = 324(41-30)v^{65-41} \cdot \ddot{a}^{(12)}_{65},$$

for a loss of

$$^{\rm act}AL_{41} - {}^{\exp}AL_{41} = 12(41-30)v^{65-41} \cdot \ddot{a}^{(12)}_{65}.$$

Note that the PUC loss from salary experience is smaller than the TUC loss because PUC contained a benefit improvement assumption (which would include an inflation assumption.)

The following chart summarizes the formulas for the Traditional Unit Credit and the Projected Unit Credit cost methods for an illustrative B_r. Recall that b_x is the unit benefit that accrues for a particular year of service. Under TUC, b_x is usually a flat dollar amount, which is typically increased every three years, usually retroactively. Under PUC, b_x is usually a function of S_{r-1} *or* the projected final average salary. Typically b_x under PUC is larger than b_x under TUC.

	TUC	PUC
B_r	$30 \times 12(r-e)$	$.02FAS(r-e)$
b_x	$B_r/(r-e)$	$B_r/(r-e)$
B_x	$b_x(x-e)$	$b_x(x-e)$
NC_x	$b_x v^{r-x} {}_{r-x}p_x \ddot{a}_r^{(12)}$	$b_x v^{r-x} {}_{r-x}p_x \ddot{a}_r^{(12)}$
AL_x	$B_x v^{r-x} {}_{r-x}p_x \ddot{a}_r^{(12)}$	$B_x v^{r-x} {}_{r-x}p_x \ddot{a}_r^{(12)}$

- The differences between TUC and PUC relate to the expected pension benefit, B_r.

- The chart assumes no death benefits; if there were death benefits (as in Section 6.7) the normal cost would be slightly larger.

DISCUSSION QUESTIONS

2-9 In Example 2.10, why is the actuarial liability assuming retirement at age 62 lower than when assuming retirement at age 65?

2-10 Is B_x higher for TUC or PUC? Write out expressions for B_x, B_{x+1}, and B_{x+2}.

2-11 Give an expression for the TUC experience loss at time 1.

2-12 What is the PUC salary experience loss at time 1, and how is it funded?

2-13 How will B_r change in the future under TUC? Under PUC?

2-14 What are the concepts behind the words (a) accrued, (b) allocated, and (c) attributed?

EXAMPLE 2.11

Normal retirement benefit: 1.5% of final 5-year average salary for each of
    the first 20 years of service, plus 1.0% of final 5-year average salary
    for each of the next 10 years of service
Actuarial cost method: Projected Unit Credit
Assumed salary increases: 6% per year
Assumed retirement age: 65
Participant data as of 1/1/94 and selected annuity values:

	Attained Age x	1994 Annual Salary	$_{65-x}\vert\,\ddot{a}_{65}^{(12)}$	Hire Age
Smith	50	$24,000	4	30
Brown	60	30,000	8	30

What is the normal cost for 1994 as of 1/1/94?

SOLUTION Let 1/1/94 be time 0. Note that TAL_0 includes 20 years of
service for Smith and 30 for Brown. The future service used for benefit
accrual is 10 years for Smith and none for Brown, since the normal
retirement benefit is based on a maximum of 30 years. Brown will not
have a normal cost at time 0 because there is no benefit accrual for future
service. Then for Smith we have

$$FAS = 24,000 \, \frac{(1.06)^{10} + \cdots + (1.06)^{14}}{5} = 48,457$$

and Smith's normal cost is

$$NC_{50} = b_{50} \cdot {}_{15}\vert\,\ddot{a}_{50}^{(12)},$$

where b_{50} is the benefit accruing in the year following time 0. This benefit
depends on the future years of service only. Thus we have

$$b_{50} = .01 FAS(r-x)/(r-x)$$

$$= .01(48,457)(10)/10 = 484.57$$

and therefore

$$NC_{50} = 484.57(4) = \$1938. \qquad \square$$

EXAMPLE 2.12

Normal retirement benefit: 1% of each year's salary as of 1/1
Actuarial cost method: Projected Unit Credit
Assumed salary increase: 6% per year
Assumed retirement age: 65
Data for sole participant as of 1/1/94:

Age of hire	30
Current age	40
Salary as of 1/1	$20,000
Accrued annual pension benefit	1,700

What is the attributed benefit as of 1/1/94?

SOLUTION The total benefit expected to be accrued at retirement is the accrued benefit at 1/1/94 plus 1% of the accumulated value of future salaries, which is

$$1700 + .01\left(20,000s_{\overline{25}|.06}\right) = 12,672.90.$$

The benefit attributed by the funding method to each year of accrual is $\frac{1}{35}(12,672.90)$, so the attributed benefit from age 30 to age 40 is

$$\frac{10}{35}(12,672.90) = \$3620.83.$$

- The "attributed benefit" as of a certain date is sometimes referred to as the "allocated benefit" or the "accrued benefit."

- If the participant *terminates* on 1/1/94, the pension commencing at age 65 is based on pre-1994 salaries, rather than post-1993 salaries! □

The final two examples in this chapter use pension plans that provide for death benefits. The preretirement and postretirement death benefits are included in the actuarial liability and the normal cost values.

EXAMPLE 2.13

Preretirement death benefit: A lump sum payment of $5000 for each year of service, payable at the end of the year of death; a year of service is granted for the year of death regardless of when within the year the participant dies

Actuarial assumptions:
  Interest rate: 7% per year
  Preretirement terminations other than deaths: None
  Retirement age: 65
Data for sole participant:
  Date of birth   1/1/34
  Date of hire   1/1/74
  Status as of 1/1/94   Active
Selected commutation values:

x	D_x	x	D_x
60	14,863	64	10,616
61	13,694	65	9,718
62	12,600	66	7,926
63	11,575		

Find the present value at age 60 of the future preretirement death benefit.

SOLUTION   At 1/1/94 the participant is age 60. If the preretirement death benefit were simply a lump sum of $5000, then we would have

$$pv_{60}DBEN = 5000A^{1}_{60:\overline{5}|} = 5000 \frac{M_{60} - M_{65}}{D_{60}},$$

where $M_{60} - M_{65} = C_{60} + C_{61} + \cdots + C_{64}$, and $C_x = vD_x - D_{x+1}$. However, the death benefit provides $5000 for each year of service, so we have

$$pv_{60}DBEN = 5000 \left[\frac{21C_{60} + 22C_{61} + \cdots + 25C_{64}}{D_{60}} \right].$$

The required numerical values are

$$
\begin{aligned}
21C_{60} &= 21(vD_{60} - D_{61}) &=& \quad 4{,}130 \\
22C_{61} &= 22(vD_{61} - D_{62}) &=& \quad 4{,}359 \\
23C_{62} &= 23(vD_{62} - D_{63}) &=& \quad 4{,}616 \\
24C_{63} &= 24(vD_{63} - D_{64}) &=& \quad 4{,}842 \\
25C_{64} &= 25(vD_{64} - D_{65}) &=& \quad 5{,}087 \\
\hline
& & & \quad 23{,}034
\end{aligned}
$$

leading to

$$pv_{60}DBEN = 5000(23{,}034/14{,}863) = \$7749.$$ $\square$

EXAMPLE 2.14

Normal retirement benefit: $500 per month

Postretirement death benefit: $5000 payable at the end of the month of death

Accrued benefit: The normal retirement benefit and the postretirement death benefit are accrued and prorated on service

Actuarial cost method: Projected Unit Credit

Actuarial assumptions:

    Interest rate: 7% per year

    Preretirement deaths and terminations: None

    Retirement age: 65

Data for sole participant:

Date of birth	1/1/34
Date of hire	1/1/69
Status as of 1/1/94	Active

Present value at age 65 of postretirement death benefit: $2100

What is the normal cost for 1994 as of 1/1/94?

SOLUTION At 1/1/94, the participant is age 60. Since there are no preretirement deaths or terminations, the participant will have 30 years of service at retirement and the accrual in 1994 is 1/30 of the benefit. The value of the death benefit is 2100 at age 65, so it is $2100v^5$ at age 60, and the normal cost for it is

$$NC_{60}^{(d)} = \frac{2100v^5}{30} = 49.91.$$

The present value of the retirement benefit is $6000\ddot{a}_{65}^{(12)}$ at age 65, the accrual in 1994 is $\frac{1}{30}$ of the benefit, and the normal cost for it at age 60 is

$$NC_{60}^{(r)} = \frac{6000\ddot{a}_{65}^{(12)} \cdot v^5}{30}.$$

To find $\ddot{a}_{65}^{(12)}$, note that we are given $5000A_{65}^{(12)} = 2100$, which implies $A_{65}^{(12)} = .42$. Next we recall the identity $A_{65}^{(12)} = 1 - d^{(12)} \cdot \ddot{a}_{65}^{(12)}$, where $d^{(12)} = 12[1 - (1.07)^{-1/12}] = .06747$. From this we can find the value of

$\ddot{a}_{65}^{(12)} = \frac{1-.42}{.06747} = 8.59641$. Finally, the normal cost for the retirement benefit is

$$\frac{6000(1.07)^{-5}(8.59641)}{30} = 1225.83,$$

and the total normal cost is

$$NC_{60} = 49.91 + 1225.83 = \$1275.74. \qquad \square$$

2.4 Exercises

2.1 Traditional Unit Credit

2-1   Plan effective date: 1/1/85
       Normal retirement benefit: $10 monthly per year of service
       Actuarial cost method: Unit Credit
       All employees were hired at age 25.
       There is one vested termination and one retired individual under the
           plan. Both are noted on the census data.
       Assumed retirement age: 65
       Assumed interest rate: 5%
       Preretirement terminations other than by death: None
       Selected annuity value: $\ddot{a}_{65}^{(12)} = 10$

       Participant data as of 1/1/94 and selected commutation functions:

Attained Age x	Service	Number of Employees	D_x
25	0	3 (all active)	40
35	10	3 (all active)	30
45	20	1 (terminated vested 12/31/93)	20
55	30	1 (active)	10
65	40	1 (retired on 12/31/93)	5

       What is the actuarial liability as of 1/1/94? (Note that the liability for
       the new entrants is zero; there is full liability for the other partici-
       pants.)

2-2   Compute the four Unit Credit actuarial liabilities for Example 2.2 if
       the entry age is 31.

2-3 Retirement benefit: 2% of each year's annual salary
Actuarial cost method: Unit Credit
Actuarial assumptions:
Interest: 7%
Retirement age: 65
Preretirement terminations other than death: None
Deaths are assumed to occur at BOY.
All benefits begin at age 65.
Actuarial value of assets as of 1/1/93: $15,000
Participant data as of 1/1/93:

Actives:

	Age at Hire	Current Age	Sex	Marital Status	Accrued Benefit as of 12/31/92	1/1/93 Annual Salary
Smith	30	30	F	Married	$ 0	$10,000
Brown	30	45	F	Married	3600	20,000

Former Participants:

	Type	Current Age	Sex	Annual Benefit	Form of Annuity
Jones	Vested terminated	50	M	$1000	Life
Green	Retired	70	M	2000	Life

Selected mortality rates and annuity values:

	Male		Female
x	$_{65-x}\|\ddot{a}_x^{(12)}$	$\ddot{a}_x^{(12)}$	$_{65-x}\|\ddot{a}_x^{(12)}$
25	.2	11.2	.3
30	.4	10.7	.5
35	.7	10.2	.8
40	1.0	9.7	1.2
45	1.5	9.2	1.7
50	2.2	8.7	2.5
55	3.4	8.2	3.7
60	5.0	7.7	5.5
65	—	7.2	—
70	—	6.7	—

(a) What is the normal cost and actuarial liability for each life as of 1/1/93?

(b) What is the unfunded actuarial liability as of 1/1/93?

(Note that the normal cost for deferred vested and retired participants is zero, since no benefit is accrued in the following year. If annuities are purchased upon termination or retirement, then the plan no longer has any financial obligations to former participants and their actuarial liability is zero.)

2-4   Retirement benefit: $35 per month for each year of service
        Actuarial cost method: Unit Credit
        Actuarial assumptions:

Interest:	6%
Mortality:	$q_{40} = .01, q_{41} = .02$
Entry:	Age 35
Retirement:	Age 65

Participants as of 1/1/93: 50, all age 40
Normal cost as of 1/1/93: $50,000
Deaths and New Entrants: None in 1993 or 1994

Calculate the total actuarial liability as of 1/1/95.

2-5   Actuarial cost method: Unit Credit
        Assumed preretirement deaths and terminations:
            Before 1993: None
            After 1992: Mortality only
        Assumed retirement age: 65
        Date of birth for sole active participant: 1/1/40
        Actuarial liability (before assumption change) as of 1/1/93: $20,000
        Selected values: $\ell_{53} = 8,980,994$ $\ell_{65} = 7,673,269$

Calculate the decrease in the accrued liability as of 1/1/93, due to the change in actuarial assumption.

2.2 Benefits with a Salary Scale
2.3 Projected Unit Credit

2-6 Retirement benefit: 1% of final salary per year of service
Actuarial cost method: Projected Unit Credit
Assumed retirement age: 65
Annuity factor: $\ddot{a}_{65}^{(12)} = 10$

There are no terminations prior to age 65 other than death.
Participant data as of 1/1/94 and selected commutation functions:

Age at Hire	Attained Age x	Number of Employees	Total Annual Salaries	s_{64}/s_x	D_x
30	30	1	$20,000	4.0	140
—	31	0	0	3.9	138
40	50	1	30,000	2.0	120
—	51	0	0	1.9	116
—	65	0	0	1.0	10

What is the normal cost for 1994 as of 1/1/94?

2-7 Using the data from Exercise 2-6, calculate the actuarial liability as of 1/1/95.

Chapter 3

Level Cost
Individual Cost Methods

This chapter discusses the cost methods which start with the total value of each participant's pension benefits (accruing from entry to retirement) and develop the equivalent level normal cost in one of the following manners:

Normal Cost each Year from	Normal Cost Expressed as
(a) Entry to Retirement	Level Dollar Amount
(b) Entry to Retirement	Level Percent of Salary
(c) Inception to Retirement	Level Dollar or Level Percent

At the inception of the plan, it is common to have past service, an initial actuarial liability, and a supplemental cost; this is discussed in Section 3.5. Case (c) only arises if entry precedes plan inception, so that age a is greater than age e. Recall that age a is the age of the participant at the inception of the plan.

3.1 Entry Age Normal (Level Dollar)

The **Entry Age Normal (level dollar)** normal cost is such that, at age e, the present value of all future normal costs equals the present value of all future benefits. Symbolically we have

entry age Normal
$PV(NC) = PV(FB)$

$$NC \cdot \ddot{a}^{(\tau)}_{e:\overline{r-e}|} = B_r \, v^{r-e} \,_{r-e}p^{(\tau)}_e \, \ddot{a}^{(12)}_r$$

or

$$NC \left(\frac{N^{(\tau)}_e - N^{(\tau)}_r}{D^{(\tau)}_e} \right) = B_r \frac{D^{(\tau)}_r}{D^{(\tau)}_e} \ddot{a}^{(12)}_r .$$

The discounting before retirement is often based on interest and a service table, but is sometimes based on interest only. (A multiple-decrement service table was assumed in writing the above formulas.) If there are no preretirement decrements other than death, a single-decrement mortality table is used, and the "upper tau" notation can be deleted. If there is no preretirement mortality either, then $\ddot{a}^{(\tau)}_{e:\overline{r-e}|}$ is replaced by $\ddot{a}_{\overline{r-e}|}$ and $_{r-e}p^{(\tau)}_e$ is deleted, since it is equal to one.

As under the Unit Credit cost method of Chapter 2, the total normal cost is the sum of the individual normal costs. Provided the projected benefit and the actuarial basis do not change, the normal cost for each individual will remain constant throughout the working lifetime. If there is any change (and there often is), the above calculation is repeated and a revised normal cost is obtained.

Note the two different uses of the word "projected." In Section 2.3, the projected final salary involves a salary scale. In Chapters 3 and 4, the projected benefit means the benefit accrued from entry to retirement. (Both are based on actuarial assumptions concerning future events.)

Note that the normal cost in the following example is calculated at the entry ages of the participants, even though the plan was not effective at that time.

EXAMPLE 3.1

Plan effective date: 1/1/94
Normal retirement benefit: $10 per month for each year of service
Actuarial cost method: Entry Age Normal
Actuarial assumptions:
    Interest: 7%
    Preretirement deaths and terminations: None
    Retirement age: 65

Participant data as of 1/1/94:

	Date of Birth	**Date of Hire**
Smith	1/1/59	1/1/89
Brown	1/1/60	1/1/85

1994 normal cost for Smith as of 1/1/94: $320

What is the normal cost for Brown as of 1/1/94?

SOLUTION The cost of Brown's retirement benefit is spread over all active years of service. As of the age of hire, which is age 25, we equate the present value of all future normal costs to the present value of future benefits, obtaining

$$NC \cdot \ddot{a}_{25:\overline{40}|} = B_{65} \, v^{40} \, {}_{40}p_{25} \, \ddot{a}_{65}^{(12)}.$$

Since there are no preretirement deaths or terminations, we can replace $\ddot{a}_{25:\overline{40}|}$ with $\ddot{a}_{\overline{40}|}$, and note that ${}_{40}p_{25} = 1$. Solving for NC we obtain

$$NC = (10 \times 12 \times 40) \, \frac{(1.07)^{-40} \, \ddot{a}_{65}^{(12)}}{\ddot{a}_{\overline{40}|}}$$

$$= 4800 \, \frac{\ddot{a}_{65}^{(12)}}{\ddot{s}_{\overline{40}|}} = 22.47 \ddot{a}_{65}^{(12)}.$$

Since we know Smith's normal cost, we can calculate $\ddot{a}_{65}^{(12)}$. For Smith, as of age 65, we have

$$320\ddot{s}_{\overline{35}|} = (10 \times 12 \times 35)\ddot{a}_{65}^{(12)},$$

from which we find

$$\ddot{a}_{65}^{(12)} = 11.27.$$

Then Brown's normal cost is $(22.47)(11.27) = \$253.23$. □

EXAMPLE 3.2

Plan effective date: 1/1/94

Normal retirement benefit: $10 per month for each year of service

Early retirement eligibility: Age 60

Early retirement benefit: Accrued retirement benefit reduced by $\frac{1}{2}$% for each month prior to age 65

Actuarial cost method: Entry Age Normal

Assumed interest rate: 7%

Assumed retirement age: 62

It is assumed that there are no deaths prior to retirement.

Data for sole participant as of 1/1/94:

       Attained age: 50

       Prior service: 5 years.

Selected annuity value: $\ddot{a}_{62}^{(12)} = 9.375$

What is the normal cost for 1994 as of 1/1/94?

SOLUTION Assuming retirement at age 62, the participant would have $5 + 12 = 17$ years of service, for an accrued benefit of

$$B_{62} = 10 \times 12 \times 17 = \$2040.$$

Since age 62 precedes age 65 by 36 months, the reduced benefit is

$$B_{62}' = 2040\,[1 - (.005)(36)] = 1672.80,$$

and at entry age 45 the present value of the reduced benefit is

$$pv_{45}B_{62}' = B_{62}'\, v^{62-45}\, \ddot{a}_{62}^{(12)}$$

$$= 1672.80\, v^{17}\, (9.375)$$

$$= \$4964.67.$$

Since $pv_{45}NC_{45} = pv_{45}B_{62}'$, then

$$NC_{45} = pv_{45}B_{62}'/\ddot{a}_{\overline{17}|} = 4964.67/10.44666 = \$475.24. \qquad \square$$

EXAMPLE 3.3

Normal retirement benefit: 1% of final five year average salary for each
      year of service, not to exceed 25%
Actuarial cost method: Entry Age Normal
Assumed retirement age: 65
Preretirement terminations other than death: None
Assumed salary increases: None
Participant data as of 1/1/94 and selected annuity values:

Age x	Number of Participants	Total of Annual Salaries	$_{65-x}|\ddot{a}_{65}^{(12)}$	$\ddot{a}_{x:\overline{65-x}|}$
35	2	$20,000	2	16
45	3	40,000	3	12
55	4	80,000	5	8
60	1	50,000	8	4

All participants were hired at age 35.

What is the normal cost for 1994 as of 1/1/94?

SOLUTION Let 1/1/94 be time 0. Since there are no assumed salary
increases, the final average salary (*FAS*) is simply the participant's current
annual salary. The total retirement benefit is the sum of each participant's
retirement benefit, and is given by

$$\sum B_r = .25 \sum FAS$$

$$= 5,000 + 10,000 + 20,000 + 12,500$$

$$= 47,500.$$

We calculate the normal cost at entry, and, since $NC_0 = NC_e$, we have

$$TNC_0 \cdot \ddot{a}_{35:\overline{30}|} = \sum B_r \cdot {}_{30}|\ddot{a}_{35}^{(12)},$$

so that

$$TNC_0 = \frac{(47,500)(2)}{16} = \$5938. \qquad \square$$

The actuarial liability is the present value of future benefits minus the present value of future normal costs. At the inception of the plan, when the participant is age a, the total actuarial liability is

Total Actuar. liab. @ inception age a

$$TAL_a = \sum pv_a B - \sum pv_a NC,$$

and this liability is amortized over a period of years as discussed in Section 3.5. On subsequent valuation dates, such as at time 0 when the participant is age x, the actuarial liability is

Act. liab. @ subsequent valuation date x

$$AL_0 = pv_0 B - pv_0 NC$$

$$= B_r \frac{D_r^{(\tau)}}{D_x^{(\tau)}} \ddot{a}_r^{(12)} - NC \left(\frac{N_x^{(\tau)} - N_r^{(\tau)}}{D_x^{(\tau)}} \right)$$

for each participant, and the total actuarial liability is the sum of each participant's liability. The actuarial liability may also be expressed retrospectively as

Retrospective

$$AL_0 = NC \cdot \ddot{s}_{e:\overline{x-e|}} = NC \left(\frac{N_e^{(\tau)} - N_x^{(\tau)}}{D_x^{(\tau)}} \right).$$

The retrospective actuarial liability is equal to the prospective liability. Because of changes in salary and other changes, the current normal cost is usually different from the historical normal costs; the equality of the retrospective and prospective liabilities is based on the current normal cost, not the historical normal cost.

For further insight into the concept of liabilities, we can state that the total actuarial liability is the accumulated value of normal costs, less any benefits paid out from age e to age x, with interest and the benefit of survivorship. A pension plan is a pure endowment policy with sum insured $B_r \cdot \ddot{a}_r^{(12)}$, where normal costs are premiums and actuarial liabilities are reserves. This is shown by the equation

$$AL_0 = B_r \cdot \ddot{a}_r^{(12)} \cdot \underset{x-e}{V} \frac{1}{e:\overline{r-e|}}.$$

EXAMPLE 3.4

Actuarial cost method: Entry Age Normal
Assumed retirement age: 65
Data for sole participant:

Date of birth	1/1/49
Date of hire	1/1/79
Status as of 1/1/94	Active

Projected annual benefit as of 1/1/94: B_r
Level annual cost from age 30: NC
Preretirement decrements other than death: None

Which of the following expressions for the accrued liability for retirement benefits as of 1/1/94 are correct?

I. $\quad NC\left(\dfrac{N_{30} - N_{45}}{D_{45}}\right)$

II. $\quad B_r\left(\dfrac{N_{65}^{(12)}}{D_{45}}\right) - NC\left(\dfrac{N_{45} - N_{65}}{D_{45}}\right)$

III. $\quad B_r\left(\dfrac{N_{65}^{(12)}}{D_{45}}\right)\left(\dfrac{N_{30} - N_{45}}{N_{30} - N_{65}}\right)$

(handwritten notes:)
$\ddot{a}_{e:\overline{x-e}|} = \dfrac{N_e - N_x}{D_e}$

$\ddot{s}_{e:\overline{x-e}|} = \dfrac{N_e - N_x}{D_x}$

SOLUTION The level annual cost from entry is

$$NC = B_r\left(\frac{N_{65}^{(12)}}{N_{30} - N_{65}}\right).$$

I. True. This is the standard retrospective definition, since there are no past benefits.

II. True. This is the standard prospective definition.

III. True. Substitute the definition of NC into expression II, and simplify.

$\square$

In the following example, the plan is introduced 10 years after the sole participant was hired. We know the normal cost is calculated as of the hire age, and the retirement benefit is funded throughout the lifetime of the participant. Thus, at the plan effective date, there will be an actuarial liability for past service. This is not the case for all funding methods, as we shall see later.

EXAMPLE 3.5

Plan effective date: 1/1/94
Normal retirement benefit: $200 per month
Actuarial cost method: Entry Age Normal
Actuarial assumptions:
>   Interest: 6%
>   Preretirement mortality and terminations: None
>   Retirement age: 65
>   Selected annuity value: $\ddot{a}_{65}^{(12)} = 10$

As of 1/1/94 there is one participant, age 45, hired on 1/1/84.

What is the plan's actuarial liability as of 1/1/94?

SOLUTION
--- At entry, equate the present value of future normal costs to the present value of future benefits, obtaining

$$NC_e \cdot \ddot{a}_{e:\overline{r-e|}} = B_r \, v^{r-e} \,_{r-e}p_e \, \ddot{a}_r^{(12)}.$$

Since entry age is 35 and there are no preretirement deaths or terminations, we have

$$NC_{35} = \frac{(200)(12)(1.06)^{-30}(1)(10)}{\ddot{a}_{\overline{30|}}} = 286.39.$$

Then, retrospectively, the actuarial liability at 1/1/94 (age 45) is

$$AL_{45} = 286.39 \ddot{s}_{\overline{10|}} = \$4001.35. \qquad \square$$

AL → take PV(ben)
→ take PV(NC) @ inception date
@ inception
not entry

| EXAMPLE 3.6 |

Normal retirement benefit: $10 per month for each year of service
Actuarial cost method: Entry Age Normal
Actuarial assumptions:
    Interest: 8%
    Preretirement terminations other than deaths: None
    Retirement age: 65
    Selected annuity value: $\ddot{a}_{65}^{(12)} = 8$

Participant data as of 1/1/94 and selected commutation functions:

	Date of Birth	Date of Hire		x	N_x	D_x
Smith	1/1/64	1/1/94		30	12,570	980
Brown	1/1/54	1/1/84		40	5,485	450
Green	1/1/44	1/1/74		50	2,255	200
				65	465	55

What is the actuarial liability as of 1/1/94?

| SOLUTION | Let 1/1/94 be time 0. Since all participants were hired at age 30 and the benefit is a flat dollar amount, the normal cost for each participant will be the same. Equating the value of normal costs at age r to the value of future benefits at age r, we have

$$NC_e \left(\frac{N_e - N_r}{D_r} \right) = B_r \cdot \ddot{a}_r^{(12)},$$

leading to

$$NC_{30} = \frac{(10 \times 12 \times 35)(8)}{220.09091} = 152.66.$$

The total actuarial liability is the sum of each participant's liability. Note that Smith is hired 1/1/94, so he has no past service, and hence no liability. Then, retrospectively, we have

$$TAL_0 = NC_e \sum_x \frac{N_e - N_x}{D_x} = 152.66 \left[\frac{7085}{450} + \frac{10,315}{200} \right] = \$10,277.$$

$\square$

EXAMPLE 3.7

Actuarial cost method: Entry Age Normal

Actuarial assumptions:

> Interest: 6%
>
> Salary increases: None
>
> Retirement age: 65
>
> Preretirement mortality and disability: None

Selected preretirement *termination* rates:

Age x	$q_x^{(w)}$
35	.5
36	.4
37	.3
38	.2
39	.1

(handwritten: AL = accumulation of past normal costs.)

Participant data and selected valuation results as of 1/1/94:

	Entry Age	**Attained Age**	**Normal Cost as of 1/1**
Smith	35	35	$1000
Brown	35	38	5000

If there is no vesting in the first five years, what is the actuarial liability as of 1/1/94?

| **SOLUTION** | Note that $AL_{35} = 0$ for Smith, since he has no past service. For Brown we have, retrospectively,

$$AL_{38} = NC_{35} \cdot \ddot{s}_{35:\overline{3|}} = 5000 \left[\frac{(1+i)^3}{{}_3p_{35}} + \frac{(1+i)^2}{{}_2p_{36}} + \frac{(1+i)}{p_{37}} \right]$$

(handwritten: $\ddot{s}_{35:\overline{3|}} = \frac{(1+i)^3}{{}_3p_{35}} + \frac{(1+i)^2}{{}_2p_{36}} + \frac{(1+i)}{p_{37}}$)

$$= 5000 \left[\frac{(1.06)^3}{(.5)(.6)(.7)} + \frac{(1.06)^2}{(.6)(.7)} + \frac{1.06}{.7} \right] = \$49,305.$$

Note that the liability is simply the accumulation of past normal costs, since there have been no past termination benefits. The values of ${}_tp_x$ and $\ddot{s}_{35:\overline{3|}}$ are taken from a single-decrement table for terminations only.   □

As with all methods, the unfunded actuarial liability for the whole plan at time 0 is $UAL_0 = AL_0 - F_0$. The expected unfunded actuarial liability at time 1 is

$$^{exp}UAL_1 = (UAL_0 + NC_0)(1+i) - C,$$

F = assets
C = contribution.

if the contribution is made at EOY. At time 1, the actual unfunded actuarial liability is $^{act}UAL_1 = AL_1 - F_1$.

There will be a gain if $^{exp}UAL_1 > {}^{act}UAL_1$, and there will be a loss if $^{exp}UAL_1 < {}^{act}UAL_1$; specifically,

$$^{tot}G = {}^{exp}UAL - {}^{act}UAL.$$

Under ideal conditions, when the actual experience (*e.g.*, interest, salary increases, and mortality) is the same as assumed, the actual unfunded actuarial liability will be the same as the expected, and there will be no resulting gain or loss. More discussion of experience gains is given in Chapter 5.

EXAMPLE 3.8

Plan effective date: 1/1/84
Normal retirement benefit: $6 per month for each year of service
All employees were hired at age 25
Retirement age: 65
Plan assets on 1/1/94: $5000
Preretirement terminations other than death: None
Census data on 1/1/94, and selected actuarial functions:

Age x	Number of Participants	D_x	$N_x - N_{65}$	$\ddot{a}_x^{(12)}$
25	8	16	320	
35	0	8	120	
45	2	4	40	
55	0	2	10	
65	0	1	0	10

Under the Entry Age Normal cost method, what is the unfunded actuarial liability as of 1/1/94?

$\boxed{\textbf{SOLUTION}}$ Let 1/1/94 be time 0. Since $UAL_0 = TAL_0 - F_0$, we first need to calculate the total actuarial liability. Prospectively we have

$$AL_0 = pv_0 B - pv_0 NC_{25}$$

$$= \sum B_{65} \frac{D_{65}}{D_x} \ddot{a}_{65}^{(12)} - \sum NC_{25} \left(\frac{N_x - N_{65}}{D_x} \right).$$

We will need to calculate the normal cost at entry, which will be the same for all participants. Therefore we have

$$NC_{25} = B_{65}\, \ddot{a}_{65}^{(12)} \left(\frac{D_{65}}{N_{25} - N_{65}} \right) = (6 \times 12 \times 40)(10) \left(\frac{1}{320} \right) = 90.$$

Those who are age 25 on 1/1/94 were just hired, so they have no past service and the plan has no liability. For each participant at age 45 we find

$$pv_0 B = B_{65} \frac{D_{65}}{D_{45}} \ddot{a}_{65}^{(12)} = (2880) \left(\frac{1}{4} \right) (10) = 7200$$

and

$$pv_0 NC = NC_{25} \left(\frac{N_{45} - N_{65}}{D_{45}} \right) = (90) \left(\frac{40}{4} \right) = 900,$$

so for each participant age 45 we have

$$AL_{45} = pv_0 B - pv_0 NC = 7200 - 900 = 6300.$$

Then the liability for all participants is

$$TAL_0 = 0 + 2(6300) = 12{,}600$$

and finally we have

$$UAL_0 = TAL_0 - F_0 = 12{,}600 - 5{,}000 = \$7600. \qquad \square$$

The calculation of the liability for each participant is more easily done retrospectively, where we have $AL_{45} = 90 \left(\frac{N_{25} - N_{45}}{D_{45}} \right) = 90 \left(\frac{320 - 40}{4} \right) = \$6300$.

3.2 Cost as a Level Percent of Salary

If the pension benefit is based on salary, then the actuarial cost will usually be expressed as a level percentage of salary. A participant's normal cost for a certain year is then a **percentage, U,** of his salary in that year. This percentage remains constant, for Entry Age Normal, from age e to age r (except that, if conditions change, a recalculation of U is necessary).

A **salary-based annuity** must be used when calculating the present value of normal costs. For one participant, we define this annuity to be

use salary-based ann. calc. when present value (NC)

$$\ddot{a}^s_{x:\overline{r-x}|} = 1 + \left(\frac{1+s}{1+i}\right)p_x + \cdots + \left(\frac{1+s}{1+i}\right)^{r-x-1}{}_{r-x-1}p_x,$$

and the present value at age x, pv_x, of future salaries is

PV (future salaries)

$$pv_x S_x = S_x \cdot \ddot{a}^s_{x:\overline{r-x}|} = S_x \cdot \frac{{}^sN_x - {}^sN_r}{{}^sD_x},$$

where s is a rate of salary increase not dependent on age. If the rate of salary increase depends on age, we replace s by s_x as described in the next section.

We have an average working-life annuity of

$$\frac{pvS}{S} = \frac{\sum pv_x S_x}{\sum S_x} = \frac{\sum S_x \cdot \ddot{a}^s_{x:\overline{r-x}|}}{\sum S_x},$$

where all active participants are included in the summations. Since the normal cost is defined as a percentage of salary, then the normal cost at age e is

$$NC_e = U_e \cdot S_e,$$

NC @ age e

the normal cost at age x is

$$NC_x = U_e \cdot S_x,$$

NC @ age x,

and the present value at age x of the normal costs from age x to age $r - 1$ is

PV of normal costs (handwritten)

$$pv_xNC = U_e \cdot S_x \cdot \ddot{a}^s_{\overline{x:r-x|}}.$$

Also at age x the present value of all future normal costs for all active participants who entered at age e is

$$pv_xNC = \sum U_e \cdot S_x \cdot \ddot{a}^s_{\overline{x:r-x|}},$$

and the total of the present values of all future normal costs for all active participants is $\sum_{A_0} pv_xNC$; the participants who entered at age e are included in the first summation in this sentence, and all participants are included in the second summation. We use A_0 to denote the set of active participants at time 0 (age x), and A_1 to denote the set of actives at time 1 (age $x+1$). Retired participants are *not* included in normal cost calculations in the methods of this chapter. The liability for inactives would be added to that for actives.

The actuarial liability is defined as the present value of the future benefits minus the present value of future normal costs. For one active participant who entered at age e and is now age x,

AL for part. entered @ age e & is now age x. (handwritten)

$$AL_x = pv_xB - pv_xNC = pv_xB - U_e \cdot S_x \cdot \ddot{a}^s_{\overline{x:r-x|}}.$$

For all active participants who entered at age e, we have

$$\sum AL_x = \sum pv_xB - U_e \sum S_x \cdot \ddot{a}^s_{\overline{x:r-x|}}.$$

For all active participants in total we have

$$TAL_0 = \sum_{A_0} pv_xB - \sum_{A_0} U_e \cdot S_x \cdot \ddot{a}^s_{\overline{x:r-x|}}.$$

For example, if there were 4 different entry ages and 5 active participants at each entry age, then there would be 20 terms in each summation in the last equation and 5 terms in each summation in the next-to-last equation.

The above calculations involve the use of the salary based commutation symbols

$$^sD_x = s_x \ell_x v^x$$

and

$$^{s}N_x = \sum_{h=x}^{\infty} {}^{s}D_h.$$

If $i = .06$ and $s = .05$, then

$$N_x = \ell_x \frac{1}{(1.06)^x} + \ell_{x+1} \frac{1}{(1.06)^{x+1}} + \cdots$$

and

$$^{s}N_x = \ell_x \left(\frac{1.05}{1.06}\right)^x + \ell_{x+1} \left(\frac{1.05}{1.06}\right)^{x+1} + \cdots .$$

The **average annuity factors** in this section will be helpful in obtaining the normal cost for the cost methods described in later sections of the text. The average annuity factor takes on slightly different forms depending on the circumstances, as shown in the following table.

Average Annuity Factors:.

Section	Method	Example	Average Annuity
3.3	EAN	3.9	$U_e \cdot S_e \cdot \dfrac{{}^{s}N_e - {}^{s}N_r}{{}^{s}D_e} = pvB$
3.4	ILP	3.27	$NC_a \cdot \dfrac{{}^{s}N_a - {}^{s}N_r}{{}^{s}D_a} = pvB$
4.1	Ind Agg	4.1	$NC_x \cdot \ddot{a}_{x:\overline{r-x}|} = pvB - F^P$
4.2	Agg	4.9	$TNC \cdot \dfrac{\sum pvS}{\sum S} = \sum pvB - F$
4.3 4.4	FIL	4.25	$TNC \cdot \dfrac{\sum \dfrac{{}^{s}N_x - {}^{s}N_r}{{}^{s}D_x} \cdot S_x}{\sum S_x} = \sum pvB - UAL - F$
4.5	Agg EAN	4.26	$TNC \cdot \dfrac{1}{n} \sum \dfrac{N_x - N_r}{D_x} = \sum pvB,$ where n is the number of actives.

3.3 Entry Age Normal (Level Percent)

The Entry Age Normal (EAN) cost method usually uses a salary-increase assumption when the pension benefit is based on career average or final average salary. Assume that the salary at age x is S_x, and that it increases annually at rate s.

When salaries are assumed to increase, the normal cost under EAN is defined as a level percentage of salary. A salary scale is used to determine a participant's salary at earlier and later dates. At and after age e, we want the normal cost to be a constant fraction, U, of salary, so that

$$NC_e = U \cdot S_e = U[S_x(1+s)^{e-x}],$$

and

$$NC_x = U \cdot S_x = U[S_e(1+s)^{x-e}].$$

This shows that

$$NC_x = NC_e(1+s)^{x-e} = NC_e \cdot \frac{S_x}{S_e}.$$

At entry age we can equate the present value of all future normal costs to the present value of future benefits, obtaining

$$NC_e \cdot \ddot{a}^s_{\overline{e:r-e|}} = U \cdot S_e \cdot \ddot{a}^s_{\overline{e:r-e|}} = B_r \frac{D_r^{(\tau)}}{D_e^{(\tau)}} \ddot{a}_r^{(12)}.$$

From the last equation we can solve for U, and then for

$$NC_e = U \cdot S_e = U \cdot S_x \cdot \frac{S_e}{S_x},$$

and

$$NC_x = U \cdot S_x = NC_0.$$

If we were to use historical salaries for all participants before age x, then we would be burdened with different U's for the same entry age. Furthermore, historical salaries are often not available, and where they are available they are not appropriate for obtaining a level normal cost where the participant has had a promotion. Hence we use projection to obtain past salaries for calculating the normal cost.

The *actuarial liability* for a *career average* plan is another matter. We are often required by the plan document to use *historical* salaries to obtain the career average pension benefit, and we wish to present a realistic actuarial liability. To do this we use historical salaries before the valuation date and projected future salaries. Hence the liability for a career average plan is the present value of realistic benefits less the present value of normal costs, where the normal costs are calculated as described in the previous paragraph.

For a *final salary* plan, we use the final expected salary.

| **EXAMPLE 3.9** |

Retirement benefit: 1% of final salary for each year of service
Accrued benefit: According to normal retirement
Actuarial cost method: Entry Age Normal
Assumed retirement age: 65
Selected annuity value: $\ddot{a}_{65}^{(12)} = 10$
Preretirement terminations other than death: None
Participant data as of 1/1/94 and selected commutation functions:

Entry Age e	Attained Age x	Number of Employees	Total Annual Salaries	$\dfrac{s_{64}}{s_x}$	^sD_x	$^sN_x - {}^sN_{65}$
30	30	2	$20,000	4.0	560	5000
—	40	0	0	2.5	325	3000
40	50	3	30,000	2.0	240	1550
—	60	0	0	1.3	143	500
—	65	0	0	1.0	10	0

What is the normal cost for 1994 as of 1/1/94?

| **SOLUTION** | Let 1/1/94 be time 0. Since $NC = U \cdot S_x$ we can find U by equating, at entry, the present value of future normal costs to the present value of future benefits, or

$$NC_e \cdot \ddot{a}^s_{\overline{e:r-e|}} = U \cdot S_e \cdot \ddot{a}^s_{\overline{e:r-e|}} = pv_e B.$$

For attained age 30, entry age 30,

$$U_{30} \cdot S_{30} \cdot \frac{{}^s N_{30} - {}^s N_{65}}{{}^s D_{30}} = .01 \times S_{64} \times 35 \times 10 \times \frac{D_{65}}{D_{30}}$$

$$U_{30} \times 20,000 \times \frac{5000}{560} = .01 \times 20,000 \times 4 \times 35 \times 10 \times \frac{10 \times 1}{560 \times 4}$$

$$U_{30} \times 5000 = .01 \times 35 \times 10 \times 10$$

$$U_{30} = .007.$$

For attained age 50, entry age 40,

$$U_{40} \cdot S_{40} \cdot \frac{{}^s N_{40} - {}^s N_{65}}{{}^s D_{40}} = .01 \times S_{64} \times 25 \times 10 \times \frac{D_{65}}{D_{40}}$$

$$U_{40} \times 30,000 \times \frac{2.0}{2.5} \times \frac{3000}{325} = .01 \times 30,000 \times 2 \times 25 \times 10 \times \frac{10 \times 1}{325 \times 2.5}$$

$$U_{40} \times 3000 = 25$$

$$U_{40} = .008\dot{3}.$$

Then

$$NC_0 = 20,000 \times .007 + 30,000 \times .008\dot{3} = \$390.$$

The following observations should be noted:

- S_{40} is obtained by projecting $S_{50} = 30,000$ *backward* for ten years.

- We are able to obtain the ratio $\frac{D_{65}}{D_x}$ when we are given values of ${}^s D_x$: since $\frac{{}^s D_{65}}{{}^s D_x} = \frac{D_{65} \cdot S_{65}}{D_x \cdot S_x}$, then

$$\frac{D_{65}}{D_x} = \frac{{}^s D_{65} \cdot S_x}{{}^s D_x \cdot S_{65}} = \frac{{}^s D_{65} \cdot \frac{S_{64}}{S_{65}}}{{}^s D_x \cdot \frac{S_{64}}{S_x}}.$$

- This example contains several elements that must be mastered for later use. □

| EXAMPLE 3.10 |

Monthly normal retirement benefit: 1% of final monthly pay rate per year
    of service
Actuarial cost method: Entry Age Normal
Actuarial assumptions:
    Interest: 6%
    Salary increases on each January 1: 5%
    Retirement age: 65
    Preretirement terminations other than death: None
Active employees as of 1/1/94:

Age at Hire	Current Age	1994 Monthly Pay Rate
25	35	$2000

Former employees as of 1/1/94:

Type	Current Age	Monthly Pension Benefit
Vested terminated	50	$100
Retired	65	300

Selected commutation functions and annuity values:

x	$\dfrac{{}^{s}D_x}{{}^{s}N_x - {}^{s}N_{65}}$	${}_{65-x\mid}\ddot{a}_x^{(12)}$	$\ddot{a}_x^{(12)}$	x	$\dfrac{{}^{s}D_x}{{}^{s}N_x - {}^{s}N_{65}}$	${}_{65-x\mid}\ddot{a}_x^{(12)}$	$\ddot{a}_x^{(12)}$
25	.07	0.4	19	50	.09	4.0	14
30	.07	0.7	18	55	.12	5.4	13
35	.08	1.0	17	60	.22	7.4	11
40	.08	1.7	16	65	—	—	10
45	.08	2.6	15	70	—	—	8

What is the normal cost for 1994 as of 1/1/94?

$\boxed{\text{SOLUTION}}$ Let $1/1/94$ be time 0. There is no normal cost for terminated vested or retired participants, since no benefit accrues in the year following time 0. At entry we have

$$pv_eB = 12(.01)(2000)(1.05)^{29} \times 40 \times 0.4 = 15{,}806$$

and

$$pv_eNC = NC_e \left(\frac{{}^sN_e - {}^sN_{65}}{{}^sD_e} \right) = \frac{NC_e}{.07} = 15{,}806$$

leading to

$$NC_e = 15{,}806 \times .07 = 1106.42.$$

The normal cost at time 0 is the normal cost at entry adjusted by the salary scale, so we have

$$NC_0 = 1106.42(1.05)^{10} = \$1802. \qquad \square$$

Under entry age normal, the actuarial liability is defined in the usual way, whether or not a salary-increase assumption is used. Thus the actuarial liability at age x is the present value of future benefits minus the present value of future normal costs, so we have

$$AL_x = pv_xB - pv_xNC$$

$$= B_r \frac{D_r}{D_x} \ddot{a}_r^{(12)} - U \cdot S_x \left(\frac{{}^sN_x - {}^sN_r}{{}^sD_x} \right)$$

The actuarial liability can also be shown retrospectively as

$$AL_x = U \cdot S_e \frac{D_e}{D_x} + U \cdot S_{e+1} \frac{D_{e+1}}{D_x} + \cdots + U \cdot S_{x-1} \frac{D_{x-1}}{D_x}.$$

Let us assume that the pension benefit is 2% of the career average salary per year of service and the salary varies with age. The retirement benefit will be

$$B_r = .02 \sum_{z=e}^{r-1} S_e \cdot \frac{S_z}{S_e}.$$

At the date of entry the actuarial liability is zero, and the normal cost can be found by equating the present value of all future normal costs to the present value of future benefits,

$$NC_e \left(\frac{{}^sN_e - {}^sN_r}{{}^sD_e} \right) = \left[.02 \sum_{z=e}^{r-1} \left(S_e \cdot \frac{S_z}{S_e} \right) \right] \frac{D_r}{D_e} \ddot{a}_r^{(12)}.$$

At time 0, which is age x, we have

$$TAL_0 = \left[.02 \sum_{z=e}^{r-1} \left(S_e \cdot \frac{S_z}{S_e} \right) \right] \frac{D_r}{D_x} \ddot{a}_r^{(12)} - NC_0 \left(\frac{{}^sN_x - {}^sN_r}{{}^sD_x} \right),$$

where $NC_0 = NC_e \cdot \frac{S_x}{S_e}$.

As discussed in the previous section, U for individual entry age cost methods depends on entry age, and TAL_0 can be obtained by summing AL_x for the participants with various entry ages. Sometimes a study will show that almost all entrants enter at about age 25, say, so the actuary can make the additional assumption that $e = 25$ for all. Then U will be the same for all participants.

EXAMPLE 3.11

Plan effective date: 1/1/94
Normal retirement benefit: 50% of final five-year average salary
Preretirement terminations other than death: None
Assumed retirement age: 65
Employee data as of 1/1/94:

	Age	Service	1994 Annual Salary
Green	45	None	$10,000

x	^sD_x	$^sN_x - {}^sN_{65}$	S_x	D_x	$N_x^{(12)}$
25	1,500	68,200	.30	5,000	
35	1,600	52,700	.40	4,000	
45	1,620	36,600	.54	3,000	
60	2,100	9,600	1.40	1,500	
61	2,100	7,500	1.50	1,400	
62	1,950	5,400	1.50	1,300	
63	1,800	3,450	1.50	1,200	
64	1,650	1,650	1.50	1,100	
65	1,500	0	1.50	1,000	10,000

What is the normal cost for Green due 1/1/94 under the Entry Age Normal
cost method (level percent of pay)?

| SOLUTION | Green's entry age, 45, is the same as his valuation age,
and

$$NC_{45}\left(\frac{^sN_{45} - {}^sN_{65}}{^sD_{45}}\right) = B_{65}\frac{D_{65}}{D_{45}}\ddot{a}_{65}^{(12)},$$

where

$$B_{65} = .5 \times 10,000 \times \frac{S_{64} + \cdots + S_{60}}{5 \cdot S_{45}}$$

$$= 5000 \times 2.74 = 13,704.$$

Green's normal cost at valuation is therefore

$$NC_{45} = 13,704 \times \frac{1000}{3000} \times \frac{10,000}{1000} \times \frac{1620}{36,600} = \$2022. \qquad \square$$

The following example uses the fact that U is calculated at hire from
the equation

$$U \cdot S_e \cdot \ddot{a}^s_{\overline{e:r-e|}} = B_r\frac{D_r}{D_e}\ddot{a}_r^{(12)}.$$

EXAMPLE 3.12

Plan effective date: 1/1/93

Normal retirement benefit: 40% of final salary

Actuarial assumptions:

    Interest: 5%

    Salary increases: None

    Retirement age: 65

All participants were hired at age 35.

Participant data and valuation results as of 1/1/93:

Attained Age	Number of Active Participants	Projected Annual Pension	PV of Future Salary	PV of Future Benefits
35	1	$4,800	$180,000	$4,000
45	1	4,560	100,000	7,600
55	1	6,000	85,000	20,000
	3	15,360	365,000	31,600

What is the actuarial liability as of 1/1/93 under the Entry Age Normal cost method?

SOLUTION At entry, $pv_eNC = pv_eB = U \cdot pv_eS$. Since U is the same for all participants, we can choose the data of the first participant to calculate it.

$$U = \frac{pvB}{pvS} = \frac{4,000}{180,000} = .0222,$$

which is 2.22% of salary. Then

$$TAL_0 = \sum AL_x = \sum pvB - \sum pvNC,$$

so we have

$$TAL_0 = 31,600 - .0222(365,000) = \$23,497. \qquad \square$$

EXAMPLE 3.13

Normal retirement benefit: 50% of final three-year average salary

Actuarial cost method: Entry Age Normal

Actuarial assumptions:

    Interest rate: 6%

    Compensation increases: 4% per year

    Preretirement terminations other than deaths: None

    Retirement age: 65

    Selected annuity value: $\ddot{a}_{65}^{(12)} = 9.345$

Data for sole participant:

    Date of birth   1/1/64

    Date of hire   1/1/89

    1994 compensation $10,000

Selected commutation functions:

x	D_x	N_x	^sD_x	^sN_x
25	22,499	366,760	59,979	1,920,504
30	16,721	266,509	54,233	1,632,341
65	1,738	17,040	22,244	296,192

What is the normal cost for 1994 as of 1/1/94?

SOLUTION   The retirement benefit is

$$B_r = .50(10,000)(1.04)^{32} \ \frac{1 + 1.04 + (1.04)^2}{3} = 18,251$$

and the normal cost is

$$NC_x = NC_e \cdot \frac{s_x}{s_e}$$

$$= B_r \ddot{a}_r^{(12)} \frac{D_r}{D_e} \left(\frac{^sD_e}{^sN_e - {}^sN_r} \right) \frac{s_x}{s_e}$$

$$= 18,251(9.345) \left(\frac{1738}{22,499} \right) \left(\frac{59,979}{1,624,312} \right) (1.04)^5 = \$592. \qquad \square$$

Note that when the benefit is based on final average salary and the data allows the calculation of both level percent and level dollar, the better answer is level percent.

EXAMPLE 3.14

Plan effective date: 1/1/84
Normal retirement benefit: 50% of final year's compensation
Preretirement terminations other than deaths: None
Actuarial cost method: Entry Age Normal
Assumed interest rate: 7% per year
Selected annuity value: $\ddot{a}_{65}^{(12)} = 8.736$
Data for sole participant:

Date of birth	1/1/59
Date of hire	1/1/84
1993 compensation	$25,000
Status as of 1/1/94	Active

Selected commutation functions:

x	s_x/s_{65}	D_x	^sD_x	N_x	^sN_x
25	.1420	1,779,168	6,024,894	25,677,330	193,660,240
35	.2314	894,190	4,932,364	12,364,650	138,500,016
45	.3769	445,008	3,998,400	5,690,850	93,472,528
55	.6139	213,953	3,131,334	2,405,025	57,406,892
65	1.0000	94,414	2,250,810	868,052	30,013,858

What is the actuarial liability as of 1/1/94?

| **SOLUTION** | The benefit is

$$B_{65} = .50 \times 25,000 \times \frac{s_{65}}{s_{35}} = 54,019.$$

At entry on 1/1/84 the participant is age 25, so the present value of benefits is

$$pv_{25}B = 54,019 \times \frac{D_{65}}{D_{25}} \ddot{a}_{65}^{(12)} = 25,043.$$

Equating $pv_{25}NC$ to $pv_{25}B$ we find

$$NC_{25} = \frac{25{,}043}{\ddot{a}^s_{25:\overline{40|}}} = 922,$$

from which we find

$$NC_{35} = NC_{25} \cdot \frac{s_{35}}{s_{25}}$$

$$= 922 \left(\frac{s_{35}}{s_{65}}\right)\left(\frac{s_{65}}{s_{25}}\right) = 1502.$$

Finally, at 1/1/94 when the participant is age 35, the actuarial liability is found retrospectively to be

$$AL_{35} = NC_{35} \cdot \ddot{s}^s_{25:\overline{10|}} = 1502(11.18333) = \$16{,}797. \qquad \square$$

The following should be noted in this solution:

- The actuary used "previous year" salaries; it is equally (or more) common to use "following year" salaries.
- The salary scale data is given as s_x/s_{65}, whereas other examples use s_{65}/s_x.
- $AL_{35} \neq NC_{25} \cdot \ddot{s}^s_{25:\overline{10|}}$
- D_x is used with pv_xB, whereas ^sD_x is used for NC_x.

EXAMPLE 3.15

Actuarial cost method: Entry Age Normal
Actuarial assumptions:
    Interest: 7%
    Salary increases: 6%
    Retirement age: 65
Preretirement terminations other than deaths: None
Data for sole participant as of 1/1/94:

    Age at hire   61
    Attained age   63
    Projected monthly benefit   \$700

Selected annuity value: $\ddot{a}^{(12)}_{65} = 10$

Selected commutation functions:

x	D_x
61	385
62	354
63	326
64	299
65	274

What is the normal cost as of 1/1/94?

SOLUTION At entry we have

$$NC_e \left(\frac{{}^s N_e - {}^s N_r}{{}^s D_e} \right) = B_r \frac{D_r}{D_e} \ddot{a}_r^{(12)}.$$

Since

$$^s N_x = \sum_{h=x}^{\infty} {}^s D_h$$

and

$$^s D_x = s_x D_x,$$

then

$$^s N_e - {}^s N_r = 385 + 354(1.06) + 326(1.06)^2 + 299(1.06)^3$$

$$= 1482.65.$$

Since $NC_e = NC_x \cdot \frac{s_e}{s_x}$,

$$NC_x (1.06)^{-2} \left(\frac{1482.65}{385} \right) = (700 \times 12)(10) \left(\frac{274}{385} \right),$$

from which we find

$$NC_x = \$17,442. \qquad \square$$

EXAMPLE 3.16

Plan effective date: 1/1/93

Normal retirement benefit: 2% of final three-year average pay for each year of service

Actuarial cost method: Entry Age Normal

Actuarial assumptions:

    Interest: 6%

    Retirement age: 65

Preretirement terminations other than deaths: None

Data for sole participant as of 1/1/93:

    Age   45

    Past service   5 years

    1993 salary $25,000

Selected annuity value: $12\ddot{a}_{65}^{(12)} = 119$

Selected commutation functions:

x	D_x	$N_x - N_{65}$	s_x	$^sN_x - {^s}N_{65}$
40	245	3200	1.82	7100
45	180	2100	2.05	5000
60	70	307	2.63	829
61	65	237	2.67	645
62	61	172	2.71	471
63	57	111	2.74	306
64	54	54	2.77	150
65	50	0	2.80	0

What is the normal cost as of 1/1/93?

| SOLUTION | At 1/1/93 the participant is age 45. The benefit is

$$B_{65} = .02 \left(\frac{25,000}{3 \cdot s_{45}} \right) (s_{62} + s_{63} + s_{64})(25) = 16,707.$$

The present value of the benefit at entry is

$$pv_{40}B = 16,707 \frac{D_{65}}{D_{40}} \ddot{a}_{65}^{(12)} = 33,812$$

so the normal cost at entry is

$$NC_{40} = \frac{33{,}812}{\ddot{a}^{s}_{40:\overline{25}|}} = 2123.49.$$

Then the normal cost at age 45 is

$$NC_{45} = NC_{40} \cdot \frac{s_{45}}{s_{40}} = (2123.49)\left(\frac{2.05}{1.82}\right) = \$2391.84. \qquad \square$$

In the following three examples, there are no preretirement deaths or terminations. Thus the present value of normal costs is based on interest only, so $\ddot{a}^{s}_{e:\overline{r-e}|}$ becomes $\ddot{a}^{s}_{\overline{r-e}|}$. This salary-based annuity can be thought of as an ordinary annuity at interest rate j, where $1 + j = \frac{1+i}{1+s} \cdot j$ is a *net-of-inflation interest rate* that is slightly less than $i - s$.

EXAMPLE 3.17

Plan effective date: 1/1/94
Normal retirement benefit: 60% of final salary
Actuarial cost method: Entry Age Normal
Actuarial assumptions:
    Interest: 7%
    Preretirement mortality and withdrawal: None
    Salary increases: 5%
    Retirement age: 65
Data for sole participant:
    Age at hire   55
    Age on 1/1/94   56
    1/1/94 salary $100,000
Selected annuity value: $12\ddot{a}^{(12)}_{65} = 100$

What is the normal cost as of 1/1/94?

SOLUTION At 1/1/94 the participant is age 56, having entered at age 55. We know that

$$NC_{e} \cdot \ddot{a}^{s}_{e:\overline{r-e}|} = B_{r}\, a^{(12)}_{r}\, \frac{D_{r}}{D_{e}},$$

where
$$B_r = .60(100{,}000)(1.05)^8 = 88{,}647.$$

Since there is no preretirement mortality, then

$$\frac{D_r}{D_e} = v^{r-e} = v_{.07}^{10} = .50834.$$

Furthermore the annuity $\ddot{a}^s_{\overline{e:r-e|}} = \ddot{a}^s_{55:\overline{10|}}$ reduces to $\ddot{a}_{\overline{10|}j}$, where

$$1+j = \frac{1+i}{1+s} = \frac{1.07}{1.05}.$$

The present value of benefits at entry is

$$pv_{55}B = 88{,}647(.50834)\left(\frac{100}{12}\right) = 375{,}523$$

and the normal cost is

$$NC_{55} = \frac{375{,}523}{\ddot{a}_{\overline{10|}j}} = \frac{375{,}523}{9.19948} = 40{,}820.$$

Finally

$$NC_{56} = NC_{55} \cdot \frac{s_{56}}{s_{55}} = 40{,}820(1.05) = \$42{,}861. \qquad \square$$

EXAMPLE 3.18

Normal retirement benefit: 50% of final three-year average salary
Actuarial cost method: Entry Age Normal
Actuarial assumptions:
    Interest: 6%
    Compensation increases: 5% per year
    Preretirement deaths and terminations: None
    Retirement age: 65
    Selected annuity value: $\ddot{a}_{65}^{(12)} = 9$

Data for sole participant as of 1/1/94:

Date of birth	1/1/44
Date of hire	1/1/79
Compensation for 1994	$50,000

What is the normal cost for 1994 as of 1/1/94?

SOLUTION At 1/1/94 the participant is age 50, having entered at age 35. The retirement benefit is

$$B_{65} = .50(50,000)(1.05)^{12} \left(\frac{1 + 1.05 + (1.05)^2}{3} \right) = 47,178.68.$$

At entry we have

$$pv_e NC = pv_e B,$$

or

$$NC_e \cdot \ddot{a}^s_{\overline{e:r-e|}} = 47,178.68 \frac{D_r}{D_e} \ddot{a}_r^{(12)},$$

or

$$NC_e \cdot \ddot{a}_{\overline{30}|j} = 47,178.68(9)(1.06)^{-30},$$

where $1+j = \frac{1.06}{1.05}$ and there are no preretirement deaths, so

$$NC_{35} = \frac{73,928.59}{26.23562} = 2818,$$

and

$$NC_{50} = 2818(1.05)^{15} = \$5858. \qquad \square$$

EXAMPLE 3.19

Normal retirement benefit: 25% of final year's compensation

Actuarial cost method: Entry Age Normal

Actuarial assumptions:

Interest rate: 6%

Compensation increases: 3% per year

Preretirement deaths and terminations: None
Retirement age: 65
Data for sole participant:
    Date of birth   1/1/44
    Date of hire   1/1/77
Present value of future benefits as of 1/1/94: $110,000

What is the actuarial liability as of 1/1/94?

$\boxed{\text{SOLUTION}}$ At 1/1/94 the participant is age 50, having entered at age
33.   At age 50 the present value of benefits is 110,000; at age 33 the
present value is $110,000(1.06)^{-17} = 40,850$. Because there is no mortality, the salary-based annuity reduces to an annuity-certain at rate j, where
$1+j = \frac{1+i}{1+s}$. Then the normal cost at age 33 is

$$NC_{33} = \frac{40,850}{\ddot{a}_{\overline{32|}j}} = 1923.77.$$

Next recall that NC_{50} and NC_{33} are a constant percent of salary.   Since
$S_{50} = S_{33}(1.03)^{17}$, we have

$$NC_{50} = NC_{33}(1.03)^{17} = 3179.70.$$

Finally the liability as of 1/1/94 is

$$AL_{50} = pv_{50}B - NC_{50} \cdot \ddot{a}_{\overline{15|}j}$$

$$= 110,000 - (3179.70)(12.36366) = \$70,687. \qquad \square$$

Note that N_{50}, not N_{33}, was used for AL_{50}.

$\boxed{\text{DISCUSSION QUESTIONS}}$

3-1   If the benefit is 2% of the final three-year average salary with a
       salary scale of 5% for all ages, write the formulae for normal cost
       and actuarial liability.

3-2 For a career average plan where the actual salaries before age x are known, write the detailed formulas at age x for (a) the EAN(LP) normal cost and (b) the actuarial liability. Is B_r the same for both normal cost and actuarial liability purposes?

3.4 Individual Level Premium — *same as Entry age normal, but @ inception*

The **Individual Level Premium** (ILP) cost method funds each participant's projected benefit with a level normal cost. There is no supplemental liability for years of service prior to plan inception for participants who become members of the plan on its inception date.

The normal cost is a level amount (occasionally level percentage) payable each year from plan inception until retirement. It is calculated the same way as under Entry Age Normal, except that the age at plan inception, a, is used in place of age at entry, e, if the participant has service before the plan was introduced. At plan inception, the present value of all future normal costs equals the present value of future benefits, so we have

NC = NC calc.

$$NC_a \left(\frac{N_a - N_r}{D_a} \right) = B_r \frac{D_r}{D_a} \ddot{a}_r^{(12)}.$$

NC$_{ILP}$ > NC$_{EAN}$
B/C PV Ben spread over shorter period

@ plan inception,
PV(FNC) = PV(FB)

The normal cost for a year can be found by solving the above equation; the result will be greater than under EAN because the pvB is spread over a shorter period.

Additional benefits arising from actual salaries being greater than expected salaries are common, and are funded by additional normal costs; each "slice of pension" has a normal cost payable from the effective date of the additional benefit until retirement (see Example 3.24). Instead of modifying the first (large) slice, we add smaller additional slices when necessary.

There will be an unfunded actuarial liability to the extent that there are non-salary gains and losses (see Example 3.23), but at the effective date $UAL_a = F_a = 0$.

EXAMPLE 3.20

Plan effective date: 1/1/94
Normal retirement benefit: $600 per month
Actuarial cost method: Individual Level Premium

Valuation date: 12/31/94
Actuarial assumptions:
    Interest: 6%
    Retirement age: 65
    Preretirement mortality and withdrawal: None
    Selected annuity value: $12\ddot{a}_{65}^{(12)} = 100$
The sole plan participant on 12/31/94 was born 1/1/60.

What is the normal cost for 1994 as of 12/31/94?

SOLUTION The age at the effective date is 34, and there are no preretirement deaths or withdrawals. Usually the normal cost is at BOY, and, at age 65,

$$NC \cdot \ddot{s}_{\overline{31|}} = 600 \times 12 \; \ddot{a}_{65}^{(12)},$$

but in this example the normal cost is at EOY, so

$$NC \cdot s_{\overline{31|}} = 600 \times 12 \; \ddot{a}_{65}^{(12)}$$

from which we find $NC = \$707.53$. ◻

EXAMPLE 3.21
Plan effective date: 1/1/85
Normal retirement benefit: $25 per month for each year of service
Actuarial cost method: Individual Level Premium
Actuarial assumptions:
    Interest rate: 7%
    Preretirement terminations other than deaths: None
    Retirement age: 65
Data for sole participant:

Date of birth	1/1/53
Date of hire	1/1/84
Status as of 1/1/94	Active

Selected annuity value: $\ddot{a}_{65}^{(12)} = 8.5$

Selected commutation functions:

x	D_x	N_x	x	D_x	N_x
31	1540	25,240	41	900	13,050
32	1500	24,000	42	860	12,150
			65	200	1,792

What is the present value of future normal costs as of 1/1/94?

$\boxed{\text{SOLUTION}}$ Note that $e = 31$, $a = 32$, and $x = 41$. To find $pv_x NC$, we must first find the normal cost. By equating $pv_{32}NC$ to pvB_{65} at plan inception, we have

$$NC\left(\frac{24,000 - 1792}{1500}\right) = 25 \times 12 \times (65-31)\left(\frac{200}{1500}\right)(8.5),$$

from which we find
$$NC = 780.80.$$

The present value of all future normal costs is

$$pv_{41}NC = 780.80\left(\frac{13,050 - 1792}{900}\right) = \$9767. \qquad \square$$

At plan inception, the actuarial liability is zero. At each subsequent valuation, the actuarial liability will equal the present value of all future benefits minus the present value of all future normal costs for all slices. Prospectively, for all slices of pension we have

$$AL_x = B_r \frac{D_r}{D_x} \ddot{a}_r^{(12)} - TNC\left(\frac{N_x - N_r}{D_x}\right),$$

and retrospectively we have

$$AL_x = NC\left(\frac{N_a - N_x}{D_x}\right)$$

for the first slice, plus additional liability for any additional slices.

EXAMPLE 3.22

Plan effective date: 1/1/89
Normal retirement benefit: $15 per month for each year of service
Actuarial cost method: Individual Level Premium
Actuarial assumptions:
    Interest rate: 6%
    Preretirement terminations other than deaths: None
    Retirement age: 65
Data for sole participant:
    Date of birth   1/1/44
    Date of hire   1/1/84
Selected annuity value: $\ddot{a}_{65}^{(12)} = 10$
Selected commutation functions:

x	D_x	N_x
40	941	13,971
45	694	9,789
50	508	6,712
55	366	4,472
65	178	1,741

What is the actuarial liability as of 1/1/94?

SOLUTION Note that $e = 40, a = 45$, and $x = 50$. We first need NC_{45} in order to find AL_{50}. At plan inception we have

$$NC_{45} \cdot \ddot{a}_{45:\overline{20}|} = B_{65} \, v^{20} \, {}_{20}p_{45} \, \ddot{a}_{65}^{(12)},$$

from which we find

$$NC_{45} = B_{65} \frac{\ddot{a}_{65}^{(12)}}{\ddot{s}_{45:\overline{20}|}} = \frac{15 \times 12 \times (65-40)(10)}{(9789 - 1741)/178} = 995.$$

Retrospectively we then find

$$AL_{50} = NC_{45} \left(\frac{N_{45} - N_{50}}{D_{50}} \right) = \$6028. \qquad \square$$

Note that in most plans, as in this example, service before the effective date is counted.

| EXAMPLE 3.23 |

Plan effective date: 1/1/84

Normal retirement benefit: $6 per month for each year of service

Actuarial cost method: Individual Level Premium

All employees were hired at age 25.

Retirement age: 65

Plan assets on 1/1/94: $5000

Preretirement terminations other than by death: None

Selected annuity value: $\ddot{a}_{65}^{(12)} = 10$

Census data on 1/1/94 and commutation functions:

	Age x	Number of Participants	D_x	$N_x - N_{65}$
	25	8	16	320
	35	0	8	120
	45	2	4	40
	55	0	2	10
	65	0	1	0

What are the normal cost and the unfunded actuarial liability as of 1/1/94?

| SOLUTION | Let 1/1/94 be time 0. The total normal cost is the sum of each participant's normal cost. For each person age 25,

$$NC_{25} = \frac{B_{65}(D_{65}/D_{25})\,\ddot{a}_{65}^{(12)}}{(N_{25} - N_{65})/D_{25}} = \frac{(6 \times 12 \times 40)(\frac{1}{16})(10)}{20} = 90.$$

For each person age 45, who was age 35 at plan inception, we have

$$NC_{35} = \frac{B_{65}(D_{65}/D_{35})\,\ddot{a}_{65}^{(12)}}{(N_{35} - N_{65})/D_{35}} = \frac{(6 \times 12 \times 40)(\frac{1}{8})(10)}{15} = 240.$$

Then the total normal cost is

$$TNC_0 = 8(90) + 2(240) = \$1200.$$

For those age 25, $AL_{25} = 0$ since there is no past service. For those age 45 we have, retrospectively,

$$AL_{45} = NC_{35} \cdot \frac{N_{35} - N_{45}}{D_{45}} = 240 \left(\frac{120-40}{4} \right) = 4800,$$

so

$$TAL_0 = 2(4800) = 9600.$$

Finally we have

$$UAL_0 = TAL_0 - F_0 = 9600 - 5000 = \$4600. \qquad \square$$

Each *increase* in the projected benefit is treated separately. For example, if the increase in the projected benefit after three years is b, then the additional normal cost, ΔNC, is such that

$$\Delta NC \left(\frac{N_{a+3} - N_r}{D_{a+3}} \right) = b \, \frac{D_r}{D_{a+3}} \, \ddot{a}_r^{(12)}.$$

Note that ΔNC is usually positive.

EXAMPLE 3.24

Plan effective date: 1/1/93
Normal retirement benefit: 50% of final year's salary
Actuarial cost method: Individual Level Premium
Valuation date: 12/31/94
Actuarial assumptions:
    Interest: 8%
    Salary increases: None
    Preretirement deaths and terminations: None
    Retirement age: 65
Selected annuity value: $\ddot{a}_{65}^{(12)} = 8.33$
Data for sole participant:

Date of birth	1/1/39
Date of hire	1/1/84
Salary for 1993	$36,000
Salary for 1994	30,000

What is the normal cost for 1994 as of 12/31/94?

SOLUTION Note that $e = 45$, $a = 54$, $x = 55$, and the calculations are at interest only. Let 1/1/93 be time 0, which is age 54. B_0 is the projected annual pension benefit at time 0. We have the values $B_0 = 36,000 \times .50$ and $B_1 = 30,000 \times .50$, so $\Delta B = 15,000 - 18,000 = -3000$. We will first calculate NC at 1/1/93, then the decrease in NC at 1/1/94, then NC at 1/1/94, and finally NC at 12/31/94.

$$NC_{54} \cdot \ddot{s}_{\overline{11|}} = B_0 \cdot \ddot{a}_{65}^{(12)} \qquad \text{so} \qquad NC_{54} = \frac{(18,000)(8.33)}{\ddot{s}_{\overline{11|}}} = 8341$$

$$\Delta NC_{55} \cdot \ddot{s}_{\overline{10|}} = \Delta B \cdot \ddot{a}_{65}^{(12)} \qquad \text{so} \qquad \Delta NC_{55} = \frac{(-3,000)(8.33)}{\ddot{s}_{\overline{10|}}} = -1597$$

$$NC_{55} \cdot \ddot{s}_{\overline{10|}} = B_1 \cdot \ddot{a}_{65}^{(12)} \qquad \text{so} \qquad NC_{55} = NC_{54} + \Delta NC_{55} = 6744$$

Then at 12/31/94 the normal cost is

$$6744(1.08) = \$7283. \qquad \square$$

EXAMPLE 3.25

Plan effective date: 1/1/89
Normal retirement benefit: 2% of final salary per year of service
Actuarial cost method: Individual Level Premium
Actuarial assumptions:
    Interest rate: 7%
    Compensation increases: None
    Preretirement deaths and terminations: None
    Retirement age: 65
    Selected annuity value: $\ddot{a}_{65}^{(12)} = 9.345$
Data for sole participant:
    Date of birth   1/1/64
    Date of hire   1/1/89
    Status as of 1/1/94   Active
Monthly compensation:

1989	$3500	1992	$4000
1990	3500	1993	4000
1991	3500	1994	4000

What is the actuarial liability as of 1/1/94?

SOLUTION Note that $e = 25$, $a = 25$, and $x = 30$ at $1/1/94$, which is time 0. To calculate the liability at time 0 prospectively, we must first calculate the normal cost at that time. Since the salary unexpectedly increases, the increased benefit will increase the normal cost. We know that $NC_0 = NC_a + \Delta NC$, where NC_a is the normal cost calculated at plan inception. The calculation is at interest only, so we have

$$NC_a = \frac{.02(3500 \times 12 \times 40)\ddot{a}_{65}^{(12)}}{\ddot{s}_{\overline{40|}}} = 1470.$$

After the salary increases, the normal cost will increase by ΔNC, where

$$\Delta NC \cdot \ddot{s}_{\overline{65-28|}} = \Delta B \cdot \ddot{a}_{65}^{(12)} = .02(500 \times 12 \times 40)\ddot{a}_{65}^{(12)},$$

leading to

$$\Delta NC = 261.46.$$

The normal cost at time 0 is the same as it was just after the salary increase on $1/1/92$, which is

$$NC_0 = NC_a + \Delta NC = 1470 + 261.46 = 1731.46.$$

The actuarial liability can be found either prospectively or retrospectively, with the latter being much easier. Prospectively,

$$AL_{30} = pvB - pvNC_0$$

$$= .02(4000 \times 12 \times 40)v^{35}\ddot{a}_{65}^{(12)} - 1731.46\ddot{a}_{\overline{35|}}$$

$$= 38,400(1.07)^{-35}(9.345) - 1731.46(13.854)$$

$$= 33,611 - 23,987 = \$9624.$$

Retrospectively, we simply accumulate the two pieces of normal cost, obtaining

$$AL_{30} = 1470\ddot{s}_{\overline{5|}} + 261.46\ddot{s}_{\overline{2|}} = \$9624. \qquad \square$$

| EXAMPLE 3.26 |

Plan effective date: 1/1/93
Normal retirement benefit: 40% of final year's compensation
Actuarial cost method: Individual Level Premium
Actuarial assumptions:
  Interest: 6%
  Preretirement deaths and terminations: None
  Retirement age: 65
  Selected annuity value: $\ddot{a}_{65}^{(12)}$ = 9.333
Data for sole participant:
  Date of birth   1/1/43
  Compensation for 1993 $100,000
  Compensation for 1994   120,000
Contribution for 1993: Normal cost as of 1/1, paid on 1/1/93
Actuarial value of assets as of 1/1/94: $15,000
Contribution for 1994: Normal cost as of 1/1, plus 10-year amortization of
    1993 experience gain or loss, paid on 1/1/94.

What is the contribution for 1994?

| SOLUTION | Let 1/1/93 be time 0, the plan inception date, where the
participant is age 50. The contribution for 1994 consists of NC_1 and the
amortization of the 1993 experience gain or loss. Recall that

$$^{tot}G_1 = {}^{exp}UAL_1 - {}^{act}UAL_1,$$

where

$$^{act}UAL_1 = AL_1 - F_1$$

and

$$^{exp}UAL_1 = (UAL_0 + NC_0 - C_0)(1 + i).$$

The normal cost at time 0 is

$$NC_{50} = \frac{B_{65} \, v^{15} \, \ddot{a}_{65}^{(12)}}{\ddot{a}_{\overline{15}|}} = \frac{.40(100,000)(1.06)^{-15}(9.333)}{10.295} = 15,131$$

and the actuarial liability at time 1, retrospectively, is

$$AL_1 = 15,131(1.06) = 16,039.$$

Then

$$^{\text{act}}UAL_1 \ = \ 16{,}039 - 15{,}000 \ = \ 1039$$

and

$$^{\text{exp}}UAL_1 \ = \ (0 + 15{,}131)(1.06) - (15{,}131)(1.06) \ = \ 0,$$

since the 1993 contribution exactly equalled the normal cost. Then

$$^{\text{tot}}G_1 \ = \ -1039.$$

Since this loss is amortized over 10 years, the portion paid in the contribution for 1994 is

$$\frac{1039}{\ddot{a}_{\overline{10}|}} \ = \ 133.18.$$

Next we need NC_1. Since the salary for 1994 increased, then

$$NC_1 \ = \ NC_0 + \Delta NC_1$$

$$= \ 15{,}131 + \frac{.40(20{,}000)(1.06)^{-14}(9.333)}{\ddot{a}_{\overline{14}|}}$$

$$= \ 15{,}131 + 3351 \ = \ 18{,}482.$$

Then the total contribution for 1994 is

$$18{,}482 + 133.18 \ = \ \$18{,}615. \qquad \square$$

The Individual Level Premium cost method may be used with a salary-increase assumption. The normal cost of the plan would then be defined as a level percentage of salary. In practice, a salary-increase assumption is rarely used with this method.

EXAMPLE 3.27

Plan effective date: 1/1/94
Normal retirement benefit: 50% of final five-year average salary
Actuarial cost method: Individual Level Premium
Preretirement terminations other than by death: None

Employee data as of 1/1/94:

	Age	Service	1994 Annual Pay
Brown	35	10 Years	$20,000

Selected commutation functions:

x	^sD_x	$^sN_x - {}^sN_{65}$	s_x	D_x	$N_x - N_{65}$	$N_x^{(12)}$
25	1,500	75,000	0.30	5,000	120,000	
35	1,600	60,000	0.40	4,000	72,000	
45	1,500	45,000	0.50	3,000	36,000	
60	2,250	9,750	1.50	1,500	6,500	
61	2,100	7,500	1.50	1,400	5,000	
62	1,950	5,400	1.50	1,300	3,600	
63	1,800	3,450	1.50	1,200	2,300	
64	1,650	1,650	1.50	1,100	1,100	
65	1,500	0	1.50	1,000	0	10,000

All normal costs are calculated as a *level percent* of salary.

What is the normal cost for Brown due 1/1/94?

SOLUTION Let 1/1/94 be time 0. At plan inception we have

$$NC_{35}\left(\frac{^sN_{35} - {}^sN_{65}}{^sD_{35}}\right) = B_{65}\frac{D_{65}}{D_{35}}\ddot{a}_{65}^{(12)},$$

where

$$B_{65} = .50S_{35}\frac{(s_{64} + \cdots + s_{60})}{5 \cdot s_{35}} = .50(20,000)\left(\frac{1.50}{.40}\right) = 37,500.$$

Then

$$NC_{35} = \frac{37,500\left(\frac{1000}{4000}\right)\left(\frac{10,000}{1000}\right)}{\frac{60,000}{1600}} = \$2500. \qquad \square$$

EXAMPLE 3.28

Plan effective date: 1/1/85

Normal retirement benefit: 50% of average of last 5 annual rates as of 1/1

Actuarial cost method: Individual Level Premium

Actuarial assumptions:

　　Interest: 6%

　　Preretirement mortality and withdrawal: None

　　Retirement age: 65

　　Salary increases: 6%

Selected annuity value: $12\,\ddot{a}_{65}^{(12)} = 110$

Salary for sole participant in the plan hired 1/1/82 at age 50:

Year	Salary	Year	Salary
1985	$10,000	1990	$15,000
1986	11,000	1991	16,000
1987	12,000	1992	17,000
1988	13,000	1993	20,000
1989	14,000		

What is the change in normal cost for 1993 as of 1/1/93, due to the excess of actual over expected salary increase?

SOLUTION Let 1/1/93 be time 0, and let ΔNC_0 be the *additional* normal cost for the additional slice of pension. Then we have

$$\Delta NC_0 \left(\frac{{}^s N_x - {}^s N_r}{{}^s D_x} \right) = \Delta B_r \frac{D_r}{D_x} \ddot{a}_r^{(12)}.$$

Since we expected the 1992 salary of $17,000 to increase by 6% each year, but the 1993 salary was actually $20,000, then the change in the retirement benefit is

$$\Delta B_{65} = \frac{.50}{5} \left[17,000 + 20,000 s_{\overline{4}|.06} - 17,000 s_{\overline{5}|.06} \right] = 866.$$

Then

$$\Delta NC_0 = 866v^4 \left(\frac{110}{12}\right) \left(\frac{1}{\ddot{a}_{\overline{4}|j}}\right),$$

where $1 + j = \frac{1+i}{1+s} = 0$, so $\ddot{a}_{\overline{4}|j} = 4$. Then

$$\Delta NC_0 = (866)(.79209)\left(\frac{110}{12}\right)\left(\frac{1}{4}\right) = \$1572. \qquad \square$$

| DISCUSSION QUESTION |

3-3   If there is an increase of b in the projected benefit after 3 years, then
        it is funded with an additional normal cost, as shown in the text of
        this section. What is the additional actuarial liability at age $a + 6$?

3.5 Supplemental Cost

The costs of all pension benefits can be broken down into normal costs, as
defined by the actuarial cost method, and **supplemental costs** (*SC*) which
amortize supplemental liabilities. Then the employer's annual cost can be
defined as

Annual Cost = Normal Cost + Supplemental Cost(s).

The supplemental liabilities may include any of the following:

(1) The liability at the inception of the plan for pension benefits
    accruing for service before the inception of the plan.

(2) Liabilities arising from improvements in plan benefits.

(3) Liabilities arising from changes in actuarial assumptions.

(4) The liability arising from a change in the actuarial cost
    method.

(5) The salary experience loss revealed at each actuarial valua-
    tion.

(6) The non-salary experience loss at each valuation.

3.5.1 Amortization of Supplemental Liabilities

The supplemental liabilities may be amortized (a) immediately, (b) over a period of years such as $5, 10, 15, \ldots, 40$, (c) over the period to the normal retirement age of each member, or (d) to infinity.

     The amortization must conform to the minimum and maximum periods contained in the applicable pension legislation. For example, the legislation might require an amortization period of at least ten years but not more than thirty years for types (1) and (2), ten years or less for types (3) and (4), and five years or less for types (5) and (6).

     The amortization is usually level dollar at interest only payable at the beginning of the year, but it could be a level percentage of payroll, it could allow for interest, mortality, and withdrawal, and it could be payable at the end of the year.

     Using the general relationship that the supplemental liability (*SL*) equals the present value of the supplemental cost (*pvSC*), we could solve for the annual supplemental cost in the amortization cases described above, as follows:

(a) $SL = SC$

(b) $SL = SC \cdot \ddot{a}_{\overline{15|}}$

(c) $SL = SC \cdot \dfrac{\sum \ddot{a}_{\overline{r-x|}}}{n}$, where there are n participants.

(d) $SL = SC \cdot \dfrac{\sum \ddot{a}_{\overline{\infty|}}}{n}$, where $\ddot{a}_{\overline{\infty|}} = \dfrac{1}{d}$, so that $\sum \ddot{a}_{\overline{\infty|}} = \dfrac{n}{d}$ and

therefore $SC = d \times SL$.

     If a pension plan using the TUC cost method is introduced when the participants are age a, the liability at the effective date will be

$$TAL = \sum_{A_0} B_a \cdot \ddot{a}_r^{(12)} \cdot \frac{D_r^{(\tau)}}{D_a^{(\tau)}} .$$

This liability will typically increase in each future year. To avoid creating a deficit at the effective date, an *asset* exactly equal to *TAL* is created; it is often called a **supplemental liability**, or an **initial unfunded liability**, and it is amortized over a reasonable number of years.

If the plan benefit is increased by, say, $2 per month for each year of service, the liability will increase by

$$\Delta TAL = \sum_{A_0} 24(x-e)\,\ddot{a}_r^{(12)} \cdot \frac{D_r^{(\tau)}}{D_x^{(\tau)}},$$

where x is the age of a participant at the time of the increase. To avoid creating a deficit, another asset is created equal to the increase in the liability, and it is amortized over a reasonable number of years. Similarly, if there is an experience loss (*e.g.*, three deaths are expected but none actually occur), an asset equal to the experience loss is set up and amortized, often over a shorter period than for the two preceding situations.

If a *contribution* to the pension fund equal to the normal cost plus the supplemental cost is made at the beginning of each year, and if actual plan benefits and experience are equal to expected, then the deficit will always be zero. (Under these conditions, the behavior of the plan is perfect, but these conditions are never experienced.) The supplemental costs amortize the supplemental liabilities, and the contributions, if sufficient, fund the supplemental liabilities.

Where the cost method is PUC, the reasoning is the same as for TUC but B_r and NC are larger for PUC, due to using a salary scale, and we can expect the supplemental costs to be smaller.

The Entry Age methods can have all six types of supplemental liabilities. The Individual Level Premium method often has "additional normal costs" due to larger than expected salary increases (see Example 3.28), and supplemental liabilities only from non-salary experience losses (see Example 3.23).

The Attained Age Normal methods (see Section 8.1.6) set up a liability at the inception of the plan for past service using the Unit Credit method, and spread the pension cost for service after the inception of the plan over the period from the age at inception to the age at retirement. The AAN methods spread an experience loss over the remaining working lifetime (unless another amortization period is specified).

Gains of types (5) and (6) from experience and type (4) from assumption changes are usually amortized and treated as negative losses; this treatment of gains "matches" the treatment of losses. When gains produce a surplus, as opposed to a reduction of the unfunded actuarial liability, consideration can be given to reducing the contribution.

Supplemental liabilities can be amortized by future supplemental costs (SC), by a portion of future normal costs (NC), or by both. Theoretically there are many different possibilities, but in practice there is a great deal of uniformity as indicated in the following table.

Cost Method	Type of Supplemental Liability					
	(1)	**(2)**	**(3)**	**(4)**	**(5)**	**(6)**
TUC, PUC, EAN	SC	SC	SC	SC	SC	SC
Ind Agg, Agg EAN, Agg	NC	NC	NC	NC	NC	NC
FIL	SC	Both	SC	NC	NC	NC
ILP	NC	NC	NC	NC	NC	SC

If there are several supplemental costs arising in different years, the amortizations will eventually run out. Alternatively, it is possible, if desired, to combine them in a reasonable way. It is common to have *contributions* each year which are equal to the annual cost. It is also common, especially in the U.S., to have contributions which are greater than or less than the annual cost, subject to maximum and minimum limits defined by the pension law.

3.5.2 Pension Fund Balance Sheet

At the end of each year, some actuaries prepare a balance sheet such as the following:

Assets at 12/31/96		Liabilities at 12/31/96	
Invested assets	50	Actuarial liabilities	145
pv of future *SC*	100	Other liabilities	4
Interest due and accrued	4	Surplus	5

The actuarial liability is typically large and increasing each year. The supplemental liability is a part of the actuarial liability, after the actuarial liability has been increased by the event which caused the supplemental liability. In addition to being part of *AL*, *SL* can be looked upon as a non-invested *asset* which decreases each year. For example, consider a plan with an effective date of 1/1/93, with an initial unfunded liability of *SL*. The non-invested asset, decreasing over time, could be as follows:

(a) SL at 1/1/93: $SC \cdot \ddot{a}_{\overline{15}|}$

(b) SL at 12/31/96: $SC \cdot \ddot{a}_{\overline{11}|}$

(c) SL at 12/31/97: $(SC \cdot \ddot{a}_{\overline{11}|} - SC)(1+i)$

(d) SL at 12/31/07: 0

It is helpful to relate the supplemental liability to the yearly balance sheet. We will use, as a typical example, an experience loss due to salary in excess of expected. The actuarial liability is, by custom, placed on the right side of the balance sheet (including the portion of the liability resulting from the unexpected salary loss). On the left side we have a receivable (or a non-invested asset), which is initially equal to the salary loss and which is amortized to zero over, say, five years. Also on the left side we show the fund, at the end of each year, which will grow over the five-year period by the actual contributions (which are often equal to the normal and supplemental costs) and by the actual interest earned. Finally we have the balancing item

$$SURPLUS = F + SC \cdot \ddot{a}_{\overline{m}|} - AL$$

included on the right side of the balance sheet if positive, *or* the balancing item

$$DEFICIT = AL - F - SC \cdot \ddot{a}_{\overline{m}|} \, ,$$

included on the left side. In these two equations, m is the number of years from the balance sheet date to the end of the amortization period. We can say that the supplemental liability is an accounting device which avoids an excessive deficit, and the supplemental cost is a funding device which spreads out the cost of the loss. Often the deficit (and surplus) is zero due to the design of the cost method; this is true for *all* cost methods at the effective date and for the Aggregate method at *all* dates.

As mentioned in Section 1.4, participant security is the primary goal of pension funding. This concept involves pension benefits, liabilities, normal costs, supplemental costs, and funds, as described above. Participant security is impaired if we have a deficit, instead of a surplus, or if future experience turns out to be worse than expected.

To clarify the interaction and the growth of the various balance sheet components, consider the following graph. Note that we are assuming that contributions are equal to the annual cost and there are no experience gains.

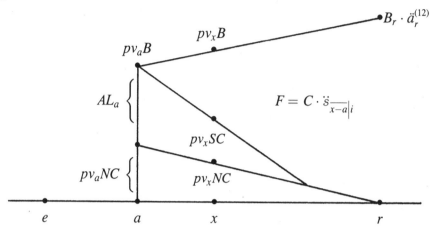

The following can be observed from the graph:

(1) $pv_x B$ grows from $B_r \cdot \ddot{a}_r^{(12)} \cdot v^{r-a} \cdot {}_{r-a}p_a$ to $B_r \cdot \ddot{a}_r^{(12)}$. It is made up of a part for service before age a and a part for service after age a.

(2) At age a, a liability of AL_a is created and an uninvested asset is also created. The uninvested asset declines from AL_a to 0.

(3) $pv_x NC$ declines from $(pv_a B - AL_a)$ to 0.

(4) The fund grows from 0 to $B_r \cdot \ddot{a}_r^{(12)}$.

(5) AL grows from $(pv_a B - pv_a NC)$ to $B_r \cdot \ddot{a}_r^{(12)}$.

(6) The deficit is $pv_x B - pv_x SC - pv_x NC - F$. The deficit is zero at all times under our assumptions.

The above scenario, where the surplus is always zero, can be easily adapted to (a) all cost methods (*e.g.*, with Aggregate, $SC = 0$), (b) experience gains and losses after creating SL, (c) contributions greater or less than annual cost, and (d) all types of supplemental liability.

To summarize, the supplemental liability is a new portion of the actuarial liability (for any one of six reasons). It is also a new equal and opposite asset which is accompanied by an amortization process which serves to avoid the otherwise pension plan deficit, except for future gains and losses which creep into this area just as they do into every other area.

To review, each new supplemental liability has two aspects: the liability and the growth thereof, and the (equal) asset and the amortization and funding thereof. In the amortization of experience gains and losses, there may be considerable cancellation. The supplemental liability is explicit in many situations in Chapters 2 and 3, but implicit (buried) in many situations in Chapter 4.

The supplemental liabilities in total, in the amount of $(AL - F)$, are often called the **unfunded actuarial liability**.

DISCUSSION QUESTIONS

3-4   Compare the amortization of a supplemental liability with the amortization of a mortgage.

3-5   Would the unamortized supplemental liability be larger if the supplemental cost were a level percent of payroll instead of a level dollar amount?

3-6   Referring to the balance sheet shown on page 96, suppose the 1997 contribution of $40 is received on 1/2/97, and consists of the normal cost of $25 plus a supplemental cost of $15. What balance sheet accounts would be increased or decreased?

3-7   Draw a graph of the balance sheet components over a six-year period, where a salary loss is experienced after one year.

3.6 Exercises

3.1 Entry Age Normal (Level Dollar)

3-1   Normal retirement benefit: $10 monthly per year of service
       Normal retirement age: Age 55 after the completion of 15 years of
            participation, but no earlier than age 55 and no later than age 65
       Plan effective date: 1/1/94
       Actuarial cost method: Entry Age Normal
       Assumed normal retirement age: Normal retirement age
       Preretirement terminations other than by death: None

	Age on 1/1/94	Date of Employment
Smith	20	1/1/94
Jones	45	1/1/89
Brown	53	1/1/91

Give an expression in commutation functions for the normal cost as
of 1/1/94.

3-2   Actuarial cost method: Entry Age Normal
       There are no decrements other than mortality and retirement at the
            normal retirement age, r, and the plan provides no benefits on
            death prior to retirement.

Which of the following expressions correctly represent the actuarial
liability for an active participant?

I. $pvB_r \left[\dfrac{D_r}{D_x} - \left(\dfrac{D_r}{N_e - N_r} \right) \left(\dfrac{N_e - N_x}{D_x} \right) \right]$

II. $pvB_r \left[\dfrac{D_r}{D_x} - \left(\dfrac{D_r}{N_e - N_r} \right) \left(\dfrac{N_x - N_r}{D_x} \right) \right]$

III. $pvB_r \left(\dfrac{D_r}{N_e - N_r} \right) \left(\dfrac{N_e - N_x}{D_x} \right)$

3-3 Effective date of plan: 1/1/94
Actuarial cost method: Entry Age Normal
Normal retirement benefit: $10 monthly per year of service
Assumed retirement age: 65
Preretirement deaths or other terminations: None
Participant data at 1/1/94:

Number of participants	10
Attained age of each	45
Past service of each	10 years

Selected annuity values:

$$\ddot{a}_{\overline{10|}} = 9 \qquad \ddot{a}_{\overline{20|}} = 15 \qquad \ddot{a}_{65}^{(12)} = 10$$

What is the past service liability at 1/1/94?

(Note that the past service is the service from the date of hire to the date of plan inception. In this problem, the pension benefit is based on years of service, not just years in the plan. Past service liability is the liability which the employer assumes at the inception of the plan.)

3-4 Plan effective date: 1/1/94
Employee data as of 1/1/94:

	Monthly Salary	Current Age	Past Service
Brown	$2500	36	1 year
Green	1000	55	15 years

Actuarial cost method: Entry Age Normal
Normal retirement benefit: 50% of final five-year average salary for 25 or more years of service
Actuarial assumptions:
    Terminations before retirement: None
    Deaths before retirement: None
    Salary increases: None
    Retirement age: 65
    Interest: 5%
    Selected annuity value: $\ddot{a}_{65}^{(12)} = 10$
From entry to retirement, the same benefit is assigned to each year of accrual.

What is the actuarial liability as of 1/1/94?

3-5   The following expressions are under consideration for the initial actuarial liability under the Entry Age Normal cost method, with respect to a given participant when applied to the projected normal retirement reserve value:

I. $$\frac{D_r}{D_x} - \left(\frac{D_r}{N_e - N_r}\right)\left(\frac{N_x - N_r}{D_x}\right)$$

II. $$\left(\frac{D_r}{N_e - N_r}\right)\left(\frac{N_e - N_x}{D_x}\right)$$

III. $$\left(\frac{D_r}{N_e - N_r}\right)\left(\frac{N_x - N_r}{D_x}\right)$$

Which of the expressions are accurate?

3-6   Plan effective date: 1/1/94
       Normal retirement benefit: $100 per month
       Actuarial cost method: Entry Age Normal
       Actuarial assumptions:
           Interest: 7%
           Preretirement deaths: GAM Table
           Postretirement deaths: GAM Table, with ages set back one year
           Preretirement terminations other than deaths: None
           Retirement age: 65
       Selected commutation functions from the GAM Table:

x	D_x	N_x	$N_x^{(12)}$
35	9,207	127,908	123,688
36	8,595	118,701	114,761
40	6,522	87,606	84,617
41	6,085	81,084	78,295
64	1,080	10,121	9,626
65	990	9,041	8,587
66	906	8,051	7,635

Data for sole participant as of 1/1/94:
    Date of birth   1/1/53
    Date of hire   1/1/89

What is the actuarial liability as of 1/1/94?

3.2 Cost as a Level Percent of Salary
3.3 Entry Age Normal (Level Percent)

3-7   Normal retirement age: 60
      Normal retirement benefit: 50% of final year's salary
      Actuarial cost method: Entry Age Normal
      Assumed retirement age: 60
      Preretirement terminations other than by death: None
      Participant data as of 1/1/94 and selected commutation functions:

	Age at Hire e	**Attained Age** x	**Monthly Salary**	$\dfrac{s_{59}}{s_e}$	$\dfrac{s_{59}}{s_x}$
Smith	35	40	$3000	2.5	2.0
Brown	25	35	1000	3.5	2.5

	^sD_e	$^sN_e - {}^sN_{60}$	$^sN_x - {}^sN_{60}$	$\ddot{a}_{60}^{(12)} \cdot \dfrac{D_{60}}{D_e}$
Smith	125	3000	2500	1.0
Brown	100	4500	3000	0.5

What is the normal cost as of 1/1/94?

3-8   Plan effective date: 1/1/94
       Normal retirement benefit: 50% of final year's salary
       Actuarial cost method: Entry Age Normal
       Assumed salary increases: 6% per year
       Preretirement terminations other than by death: None
       Assumed retirement age: 65
       Data for sole participant as of 1/1/94:

       Date of birth   1/1/54
       Date of hire   1/1/89
       Annual salary for 1993 $30,000

       Selected annuity value: $\ddot{a}_{65}^{(12)} = 10$
       Selected commutation functions:

x	D_x	^sD_x	^sN_x
35	921	7,077	239,735
40	652	6,708	205,091
65	99	4,371	62,569

       What is the normal cost as of 1/1/94?

3-9   Normal retirement benefit: $20 monthly per year of service
       Actuarial cost method: Entry Age Normal
       Preretirement deaths and other terminations: None
       Assumed retirement age: 65
       Data for sole participant:

       Date of birth   1/1/39
       Date of hire   1/1/84

       Valuation results as of 1/1/94 under Entry Age Normal:

       Actuarial value of assets $8,000.00
       Unfunded actuarial liability   9,700.00
       pv of $1.00 per year of future employment   7.90
       Normal cost as of 1/1/94   1,300.00

       What is the unfunded liability as of 1/1/94 if the Unit Credit cost
       method is used instead of Entry Age Normal?

3-10 Normal retirement benefit: 1% of final salary per year of service
Actuarial cost method: Entry Age Normal
Actuarial assumptions:
Interest rate: 7%
Compensation increases: 5% per year
Preretirement deaths and terminations: None
Retirement age: 65
Data for sole participant:
Date of birth   1/1/39
Date of hire   1/1/74
1993 compensation $30,000
Selected annuity value: $\ddot{a}_{65}^{(12)} = 10$

What are the normal cost and actuarial liability as of 1/1/94?

3.4 Individual Level Premium

3-11 Plan effective date: 1/1/93
Normal retirement benefit: 30% of final year's salary
Actuarial cost method: Individual Level Premium
Valuation date: 12/31/93
Actuarial assumptions:
Interest: 8%
Salary increases: None
Preretirement deaths and terminations: None
Retirement age: 65
Selected annuity value: $\ddot{a}_{65}^{(12)} = 8.40$
Data for sole participant:
Date of birth   1/1/49
Salary for 1993 $200,000

What is the normal cost for 1993 as of 12/31/93?

3-12   Normal retirement benefit: $10 monthly per year of service
Plan effective date: 1/1/94
Plan covers one employee, age 45 with 10 years of service on
1/1/94.
Actuarial assumptions:
   Preretirement terminations other than death: None
   Interest: 5%
   Retirement age: 65
Selected annuity value: $\ddot{a}_{45:\overline{20}|} = 10$
Normal cost as of 1/1/94 under Unit Credit: $840

What is the normal cost as of 1/1/94 under the Individual Level
Premium cost method?

3-13   Plan effective date: 1/1/93
Normal retirement benefit: $10 monthly per year of service
Actuarial cost method: Unit Credit
Assumed interest rate: 8%
Assumed retirement age: 65
Preretirement deaths and terminations: None
If the Individual Level Premium cost method had been used, the nor-
mal cost as of 1/1/93 would have been $18,000.
Participant data as of 1/1/93:

Number of participants	30
Attained age of each participant	45
Prior service of each participant	10 years

What is the normal cost for 1993?

3-14   Plan effective date: 1/1/93
        Normal retirement benefit: 50% of final salary
        Actuarial cost method: Individual Level Premium
        Actuarial assumptions:
            Interest: 6%
            Assumed retirement age: 65
            Salary increases: None
            Preretirement deaths and terminations: None
        Participant data:

	Age as of 1/1/93	Annual Salary 1993	1994	Normal Cost as of 1/1/93
Smith	53	$30,000	$30,000	$7,775
Brown	47	15,000	12,000	2,122

What is the 1994 normal cost as of 1/1/94?

3-15   Plan effective date: 1/1/93
        Normal retirement benefit: 40% of highest three-year average compensation
        Actuarial cost method: Individual Level Premium
        Actuarial assumptions:
            Interest rate: 6%
            Compensation increases: None
            Preretirement deaths and terminations: None
            Retirement age: 65
        Selected annuity value: $\ddot{a}_{65}^{(12)} = 9.35$
        Data for sole participant:
            Date of birth   1/1/50
            Date of hire   1/1/93
            1993 compensation $200,000
            1994 compensation   170,000

What is the normal cost for 1994 as of 1/1/94?

3-16   Plan effective date: 1/1/93
        Normal retirement benefit: 75% of final 3-year average pay
        Actuarial cost method: ILP (level dollar)
        Actuarial assumptions:
            Interest rate: 8% per year
            Compensation increases: 4% per year
            Preretirement deaths and terminations: None
            Retirement age: 65
        Selected annuity value: $\ddot{a}_{65}^{(12)}$ = 8.5
        Data for sole participant:
            Date of birth   1/1/51
            1993 compensation $43,500
            1994 compensation   46,000
            Status as of 1/1/94   Active

        Find the increase in the normal cost for 1994 as of 1/1/94 over the
        normal cost for 1993 as of 1/1/93.

3-17   Plan effective date: 1/1/91
        Normal retirement benefit: 50% of final 3-year average salary
        Actuarial cost method: Individual Level Premium
        Actuarial assumptions:
            Interest rate: 7% per year
            Compensation increases: None
            Preretirement deaths and terminations: None
            Retirement age: 65
        Selected annuity value: $\ddot{a}_{65}^{(12)}$ = 8.74
        Data for sole participant:
            Date of birth   1/1/51
            Date of hire   1/1/91
            Compensation used in 1/1/91 valuation   60,000
        Normal cost for 1992 as of 1/1/92: 3032

        What is the participant's projected 3-year average compensation
        used in the 1/1/92 actuarial valuation?

3-18   Plan effective date: 1/1/91
Normal retirement benefit: 50% of final 5-year average salary
Actuarial cost method: Individual Level Premium
Actuarial assumptions:
Interest rate: 7% per year
Compensation increases: None
Preretirement deaths and terminations: None
Retirement age: 65
Selected annuity value: $\ddot{a}_{65}^{(12)} = 8.74$

Valuation data for sole participant:

Date of birth	1/1/40
Date of hire	1/1/91
1991 compensation for 1/1/91 valuation	100,000
1992 compensation for 1/1/92 valuation	92,000

What is the accrued liability as of 1/1/93?

3-19   Plan effective date: 1/1/90
Normal retirement benefit: 50% of highest 3-year average salary
Compensation: Base rate of pay as of 1/1
Actuarial cost method: Individual Level Premium
Actuarial assumptions:
Interest rate: 7% per year
Compensation increases: None
Pretirement deaths and terminations: None
Retirement age: 65
Selected annuity value: $\ddot{a}_{65}^{(12)} = 8.786$
Valuation data for sole participant:

Date of birth	1/1/30
Date of hire	1/1/90
Base rate of pay as of 1/1/90	$60,000
Base rate of pay as of 1/1/91	60,000
Base rate of pay as of 1/1/92	80,000
Base rate of pay as of 1/1/93	80,000
Base rate of pay as of 1/1/94	65,000

What is the normal cost for 1994 as of 1/1/94?

Chapter 4

Aggregate Cost Methods

4.1 Individual Aggregate

As its name suggests, the **Individual Aggregate** cost method has character-istics of both individual and aggregate methods. We could have presented it in Chapter 3, but it appears to fit better pedagogically in this chapter. The method is similar to other *individual* methods in that the total normal cost is the sum of the individual normal costs. It is similar to other *aggregate* methods (*c.f.*, Section 4.2) in that all such methods involve a **pension fund**, and the larger the fund, the smaller the normal cost.

For every individual participant at every valuation, we have

$$pvNC \ = \ pvB - F^P,$$

where the normal cost for the participant can be level dollar or level percent from valuation to retirement, B is the projected benefit often with salary scale, and F^P is the participant's share of the fund. This formula is the key concept in aggregate cost methods. The philosophy is that for each participant, future normal costs will pay for the excess of pvB over the existing funds.

The share of the fund for all retired participants is normally the present value of benefits for such participants; the balance of the fund for the active participants can be (a) divided by the number of participants, (b) prorated by the present value of the projected benefit, (c) prorated by the present value of the accrued benefit, (d) prorated by AL^{EAN} or AL^{ILP}, or (e) prorated by any other reasonable measure.

With the Individual Aggregate method, as with the Individual Level Premium method, at the inception of the plan there is *no* actuarial liability for past service and presumably no fund. There is never an unfunded actuarial liability.

DISCUSSION QUESTION

4-1   Develop an expression for the actuarial liability under this method.

EXAMPLE 4.1

Plan effective date: 1/1/89
Normal retirement benefit: $10 per month for each year of service
Actuarial cost method:
    Before 1994: Aggregate
    After 1993: Individual Aggregate, with assets allocated in proportion
                    to present value of accrued benefits as of 1/1/94
Actuarial assumptions:
    Interest: 6%
    Preretirement deaths and terminations: None
    Retirement age: 65
Actuarial value of assets as of 1/1/94: $10,000
Selected annuity value: $\ddot{a}_{65}^{(12)} = 10$
Participant data as of 1/1/94:

	Smith	Brown
Date of birth	1/1/44	1/1/34
Date of hire	1/1/89	1/1/79

What is Smith's normal cost for 1994 as of 1/1/94?

SOLUTION   Let 1/1/94 be time 0. For Smith at time 0 (age 50) we have

$$NC_{50} \cdot \ddot{a}_{50:\overline{15|}} = pv_{50}B - F_0^S,$$

where F_0^S is the amount of the fund that is allocated to Smith. We are told that the fund is allocated to participants in proportion to the present value, at time 0, of the benefits accrued from date of hire to 1/1/94. For Brown, who is age 60, the accrued benefit is

$$B_{60} = 10 \times 12 \times 15 = 1800,$$

and the present value of this accrued benefit is

$$pv_{60}B_{60} = 1800v^5 \, \ddot{a}_{65}^{(12)} = 13,450.65.$$

For Smith we have

$$B_{50} = 10 \times 12 \times 5 = 600$$

and

$$pv_{50}B_{50} = 600 \, v^{15} \, \ddot{a}_{65}^{(12)} = 2503.59,$$

so the amount of the fund allocated to him is

$$\left(\frac{2503.59}{2503.59 + 13,450.65} \right) (10,000) = 1569.23.$$

Then Smith's normal cost is

$$NC_{50} = \frac{(10 \times 12 \times 20)(v^{15})(10) - 1569.23}{\ddot{a}_{\overline{15|}}} = \$820. \qquad \square$$

EXAMPLE 4.2

Plan inception date: 1/1/94

Normal retirement benefit: $10 per month for each year of service

Actuarial cost method: Individual Aggregate, with assets allocated to individuals in proportion to their respective actuarial liabilities under the Individual Level Premium method

Assumed interest rate: 7%

Assumed retirement age: 65

Assumed preretirement mortality and terminations: None

Actuarial value of assets as of 1/1/95: $10,000

Participant data and valuation results at 1/1/94:

	Smith	Brown	Green
Age a at inception	29	49	59
Normal cost as of 1/1	$301	1609	6271

Green died on 12/1/94.

What is the normal cost for 1995 as of 1/1/95?

SOLUTION Let 1/1/95 be time 1 and age at valuation x. (Note that $x = a+1$.) Since Green died on 12/1/94, he has no normal cost for 1995. We must calculate Smith's and Brown's actuarial liabilities under ILP to find the amount of the fund allocated to each of them. The liability under ILP is, retrospectively,

$$AL_x = NC_a \left(\frac{N_a - N_x}{D_x} \right).$$

The calculation is at interest only and $x = a + 1$, so the accumulation factor is simply $1 + i = 1.07$. Thus for Smith we have

$$AL_1^S = 301(1.07) = 322.07$$

and for Brown we have

$$AL_1^B = 1609(1.07) = 1721.63.$$

The proportion of the fund allocated to Smith is therefore

$$F_1^S = \left(\frac{322.07}{322.07 + 1721.63} \right) (10,000) = 1575.92,$$

and the proportion of the fund allocated to Brown is

$$F_1^B = \left(\frac{1721.63}{322.07 + 1721.63} \right) (10,000) = 8424.08.$$

At time 1 we have

$$NC_1 \cdot \ddot{a}_{x:\overline{r-x|}} = pvB - F_1^P.$$

For Smith we have

$$pvB = NC \cdot \ddot{s}_{\overline{r-a|}} (1.07)^{-(r-x)} = 301 \ddot{s}_{\overline{36|}} (1.07)^{-35}$$

and

$$NC_1^S = \frac{(301)(159.34)(1.07)^{-35} - 1575.92}{\ddot{a}_{\overline{35|}}} = 211.$$

For Brown we have

$$pvB = 1609 \ddot{s}_{\overline{16|}} (1.07)^{-15}$$

and

$$NC_1^B = \frac{(1609)(29.84)(1.07)^{-15} - 8424.08}{\ddot{a}_{\overline{15|}}} = 921.$$

Then the total normal cost is

$$NC_1 = 211 + 921 = \$1132. \qquad \square$$

EXAMPLE 4.3

Actuarial cost method: Individual Aggregate, with assets allocated to each
  active participant in proportion to the sum, as of the prior valuation
  date, of normal cost and allocated assets

Actuarial assumptions:
  Interest: 6%
  Preretirement deaths and terminations: None
  Retirement age: 65
  Selected annuity value: $\ddot{a}_{65}^{(12)} = 10$

Valuation results as of 1/1/93:

	Normal Cost as of 1/1	Allocated Assets
Smith	$2,000	$10,000
Brown	1,000	3,000
Green	1,000	2,000

During 1993 Green terminated with no vested benefit.
Participant data as of 1/1/94:

	Age	Projected Monthly Benefit
Smith	50	$800
Brown	45	600

Actuarial value of assets as of 1/1/94: $22,000

What is Smith's normal cost for 1994 as of 1/1/94?

$\boxed{\text{SOLUTION}}$ Let 1/1/94 be time 1, which is age $x = 50$ for Smith. We have

$$NC_{50} \cdot \ddot{a}_{\overline{15|}} = pvB - F_1^S.$$

We need the sum of the normal cost and allocated assets at time 0 for each participant to determine the amount of assets allocated to Smith at time 1. However, Green's sum of $3000 will not be used to determine the allocation of assets at time 1, because he terminated with no vested benefits during 1993. The sum for Smith is 12,000 and the sum for Brown is 4,000. Then the amount of the assets allocated to Smith on 1/1/94 (time 1) is

$$F_1^S = \left(\frac{12}{16}\right)(22,000) = 16,500$$

and the present value of Smith's benefit at time 1 is

$$pvB = (800)(12)(1.06)^{-15}(10) = 40,057.44.$$

Smith's normal cost at time 1 is

$$NC_{50} = \frac{40,057.44 - 16,500}{10.29} = \$2288.   \qquad \square$$

4.2 Aggregate

The philosophy of the **Aggregate** cost method is that, in the aggregate, the future normal costs will pay for the value of the benefits in excess of the funds on hand. Thus we have

$$TNC \cdot \ddot{a} = \sum pvB - F,$$

where TNC now denotes the total normal cost for the *group*, $\ddot{a}$ is the *average* working-life annuity, $\sum pvB$ is the value of the future benefits at the date of valuation for *all* participants, active, deferred vested, and retired, and F is the total fund at the valuation date.

For the level percent case (see Section 3.2), the average annuity is defined as

$$\ddot{a} = \frac{\sum \left(\dfrac{{}^sN_x - {}^sN_r}{{}^sD_x} \right) S_x}{\sum S_x} = \frac{\sum pv \text{ (future salaries)}}{\text{total salaries}}.$$

We often wish to express the total normal cost as a proportion, U, of total salaries (see Example 4.13); U is then such that

$$TNC = U \cdot \sum S_x$$

at the valuation date. Level dollar is a special case of level percent, where the salaries all equal one, ^sD_x becomes D_x, U becomes the normal cost per participant, and $\sum S_x$ becomes n, if there are n active participants.

Like Individual Aggregate, the unfunded actuarial liability is always zero, but we do not need to divide the fund into n pieces.

If we look at the first formula in this section, we can see that the normal cost for the entire group is "aggregate," and cannot easily be broken down (and does not need to be broken down) into a normal cost for each participant. This "aggregate" characteristic applies to the Aggregate method of this section and also to the three remaining *aggregate methods* in this chapter. Recall that with *individual methods* we obtain the total normal cost and total actuarial liability by making calculations for each participant and summing the individual results.

| DISCUSSION QUESTIONS |

4-2   What is the actuarial liability under the Aggregate method?

4-3   With Individual Aggregate and ILP, how does the balance sheet provide for retired lives?

4-4   Compare and contrast Individual Aggregate and Aggregate.

4-5   Is U^{EAN} different for each entry age? Is U^{AGG} different for each entry age?

| EXAMPLE 4.4 |

Plan effective date: 1/1/94
Normal retirement benefit: $10 per month for each year of service
Assumed interest rate: 6%
Assumed retirement age: 65
Preretirement terminations other than by death: None
All employees were hired at age 25.
Selected annuity value: $\ddot{a}_{65}^{(12)} = 10$

Participant data as of 1/1/94 and selected commutation functions:

Attained Age x	Number of Employees Employees	D_x	$N_x - N_{65}$
25	0	15	240
35	1	8	120
45	2	4	48
55	0	2	15
65	0	1	0

What is the normal cost for 1994 as of 1/1/94 under the Aggregate cost method?

   SOLUTION Let 1/1/94 be time 0 and age x. To calculate the normal cost for the plan we need the values of

$$\sum pvB = (10 \times 40)(120)\left(\frac{1}{8}\right) + 2(10 \times 40)(120)\left(\frac{1}{4}\right) = 30,000$$

and

$$\sum \frac{N_x - N_r}{D_x} = \left(\frac{120}{8}\right) + 2\left(\frac{48}{4}\right) = 39.$$

Assuming that the value of the fund is zero at plan inception, the total normal cost is such that

$$TNC_0 \cdot \frac{39}{3} = 30,000 - 0,$$

so we have

$$TNC_0 = \$2307. \qquad \square$$

   EXAMPLE 4.5
Plan effective date: 1/1/94
Normal retirement benefit: $1000 per month
Actuarial cost method: Aggregate
Assumed interest rate: 7%
Preretirement terminations other than by death: None
Assumed retirement age: 65
Sole participant's date of birth: 1/1/54
Normal cost as of 1/1/94: $1500
Actuarial value of assets as of 1/1/95: $1675

Selected commutation functions:

x	D_x	$N_x - N_{65}$
40	67	787
41	62	720
65	10	0

What is the normal cost for 1995 as of 1/1/95?

SOLUTION Let 1/1/94 be time 0 and age $x - 1$. The normal cost at time 1 is such that

$$NC_1 \cdot \ddot{a}_{41:\overline{24|}} = pvB - F_1,$$

where

$$F_1 = 1675,$$

$$\ddot{a}_{41:\overline{24|}} = \frac{N_{41} - N_{65}}{D_{41}} = 11.61,$$

and

$$pvB = (1000 \times 12) \frac{D_{65}}{D_{41}} \ddot{a}_{65}^{(12)} = 1935.48 \, \ddot{a}_{65}^{(12)}.$$

We are not given the value of $\ddot{a}_{65}^{(12)}$, but we can find it from the value of the normal cost at plan inception. At time 0 we have

$$NC_0 \cdot \ddot{a}_{40:\overline{25|}} = pvB - F_0,$$

where $NC_0 = 1500$ and $F_0 = 0$. Thus we have

$$1500 \left(\frac{787}{67} \right) = (1000 \times 12) \left(\frac{10}{67} \right) \ddot{a}_{65}^{(12)},$$

from which we find $\ddot{a}_{65}^{(12)} = 9.8375$. Finally we can calculate the normal cost at time 1 as

$$NC_1 = \frac{1935.48(9.8375) - 1675}{11.61} = \$1495. \qquad \square$$

| EXAMPLE 4.6 |

Normal retirement benefit: $10 per month for each year of service
Actuarial cost method: Aggregate
Actuarial assumptions:
    Interest rate: 7% per year
    Preretirement terminations other than deaths: None
    Retirement age: 65
Data for all participants as of 1/1/94:

Age	Number of Participants	Past Service	Status
45	15	20	Active
55	10	30	Active
65	5	40	Retired

Value of assets as of 1/1/94: $300,000
Selected commutation functions:

x	D_x	N_x
45	4528	58,163
55	2187	24,581
65	965	8,872

What is the normal cost for 1994 as of 1/1/94?

| SOLUTION | Let 1/1/94 be time 0 and age x. Since all participants were hired at age 25, the projected benefit for each participant is

$$B_{65} = 10 \times 12 \times 40 = 4800,$$

and the sum of the present value of each participant's projected benefit at time 0 is

$$\sum pvB = 4800 \left[15 \left(\frac{N_{65}^{(12)}}{4528} \right) + 10 \left(\frac{N_{65}^{(12)}}{2187} \right) + 5 \left(\frac{N_{65}^{(12)}}{965} \right) \right].$$

Using the standard approximation

$$N_{65}^{(12)} = N_{65} - \frac{11}{24} D_{65} = 8429.71,$$

the above expression evaluates to

$$\sum pvB = 528,707.$$

We know that the normal cost for retired members is zero, so we have

$$\sum \ddot{a}_{x:\overline{r-x}|} = 15 \left(\frac{58,163 - 8,872}{4528} \right) + 10 \left(\frac{24,581 - 8,872}{2187} \right) = 235.12,$$

so the average annuity value is

$$\ddot{a} = \frac{235.12}{25} = 9.40.$$

Then the total normal cost at time 0 is

$$TNC_0 = \frac{528,707 - 300,000}{9.40} = \$24,318. \qquad \square$$

EXAMPLE 4.7

Plan effective date: 1/1/94
Normal retirement benefit: \$10 per month for each year of service
Actuarial cost method: Aggregate
Actuarial assumptions:
    Interest: 6%
    Preretirement mortality and withdrawal: None
    Retirement age: 65
    Selected annuity value: $12 \, \ddot{a}_{65}^{(12)} = 110$
Normal cost for 1994 as of 1/1/94: \$1000
1994 contribution of normal cost plus interest was paid 12/31/94.
There were no actual deaths or other terminations during 1994.
As of 1/1/95, there are the two original plan participants, whose ages are
    now 35 and 45, and a new participant hired 1/1/95 at age 30.

What is the normal cost for 1995 as of 1/1/95?

SOLUTION Let 1/1/94 be time 0 and age x. Since the plan inception date is 1/1/94, the fund at time 0 is $F_0 = 0$. The amount in the fund at time 1 is

$$F_1 = 1000(1.06) = 1060,$$

since the contribution for 1994 was $1000 plus interest at time 1. We do not know the number of years of service for the two original participants, so we cannot calculate ΣpvB_1 at time 1 in the usual way.

We are given the normal cost at time 0, so we can calculate $\Sigma pv_x B$. At time 0,

$$TNC_0 \sum \frac{N_x - N_r}{D_x} \div n = \sum pv_x B - F_0,$$

or

$$1000 \left[\ddot{a}_{\overline{31|}} + \ddot{a}_{\overline{21|}} \right] \div 2 = \sum pv_x B - F_0.$$

Since $F_0 = 0$, then

$$\sum pv_x B = 13,617.$$

Since there were no deaths or other terminations during 1994, $\Sigma pv_x B$ only increases with interest during the year, and, allowing for the new participant,

$$\sum pv_{x+1} B = \left(\sum pv_x B \right)(1+i) + (10 \times 35)(110)(1+i)^{-35}.$$

$$= 13,617(1.06) + 5009 = 19,443.$$

Finally the normal cost at time 1 is

$$TNC_1 = 3 \left[\frac{19,443 - 1060}{\ddot{a}_{\overline{20|}} + \ddot{a}_{\overline{30|}} + \ddot{a}_{\overline{35|}}} \right] = \$1309. \qquad \square$$

EXAMPLE 4.8

Actuarial cost method: Aggregate

Valuation date: 1/1/94

Normal retirement benefit: $10 per month per year of service

Vesting: Full vesting in the accrued benefit upon termination after 10 or more years of service; no prior vesting

All decrements among active participants are assumed to occur at EOY.
Active participant Smith was born 1/1/54, employed 1/1/78, and is active
on 1/1/94 at age 40 with 16 years of service.

Give an expression in standard actuarial notation for the present value on
1/1/94 of Smith's future vested termination benefits.

| SOLUTION | Let 1/1/94 be time 0, at which time Smith is age 40. His
accrued benefit is fully vested since he has 16 years of service. If he
withdraws at the end of any year before age 65, he will receive a monthly
benefit, commencing at age 65, based on his actual number of years of
service. Retirement at age 65 eliminates the withdrawal decrement at age
65. The present value of Smith's future vested termination benefit is

$$(120 \times 17)v^0 \; {}_0p_{40}^{(\tau)} \; q_{40}^{(w)} \; {}_{25|}\ddot{a}_{40}^{(12)} + (120 \times 18)v^1 \; {}_1p_{40}^{(\tau)} \; q_{41}^{(w)} \; {}_{24|}\ddot{a}_{41}^{(12)}$$

$$+ \cdots + (120 \times 41)v^{24} \; {}_{24}p_{40}^{(\tau)} \; q_{64}^{(w)} \; {}_{1|}\ddot{a}_{64}^{(12)}$$

$$= 120\sum_{x=40}^{64}(x-23) \; \frac{v^x}{v^{40}} \; \frac{\ell_x^{(\tau)}}{\ell_{40}^{(\tau)}} \; q_x^{(w)} \; {}_{65-x|}\ddot{a}_x^{(12)}$$

$$= \frac{120}{D_{40}^{(\tau)}} \sum_{x=40}^{64}(x-23)v^x \; \ell_x^{(\tau)} \; q_x^{(w)} \; {}_{65-x|}\ddot{a}_x^{(12)}. \qquad \square$$

| EXAMPLE 4.9 |
Plan effective date: 1/1/94
Normal retirement benefit: 50% of final five-year average salary
Assumed retirement age: 65
Employee data as of 1/1/94:

	Age	Service	1994 Salary
Brown	35	10 years	$20,000
Green	45	None	10,000

Preretirement terminations other than by death: None

Selected commutation functions:

x	^sD_x	$^sN_x - {}^sN_{65}$	S_x	D_x	$N_x - N_{65}$	$N_x^{(12)}$
25	1,500	75,000	.30	5,000	120,000	
35	1,600	64,000	.40	4,000	72,000	
45	1,500	45,000	.50	3,000	36,000	
60	2,250	9,750	1.50	1,500	6,500	
61	2,100	7,500	1.50	1,400	5,000	
62	1,950	5,400	1.50	1,300	3,600	
63	1,800	3,450	1.50	1,200	2,300	
64	1,650	1,650	1.50	1,100	1,100	
65	1,500	0	1.50	1,000	0	10,000

All normal costs are calculated as a level percent of the appropriate pay.

What is the normal cost for the plan due 1/1/94 under the Aggregate cost method?

SOLUTION Let 1/1/94 be time 0 and age x. Using a salary increase assumption, the total normal cost at time 0 is such that

$$TNC_0 \cdot \frac{\sum pv_0 S}{\sum S_x} = \sum pv_0 B - F_0.$$

A participant's final five-year average salary is

$$FAS = \frac{1}{5}\left(S_{60}+S_{61}+\cdots+S_{64}\right) = \frac{S_{60}}{5 \cdot s_{60}}\left(s_{60}+s_{61}+\cdots+s_{64}\right) = S_{60},$$

since $s_x = 1.5$ for $x = 60, \dots, 64$. The present value of all future benefits at time 0 is

$$\sum pv_0 B = .50 \sum FAS \frac{D_{65}}{D_x} \ddot{a}_{65}^{(12)}$$

$$= .50 \left[\left(20{,}000\frac{1.5}{.4}\right)\left(\frac{1000}{4000}\right)\right.$$

$$\left. +\left(10{,}000\frac{1.5}{.5}\right)\left(\frac{1000}{3000}\right)\right]\left(\frac{10{,}000}{1{,}000}\right)$$

$$= 143{,}750$$

and the present value of all future salaries is

$$\sum pv_0 S = 20,000 \left(\frac{{}^sN_{35} - {}^sN_{65}}{{}^sD_{35}} \right) + 10,000 \left(\frac{{}^sN_{45} - {}^sN_{65}}{{}^sD_{45}} \right)$$

$$= 20,000 \left(\frac{64,000}{1,600} \right) + 10,000 \left(\frac{45,000}{1,500} \right) = 1,100,000.$$

The total normal cost at time 0 is therefore

$$TNC_0 = \left(\frac{143,750 - 0}{1,100,000} \right) (30,000) = \$3920.45. \qquad \square$$

Note that the question arises as to whether salaries are paid at BOY or throughout the year. We will assume BOY if not clearly stated.

EXAMPLE 4.10

Plan effective date: 1/1/94
Normal retirement benefit: 50% of final year's salary
Actuarial cost method: Aggregate
Actuarial assumptions:
   Interest: 5%
   Salary increases: 5% per year effective 1/1 of each year
   Preretirement terminations or deaths: None
   Selected annuity value: $12\ddot{a}_{65}^{(12)} = 100$
Participant data:
   The only participant on 1/1/94 is age 54, with an annual salary of
      $30,000 per year. On 1/1/95 he is still the only participant.
The contribution paid on 1/1/94 is the normal cost.
Experience rates for 1994:
   Interest: 10%
   Salary increases: 10%

What is the normal cost for 1995 as of 1/1/95?

SOLUTION Let 1/1/94 be time 0 and age $x - 1$. The amount of the fund at time 1 is the normal cost for 1994 together with one year's interest. The normal cost at time 0 is

$$NC_0 = \left(\frac{pv_0 B - F_0}{pv_0 S} \right) S_{54},$$

where

$$pv_0 B = .50[(30,000)(1.05)^{10}]\,\ddot{a}_{65}^{(12)}(1.05)^{-11} = 119,047.62.$$

We can use a net interest rate of zero because the salary and interest assumptions are the same. Then the expression

$$pv_0 S = 30,000\ddot{a}_{\overline{11}|j}$$

at rate $j = 0$ reduces to

$$pv_0 S = 30,000(11) = 330,000.$$

The normal cost at time 0 is

$$NC_0 = \frac{119,047.62}{11} = 10,822.51.$$

Since the actual interest rate and salary increase rate for 1994 was 10%, then at time 1 we have

$$F_1 = (10,822.51)(1.10) = 11,904.76$$

and

$$pv_1 B = .50\,[(30,000)(1.10)(1.05)^9]\,(1.05)^{-10}\left(\frac{100}{12}\right) = 130,952.38,$$

so the normal cost at time 1 is

$$NC_1 = \frac{130,952.38 - 11,904.76}{\ddot{a}_{\overline{10}|}} = \$11,905. \qquad \square$$

| **EXAMPLE 4.11** |

Normal retirement benefit: 60% of final salary
Actuarial cost method: Aggregate
Asset valuation method: Market
Actuarial assumptions:
    Interest: 7%
    Retirement age: 65 (no retirements are scheduled for 1994)
    Preretirement terminations and deaths: None
    Salary increases: 6%

Valuation results as of 1/1/94:

Annual salaries	$ 10,000,000
Present value of future salaries (paid BOY)	200,000,000
Present value of benefits (none paid in 1994)	30,000,000
Assets	10,000,000

The contribution for 1994 is the normal cost, paid at BOY. During 1994 the experience of the plan is according to the assumptions, except that each employee's salary increases 10%.

What is the normal cost for 1995 as of 1/1/95?

$\boxed{\textbf{SOLUTION}}$ Let 1/1/94 be time 0 and age $x - 1$. First we must find the normal cost at time 0 since the fund at time 1 is the sum of the fund at time 0 and the contribution at time 0, together with interest. Using a salary increase assumption of 6% for all ages,

$$TNC_0 \left(\frac{200,000,000}{10,000,000} \right) = 30,000,000 - 10,000,000$$

from which we find

$$TNC_0 = 1,000,000.$$

The fund at time 1 is

$$F_1 = (10,000,000 + 1,000,000)(1.07) = 11,770,000.$$

We know that if there are no preretirement deaths or terminations, then the present value of future benefits at time 0 is the present value at time 1 discounted with interest, so

$$\sum pv_1 B = (1+i) \sum pv_0 B.$$

However the benefit is based on salary, and $\sum pv_0 B$ at time 0 was calculated assuming a salary increase of 6% in the year following time 0. Since all salaries increased by 10% during the year, then at time 1 we have

$$\sum pv_1 B = 30,000,000(1.07) \left(\frac{1.10}{1.06} \right) = 33,311,321.$$

Finally we need the present value of future salaries at time 1. Using the same logic as we did for $\Sigma pv_1 B$ and recognizing that one year's worth of salaries have been paid during 1994, at time 1 we have

$$\sum pv_1 S = (200,000,000 - 10,000,000)(1.07)\left(\frac{1.10}{1.06}\right)$$
$$= 210,971,698.$$

Then the normal cost at time 1 is

$$TNC_1 = (33,311,321 - 11,770,000)\left(\frac{10,000,000(1.10)}{210,971,698}\right)$$
$$= \$1,123,158. \qquad \Box$$

Note that in this example, as with all aggregate methods (but not with individual methods), pvB includes the future benefits for all deferred vested and retired lives. Note also how pvB increases from BOY to EOY.

| **EXAMPLE 4.12** |

Actuarial cost method: Aggregate
Actuarial assumptions:
    Interest rate: 6%
    Compensation increases: 5% per year
    Preretirement deaths and terminations: None
    Retirement age: 65
Valuation results as of 1/1/94:

Normal cost as of 1/1	$ 31,250
Present value of future benefits:	
Active participants	900,000
Inactive participants	100,000
Actuarial value of assets	500,000
Annual compensation	1,000,000

Contribution for 1994: $31,250 paid on 1/1/94
During 1994, the experience of the plan is according to the assumptions, except that three retired participants died, resulting in an experience gain of $30,000. During 1994, there are no new entrants, and no benefits are paid. (Note that the gain of $30,000 consists of the excess of actual over expected retiree liability released *and* the excess of expected over actual retiree monthly benefits, all at EOY.)

What is the normal cost for 1995 as of 1/1/95?

SOLUTION Let 1/1/94 be time 0 and age $x - 1$. We do not know the ages of the participants. In order to calculate $\sum pv_1 S$ at time 1, we can calculate it at time 0 using the information given and increase it with interest. To find $\sum pv_0 S$ at time 0, we equate

$$TNC_0 \left[\frac{\sum pv_0 S}{\sum S_{x-1}} \right] = \sum pv_{x-1} B - F_0.$$

Then

$$(31{,}250) \frac{\sum pv_0 S}{1{,}000{,}000} = (900{,}000 + 100{,}000) - 500{,}000$$

leading to

$$\sum pv_0 S = 16{,}000{,}000.$$

At time 1 we have

$$\sum pv_1 S = (16{,}000{,}000 - 1{,}000{,}000)(1.06) = 15{,}900{,}000$$

$$F_1 = (500{,}000 + 31{,}250)(1.06) = 563{,}125$$

$$\sum S_x = 1{,}000{,}000(1.05) = 1{,}050{,}000$$

and $\sum pv_1 B = \sum pv_0 B$ plus interest and minus the gain, leading to

$$\sum pv_1 B = (900{,}000 + 100{,}000)(1.06) - 30{,}000 = 1{,}030{,}000.$$

Then the normal cost at time 1 is

$$TNC_1 = (1{,}030{,}000 - 563{,}125) \left(\frac{1{,}050{,}000}{15{,}900{,}000} \right) = \$30{,}831. \qquad \square$$

EXAMPLE 4.13
Retirement benefit: 50% of final year's salary
Actuarial cost method: Aggregate
Participant data as of 1/1/94:

Attained Age	Salary for 1994
47	$35,000
47	45,000
47	55,000
47	65,000

Original valuation results as of 1/1/94:

Present value of future benefits	$500,000
Actuarial value of assets	100,000
Normal cost as of 1/1	40,000

After the 1/1/94 valuation, it was discovered that an employee with the following data had been omitted:

Attained Age	Salary for 1994
47	$25,000

The valuation was revised to include the previously omitted employee.

What is the revised normal cost for 1994 as of 1/1/94?

SOLUTION Let 1/1/94 be time 0. U was defined in the introduction to this section as a proportion of salaries such that $U \cdot \Sigma S$ is the normal cost. Therefore U is such that

$$TNC \cdot \ddot{a}_0 = U \sum S_0 \frac{\sum pv_0 S}{\sum S_x} = \sum pv_0 B - F_0.$$

In the previous example, ΣpvB was affected by the deaths of retired participants; similarly in this example, $\Sigma pv_0 B$ and $\Sigma pv_0 S$ are affected by omitting an active participant. To find $\Sigma pv_0 S$ for all the participants, we can calculate it for the 4 original participants using the given data, and then adjust the result to include the omitted participant. For the 4 participants at time 0 we have

$$\sum pv_0 S = \frac{\sum pv_0 B - F_0}{TNC_0} \sum S_x$$

$$= \frac{500,000 - 100,000}{40,000} (200,000) = 2,000,000.$$

Since all the participants are the same age at time 0, then

$$\sum pv_0 S = \ddot{a}^s_{x:\overline{r-x}|} \left(\sum S_x \right),$$

and for all 5 participants we have

$$\sum pv_0 S = 2,000,000 \left(\frac{225,000}{200,000} \right) = 2,250,000.$$

Using the same reasoning, for the 5 participants at time 0 we have

$$\sum pv_0B \ = \ 500,000 \left(\frac{225,000}{200,000}\right) \ = \ 562,500$$

since the benefit is based on salary and the participants are all the same age. Now we can find the value of U as

$$U \ = \ \frac{562,500 - 100,000}{2,250,000} \ = \ .20555,$$

and the revised normal cost at time 0 is

$$.20555(225,000) \ = \ \$46,250. \qquad \square$$

| **EXAMPLE 4.14** |

Normal retirement benefit: 50% of final year's compensation
Preretirement death benefits: None
Actuarial cost method: Aggregate
Actuarial assumptions:
    Interest rate: 7% per year
    Compensation increases:
        Assumption before 1994: None
        Assumption after 1993: 5% per year
    Preretirement terminations other than deaths: None
    Retirement age: 65
Data for sole participant:
    Date of birth   1/1/32
    1994 compensation $40,000
    Status as of 1/1/94   Active
Normal cost for 1994 as of 1/1/94, before change in assumed compensation
    increases: 23,615
Selected commutation functions:

x	D_x	N_x
62	365	3514
63	335	3149
64	306	2814
65	279	2508
66	254	2229

What is the normal cost for 1994 as of 1/1/94?

$\boxed{\text{SOLUTION}}$ Let 1/1/94 be time 0. To calculate the normal cost after the change in assumed compensation increases, we need to find the value of the fund. Before the change in the assumed compensation increases we had

$$pv_0 NC = pv_0 B - F_0,$$

or

$$23{,}615 \left(\frac{N_{62} - N_{65}}{D_{62}} \right) = .50(40{,}000) \frac{N_{65}^{(12)}}{D_{62}} - F_0,$$

or

$$23{,}615 \left(\frac{3514 - 2508}{365} \right) = 20{,}000 \left[\frac{2508 - \left(\frac{11}{24}\right) 279}{365} \right] - F_0.$$

This equation solves for

$$F_0 = 130{,}418 - 65{,}087 = 65{,}331.$$

Using the 5% salary scale we have

$$NC_0 \left(\ddot{a}^s_{62:\overline{3}|} \right) = pv_0 B - F_0,$$

or

$$NC_0 (1 + 1.05 v p_{62} + (1.05)^2 v^2 \, _2p_{62}) = 130{,}418(1.05)^2 - 65{,}331.$$

The value of the salary-based annuity is

$$\ddot{a}^s_{62:\overline{3}|} = \frac{D_{62} + 1.05 D_{63} + (1.05)^2 D_{64}}{D_{62}} = 2.8880,$$

so the normal cost is

$$NC_0 = \frac{78{,}455}{2.8880} = \$27{,}166. \qquad \Box$$

4.3 Frozen Initial Liability (Entry Age Normal)

For a new pension plan, the Aggregate normal cost is sometimes a high percentage of payroll because some participants with high salaries are close to retirement. A common way to alleviate this problem is to set up a **frozen initial liability** with amortization over 15, 20 or 30 years. The resulting total annual cost (normal cost plus supplemental cost) will presumably be less than NC^{AGG}. If the employer can manage contributions which exceed the annual cost, the amortization will be accelerated; when the amortization is complete, this cost method will become the Aggregate cost method.

The cost method in this section is called the **Frozen Initial Liability (Entry Age Normal)** cost method, and is abbreviated as FIL (EAN). It is sometimes referred to as Frozen-Entry-Age, Frozen Initial Liability, or simply FIL. The initial (age a, time 0) actuarial liability is

$$AL_0 = \sum pv_0 B - \sum NC \cdot \ddot{a}_0^s = FIL = UAL_0,$$

where NC and AL_0 are computed by the EAN cost method; the summation is normally over all active lives, and we assume that no retired lives are covered by the plan at inception.

The normal cost at age a (time 0) for the method is such that

$$NC_0 \cdot \ddot{a}_0^s = \sum pv_0 B - FIL - F_0,$$

where F_0 is normally zero.

The frozen initial liability will be amortized (run down to zero) over some period of time; if the period is 20 years and if the amortization is a level dollar amount, then $SC = UAL_0 \cdot \ddot{a}_{\overline{20}|}^{-1}$. If the contribution at the beginning of each year is the normal cost plus the supplemental cost, then the amortization will be orderly and we will have

$$UAL_1 = SC \cdot \ddot{a}_{\overline{19}|},$$

$$UAL_2 = SC \cdot \ddot{a}_{\overline{18}|},$$

and eventually

$$UAL_{20} = SC \cdot \ddot{a}_{\overline{0}|} = 0.$$

If the contribution is more than the normal cost plus the supplemental cost each year, then the amortization will take less than 20 years. If C is paid at BOY, then

$$UAL_1 = (UAL_0 + NC_0 - C)(1+i).$$

If we allow for C to be paid later in the year, then

$$UAL_1 = (UAL_0 + NC_0)(1+i) - {}^i C,$$

$$UAL_2 = (UAL_1 + NC_1)(1+i) - {}^i C,$$

and so on. Recalling that

$$F_1 = F_0 + C - BEN + {}^{act}I,$$

$$F_2 = F_1 + C - BEN + {}^{act}I,$$

and so on, where BEN is any death, withdrawal, or pension benefit paid out during the year and ${}^{act}I$ is the actual interest earned, we can now state that the normal cost is such that

$$NC_1 \cdot \ddot{a}_1^s = pv_1 B - UAL_1 - F_1,$$

$$NC_2 \cdot \ddot{a}_2^s = pv_2 B - UAL_2 - F_2,$$

and so on, where $\ddot{a}_i^s$ is the average working-life annuity for working lives (for the level dollar case the salaries can be taken as 1) and pvB is the value for all active, deferred vested, and retired participants as discussed in the previous section.

The philosophy of this method is that the supplemental costs amortize the frozen initial liability, and the future normal costs provide for the value of the benefits in excess of the unamortized portion of the frozen initial liability and the funds on hand. Thus at each valuation date we have

$$NC \cdot \ddot{a}^s = pvB - UAL - F.$$

As with the Aggregate method, there is *no explicit gain* in any year, but, rather, good experience tends to depress the normal cost and bad experience tends to raise it. If ${}^{act}I > {}^{exp}I$, then ${}^{act}F > {}^{exp}F$, and the implicit interest gain results in a reduced normal cost. If actual mortality is higher than expected, then pvB is reduced, and the implicit mortality gain results in a reduced normal cost.

The following relationships follow from the foregoing, where time 1 is the end of any year, and time 0 is the beginning of that year:

(1) $^{\exp}F_1 = (F_0 + NC_0 + SC_0)(1+i) - {^i}BEN$

(2) $^{\exp}UAL_1 = (UAL_0 - SC_0)(1+i) = (UAL_0 + NC_0)(1+i) - {^i}C$

(3) $^{\text{act}}UAL_1 = (UAL_0 + NC_0)(1+i) - {^i}C - G_1$

(4) $G_1 = {^{\exp}}UAL_1 - {^{\text{act}}}UAL_1 = 0$

Note that ^iC and ^iBEN include interest at the expected earned rate, not the actual earned rate. If the actual interest earned during the year is other than expected, UAL_1 will not be affected; similarly, if actual mortality and salary experience during the year are other than expected, UAL_1 will not be affected. As stated earlier, FIL gains during the year result in a lower normal cost at the beginning of the next year. With Aggregate and FIL methods, the implicit gain or loss is spread over future working lifetimes.

To the extent that the *contribution* exceeds the annual cost, the EOY actual unfunded actuarial liability will be correspondingly lower and the EOY actual fund will be correspondingly higher, but the following year's normal cost will not be affected!

When a *change* in benefits or assumptions occurs, the FIL (EAN) unfunded actuarial liability is adjusted by the amount of the change in the EAN actuarial liability. (See Example 4-16.)

| DISCUSSION QUESTION |

4-6 Suppose a participant withdraws and produces a large gain from withdrawal for the fund. Suppose this FIL gain is amortized over the aggregate period to retirement of ten years. Suppose the amortization period under EAN level percent is five years. Would the gain result in a decrease in normal cost under EAN? Would it result in a larger decrease in normal cost under FIL?

EXAMPLE 4.15

Actuarial cost method: Frozen Initial Liability (level dollar)
Actuarial assumptions:
    Interest rate: 7%
    Preretirement deaths and terminations: None
    Retirement age: 65
Data for all participants:

	Smith	Brown	Green
Age	45	55	65
Annual projected benefit	$20,000	20,000	20,000
Status as of 1/1/94	Active	Active	Retired

Unfunded liability as of 1/1/94: $12,000
Value of assets as of 1/1/94: $208,800
The contribution for 1994 is equal to the normal cost for 1994 as of 1/1/94,
    plus a 10-year amortization payment as of 1/1/94 toward the unfunded
    liability as of 1/1/94.
Selected annuity values:

x	$\ddot{a}_x^{(12)}$
45	12.33
55	10.78
65	8.74

What is the contribution for 1994 as of 1/1/94?

SOLUTION Let 1/1/94 be time 0 and age x. The 10-year amortization
payment is

$$\frac{12,000}{\ddot{a}_{\overline{10|}}} = 1597.$$

To calculate the normal cost we first need the pvB. At time 0 we have

$$\sum pv_x B = 20,000\ddot{a}_{65}^{(12)}[(1.07)^{-20} + (1.07)^{-10} + 1] = 308,831.$$

From the basic equation

$$TNC_0 \cdot \frac{1}{n} \cdot \sum \frac{N_x - N_r}{D_x} = \sum pv_x B - UAL_0 - F_0$$

we can solve for TNC_0, obtaining

$$TNC_0 = 2[308,831 - 12,000 - 208,800] \left(\frac{1}{\ddot{a}_{\overline{10}|} + \ddot{a}_{\overline{20}|}} \right) = 9340.$$

Then the total contribution is

$$C_0 = 9340 + 1597 = \$10,937. \qquad \square$$

EXAMPLE 4.16

Normal retirement benefit: $10 per month for each year of service
Actuarial cost method: Frozen Initial Liability (EAN)
Actuarial assumptions:

  Interest: 7%
  Preretirement deaths and terminations: None
  Retirement age: 65

The sole plan participant is age 50 as of 1/1/94. Due to a plan amendment
  effective 1/1/94 which changed the normal retirement age from 65 to
  62, the *assumed* retirement age is changed to 62. The unfunded
  liability is adjusted as of 1/1/94 to reflect the change in assumptions.
Selected valuation results as of 1/1/94:

	Assumed Retirement Age	
	65	62
Present value of future benefits	15,000	18,400
Unfunded liability	6,150	
Actuarial value of assets	5,000	5,000
Entry Age Normal accrued liability	13,100	16,350

Find the 1/1/94 normal cost under the revised retirement age assumption?

SOLUTION Let 1/1/94 be time 0 and age x. We are given that the
unfunded liability is adjusted to reflect the change in assumptions. At plan
inception, $UAL = AL$ since the fund will normally be 0 at this time.
Furthermore, at the time when the normal retirement age is changed,
$\Delta UAL = \Delta AL$ because $UAL = AL - F$, and F is not affected by this

change. The unfunded actuarial liability at time 0, after the normal retirement age is changed to 62, is

$$UAL_0 = 6150 + (16{,}350 - 13{,}100) = 9400.$$

The revised normal cost is

$$NC_0 = \frac{pvB - UAL_0 - F_0}{\ddot{a}_{\overline{12}|}} = \frac{18{,}400 - 9400 - 5000}{8.499} = \$470.64. \qquad \square$$

EXAMPLE 4.17

Actuarial cost method: Frozen Initial Liability (EAN)
Assumed interest rate: 6% (use simple interest for part of a year)
Selected valuation results:

	1/1/93	1/1/94
Normal cost as of 1/1	$ 25,000	—
Present value of future benefits	500,000	$565,000
Present value of future normal costs	210,000	—
Actuarial value of assets	80,000	—

Contributions for 1993: $25,000 on 6/30/93; $20,000 on 12/31/93
Benefit payments for 1993: $0
The rate of return on the actuarial value of assets during 1993 was 8.4%
    (simple interest can be used for part of a year).

What is the present value of future normal costs as of 1/1/94?

SOLUTION Let 1/1/93 be time 0. At time 1 we have

$$pv_1NC = pv_1B - UAL_1 - F_1.$$

During 1993, the fund at time 0 will increase by the contributions made during the year and by interest earned on the initial fund and the contributions. Thus we have

$$F_1 = 80{,}000(1.084) + 25{,}000\,[1 + .5(.084)] + 20{,}000 = 132{,}770.$$

Recall that the unfunded actuarial liability at time 1 can be defined as

$$UAL_1 = (UAL_0 + NC_0)(1+i) - {}^iC$$

$$= \left[(AL_0 - F_0) + NC_0\right](1+i) - {}^iC,$$

where

$$AL_0 = pvB_0 - pvNC_0 = 500,000 - 210,000 = 290,000.$$

Using the given information, we find

$$UAL_1 = [(290,000 - 80,000) + 25,000](1.06) - 25,000(1.03) - 20,000$$

$$= 203,350.$$

Finally, we have

$$pv_1NC = 565,000 - 203,350 - 132,770 = \$228,880. \qquad \square$$

EXAMPLE 4.18

Normal retirement benefit: $10 per month for each year of service
Actuarial cost method: Frozen Initial Liability (EAN)
Actuarial assumptions:
    Interest: 8%
    Preretirement deaths and terminations: None
    Retirement age: 65
Actual experience for 1993: Same as assumptions
Valuation dates:
    For 1993 plan year: 12/31/93
    For 1994 plan year: 1/1/94
Selected valuation results as of 12/31/93:

Present value of future benefits	$900,000
Unfunded liability	400,000
Normal cost as of 12/31	30,000

Value of assets on 12/31/93: $200,000 prior to 1993 contribution
Contribution for 1993: $60,000 paid at 12/31/93

What is the normal cost for 1994 as of 1/1/94?

SOLUTION Let 1/1/93 be time 0. Since the normal cost at the end of the year is $30,000, the normal cost at the beginning of the year is

$$TNC_0 = \frac{30,000}{1.08} = 27,778.$$

We are not using a salary increase assumption, so the normal cost remains the same flat dollar amount each year. Thus we have

$$TNC_1 = \$27,778. \qquad\qquad \square$$

ALTERNATE SOLUTION Let 1/1/93 be time 0. We have

$$TNC_0 \cdot \ddot{a}_{\overline{r-x|}} = \sum pv_0 B - UAL_0 - F_0,$$

and at 12/31/93 we have

$$TNC_0 \cdot \ddot{a}_{\overline{r-x|}} (1.08) = \sum pv_1 B - UAL_1 - F_1,$$
$$= 900,000 - 400,000 - 200,000 = 300,000.$$

We know that

$$TNC_0(1.08) = 30,000$$

from which we easily find $\ddot{a}_{\overline{r-x|}} = 10$. Then at time 1, which is 1/1/94, we have

$$TNC_1 \cdot \ddot{a}_{\overline{r-x-1|}} = \sum pv_1 B - UAL_1' - F_1',$$

where

$$\ddot{a}_{\overline{r-x-1|}} = (10-1)(1.08) = 9.72,$$

$$UAL_1' = 400,000 + 30,000 - 60,000 = 370,000$$

and

$$F_1' = 200,000 + 60,000 = 260,000.$$

Then

$$TNC_1 = \frac{900,000 - 370,000 - 260,000}{9.72} = \$27,778. \qquad \square$$

4.4 Frozen Initial Liability (Attained Age Normal)

The actuarial cost method described in this section, called **Frozen Initial Liability (Attained Age Normal)**, abbreviated FIL (AAN), is sometimes referred to as Frozen-Attained-Age, Attained Age Normal with FIL, or, ambiguously, Attained Age Normal. In practice, it is used more frequently than the IAAN method (see Section 8.1.6), but less frequently than FIL (EAN).

This method is the same as FIL (EAN), except that here the frozen initial liability is computed by the Unit Credit method instead of the EAN method; the frozen initial liability is based on the accrued pension benefit. At each valuation date we have

$$TNC \cdot \ddot{a}^s \ = \ pvB - UAL - F.$$

The resulting *normal cost* is higher than it is under FIL (EAN), because the unfunded actuarial liability is smaller, but the initial normal cost is lower than under ILP which has a zero initial unfunded actuarial liability. The resulting *supplemental cost* is smaller than under FIL (EAN) due to the smaller unfunded actuarial liability.

Because of new entrants and withdrawals, it is standard practice to recalculate the normal cost (with this method and all methods) at each valuation. The supplemental cost is almost always a level dollar amount, and is usually not recalculated at each valuation.

Whenever there is a *change* in the plan, the assumptions, or the asset valuation method, the FIL (AAN) unfunded actuarial liability is increased by the increase (positive or negative) in the Unit Credit unfunded liability.

EXAMPLE 4.19

Plan effective date: 1/1/94
Normal retirement benefit:
    $10 per month for each year of service before 1/1/94, plus
    $15 per month for each subsequent year of service
Actuarial cost method: Frozen Initial Liability (AAN)
Actuarial assumptions:
    Interest: 6%
    Preretirement deaths and terminations: None
    Retirement age: 65
    Selected annuity value: $\ddot{a}^{(12)}_{65} = 9$

Participant data as of 1/1/94:

	Smith	Brown
Date of birth	1/1/49	1/1/34
Date of hire	1/1/79	1/1/74

What is the normal cost for 1994 as of 1/1/94?

SOLUTION Let 1/1/94, the plan effective date, be time 0. To calculate the normal cost under FIL (AAN), we need the values of F_0, UAL_0, and $\sum pvB$. We know that $F_0 = 0$ since time 0 is plan inception, and therefore $UAL_0 = TAL_0$. The liability at plan inception is calculated under Unit Credit, obtaining

$$TAL_0 = (10 \times 12 \times 15)v^{20}\ddot{a}_{65}^{(12)} + (10 \times 12 \times 20)v^5\ddot{a}_{65}^{(12)}$$

$$= 5,051.24 + 16,140.78$$

$$= 21,192.02.$$

Since the plan provides \$10 per month for any service prior to plan inception and \$15 per month thereafter, then

$$\sum pvB = (120 \times 15 + 180 \times 20)v^{20}\ddot{a}_{65}^{(12)} + (120 \times 20 + 180 \times 5)v^5\ddot{a}_{65}^{(12)}$$

$$= 15,153.71 + 22,193.57$$

$$= 37,347.28.$$

The total normal cost is such that

$$TNC_0 \cdot \frac{\ddot{a}_{\overline{20|}} + \ddot{a}_{\overline{5|}}}{2} = \sum pvB - AL_0,$$

from which we find

$$TNC_0 = 2\left(\frac{37,347.28 - 21,192.02}{12.158 + 4.465}\right) = \$1944. \qquad \square$$

EXAMPLE 4.20

Plan effective date: 1/1/94

Normal retirement benefit: $5 per month for each year of service

Actuarial cost method: Frozen Initial Liability (AAN)

Assumed retirement age: 65

Selected annuity value: $\ddot{a}_{65}^{(12)} = 10$

Preretirement terminations other than death: None

Participant data 1/1/94 and selected commutation functions:

Age at hire	Attained Age x	Number of Participants	D_x	$N_x - N_{65}$
30	30	10	600	9900
30	40	5	350	4600
—	50	0	200	1900
40	60	10	125	575
50	65	2	100	0

What is the actuarial liability as of 1/1/94?

SOLUTION Let 1/1/94 be time 0, the plan effective date. Under AAN, the liability is calculated as under Unit Credit. By summing each participant's liability, the total liability is

$$TAL_0 = \sum B_x \frac{D_r}{D_x} \ddot{a}_r^{(12)}$$

$$= 5(5 \times 12 \times 10)\left(\frac{100}{350}\right)(10) + 10(5 \times 12 \times 20)\left(\frac{100}{125}\right)(10)$$

$$+ 2(5 \times 12 \times 15)\left(\frac{100}{100}\right)(10) = \$122{,}571. \qquad \square$$

EXAMPLE 4.21

Plan effective date: 1/1/94

Normal retirement benefit: $10 per month for each year of service

Assumed retirement age: 65

Selected annuity value: $\ddot{a}_{65}^{(12)} = 10$

Preretirement terminations other than death: None

Participant data at 1/1/94 and selected commutation functions:

Age at hire	Attained Age x	Number of Participants	D_x	$N_x - N_{65}$
35	35	40	92	1190
35	45	60	46	500
—	55	0	22	160
—	65	0	10	0

What is the difference between the actuarial liability under the Entry Age Normal method and that under the Attained Age Normal method?

$\boxed{\text{SOLUTION}}$ Let 1/1/94, the plan effective date, be time 0. The liability under Entry Age Normal is, retrospectively,

$$TAL_0^{EA} = \sum B_r \frac{D_r}{D_x} \ddot{a}_r^{(12)} \left(\frac{N_e - N_x}{N_e - N_r} \right)$$

$$= 60(10 \times 12 \times 30)\left(\frac{10}{46}\right)(10)\left(\frac{690}{1190}\right) = 272{,}268.91.$$

The liability under Attained Age Normal is zero for the first 40 participants; for the next 60 participants it is

$$TAL_0^{AA} = \sum B_x \frac{D_r}{D_x} \ddot{a}_r^{(12)}$$

$$= 60(10 \times 12 \times 10)\left(\frac{10}{46}\right)(10) = 156{,}521.74.$$

The difference is

$$TAL_0^{EA} - TAL_0^{AA} = 272{,}268.91 - 156{,}521.74 = \$115{,}747.17. \quad \square$$

$\boxed{\text{EXAMPLE 4.22}}$

Plan effective date: 1/1/94
Normal retirement benefit: $10 monthly per year of service up to 30 years
Actuarial cost method: Attained Age Normal with FIL

Actuarial assumptions:
    Preretirement terminations other than deaths: None
    Retirement age: 65
Data for sole participant:
    Date of birth   1/1/44
    Date of hire   1/1/74
    Status as of 1/1/94   Active
Selected commutation functions:

x	D_x	$N_x^{(12)}$
30	1238	28,056
50	320	3,716
65	97	849

What is the normal cost for 1994 as of 1/1/94?

SOLUTION   Let 1/1/94, the plan effective date, be time 0. The pension
will be based on 30 years of service, of which 20 will be funded by the
supplemental cost and 10 by the normal cost. (Supplemental cost is discussed in Section 3.6.) Equating $pvNC$ to pvB gives us

$$NC_0 \left(\frac{N_{50} - N_{65}}{D_{50}} \right) = (10 \times 12 \times 10)\frac{N_{65}^{(12)}}{D_{50}}.$$

Note that pvB here refers to only future service benefits. Recall that
$N_x^{(12)} \approx N_x - \frac{11}{24} \cdot D_x$. Then we have

$$NC_0 = \frac{(1200)(849)}{N_{50}^{(12)} + .458 D_{50} - N_{65}^{(12)} - .458 D_{65}}$$

$$= \frac{(1200)(849)}{3862.7 - 893.5} = \$343. \qquad \square$$

Note that the service before the inception date is funded by the supplemental cost, and the service from age 50 to age 60 is funded by the normal
cost. No pension benefit accrues from service after age 60. The normal
cost is payable from age 50 to age 64. The actuarial liability is defined
exactly as under the Unit Credit cost method, which is

$$AL = B_x \frac{D_r}{D_x} \ddot{a}_r^{(12)},$$

where the accrued benefit, B_x, uses the number of past years of employment, which is $x - e$.

EXAMPLE 4.23

Plan effective date: 1/1/93
Normal retirement benefit: $25 per month for each year of service
Actuarial cost method: Attained Age Normal with FIL
Actuarial assumptions:
    Interest rate: 8%
    Preretirement terminations other than deaths: None
    Retirement age: 65
Data for sole participant:
    Date of birth   1/1/43
    Date of hire   1/1/70
Contribution for 1993: $3000 paid on 12/31/93
Selected annuity value: $\ddot{a}_{65}^{(12)} = 8.67$
Selected commutation functions:

x	D_x	N_x
50	322	3902
51	298	3508
65	99	904

What is the normal cost for 1994 as of 1/1/94?

SOLUTION Let 1/1/93 be time 0. We must calculate F_1 and UAL_1, since the valuation is being performed at a date later than plan inception. The fund increases by contributions and interest, and decreases by amounts withdrawn as benefits. Thus we have

$$F_1 = F_0(1+i) + {}^iC - B = 3000.$$

We know that the unfunded liability at time 1 is

$$UAL_1 = (UAL_0 + NC_0)(1+i) - {}^iC,$$

where

$$UAL_0 = AL_0 - F_0 = (25 \times 12 \times 23)\left(\frac{99}{322}\right)(8.67) - 0 = 18{,}393$$

as calculated under Unit Credit, and

$$NC_0 = \frac{(25 \times 12 \times 38)(99/322)(8.67) - 0 - 18{,}393}{(3902 - 904)/322} = 1288$$

as calculated under AAN (FIL). Then

$$UAL_1 = (18{,}393 + 1288)(1.08) - (3000) = 18{,}255.$$

Finally the normal cost at time 1 is

$$NC_1 = \frac{(25 \times 12 \times 38)(99/298)(8.67) - 3000 - 18{,}255}{(3580 - 904)/298} = \$1290. \quad \square$$

Note that $NC_0 = 1288$, so $NC_1 = 1288$ as well. The calculated answer of 1290 differs due to rounding.

EXAMPLE 4.24

Plan effective date: 1/1/93
Normal retirement benefit: $13 per month for each year of service
Actuarial cost method: Attained Age Normal with FIL
Actuarial assumptions:
    Interest: 7%
    Retirement age: 65
    Selected annuity value: $\ddot{a}_{65}^{(12)} = 9.542$
1993 contribution: $3000 paid at 12/31/93

Participant data 1/1/93 and selected commutation functions:

Age at Hire	Attained Age x	Number of Participants	D_x	N_x
—	35	0	27	386
—	36	0	26	359
35	45	1	14	181
—	46	0	13	167
35	55	1	7	79
—	56	0	6	72
—	65	0	3	30

What is the unfunded liability as of 1/1/94?

$\boxed{\textbf{SOLUTION}}$ Let 1/1/93 be time 0. We know $UAL_1 = AL_1 - F_1$, but we can only calculate the liability at plan inception using Unit Credit, so we must use the formula

$$UAL_1 = (UAL_0 + NC_0)(1+i) - {}^iC.$$

At time 0, $UAL_0 = TAL_0$ since the amount of the fund is 0. The unfunded liability at time 0 for the 2 participants is

$$UAL_0 = [(13 \times 12 \times 10)(3/14) + (13 \times 12 \times 20)(3/7)](9.542) = 15,949.$$

Using FIL (AAN), the normal cost at time 0 can be found from

$$TNC \cdot \sum \left(\frac{N_x - N_r}{D_x} \right) \div 2 = \sum pvB - UAL_0,$$

where

$$\sum pvB = (13 \times 12 \times 30)(9.542)\left(\frac{3}{14} + \frac{3}{7} \right) = 28,708$$

and

$$\sum \frac{N_x - N_r}{D_x} = \frac{181-30}{14} + \frac{79-30}{7} = 17.79.$$

The normal cost at time 0 for the 2 participants is

$$TNC_0 = \frac{2[28,708 - 15,949]}{17.79} = 1435.$$

Then the unfunded actuarial liability at time 1 is

$$UAL_1 = (15,949+1435)(1.07) - 3000 = \$15,601. \qquad \square$$

| **EXAMPLE 4.25** |

Plan effective date: 1/1/93
Actuarial cost method: Frozen Initial Liability
Assumed interest rate: 8%
Results of 1/1/93 valuation:
    Actuarial liability   \$100,000
    Normal cost as of 1/1   10,000
Contribution for 1993: \$20,000 at 1/1/94
Beginning 1994, the valuation date is changed from 1/1 to 12/31.
Results of 12/31/94 valuation:
    Present value of future benefits   \$ 265,000
    Present value of future salary   2,400,000
    Total annual salary   200,000
Contribution for 1994: \$25,000 at 1/1/95
The fund earned 8% interest in 1994.
There were no benefit payments in 1993 or 1994.

What is the normal cost for 1994 as of 12/31/94?

| **SOLUTION** | Let time 2 be 12/31/94 so time 0 is 1/1/93. To calculate the normal cost under FIL, we need the values of UAL_2 and F_2. These are found to be

$$UAL_2 = (UAL_0+NC_0)(1+i)^2 - {}^iC$$

$$= (100,000+10,000)(1.08)^2 - 20,000(1.08) = 106,704$$

and

$$F_2 = F_0 + I + C - P = 0 + 20,000(1.08) - 0 = 21,600.$$

Under FIL at time 2,

$$TNC\left(\frac{pvS}{S}\right) = pvB_2 - UAL_2 - F_2,$$

or

$$TNC\left(\frac{2,400,000}{200,000}\right) = 265,000 - 106,704 - 21,600$$

from which we find

$$TNC = \$11,391. \qquad \qquad \square$$

Note that the contribution received on 1/1/95 is not included in F_2.

4.5 Aggregate Entry Age Normal

Recall that for Individual EAN, for each entry age, each participant has a normal cost at entry such that

$$NC_e \cdot \frac{pv_e S}{S_e} = pv_e B_r,$$

where $pv_e S$ denotes the present value at entry age of the salary scale salaries from age e to age $r-1$, and $pv_e B_r$ denotes the present value at entry of the expected projected benefit. Then

$$NC_e = \frac{pv_e B_r}{pv_e S} \cdot S_e = U_e \cdot S_e.$$

The value $U_e = \dfrac{pv_e B_r}{pv_e S}$ is the level proportion of salary needed to provide the pension (*e.g.*, 8%, 9%, 10% for entry ages 20, 25, 30, respectively). At valuation age x we have

$$NC_x = U_e \cdot S_x.$$

For all participants with entry age e we have

$$TNC_e = U_e \cdot \sum S_x = \frac{pv_e B_r}{pv_e S_e} \cdot \sum S_x$$

and

$$TAL_e = \sum pv_x B_r - U_e \cdot \sum S_x \cdot \frac{{}^s N_x - {}^s N_r}{{}^s D_x}.$$

We have now dealt with a typical entry age, and must deal with each entry age in a similar fashion.

For *level dollar* normal cost, we set all salaries equal to one dollar, and $\dfrac{pv_eS}{S_e}$ becomes $\dfrac{N_e - N_r}{D_e}$.

For **Aggregate Entry Age Normal**, for all entry ages combined, the aggregate normal cost on the valuation date (age x) is such that

$$TNC \cdot \frac{\sum pv_eS}{\sum S_x} = \sum pv_eB_r,$$

where the numerator is the present value at entry of the salary scale salaries before and after age x of all active participants on the valuation date, and the benefit term is the present value at entry of the expected projected benefit, accrued before and after age x, for all active participants. Then

$$TNC = U \cdot \sum S_x = \frac{\sum pv_eB_r}{\sum pv_eS} \cdot \sum S_x,$$

where $U = \dfrac{\sum pv_eB_r}{\sum pv_eS}$ is a proportion of salary, such as 9%. The liability

for all participants at all entry ages is

$$TAL = \sum pv_xB_r - U \cdot \sum S_x \cdot \frac{{}^sN_x - {}^sN_r}{{}^sD_x}.$$

If the aggregate normal cost is *level dollar*, then set all salaries equal to one dollar (see Example 4.26). Alternatively,

$$TNC \cdot \sum \ddot{a}^s_{e:\overline{r-e}|} \cdot \frac{1}{n} = \sum pv_eB_r$$

and

$$TAL = \sum pv_xB_r - \frac{TNC}{n} \cdot \sum \ddot{a}^s_{x:\overline{r-x}|}.$$

For both Individual and Aggregate EAN, the normal cost does not depend on the size of the fund or the benefits for retired lives. The value of $\sum pvB$ for retired lives and deferred vesteds is an additional liability. The fund for actives, retired lives, and deferred vesteds is an asset.

EXAMPLE 4.26

Plan effective date: 1/1/94
Normal retirement benefit: $10 per month for each year of service
Preretirement death benefit: None
Actuarial Assumptions:
  Preretirement terminations other than deaths: None
  Retirement age: 65
Data for all active participants as of 1/1/94:

Age	Number of Participants	Past Service	D_x	N_x	$N_x^{(12)}$
30	0	—	1336	18,946	18,334
40	2	10	670	8,953	8,646
50	0	—	329	3,974	3,823
60	2	10	153	1,571	1,501
65	0	—	100	919	873

There are no inactive participants as of 1/1/94.

What is the difference in the normal cost for 1994 as of 1/1/94 determined under the Entry Age Normal method applied on an individual basis (NC), versus that determined under the Entry Age Normal method applied on an aggregate basis (NC^{AGG})?

SOLUTION Let 1/1/94 be time 0. For those who entered at age 30, under the Individual EAN we have

$$B = 10 \times 12 \times 35 = 4200$$

and

$$NC_{30}\left(\frac{18,946 - 919}{1336}\right) = 4200\left(\frac{873}{1336}\right),$$

from which we find

$$NC_{30} = 203.39.$$

For those who entered at age 50 we have

$$B = 10 \times 12 \times 15 = 1800$$

and

$$NC_{50} \left(\frac{3974 - 919}{329} \right) = 1800 \left(\frac{873}{329} \right),$$

from which we find

$$NC_{50} = 514.37.$$

Then the total individual normal cost is

$$TNC_0 = 2(203.39) + 2(514.37) = 1436.$$

Under Aggregate EAN,

$$TNC_0^{AGG} \cdot \frac{1}{4} \sum \ddot{a} = 4200 \frac{N_{65}^{(12)}}{D_{30}}(2) + 1800 \frac{N_{65}^{(12)}}{D_{50}}(2)$$

or

$$TNC_0^{AGG} \cdot \frac{1}{4} \left[2 \left(\frac{18,946 - 919}{1336} \right) + 2 \left(\frac{3974 - 919}{329} \right) \right]$$

$$= 8400 \left(\frac{873}{1336} \right) + 3600 \left(\frac{873}{329} \right),$$

which solves for

$$TNC_0^{AGG} = 1320.$$

The difference is

$$TNC_0 - TNC_0^{AGG} = 1436 - 1320 = \$116. \qquad \square$$

Note the similarities and differences for the two methods, which are made clear in this example. Note also that if 2 participants entered at age 30 and 7 at age 50, the four terms would be weighted 2, 7, 2, 7 in order to get the normal cost per participant.

EXAMPLE 4.27

Plan effective date: 1/1/94
Normal retirement benefit: $10 per month for each year of service
Actuarial cost method: Aggregate Entry Age Normal
Actuarial assumptions:
      Preretirement terminations other than deaths: None
      Retirement age: 65
Participant data as of 1/1/94:

	Smith	Brown
Date of birth	1/1/59	1/1/49
Date of hire	1/1/84	1/1/84

Selected commutation and annuity values:

x	D_x	$\ddot{a}_{x:\overline{65-x}|}$	$\ddot{a}_x^{(12)}$
25	2441	15.62	
35	1348	14.22	
45	737	11.84	
65	189	0.00	9.35

Calculate the normal cost and the actuarial liability as of 1/1/94.

SOLUTION Let 1/1/94 be time 0. The aggregate entry age normal cost is such that

$$TNC_0 \left(\frac{15.62+14.22}{2} \right)$$

$$= \left[(10 \times 12 \times 40) \left(\frac{189}{2441} \right) + (10 \times 12 \times 30) \left(\frac{189}{1348} \right) \right] (9.35),$$

which solves for $TNC_0 = 549.22$. Then

$$TAL = \sum pvB - TNC \cdot \ddot{a}_0$$

$$= \left[(10 \times 12 \times 40) \left(\frac{189}{1348} \right) + (10 \times 12 \times 30) \left(\frac{189}{737} \right) \right] (9.35)$$

$$- 549.22 \left(\frac{14.22+11.84}{2} \right) = \$7768. \qquad \square$$

EXAMPLE 4.28

Plan effective date: 1/1/94
Actuarial valuation date: 1/1/94
Actuarial cost method: Aggregate Entry Age Normal
Actuarial valuation results:

Past service liability, 1/1/94	$ 300,000
Assets, 1/1/94	0
Normal cost, due 1/1/94	40,000
Annual payroll of participants	250,000
Present value of future payroll	4,000,00

What would the normal cost (payable 1/1/94) be, if the Aggregate cost method were used with the same actuarial assumptions?

| **SOLUTION** | Let 1/1/94 be time 0. The value of the salary-based annuity is

$$\ddot{a}_0^s = \frac{4,000,000}{250,000} = 16.$$

Under Aggregate Entry Age Normal, the actuarial liability at time 0 is

$$AL_0 = \sum pvB_0 - NC_0 \cdot \ddot{a}_0^s,$$

so

$$\sum pvB = 300,000 + 40,000(16) = 940,000.$$

The normal cost at time 0, using the Aggregate method, is

$$NC_0 = \frac{940,000}{16} = = \$58,750. \qquad \square$$

Note that with Individual EAN, the supplemental cost provides for the past service liability; with Aggregate EAN, the normal cost provides for the pvB of active lives for service before *and* after the effective date.

4.6 Review

The following observations review some basic ideas presented thus far in the text.

- Pension benefits are created by the plan document, not by the cost method. But expected pension benefits, B_r, are affected by the salary scale.

- The present value of expected pension benefits is the same for all methods (but the higher the discounting for interest, mortality and withdrawal, the lower will be the value of pv_0B_r).

- The actuarial liability at time 0 (age x) for all methods can be expressed as

$$AL_0 = pv_0B_r - pv_0NC$$

or

$$TAL_0 = \sum pv_0B_r - \sum pv_0NC.$$

- A method (or a participant) with relatively high future normal costs will have a low actuarial liability. (For example, TUC has high future normal costs and a low actuarial liability.)

- For individual cost methods,

$$TNC_0 = \sum_{A_0} NC_0.$$

For Aggregate and FIL, TNC_0 is such that

$$TNC_0 \cdot \sum_{A_0} \ddot{a} = \sum_{A_0} pv_0NC = \sum pv_0B_r - UAL_0 - F_0$$

and

$$TAL_0 = \sum pv_0B_r - \sum_{A_0} pv_0NC = UAL_0 + F_0.$$

- "Immediate gain" cost methods are those where the experience gain or loss is explicitly calculated (and usually amortized as described in Section 3.5).

- "Spread gain" cost methods are those where the experience gain or loss is spread over the future normal costs. The explicit gain, G_1, is zero. In Sections 4.1-4.4, the implicit gain (loss) leads to lower (higher) normal costs from time 1 to retirement.

- The following table shows, for each cost method, the formula for determining the normal cost, and whether the gain or loss is immediate (explicit) or spread (implicit, with $G_1 = 0$).

Method	Formula for Determining Normal Cost	Experience Gain or Loss
Unit Credit	$NC_x = b_x \dfrac{D_r}{D_x} \ddot{a}_r^{(12)}$	Immediate
EAN	$NC_e \cdot \dfrac{N_e - N_r}{D_e} = B_r \dfrac{D_r}{D_e} \ddot{a}_r^{(12)}$ $U \cdot S_e \cdot \ddot{a}_{e:\overline{r-e}|}^s = B_r \dfrac{D_r}{D_e} \ddot{a}_r^{(12)}$	Immediate
ILP	$NC \cdot \dfrac{N_a - N_r}{D_a} = B_r \dfrac{D_r}{D_a} \ddot{a}_r^{(12)}$ $\Delta NC \cdot \dfrac{N_x - N_r}{D_x} = \Delta B_r \dfrac{D_r}{D_x} \ddot{a}_r^{(12)}$ $UAL_a = 0$	Immediate if non-salary $^{sal}G_1 = 0$
Aggregate EAN	$TNC \cdot \displaystyle\sum_{A_0} \dfrac{N_e - N_r}{n \cdot D_e} = \sum_{A_0} B_r \dfrac{D_r}{D_e} \ddot{a}_r^{(12)}$	
Individual Aggregate	$NC_0 \cdot \dfrac{N_x - N_r}{D_x} = B_r \dfrac{D_r}{D_x} \ddot{a}_r^{(12)} - F^P$ $UAL_x = 0$	$G_1 = 0$
Aggregate	$TNC_0 \cdot \displaystyle\sum_{A_0} \dfrac{N_x - N_r}{n \cdot D_x} = \sum_{A_0} B_r \dfrac{D_r}{D_x} \ddot{a}_r^{(12)} - F$ $UAL_x = 0$	$G_1 = 0$
FIL	$TNC_0 \cdot \displaystyle\sum_{A_0} \dfrac{N_x - N_r}{n \cdot D_x} = \sum_{A_0} B_r \dfrac{D_r}{D_x} \ddot{a}_r^{(12)} - UAL_0 - F_0$ $UAL_a^{FIL(EAN)} = AL_a^{EAN}$ $UAL_a^{FIL(AAN)} = AL_a^{UC}$	$G_1 = 0$
All	$UAL_1 = (UAL_0 + NC_0)(1 + i) - {}^iC - G_1$	

4.7 Exercises

4.1 Individual Aggregate

4-1   Actuarial cost method: Individual Aggregate, with assets allocated
       to each active participant in proportion to the sum, as of the prior
       valuation date, of normal cost and allocated assets
       Actuarial assumptions:
            Interest: 6%
            Preretirement deaths and terminations: None
            Retirement age: 65
            Selected annuity value: $\ddot{a}_{65}^{(12)} = 10$
       Selected valuation results as of 1/1/93:

	Normal Cost as of 1/1	Allocated Assets
Smith	$1705	$30,000
Brown	858	4,000

Participant data as of 1/1/94:

	Age	Projected Monthly Benefit
Smith	55	$700
Brown	40	600
Green (new entrant)	55	200

Actuarial value of assets as of 1/1/94: $40,000

What is the total normal cost as of 1/1/94?

4-2   Normal retirement benefit: $600 per month
       Actuarial cost method: Individual Aggregate, with assets allocated
             to each active participant in proportion to the sum, as of the
             prior valuation date, of the participant's normal cost and
             allocated assets
       Actuarial assumptions:
             Interest: 8%
             Preretirement deaths and terminations: None
             Retirement age: 65
       Selected valuation results as of 1/1/93:

	Age	Normal Cost as of 1/1	Allocated Assets
Smith	40	$510	$ 2,705
Brown	50	274	16,000

       Actuarial value of assets as of 1/1/94: $20,000
       There were no deaths, terminations, retirements, or new entrants
             during 1993.

       What is the normal cost for 1994 as of 1/1/94?

4-3   Valuation date: 12/31/92
       Normal retirement benefit: 50% of final year's compensation
       Actuarial cost method: Individual Aggregate
       Actuarial assumptions:
             Interest rate: 7% per year
             Compensation increases: 3% per year
             Preretirement deaths and terminations: None
             Retirement age: 65
       Valuation data for participant Smith:
             Date of birth   1/1/40
             1992 compensation   50,000
             Allocated assets as of 12/31/92   10,000

       Selected annuity value: $\ddot{a}_{65}^{(12)} = 8.74$

       What is Smith's normal cost for 1992 as of 12/31/92?

4.2 Aggregate

4-4   Normal retirement benefit: $10 monthly per year of service
       Normal retirement age: 65 *or* after 10 years of participation, if later
       Actuarial cost method: Aggregate
       Actuarial assumptions:
           Interest: 8%
           Preretirement deaths and terminations: None
           Retirement age: Normal retirement age
       Participant data as of 1/1/94:

	Date of Birth	Date of Hire	Date of Participation
Smith	1/1/44	1/1/77	1/1/86
Brown	1/1/29	1/1/69	1/1/86

Actuarial value of assets as of 1/1/94: $10,000
Selected annuity values:

x	$\ddot{a}_x^{(12)}$
65	8.142
66	7.951
67	7.702

What is the normal cost for 1994 as of 1/1/94?

4-5   Plan effective date: 1/1/84
       Normal retirement benefit: $6 monthly per year of service
       All employees were hired at age 25.
       There are no retired or terminated vested participants.
       Plan assets on 1/1/94: $5000
       Preretirement terminations other than by death: None
       Selected annuity value: $\ddot{a}_{65}^{(12)} = 10$
       Census data on 1/1/94, and commutation functions:

Age x	Number of Participants	D_x	$N_x - N_{65}$
25	8	16	320
35	0	8	120
45	2	4	40
55	0	2	10
65	0	1	0

Under the Aggregate cost method, what is the normal cost due on 1/1/94 and the unfunded actuarial liability as of 1/1/94?

4-6 Valuation date: 12/31
Normal retirement benefit: 50% of final 3-year average salary
Actuarial cost method: Aggregate
Actuarial assumptions:
   Interest rate: 7% per year
   Compensation increases: None
   Preretirement deaths and terminations: None
   Retirement age: 65
   Selected annuity value: $\ddot{a}_{65}^{(12)} = 8.74$
Data for only participants:

	Smith	Brown
Date of birth	1/1/30	1/1/49
1994 compensation	—	$30,000
Status as of 12/31/94	Retired	Active
Monthly benefit	$1000	—

Value of assets as of 12/31/94: $94,650

What is the normal cost for 1994 as of 12/31/94?

4-7   Plan effective date: 1/1/93
        Normal retirement benefit: $500 per month
        Actuarial cost method: Aggregate
        Actuarial assumptions:
                Interest: 6%
                Salary increases: None
                Retirement age: 65
                Selected annuity value: $\ddot{a}_{65}^{(12)} = 10$
        Preretirement mortality and terminations: None
        Data for sole participant:
                Date of birth   1/1/53
                Annual salary $15,000
        Normal cost for 1994 as of 1/1/94: $1000

        What is the actuarial value of assets as of 1/1/94?

4-8   Actuarial valuation date: 1/1/94
        Actuarial cost method: Aggregate
        Actuarial assumptions:
                Interest: 5%
                Salary scale: None
                Mortality and other decrements prior to age 65: None
                Selected annuity value: $\ddot{a}_{65}^{(12)} = 10$
                Normal cost: 10% of salary
        Data for sole participant age 45:
                Current salary: $20,000 per year
                Expected monthly benefit at age 65: $1000

        What is the actuarial value of assets as of 1/1/94?

4-9   Plan effective date: 1/1/94
        Normal retirement benefit: 40% of final salary
        Actuarial assumptions:
                Interest: 5%
                Salary increases: None
                Retirement age: 65
        There are no retired or vested terminated employees.

Participant data and valuation results as of 1/1/94:

Attained Age	Number of Participants	Projected Annual Pension	pv of Future Salary	pv of Future Benefits
35	1	$ 4,800	$180,000	$ 4,000
45	1	4,560	100,000	7,600
55	1	6,000	85,000	20,000
	3	15,360	365,000	31,600

All participants were hired at age 35.

What is the 1994 normal cost as of 1/1/94 under the Aggregate cost method?

4-10 Normal retirement benefit: 40% of final five-year average salary
Actuarial cost method: Aggregate
Actuarial assumptions:
   Interest: 8%
   Salary increases: 6% per year
   Preretirement deaths and terminations: None
   Retirement age: 65
   Selected annuity value: $\ddot{a}_{65}^{(12)} = 8.65$
Data for sole participant as of 1/1/94:
   Date of birth   1/1/39
   Date of hire   1/1/84
   Salary for 1993 $32,000
Actuarial value of assets as of 1/1/94: $30,000

What is the normal cost for 1994 as of 1/1/94?

4-11 Refer to the data given in Exercise 2-3. Under the Aggregate cost method, what are the normal cost, actuarial liability, and unfunded actuarial liability as of 1/1/93? (For female values of $\ddot{a}_{x}^{(12)}$, use the male values rated down five years.)

4-12 Plan effective date: 1/1/94
      Normal retirement benefit: 2% of final salary per year of service
      Actuarial assumptions:
           Interest rate: 8% per year
           Compensation increases: None
           Preretirement deaths and terminations: None
           Retirement age: 65
           Selected annuity value: $\ddot{a}_{65}^{(12)} = 9.345$
      Data for all participants:

	Smith	Brown
Date of birth	1/1/34	1/1/64
Date of hire	1/1/69	1/1/94
1994 compensation	$90,000	$12,000
Status as of 1/1/94	Active	Active

What is the excess (shortfall) of the normal cost for 1994 as of
1/1/94 determined under the level dollar Aggregate method over that
determined under the level dollar Individual Aggregate method?

4.3 Frozen Initial Liability (Entry Age Normal)

4-13 Actuarial cost method: Frozen Initial Liability (level dollar)
      Actuarial assumptions:
           Interest rate: 7% per year
           Preretirement deaths and terminations: None
           Retirement age: 65
      Data and valuation results for only participants at 1/1/94:

	Smith	Brown	Green
Date of birth	1/1/24	1/1/59	1/1/49
Status	Retired	Active	Active
Monthly accrued benefit	$1000	—	—
Monthly projected benefit	—	$5000	$3000

Unfunded liability as of 1/1/94: $10,000

Value of assets as of 1/1/94: $91,200

Selected annuity values: $\ddot{a}_{65}^{(12)} = 8.74$; $\ddot{a}_{70}^{(12)} = 7.60$

What is the normal cost for 1994 as of 1/1/94?

4-14 Plan effective date: 1/1/91

Normal retirement benefit: 50% of final five-year average salary

Actuarial cost method: Frozen Initial Liability

Valuation results as of 1/1/94:

Present value of future benefits	1,700,000
Unfunded actuarial liability	300,000
Actuarial value of assets	200,000
Normal cost as of 1/1	80,000

As of 1/1/94, there are no retired or terminated vested participants, and it is assumed that there will not be any in the next 5 years. After the above results were determined, it was discovered that all *salaries* were 10% higher than reported. The normal cost for 1994 was then recalculated.

What is the recalculated normal cost for 1994 as of 1/1/94?

4-15 Normal retirement benefit: 50% of final salary

Actuarial cost method: Frozen Initial Liability

Selected valuation results as of 1/1/94:

Present value of future salaries	$2,500,000
Normal cost as of 1/1	15,000
Annual salaries	200,000

After the valuation was done, it was discovered that a new entrant *had been omitted*. A revised valuation included the following information for the omitted participant as of 1/1/94:

Present value of future benefits	$ 39,000
Annual salary	30,000
Present value of future salaries	850,000

What is the revised normal cost for 1994 as of 1/1/94?

4-16   Plan effective date: 1/1/93
        Actuarial cost method: Frozen Initial Liability
        Assumed interest rate: 8%
        Results of 1/1/93 valuation:
            Accrued liability $ 100,000
            Normal cost as of 1/1   10,000
        Contribution for 1993: $20,000 at 1/1/94
        Beginning in 1994, the valuation date is *changed* from 1/1 to 12/31.
        Results of 12/31/94 valuation:
            Present value of future benefits $ 265,000
            Present value of future salary   2,400,000
            Total annual salary   200,000
        Contribution for 1994: $25,000 at 1/1/95
        The fund earned 8% in 1994.
        There were no benefit payments in 1993 or 1994.

        What is the normal cost for 1994 as of 12/31/94?

4-17   Plan effective date: 1/1/93
        Normal retirement benefit: $10 monthly per year of service
        Actuarial assumptions (in use since plan effective date):
            Interest: 7%
            Mortality: Group Annuity Table (females)
            Retirement: Age 65
            Withdrawals: None
        1993 experience:
            Investment return: 7%
            Mortality, withdrawals, and retirements: None
        On 1/1/94, the only participant the plan has ever had is a female age
            62, who was hired at age 35.

        Consider the actuarial liability and normal cost on 1/1/94 under dif-
        ferent cost methods. For each of the following pairs, which is
        greater:

        (a) NC^{UC} or NC^{EAN}?   (c) NC^{EAN} or NC^{FIL}?

        (b) AL^{UC} or AL^{EAN}?   (d) AL^{EAN} or AL^{FIL}?

4-18   Plan effective date: 1/1/82
       Normal retirement benefit:
           Before 1993: $15 per month for each year of service
           After 1992: $20 per month for each year of service
       Actuarial cost method: Frozen Initial Liability
       Asset valuation method:
           Before 1993: Actuarial value
           After 1992:   Market value
       Assumed interest rate:
           Before 1993: 7% per year
           After 1992:   8% per year
       Selected valuation results as of 1/1/93 (based on $15 benefit level):

	7%	8%
Present value of future benefits	$450,000	$350,000
Unfunded liability	60,000	
Actuarial value of assets	225,000	225,000
Market value of assets	250,000	250,000
Accrued liability under entry age normal method	270,000	225,000
Ratio of present value of future working lifetime to number of active participants	11	10

There were no inactive participants as of 1/1/92 and 1/1/93.

What is the normal cost for 1993 as of 1/1/93?

4.4 Frozen Initial Liability (Attained Age Normal)

4-19   Plan effective date: 1/1/83
       Eligibility: Age 25 and one year of service
       Normal retirement benefit: $9 per month for each year of service pri-
           or to 1994: $13 per month for each year of service after 1993
       Actuarial cost method: Attained Age Normal with FIL
       Actuarial assumptions:
           Interest: 6%
           Preretirement termination other than by death: None
           Retirement age: 65.
       Valuation results as of 1/1/93:
           Unfunded liability $5500
           Normal cost as of 1/1   500
           Actuarial value of assets   5000
       Contribution for 1993: $800 paid at 12/31/93
       1993 investment return: 8%
       The sole participant, hired at age 20, is age 50 as of 1/1/94.
       Selected annuity value: $\ddot{a}_{65}^{(12)} = 8.75$
       Selected commutation functions:

x	D_x	$N_x - N_{65}$
20	94	1519
21	89	1424
25	70	1098
26	66	1028
50	16	154
51	15	138
65	6	

What is the normal cost for 1994 as of 1/1/94?

4-20 Plan effective date: 1/1/93
Actuarial cost method: Attained Age Normal with FIL
Assumed interest rate: 6%
Valuation results:

	1/1/93	1/1/94
Present value of future benefits	$1,000,000	$1,200,000
Actuarial liabililty	400,000	—
Ratio of present value of future salaries to current salaries	10	11

Contribution for 1993, paid at 12/31/93: $100,000
Benefits for 1993: None

What is the normal cost for 1994 as of 1/1/94?

4-21 Normal retirement benefit: $10 monthly per year of service
Normal retirement age: 65
Plan effective date: 1/1/94
Plan covers one employee, age 45 with 10 years of service on 1/1/94
Actuarial assumptions:
    Preretirement terminations other than death: None
    Interest: 5%
Selected annuity value: $\ddot{a}_{45:\overline{20|}} = 10$
Normal cost as of 1/1/94 under Unit Credit: $840

Find the actuarial liability on 1/1/94 under the FIL (AAN) cost method.

4-22   Plan effective date: 1/1/92
        Actuarial cost method: Frozen Initial Liability
        Assumed interest rate: 6%
        Initial accrued liability: $10,000,000
        Normal cost for 1992 as of 1/1/92: $3,000,000
        Normal cost for 1993 as of 1/1/93: $3,200,000
        Normal cost for 1994 as of 1/1/94 (after plan amendment):
             $3,500,000
        Increase in unfunded liability as of 1/1/94 due to plan amendment:
             $5,000,000
        Investment fund activity for 1992 through 1994:

Year	Contribution	Date of Contribution	Actual Investment Return
1992	$4,500,000	1/1/92	8.0%
1993	5,000,000	4/1/93	7.5
1994	5,500,000	4/1/94	5.5

What is the unfunded liability as of 1/1/95?

4-23   Normal retirement benefit: 10 per month for each year of service
       Actuarial cost method: Frozen Initial Liability
       Actuarial assumptions:
            Interest rate: 7% per year
            Preretirement deaths and terminations: None
            Retirement age: 65
       Unfunded liability as of 1/1/92: 10,000
       Value of assets as of 1/1/92: 41,952
       Data and valuation results for the only participants:

	Smith	Brown
Date of birth	1/1/47	1/1/27
Date of hire	1/1/72	1/1/52
Date of retirement		12/31/91
Present value of future benefits as of 1/1/92	10,841	41,952

Contribution for 1992:

    Normal cost for 1992 as of 1/1, plus an amount to amortize the
        unfunded 1/1/92 liability over 10 years; paid on 1/1/92

Investment rate of return for 1992: 7%, compounded annually

As of 1/1/93 Smith is active and Brown is retired

Selected annuity values: $\ddot{a}_{65}^{(12)} = 8.74$ $\ddot{a}_{66}^{(12)} = 8.51$

What is the normal cost for 1993 as of 1/1/93?

4-24 Normal retirement benefit: 50% of final year's compensation

    Actuarial cost method: Frozen Initial Liability

    Actuarial assumptions:

        Interest rate: 7% per year

        Compensation increases: 4% per year

        Preretirement deaths and terminations: None

        Retirement age: 65

    As of 1/1/92, all participants are active and under age 63.

    Selected valuation results as of 1/1/92:

Present value of future benefits	$1,200,000
Value of assets	500,000
Present value of future compensation	9,500,000

    Contribution for 1992: $60,000 paid on 1/1/92.

    There were no deaths, terminations, or retirements during 1992, and
        there are no new participants on 1/1/93.

    There were no investment experience gains or losses for 1992, and
        there was a 10% increase in compensation for all participants
        from 1992 to 1993.

    Selected valuation results as of 1/1/93:

Unfunded liability	$400,000
1993 compensation	750,000

What is the normal cost for 1993 as of 1/1/93?

4-25 Normal retirement benefit: $900 per month
      Preretirement death benefit: None
      Actuarial cost method: Attained Age Normal
      Actuarial assumptions:
              Interest rate: 7% per year
              Preretirement deaths and terminations: None
              Retirement age: 65
      Valuation data for sole participant:
              Date of birth   1/1/48
              Date of hire   1/1/83

      Normal cost for 1993 as of 1/1/93: $1231

      Value of assets as of 1/1/93: $10,000
      Selected annuity value: $\ddot{a}_{65}^{(12)} = 10.0$

      What is the unfunded liability as of 1/1/93?

4.5 Aggregate Entry Age Normal

4-26 Normal retirement benefit: $10 monthly per year of service
      Actuarial cost method: Aggregate Entry Age Normal
      Preretirement terminations other than by death: None
      Assumed retirement age: 65
      Selected annuity value: $\ddot{a}_{65}^{(12)} = 10$
      Participant data as of 1/1/94 and selected commutation functions:

Attained Age x	Age at hire	Number of Participants	D_x	$N_x - N_{65}$
45	—	0	1000	9012
50	45	1	585	4945
55	50	1	362	2522
65	—	0	147	0

      What is the normal cost for 1994 as of 1/1/94?

4-27 Plan effective date: 1/1/94
  Normal retirement benefit: $10 monthly per year of service
  Actuarial cost method: Entry Age Normal
  Assumed retirement age: 65
  Preretirement terminations other than by death: None
  Participant data as of 1/1/94 and selected annuity values:

Age x	Number of Participants	Past Service of Each Participant	$\ddot{a}_{x:\overline{65-x}|}$	$_{65-x|}\ddot{a}_x^{(12)}$
25	0	—	15.0	1.0
35	1	10	13.5	2.0
45	0	—	11.0	4.0
55	1	10	7.0	7.0

What is the sum of (a) the normal cost for 1994 as of 1/1/94 under the Entry Age Normal method on an *individual* basis, and (b) the normal cost for 1994 as of 1/1/94 under the Entry Age Normal method applied on an *aggregate* basis?

4-28 Plan effective date: 1/1/94
  Normal retirement benefit: 50% of final five-year average pay
  Preretirement terminations other than by death: None
  Selected commutation functions:

x	^sD_x	$^sN_x - {}^sN_{65}$	s_x	D_x	$N_x - N_{65}$	$N_x^{(12)}$
25	1500	75,000	.30	5000	120,000	
35	1600	64,000	.40	4000	72,000	
45	1500	45,000	.50	3000	36,000	
60	2250	9,750	1.50	1500	6,500	
61	2100	7,500	1.50	1400	5,000	
62	1950	5,400	1.50	1300	3,600	
63	1800	3,450	1.50	1200	2,300	
64	1650	1,650	1.50	1100	1,100	
65	1500	0	1.50	1000	0	10,000

Employee data as of 1/1/94:

Name	Age	Past Service	1994 Salary
Brown	35	10 years	$20,000
Green	45	None	10,000

Assumed retirement age: 65
All normal costs are calculated as a level percent of pay.

What is the normal cost for the plan due 1/1/94 under the Aggregate
Entry Age Normal method?

Chapter 5

Experience Gains and Losses

Experience gains and losses occur when the actuarial assumptions for a pension plan are not exactly realized. For example, if the plan does not provide for a death benefit, a gain will result if more participants than expected die during the year. The **total experience gain** can be broken down into the two components of (a) asset or **investment gain** and (b) **liability gain**, so we have

$$^{\text{tot}}G = {}^{\text{inv}}G + {}^{\text{liab}}G.$$

Liability gains are made up of experience gains from mortality, salary, withdrawal, early retirement and late retirement. Investment gains occur when the investment earnings of the fund are greater than expected.

Section 5.1 develops the concept of gain and Section 5.2 discusses total gain. Then Section 5.3 discusses investment gains and Sections 5.4 - 5.7 discuss liability gains. Numerical examples are included in all sections.

5.1 Unfunded Liabilities and Gains

In this section we will develop (a) the relationship between UAL_0 and UAL_1 (which was briefly mentioned earlier in the text), (b) an expression for the total gain, and (c) expressions for mortality, interest, withdrawal, and retirement gains.

5.1.1 Relationships

We begin with some common actuarial relationships from the field of life insurance and then switch to the analogous relationships in the pension area. Each symbolic relationship is then explained in words.

(a) $(\ell_x^{(\tau)} \cdot {}_t V + \ell_x^{(\tau)} \cdot P)(1+i) = DBEN \cdot d_x + WBEN \cdot w_x + {}_{t+1}V \cdot \ell_{x+1}^{(\tau)}$

(a') $({}_t V + P)(1+i) = DBEN \cdot q_x^{(d)} + WBEN \cdot q_x^{(w)} + {}_{t+1}V \cdot p_x^{(\tau)}$

(b) $({}_t V + P)(1+i) = {}_{t+1}V + (DBEN - {}_{t+1}V)q_x^{(d)} + (WBEN - {}_{t+1}V)q_x^{(w)}$

(c) $\sum_{A_0}(AL_0 + NC_0)(1+i) = \sum_{A_0}q_x^{(d)} \cdot {}^i DBEN + \sum_{A_0}q_x^{(w)} \cdot {}^i WBEN + \sum_{A_0}p_x^{(\tau)} \cdot AL_1$

(c') $\sum_{A_0}(AL_0 + NC_0)(1+i) = \sum_{A_0} AL_1 - \sum_{A_0}q_x^{(d)}(AL_1 - {}^i DBEN) - \sum_{A_0}q_x^{(w)}(AL_1 - {}^i WBEN)$

(c'') $\sum_{A_0}(AL_0 + NC_0)(1+i) = \sum_{A_0}AL_1 - \sum_{A_0}q_x^{(d)}(AL_1 - {}^i DBEN) - \sum_{A_0}q_x^{(w)}(AL_1 - {}^i WBEN)$

$$- \left[\sum_D (AL_1 - {}^i DBEN) - \sum_{A_0}q_x^{(d)}(AL_1 - {}^i DBEN) \right]$$

$$- \left[\sum_W (AL_1 - {}^i WBEN) - \sum_{A_0}q_x^{(w)}(AL_1 - {}^i WBEN) \right]$$

(d) $\sum_{A_0}(AL_0 + NC_0)(1+i) = \sum_{A_1}AL_1 + \sum_D {}^i DBEN + {}^{mort}G_1 + \sum_W {}^i WBEN + {}^{with}G_1$

(e) $F_0(1+i) + {}^i C - \sum_{A_0}q_x^{(d)} \cdot {}^i DBEN - \sum_{A_0}q_x^{(w)} \cdot {}^i WBEN = {}^{exp}F_1$

(f) $\left(\sum_{A_0}AL_0 - F_0 \right)(1+i) + \sum_{A_0} NC_0 (1+i) - {}^i C = {}^{exp}AL_1 - {}^{exp}F_1$

(f') $UAL_0(1+i) + \sum_{A_0}NC_0(1+i) - {}^i C = {}^{exp}UAL_1$

(g) $F_0 + C - \sum_D {}^i DBEN - \sum_W {}^i WBEN + {}^{act}I = {}^{act}F_1$

(h) ${}^{act}AL_1 - {}^{act}F_1 = {}^{act}UAL_1$

(i) ${}^{tot}G_1 = {}^{exp}UAL_1 - {}^{act}UAL_1$

5.1.2 Explanations of the Relationships

(a) The premium is net of expense and is actuarially calculated to purchase the stated benefits using the stated assumptions. The total reserve at BOY plus premium plus interest is sufficient to provide the death benefit for the expected deaths, the withdrawal benefit for the expected withdrawals, and the new reserve at EOY for the expected survivors. Expected benefits are assumed payable at EOY. Actual benefits may be paid earlier with different frequency; this concept is introduced in (c″) and (d), below.

(a′) The reserve per survivor at BOY plus premium plus interest provides the expected death and withdrawal benefits plus the *expected* reserve at EOY, which is $_{t+1}V \cdot p_x^{(\tau)}$. If $q_x^{(w)} = 0$, as is often the case, we have a single-decrement model.

(b) In (a′), let $p_x^{(\tau)} = 1 - q_x^{(d)} - q_x^{(w)}$ and group the q_x terms. The left side of (b) provides the EOY reserve for all who *start* the year, and the amount at risk for those who are expected to die and withdraw. (Note that life insurance benefits are normally larger than the reserve liabilities.)

(c) Next we rewrite (a′) using pension terminology. The benefits ^iDBEN and ^iWBEN are assumed payable at EOY; recall Section 1.6.3. (The accrued interest is normally zero.) Let the number of active participants at time 0 and time 1 be A_0 and A_1, respectively, so the notation $\sum\limits_{A_0}$ denotes summation over all active BOY participants. The left side provides the benefits at EOY for those expected to die and withdraw, and the expected EOY liability, $\sum\limits_{A_0} p_x^{(\tau)} \cdot AL_1$, for all who *start* the year. Under the TUC method, $AL_0 = B_x \cdot {}_{r-x|}\ddot{a}_x^{(12)}$ and equation (c) defines, and can be used to derive, the normal cost for each participant each year. Under the EAN cost method, the normal cost is such that $pv_eNC = pv_eB$, and equation (c) defines the actuarial liability for each participant each year.

(c′) We rewrite (b) in pension terminology, keeping in mind that death and withdrawal benefits are usually *smaller* than the liabilities.

(c″)   We assume for equation (c″) that the actual benefits are the *same* as
        the expected benefits, so the additional terms in square brackets are
        zero. $\sum_{D}$ and $\sum_{W}$ mean summation over the actual deaths and with-
        drawals. $^{i}DBEN$ and $^{i}WBEN$ denote the actual EOY equivalent
        benefits; if *DBEN* is paid before EOY, then the EOY equivalent is
        DBEN plus appropriate interest at the expected interest rate.

(d)   This equation shows that the expected EOY fund, shown on the left,
        will provide the new liability for the A_1 actual survivors and the
        benefits for the actual deaths and withdrawals. Any money left in
        the fund represents a mortality and/or withdrawal gain. Conversely,
        if the EOY fund is not sufficient to provide the required liability and
        benefits, then we have a loss. The A_0 persons who start the year
        must either die, withdraw, or survive to the end of the year, so we
        have the important relationship $A_0 - D - W = A_1$. We can derive
        an expression for $^{mort}G_1$ by letting $q_x^{(w)} = 0$ and comparing equa-
        tions (c″) and (d). Since their left sides are identical, their right
        sides must be equal, so we have

$$\sum_{A_0} AL_1 - \sum_{A_0} q_x^{(d)}(AL_1 - {}^iDBEN) \;=\; \sum_{A_1} AL_1 + \sum_{D} {}^iDBEN + {}^{mort}G_1.$$

If $W = 0$, then $A_0 = A_1 + D$, and the above equation can be rewrit-
ten as

$$\sum_{A_1} AL_1 + \sum_{D} AL_1 - \sum_{A_0} q_x^{(d)}(AL_1 - {}^iDBEN) = \sum_{A_1} AL_1 + \sum_{D} {}^iDBEN + {}^{mort}G_1.$$

We can now cancel the first term on each side and solve the equation
for

$$^{mort}G_1 \;=\; \sum_{D}(AL_1 - {}^iDBEN) - \sum_{A_0} q_x^{(d)}(AL_1 - {}^iDBEN).$$

This is our *first* important result. Similarly,

$$^{with}G_1 \;=\; \sum_{W}(AL_1 - {}^iWBEN) - \sum_{A_0} q_x^{(w)}(AL_1 - {}^iWBEN).$$

(e) F_0 plus contributions plus interest on both at the valuation rate, minus expected benefits, equals expected funds at EOY.

(f) Subtracting equation (e) from equation (c), we are pleased to discover that the expected benefit terms cancel.

(f′) Equation (f′), which follows directly from equation (f), connects UAL_0 and $^{\text{exp}}UAL_1$. This is our *second* important result.

(g) Funds at BOY plus actual contributions less actual benefits paid out plus actual interest earned on the foregoing equals actual funds at EOY. Subtracting equation (e) from equation (g) and canceling the mortality gain from both sides we obtain

$$^{\text{inv}}G_1 \;=\; {}^{\text{act}}I - (i \cdot F_0 + {}^{i}C - C),$$

which defines the investment gain as the excess of actual interest over expected interest. This is our *third* important result.

(h) At EOY it is easy to determine the actual unfunded liability.

(i) The total gain is the excess of the expected unfunded liability over the actual unfunded liability. This is our *fourth* important result.

5.1.3 Observations

The following observations add insight to the material presented above:

(1) The concept of gain and loss is similar in the various areas of actuarial science. Gain and loss analysis gives the actuary an independent check on the accuracy of the valuation, and it identifies areas of concern to the actuary and the plan sponsor.

(2) If $^{i}C - {}^{i}NC = X$, then UAL_1 is reduced by X but the gain is not affected. X is referred to as an **excess contribution**, not as a "contribution gain." Note that C in all the equations is the *actual* contribution and the amount may not be known until EOY.

(3) Relationship (c) not only connects AL_0 and AL_1, it also allows the derivation of AL_1 from AL_0.

(4) If the gain is negative, it is called a loss; if the unfunded liability is negative, it is called a surplus.

(5) The *investment gain* is the excess of the actual over the expected investment earnings. If no benefits are expected or paid out, the investment gain is $^{\text{act}}F_1 - {}^{\text{exp}}F_1$.

(6) The *mortality gain* is given by $\sum_D AL_1 - \sum_{A_0} q_x^{(d)} \cdot AL_1$ if there is no death benefit. If there is a death benefit, then the gain is given by

$$^{\text{mort}}G_1 = \sum_D (AL_1 - {}^iDBEN) - \sum_{A_0} q_x^{(d)} \cdot (AL_1 - {}^iDBEN),$$

which is the actual net release of liability minus expected net release of liability. (Relationship (d) will facilitate the alternate solution to Example 5.14 on page 199.)

For example, suppose the preretirement death benefit is the actuarial liability discounted from EOY back to the date of death. Then for death at age $x + \frac{1}{2}$ ($t = \frac{1}{2}$), we have $DBEN = AL_1 \cdot v^{\frac{1}{2}}$ and $^iDBEN = AL_1$. If death benefits are assumed payable at EOY (age $x + 1$), then $^iDBEN = AL_1$. In general, we expect ^iDBEN at age $x + 1$ to be the *same* for both actual and expected deaths, except, of course, that the *number* of actual and expected deaths at each age will usually be different.

(7) Similarly, the *withdrawal gain* is

$$^{\text{with}}G_1 = \sum_W (AL_1 - {}^iWBEN) - \sum_{A_0} q_x^{(w)} \cdot (AL_1 - {}^iWBEN),$$

the actual net release of liability minus the expected. For example, if all participants have identical liabilities, and if Virginia is vested and withdraws with $^iWBEN = AL_1$ and Norm is not vested and withdraws with $^iWBEN = 0$, and if we expect .4 vested and .2 nonvested withdrawals, then the withdrawal gain (actual net for vested and nonvested minus expected net for vested and nonvested) is

$$(AL_1 - AL_1) + (AL_1 - 0) - .4(AL_1 - AL_1) - .2(AL_1 - 0) = .8AL_1.$$

(8) The *retirement gain* is the actual net release of liability minus expected. Thus we have

$$^{\text{ret}}G_1 \;=\; \sum_R (AL_1 - {}^iPBEN) - \sum_{A_0} q_x^{(r)}(AL_1 - AL_1)$$

$$=\; \sum_R (AL_1 - {}^iPBEN).$$

For example, if Roger is the only participant actually retiring this year and his accrued benefit is purchased from a life insurance company for *PBEN*, then the retirement gain to the pension fund is $AL_1 - {}^iPBEN$.

(9) Relationship (c) assumes there is no pension benefit payout during the year. If $DBEN = WBEN = 0$, and if the *pension benefit payout* is *PBEN*, then (c) becomes

$$\sum_{A_0} (AL_0 + NC_0)(1+i) = \sum_{A_0} q_x^{(r)} \cdot {}^iPBEN + \sum_{A_0} p_x^{(\tau)} \cdot AL_1.$$

The pension benefit payout can be as a lump sum or as monthly payments.

(10) In order to calculate gains at EOY, it is often necessary to first calculate liabilities at EOY. Relationship (c) is often helpful. $\sum_{A_0} p_x^{(\tau)} \cdot AL_1$ is normally the *expected liability*. Often no benefits are payable, and the left side of (c) is then a convenient expression for the expected liability; but if the interest rate is unknown, then it is necessary to find the expected liability from $\sum_{A_0} p_x^{(\tau)} \cdot AL_1$. Note that the value of a postponed retirement benefit may be less than the expected liability; in that case, if no pension benefits are payable during the year, the left side of (c) again becomes an expression for the expected liability. AL_1 is the *actual liability per survivor* (resulting from the plan benefits, the actuarial cost method, and the assumptions). See Exercises 5-30 and 5-31, Examples 5.33 and 5.35, and Section 5.4.3.

(11) The *total gain* is the excess of the expected over the actual unfunded liability. If the total gain is not equal to the sum of the components, a mistake has been made and must be corrected. This is illustrated in the first three examples below.

(12) Recall that

$$^{\exp}UAL_1 = (UAL_0 + NC_0)(1+i) - {}^iC$$

and

$$^{\text{act}}UAL_1 = (UAL_0 + NC_0)(1+i) - {}^iC - {}^{\text{tot}}G_1,$$

but with Aggregate and FIL methods, the implicit gain or loss is spread over the future working lifetimes, so

$$^{\text{act}}UAL_1 = (UAL_0 + NC_0)(1+i) - {}^iC.$$

5.1.4 Experience Gain Summary

To summarize the material on experience gains presented so far, the following simple relationships and ideas are presented. These will be very helpful in the solution of the listed examples.

- $^{\text{tot}}G = {}^{\text{inv}}G + {}^{\text{liab}}G$ (Examples 5.1 and 5.12)

- $^{\text{inv}}G = {}^{\text{tot}}G - {}^{\text{liab}}G$ (Examples 5.8 and 5.14)

- $^{\text{liab}}G = {}^{\text{tot}}G - {}^{\text{inv}}G$ (Examples 5.10 and 5.11)

- If $^{\text{inv}}G = 0$, then $^{\text{tot}}G = {}^{\text{liab}}G = {}^{\exp}AL_1 - {}^{\text{act}}AL_1$ (Examples 5.4 and 5.27)

- If $^{\text{liab}}G = 0$, then $^{\text{act}}AL_1 = {}^{\exp}AL_1$ and $^{\text{tot}}G = {}^{\text{inv}}G = {}^{\text{act}}F_1 - {}^{\exp}F_1$ (Examples 5.9, 5.14 (Alternate Solution), and 5.18)

- Benefits paid out reduce F_1 and AL_1, but not G_1 (Example 5.6)

- Excess contributions increase F_1, but not G_1 and normally not AL_1 (Example 5.7)

| **EXAMPLE 5.1** |

Normal retirement benefit: $600 per year for each year of service
Preretirement death benefit: None
Actuarial cost method: Unit Credit
Actuarial assumptions:
    Interest rate: 6%
    Mortality: $q_{59}^{(d)} = .02$ and $q_{60}^{(d)} = .03$
    Preretirement terminations other than death: None
    Retirement age: 61
    Selected annuity value: $\ddot{a}_{61} = 10$
Data for each of two participants:
    Date of birth   1/1/35
    Date of hire   1/1/70
    Status as of 1/1/94   Alive
Value of fund as of 1/1/94: $80,000
Total contribution: $6000 at BOY
Actual earned interest rate in 1994: 10%
One participant died at the end of 1994.

Find the total experience gain for 1994. Calculate the gain for each separate component and show that they sum to the total gain.

| **SOLUTION** | Let 1/1/95 be time 1 (age 60). The total gain is

$$^{exp}UAL_1 - {}^{act}UAL_1 = {}^{exp}AL_1 - {}^{exp}F_1 - {}^{act}AL_1 + {}^{act}F_1.$$

At retirement, $AL_2 = 600 \times 26 \times \ddot{a}_{61} = 156{,}000$ per survivor. At age 60 we have

$$AL_1 = 600 \times 25 \times 10 \div 1.06 \times .97 = 137{,}264.$$

The expected number of survivors at time 1 is $2 \times .98 = 1.96$, and we have the following values at time 1:

$$^{exp}AL_1 = 137{,}264 \times 2 \times .98 = 269{,}037$$

$$^{exp}F_1 = (80{,}000 + 6000)1.06 = 91{,}160$$

$$^{act}F_1 = (80{,}000 + 6000)1.10 = 94{,}600$$

$$^{act}AL_1 = 137{,}264$$

Then the total gain is

$$269,037 - 91,160 - 137,264 + 94,600 = \$135,213.$$

The interest gain is

$$(80,000 + 6000)(.10 - .06) = \$3440.$$

The mortality gain (if there is no death benefit) is the actual minus the expected release of liability. In this example we have an actual release of AL_1 for one person, so the gain is

$$137,264 - 137,264 \times 2 \times .02 = \$131,773.$$

The total of the interest and mortality gains is 135,213 which agrees with the total gain. ☐

EXAMPLE 5.2
Calculate the mortality gain or loss in Example 5.1 if there are 0 or 2 deaths.

SOLUTION If there are 2 deaths, the mortality gain at time 1 is the actual release minus the expected release, which is

$$137,264 \times 2 - 137,264 \times 2 \times .02 = 269,037.$$

If there are no deaths, the mortality gain is

$$0 - 137,264 \times 2 \times .02 = -5491.$$

We can verify that the total expected gain is zero:

Number of Deaths	Probability	Gain	Weighted Gain
0	.98 × .98	−5491	−5274
1	.02 × .98 × 2	131,773	5166
2	.02 × .02	269,037	108
	1.00		0

☐

EXAMPLE 5.3

What is the mortality gain in Example 5.1 if the death benefit is 60% of the EOY liability instead of 0?

SOLUTION First we find the values of

$$AL_2 = 600 \times 26 \times 10 = 156,000$$

and

$$NC_1 = 600\ddot{a}_{61} \times vp_{60} + .60AL_2 \times vq_{60} = 8139.63.$$

From relationship (c) we have

$$(AL_1 + NC_1)(1.06) = DBEN \cdot q_{60} + AL_2 \cdot p_{60}$$

or

$$(AL_1 + 8139.63)(1.06) = .60 \times 156,000 \times .03 + 156,000 \times .97,$$

which solves for $AL_1 = 137,264$. The liability released, net of *DBEN*, for each actual death in 1994 is

$$AL_1 - DBEN = AL_1 - .60AL_1 = .40AL_1,$$

so the actual net release is $.40AL_1$. The expected net release for all exposed is $2 \times q_{59} \times .40AL_1$. Finally, the mortality gain, the excess of actual net release over expected net release, is

$$.40AL_1(1 - 2 \times q_{59}) = .40(137,264)(1 - .04) = \$52,709.$$

$\square$

Note that NC_1 provides for pension and insurance benefits. The insurance benefit is on a one-year-term basis, so the EOY liability is not affected.

DISCUSSION QUESTIONS

5-1 What is the difference in the method of calculating AL_1 between Examples 5.1 and 5.3? Is AL_1 and the mortality gain greater in Example 5.1 or 5.3 and why?

5-2   How are relationships (c) and (c′) simplified in the case where $DBEN = WBEN = 0$? What if $DBEN = WBEN = AL_1$?

5-3   The benefits include accrued interest to EOY. This accrued interest could be part of the interest gain or the benefit gain. Which alternative was used in Section 5.1.2?

5-4   Give three reasons why $^{act}F_1$ could be relatively high.

5-5   Does *WBEN* represent actual or expected withdrawal benefit?

5.2 Total Experience Gains

At time 0 we can calculate the BOY actual unfunded actuarial liability as

$$UAL_0 = AL_0 - F_0,$$

and we can predict the EOY unfunded actuarial liability as

$$^{exp}UAL_1 = (UAL_0 + NC_0)(1+i) - {}^iC.$$

The total experience gain is the difference between the expected and the actual unfunded actuarial liabilities. It arises when the overall actual experience is better than expected. The total experience gain at time 1 is defined as

$$^{tot}G_1 = {}^{exp}UAL_1 - {}^{act}UAL_1$$

$$= (UAL_0 + NC_0)(1+i) - {}^iC - UAL_1.$$

Note that we use the notation $^{act}UAL_1$ to distinguish the *actual* value of UAL_1, determined at time 1, from its *expected* value, denoted $^{exp}UAL_1$, which was determined at time 0. When it is no longer necessary to distinguish $^{act}UAL_1$ from $^{exp}UAL_1$, the superscript is deleted, and we use simply UAL_1.

The total experience gain is the sum of several components. These will be discussed, in turn, in the remaining sections of this chapter. The use of a plus or minus sign indicates whether the amount is a gain or a loss.

Increases in actuarial liability will occur if (a) plan benefits are improved, (b) the cost method is changed from Unit Credit to, say, EAN, or (c) the actuarial assumptions are made more conservative. These issues will be discussed in Chapter 6 which deals, in part, with the cost of changes.

| EXAMPLE 5.4 |

Normal retirement benefit: 1% of final salary per year up to 30 years
Actuarial cost method: Projected Unit Credit
Actuarial assumptions:
    Interest rate: 7% per year
    Compensation increases: 5% per year
    Preretirement terminations other than deaths: None
    Retirement age: 65
Data for sole participant:

Date of birth	1/1/44
Date of hire	1/1/84
1993 compensation	$40,000
Status as of 1/1/94	Active

Valuation results as of 1/1/93:

Normal cost as of 1/1	$ 2,000
Accrued liability	21,000
Value of assets	12,000

Contribution for 1993: $2500 paid on 12/31/93
Investment experience gain or loss for 1993: 0
Commutation functions: $D_{49} = 344$; $D_{50} = 320$; $N_{65}^{(12)} = 849$

What is the experience gain for 1993?

| SOLUTION | Let 1/1/93 be time 0. The total experience gain is defined by

$$^{tot}G_1 = {}^{exp}UAL_1 - {}^{act}UAL_1$$

$$= [(AL_0 - F_0 + NC_0)(1+i) - {}^iC] - (AL_1 - F_1).$$

No investment experience gain or loss for 1993 means that the value of the fund at time 1 is exactly what was expected, which is

$$F_1 = F_0(1+i) + {}^iC$$

$$= 12,000(1.07) + 2500 = 15,340.$$

Under Projected Unit Credit, the actuarial liability at time 1 is

$$AL_1 \; = \; .01(40,000)(1.05)^{15}(10)\left(\frac{849}{320}\right) \; = \; 22,063.$$

Then

$$^{tot}G_1 \; = \; [(21,000-12,000+2,000)(1.07) - 2500] - (22,063-15,340)$$

$$= \; \$2547. \qquad\qquad \square$$

$\boxed{\textbf{ALTERNATE SOLUTION}}$ Because the investment gain is zero, the experience gain is $^{exp}AL_1 - {^{act}}AL_1$, where $^{act}AL_1 = 22,063$ (see first solution). Since $DBEN = WBEN = 0$, then

$$^{exp}AL_1 \; = \; (AL_0 + NC_0)(1 + i)$$

from relationship (c), so the gain is

$$^{tot}G_1 \; = \; (21,000+2,000)(1.07) - 22,063 \; = \; \$2547.$$

$\qquad\qquad\qquad\qquad\qquad\qquad\qquad\qquad\qquad\qquad\qquad\qquad\qquad \square$

$\boxed{\textbf{EXAMPLE 5.5}}$
Actuarial cost method: Projected Unit Credit
Assumed interest rate: 8%
Valuation results:

	1/1/94	1/1/95
Normal cost as of 1/1	$ 50,000	$ 65,000
Accrued liability	400,000	500,000
Experience gain for previous year	20,000	10,000

Contributions for 1994:

Date	Amount
7/1/94	$75,000
12/31/94	25,000

Benefit payments for 1994, paid 7/1/94: $15,000
Actuarial value of assets as of 1/1/95: $300,000

What is the actuarial value of assets as of 1/1/94?

SOLUTION Let 1/1/94 be time 0. We are given the value of the fund at time 1 and the experience gain for 1994. We can solve for F_0 from

$$^{tot}G_1 = {}^{exp}UAL_1 - {}^{act}UAL_1$$
$$= (AL_0 - F_0 + NC_0)(1.08) - {}^iC - (AL_1 - F_1).$$

Substituting numerical values we have

$$10,000 = (400,000 - F_0 + 50,000)(1.08)$$
$$- [(75,000)(1.04) + 25,000] - [500,000 - 300,000],$$

from which we find

$$F_0 = \$160,185. \qquad \square$$

EXAMPLE 5.6

Normal retirement benefit for all active and inactive participants:
     Before 1994: $12.00 per month for each year of service
     After 1993: $12.50 per month for each year of service
Actuarial cost method: Entry Age Normal
Assumed interest rate: 7% per year
Selected valuation results as of 1/1/93:
     Normal cost as of 1/1 $ 50,000
     Actuarial liability   800,000
     Value of assets   420,000
Contribution for 1993: $80,000 paid on 7/1/93
Benefit payments for 1993: $15,000 paid on 7/1/93
Selected valuation results as of 1/1/94, after amendment:
     Actuarial liability $890,000
     Value of assets   500,000

What is the experience gain for 1993?

SOLUTION Let 1/1/93 be time 0. Since the amendment took place at the beginning of 1994, we are to find the experience gain for 1993 using the original benefit. The actual unfunded liability before the amendment is

$$^{act}UAL_1 = 890,000 \left(\frac{12}{12.50} \right) - 500,000 = 354,400.$$

The expected unfunded liability is

$$^{\exp}UAL_1 = (800,000-420,000+50,000)(1.07) - 80,000(1.035) = 377,300$$

so the total gain is

$$^{\mathrm{tot}}G_1 = 377,300 - 354,400 = \$22,900. \qquad \square$$

EXAMPLE 5.7

Actuarial cost method: Entry Age Normal
Actuarial liability, 1/1/93: $400,000
Assets, 1/1/93: $300,000
Normal cost for 1993, due 1/1/93: $40,000
Contribution for 1993, paid 6/1/93: $50,000
Benefits for 1993, all paid 7/1/93: $10,000
Actuarial liability, 1/1/94: $500,000
Assets, 1/1/94: $350,000
Valuation rate of interest: 4%

What would the actuarial liability have been as of 1/1/94 if all assumptions had been realized during 1993?

SOLUTION Let 1/1/93 be time 0. The desired liability is

$$(AL_0+NC_0)(1+i) - {}^iB$$
$$= (400,000+40,000)(1.04) - 10,000(1.02) = \$447,400. \qquad \square$$

The following observations arise from Example 5.7:

(1) Contributions and actual interest earnings normally increase the fund but not the liability.

(2) Benefits normally decrease the actual and expected liabilities and the fund.

(3) If, as in Exercise 5-1, the liability and the fund are decreased by the benefits, the net effect on the gain is zero.

(4) The fact that the actual liability is $500,000 suggests that there were fewer actual deaths and withdrawals than expected, and/or more new entrants and salary increases than expected.

5-6   Write a formula for the expected unfunded actuarial liability if the contribution is made halfway through the year.

5.3 Investment Gains

Investment gains are often referred to as **interest gains** or **asset gains**. When the actual investment income exceeds the expected investment income, there is an investment gain of

$$^{inv}G = {}^{act}I - {}^{exp}I.$$

The expected investment income is calculated using the interest rate assumed for the valuation year. We expect to earn interest on the fund and on any contributions made during the year, and to lose interest on any amount withdrawn from the fund for benefits. If the contributions, C, and the benefit payments, BEN, are made halfway through the year, then the expected investment income is

$$^{exp}I = i\left(F_0 + \frac{C}{2} - \frac{BEN}{2}\right),$$

where i the assumed interest rate. The actual investment income is based upon the actual interest rate that the fund earns during the year. Thus

$$^{act}I = i'\left(F_0 + \frac{C}{2} - \frac{BEN}{2}\right),$$

where i' is the actual earned interest rate, if the contributions and benefit payments are made halfway through the year. Obviously there is a gain if the actual interest rate exceeds the assumed interest rate.

If we take into consideration the contributions made to the fund and the benefits withdrawn from the fund, the investment income can be calculated using the growth of the fund during the year; often the actual investment income is the unknown, and can be obtained by solving the equation

$$F_0 + C - {}^{act}BEN + {}^{act}I = {}^{act}F_1.$$

Also,

$$F_0 + C - {}^{exp}BEN + {}^{exp}I = {}^{exp}F_1.$$

When $^{act}BEN = {}^{exp}BEN$, the investment gain is the excess of the actual fund over the expected fund; that is,

$$^{inv}G_1 = {}^{act}I - {}^{exp}I$$

$$= ({}^{act}F_1 + {}^{act}BEN - C - F_0) - ({}^{exp}F_1 + {}^{exp}BEN - C - F_0)$$

$$= {}^{act}F_1 - {}^{exp}F_1,$$

as already stated.

EXAMPLE 5.8

Plan effective date: 1/1/93
Normal retirement age: 63
Normal retirement benefit: 2.5% of final salary per year of service
Actuarial cost method: Projected Unit Credit
Actuarial assumptions:
   Interest rate: 8% per year
   Compensation increases: 4% per year
   Preretirement deaths and terminations: None
   Retirement age: 63
   Selected annuity value: $\ddot{a}_{63}^{(12)} = 8.582$

Data for sole participant:
   Date of birth   1/1/59
   Date of hire   1/1/84
   1992 compensation $40,000
   Status as of 1/1/94   Active
Value of assets as of 1/1/93: 0
Contribution for 1993: $6000 paid on 4/1/93
Noninvestment experience gain or loss for 1993: 0
Unfunded actuarial liability as of 1/1/94: $25,000

What is the investment gain or loss for 1993?

SOLUTION Let 1/1/93 be time 0. Since there is no noninvestment gain, the total experience gain is made up of the gain from investment only. We can use the formula

$$^{tot}G_1 = {}^{exp}UAL_1 - {}^{act}UAL_1$$

$$= (AL_0 - F_0 + NC_0)(1+i) - {}^{i}C - {}^{act}UAL_1,$$

where

$$AL_0 = .025[(40,000)(1.04)^{29}(9)](1.08)^{-29}(8.582) = 25,853$$

and

$$NC_0 = .025[(40,000)(1.04)^{29}](1.08)^{-29}(8.582) = 2873.$$

The investment gain for 1993 is

$$^{\text{inv}}G_1 = (25,853-0+2873)(1.08) - 6000\left[1+\frac{9}{12}(.08)\right] - 25,000 = -336,$$

which is a loss of $336. □

| **EXAMPLE 5.9** |

Benefits of $10,000 are paid on the first day of each month.
No other disbursements are made from the fund during 1994.
Assumed interest rate: 6%
Actuarial value of assets as of 1/1/94: $3,000,000
Actuarial value of assets as of 12/31/94: $3,400,300
Contribution for 1994 paid at 7/1/94: $300,000
Use the approximation $(1+i)^t = 1 + ti, 0 < t < 1$.

What is the amount of the investment gain during 1994?

| **SOLUTION** | Let 1/1/94 be time 0. Since $^{\text{act}}BEN = {}^{\text{exp}}BEN$, then

$$^{\text{inv}}G_1 = {}^{\text{act}}F_1 - {}^{\text{exp}}F_1 = 3,400,300 - {}^{\text{exp}}F_1,$$

where

$$^{\text{exp}}F_1 = 3,000,000(1.06) + 300,000(1.03)$$

$$- 10,000\left[\left(1+\frac{12}{12}(.06)\right)+\left(1+\frac{11}{12}(.06)\right)+\cdots+\left(1+\frac{1}{12}(.06)\right)\right]$$

$$= 3,489,000 - 10,000\left[12+\frac{.06}{12}(12+11+\cdots+1)\right] = 3,365,100.$$

Then

$$^{\text{inv}}G_1 = 3,400,300 - 3,365,100 = \$35,200. \qquad □$$

In this text we will not emphasize the difference between the *market values* and the *actuarial values* of assets, but it can be noted that market values of bonds and stocks often fluctuate unduly. Actuarial values are market values which are often dampened with an averaging device, similar to graduated values. Investment gains and losses based on actuarial values do not fluctuate as much.

EXAMPLE 5.10

Actuarial cost method: Unit Credit
Assumed interest rate: 7%
Valuation results:

Normal cost as of 1/1/93	$ 14,000
Actuarial liability as of 1/1/93	125,000
Actuarial value of assets as of 1/1/93	35,000

1993 contribution: $24,000 paid at 12/31/93
There were no benefits paid in 1993.
Investment earnings for 1993: $2000 less than assumed
Actuarial liability as of 1/1/94: $153,000

What is the experience gain or loss for 1993?

SOLUTION Let 1/1/93 be time 0. We know that there was a $2000 investment loss. We also have $BEN = 0$ and $^iC = C$, so

$$^{inv}G_1 \ = \ ^{act}I - {}^{exp}I.$$

Then we have

$$-2000 \ = \ ^{act}I - i \cdot F_0 = {}^{act}I - (.07)(35,000),$$

from which we find

$$^{act}I = 450.$$

The fund at time 1 is

$$F_1 \ = \ F_0 + {}^{act}I + C - BEN \ = \ 35,000 + 450 + 24,000 - 0 = 59,450.$$

Then the experience gain is

$$^{tot}G_1 \ = \ ^{exp}UAL_1 - {}^{act}UAL_1$$

$$= \ (AL_0 - F_0 + NC_0)(1+i) - {}^iC - UAL_1$$

$$= \ (125,000 - 35,000 + 14,000)(1.07) - 24,000 - (153,000 - 59,450)$$

$$= \ -6270,$$

which means that there was a total experience loss of $6270.   □

EXAMPLE 5.11

Plan effective date: 1/1/93
Actuarial cost method: Unit Credit
Assumed interest rate: 7%
Valuation results:

	1/1/93	1/1/94
Normal cost as of 1/1	$ 8,000	$ 9,000
Accrued liability	40,000	53,000
Actuarial value of assets	0	12,840

Contribution paid at 1/1/93: $6000
Contribution paid at 7/1/93: $6000
Benefit payments during 1993: None

What is the net experience loss for 1993 attributable to experience other than investment return?

SOLUTION Let 1/1/93 be time 0. The total loss is

$$^{\text{act}}UAL - {}^{\text{exp}}UAL$$

$$= (AL_1 - F_1) - [(AL_0 - F_0 + NC_0)(1+i) - {}^iC]$$
$$= (53,000 - 12,840) - (40,000 - 0 + 8,000)(1.07) + 6,000(1.035 + 1.07)$$
$$= 1430.$$

The gain due to investment return, where $BEN = 0$, is

$$^{\text{act}}F_1 - {}^{\text{exp}}F_1 = 12,840 - [0 + 6000(1.07 + 1.035)] = 210.$$

Finally, the non-investment loss is

$$1430 + 210 = \$1640. \qquad \square$$

EXAMPLE 5.12

Actuarial cost method: Unit Credit
Assumed interest rate: 6%
Normal cost for 1992 as of 12/31/92: $50,000

Valuation results as of 1/1/93:

Actuarial value of assets as of 1/1/93	$425,000
Unfunded actuarial liability as of 1/1/93	450,000
Experience gain attributable to investment return	42,600
Experience gain attributable to experience	
other than investment return	13,400

Contribution for 1992: $75,000 paid at 12/31/92
Benefit payments for 1992: $10,000 paid at 1/1/92

What is the actuarial liability as of 1/1/92?

SOLUTION Let 1/1/92 be time 0. The total gain is

$$^{tot}G_1 \;=\; ^{exp}UAL_1 - {}^{act}UAL_1 \;=\; UAL_0(1+i) + NC_1 - C_1 - {}^{act}UAL_1,$$

since the normal cost and the contribution are made at the end of the year. Since the total gain is composed of investment and non-investment gain, we have

$$42,600 + 13,400 \;=\; [UAL_0(1.06)+50,000-75,000] - 450,000$$

from which we find

$$UAL_0 \;=\; 500,943.$$

We need the value of the fund at time 0, since $AL_0 = F_0 + UAL_0$. The fund at time 1 is

$$F_1 \;=\; F_0 + (C_1 - BEN_0) + {}^{act}I,$$

where $^{act}I = {}^{exp}I + {}^{inv}G$. Substituting numerical values we find

$$425,000 = F_0 + (75,000-10,000) + .06F_0 - .06(10,000) + 42,600$$

from which we find

$$F_0 \;=\; 300,000.$$

Finally, we can find

$$AL_0 = F_0 + UAL_0 \;=\; 300,000 + 500,943 \;=\; \$800,943. \qquad \square$$

EXAMPLE 5.13

Actuarial cost method: Frozen Initial Liability
Assumed interest rate: 7%
Valuation results:

	1/1/93	1/1/94
Present value of future benefits	$850,000	$901,000
Present value of future normal costs	420,000	—
Actuarial value of assets (market)	125,000	—
Normal cost as of 1/1	23,000	—

Contributions of $50,000 for 1993 were paid in two installments of $25,000 each at 1/1/93 and 12/31/93. There were no benefits payable in 1993. Actual investment earnings exceeded assumed investment earnings by $3000 in 1993.

What is the present value of future normal costs as of 1/1/94?

| SOLUTION | Let 1/1/93 be time 0. The present value of future normal costs under FIL is

$$pvNC_1 \ = \ pvB_1 - UAL_1 - F_1.$$

To calculate the expected unfunded liability, we first need the value of UAL_0, which is

$$UAL_0 \ = \ pvB_0 - F_0 - pvNC_0$$
$$= \ 850,000 - 125,000 - 420,000 \ = \ 305,000.$$

Then we can find

$$^{\exp}UAL_1 \ = \ (UAL_0 + NC_0)(1+i) - {}^{i}C$$
$$= \ (305,000 + 23,000)(1.07) - 25,000(1.07 + 1) \ = \ 299,210.$$

The value of the fund at time 1 is

$$F_1 \ = \ F_0 + {}^{\text{act}}I + C - BEN,$$

where

$$^{\text{act}}I \ = \ 125,000(.07) + 25,000(.07) + 3,000 \ = \ 13,500.$$

Now we can find

$$F_1 = 125,000 + 13,500 + 50,000 - 0 = 188,500$$

and finally

$$pvNC_1 = 901,000 - 299,210 - 188,500 = \$413,290. \qquad \square$$

EXAMPLE 5.14

Actuarial cost method: Unit Credit
Assumed interest rate: 8%
Valuation results as of 1/1/93:

    Actuarial liability   \$850,000
    Actuarial value of assets   420,000
    Normal cost as of 1/1   70,000

Benefit payments during 1993: \$500 at the beginning of each month
1993 experience gains and losses:

    Investment: \$600 gain
    All other sources: 0

Actuarial value of assets as of 1/1/94: \$573,000

What is the unfunded actuarial liability as of 1/1/94?

SOLUTION Let 1/1/94 be time 1. First we calculate

$$^{i}BEN = 500 \times 12 + 500 \times .08\left(\frac{1}{12}+\frac{2}{12}+\cdots+\frac{11}{12}\right) = 6260.$$

The equation connecting F_0 and F_1 is

$$F_0(1+i) + {}^{i}C - {}^{i}BEN + {}^{inv}G = F_1.$$

Substituting values we have

$$(420,000)(1.08) + {}^{i}C - 6260 + 600 = 573,000$$

from which we find ${}^{i}C = 125,060$. Next we have

$${}^{tot}G_1 = {}^{exp}UAL_1 - {}^{act}UAL_1 = (UAL_0+NC_0)(1+i) - {}^{i}C - {}^{act}UAL_1.$$

Substituting values we have

$$600 = (850,000 - 420,000 + 70,000)(1.08) - 125,060 - {}^{\mathrm{act}}UAL_1$$

from which we find

$$\mathrm{}^{\mathrm{act}}UAL_1 = 414,340. \qquad \square$$

$\boxed{\text{ALTERNATE SOLUTION}}$ Since there is no liability gain, then, from Section 5.1.4,

$$\mathrm{}^{\mathrm{act}}AL_1 = {}^{\mathrm{exp}}AL_1 = (AL_0 + NC_0)(1 + i) - {}^i BEN$$

$$= (850,000 + 70,000)(1.08) - 6000\left(1 + \frac{13}{24}(.08)\right)$$

$$= 987,340.$$

Then

$$UAL_1 = AL_1 - F_1 = 987,340 - 573,000 = \$414,340. \qquad \square$$

Note that the first solution utilizes the investment gain, whereas the alternate solution does not.

$\boxed{\textbf{EXAMPLE 5.15}}$
Plan effective date: 1/1/94
Normal retirement benefit: $20 per month for each year of service
Actuarial assumptions:
    Interest: 7%
    Preretirement deaths and terminations: None
    Retirement age: 65
Participant data as of 1/1/94:

	Attained Age	Age at Hire
Smith	30	30
Brown	50	50
Green	55	55

Contributions for 1994 and 1995: Normal cost, paid at 12/31
Experience:
    For 1994: In accordance with assumptions
    For 1995: In accordance with assumptions, except that investment
          return is 14%

Which of the following statements regarding the Aggregate cost method and the Entry Age Normal cost method (individual) are true?

I.   The normal cost for 1994 under the Aggregate method is less than the normal cost for 1994 under the Entry Age Normal method.

II.   The normal cost for 1996 under the Aggregate method is less than the normal cost for 1995 under the Aggregate method.

III.   The normal cost for 1996 under the Entry Age Normal method is less than the normal cost for 1995 under the Entry Age Normal method.

SOLUTION Note that $x = e$ and no mortality is assumed. Under the Aggregate cost method,

$$TNC_e \left[\frac{\ddot{a}_{\overline{35|}} + \ddot{a}_{\overline{15|}} + \ddot{a}_{\overline{10|}}}{3} \right] = \sum p v_e B - 0,$$

where

$$\sum pvB = 20 \times 12[35(1.07)^{-35} + 15(1.07)^{-15} + 10(1.07)^{-10}] \, \ddot{a}_r^{(12)}$$

$$= 3311.60 \ddot{a}_r^{(12)}.$$

Then

$$TNC = \frac{3311.60 \ddot{a}_r^{(12)} - 0}{(31.12/3)} = 319.24 \ddot{a}_r^{(12)}.$$

Under EAN,

$$NC_e \cdot \ddot{a}_{\overline{r-e|}} = pvB.$$

Then for Smith we have

$$NC = (240 \times 35) v^{35} \, \ddot{a}_r^{(12)} \div 13.85 = 56.81 \ddot{a}_r^{(12)},$$

for Brown we have

$$NC = (240 \times 15) v^{15} \, \ddot{a}_r^{(12)} \div 9.75 = 133.82 \, \ddot{a}_r^{(12)},$$

and for Green we have

$$NC = (240 \times 10) v^{10} \, \ddot{a}_r^{(12)} \div 7.52 = 162.24 \, \ddot{a}_r^{(12)}.$$

The total EAN normal cost is therefore

$$TNC = 352.87 \, \ddot{a}_r^{(12)},$$

so Statement I is *true*.

If everything proceeds as expected in 1994, then $NC_1^{Agg} = NC_0^{Agg}$. In 1995, the investment return is better than expected (14% instead of 7%), so $^{act}F_2 > {}^{exp}F_2$ which implies that NC_2^{Agg} will be less than expected, so Statement II is *true*.

$NC^{EAN} = \Sigma B_r \ddot{a}_r^{(12)} \left(\dfrac{D_r}{N_e - N_r} \right)$. The normal cost will not change from NC_1 to NC_2 since there is no change in B_r, $\ddot{a}_r^{(12)}$, or $\dfrac{D_r}{N_e - N_r}$. The investment return of 14% will produce an investment gain, but will not affect the normal cost. Therefore Statement III is *false*. □

EXAMPLE 5.16

The 1/1/94 actuarial valuation identifies an actuarial loss for the 1993 plan year due to interest earnings below the assumed rate. There are no other current or prior experience gains or losses being amortized.

Which of the following statements are true?

I. Under the Aggregate cost method, the loss increases the present value of future normal costs.

II. Under the Unit Credit cost method, the loss increases the 1994 normal cost.

III. Under the Frozen Initial Liability cost method, the loss increases the unfunded frozen initial liability.

SOLUTION

I. *True*. $pvNC = pvB - F$, so F suffers the loss.

II. *False*. The interest loss may be amortized with a supplemental cost, in which case the normal cost is not affected.

III. *False*. $pvNC = pvB - UAL - F$, so F is affected but UAL is not. □

EXAMPLE 5.17

Three identical pension plans, Plan UC, Plan EAN, and Plan FIL, were established 1/1/76 for three employers, each of which had only one employee. The three employees are identical in all respects for plan valuation purposes. Assume that, for the 19 years before 1995, the three employees have the same salary.

The same actuarial assumptions have been used for all three plans. The Unit Credit cost method has been used for Plan UC, the Entry Age Normal cost method has been used for Plan EAN, and the Frozen Initial Liability (EAN) cost method has been used for Plan FIL. There has been no change in assumptions or cost method for any of the plans before 1995. Further assume that there are no deaths, terminations, retirements, or new entrants before 1995.

With the exception of investment return, the experience of each plan has been in accordance with actuarial assumptions. The investment return has, however, been the same in each of the 19 years 1976 through 1994 and has been the same for all three plans.

The 1/1/95 valuations show the following normal costs (due 1/1/95 in each case):

$$
\begin{array}{ll}
\text{Plan UC:} & \$1000 \\
\text{Plan EAN:} & 900 \\
\text{Plan FIL:} & 800
\end{array}
$$

Which of the following statements are true?

I.   The fact that the normal cost for Plan UC exceeds the normal cost for Plan EAN shows that there have been investment gains.

II.   The fact that the normal cost for Plan UC exceeds the normal cost for Plan FIL shows that there have been investment gains.

III.   The fact that the normal cost for Plan EAN exceeds the normal cost for Plan FIL shows that there have been investment gains.

SOLUTION The normal cost for Plan UC may be higher because the employee is older, so Statements I and II are *false*. Investment gains depress the FIL normal cost but do not affect the EAN normal cost, so Statement III is *true*.   □

EXAMPLE 5.18

Plan effective date: 1/1/93
Normal retirement benefit: $35 per month for each year of service
Actuarial cost method: Attained Age Normal with FIL
Actuarial assumptions:
    Interest rate: 8% per year
    Preretirement deaths and terminations: None
    Retirement age: 65
Data for sole participant:
    Date of birth   1/1/48
    Date of hire   1/1/72
    Status as of 1/1/94   Active
Selected valuation results as of 1/1/93:
    Normal cost as of 1/1 $ 1,296
    Unfunded liability   12,818
    Value of assets   3,000
Contribution for 1993: $3000 paid on 12/31/93
Benefit payments for 1993: 0
There were no experience gains in 1993 other than an investment
    gain of $500.
Selected annuity value: $\ddot{a}_{65}^{(12)} = 8.00$

What is the normal cost for 1994 as of 1/1/94?

| **SOLUTION** | Let 1/1/93 be time 0. The normal cost for 1993 is given
by

$$NC_0 \cdot \ddot{a}_{\overline{20|}} = pvB - UAL - F,$$

which solves for

$$NC_0 = 1296.$$

NC_1 is the same as NC_0 except for the unexpected increase in the fund of
500. Amortizing from time 1 to retirement reduces NC_0 by $\dfrac{500}{\ddot{a}_{\overline{19|}}} = 48.21$,
so we have

$$NC_1 = 1296 - 48.21 = \$1247.79. \qquad \square$$

Note that the same answer can be obtained by solving the equation
$NC \cdot \ddot{a}_{\overline{19|}} = pvB - UAL - F$ as of time 1. Note also that the large
contribution of 3000 increases the fund and decreases the unfunded liability,
but does not reduce the normal cost!

5.4 Retirement Gains

In this section, we discuss gains due to (a) normal retirement, (b) early retirement, and (c) postponed retirement. The text will be followed by several examples.

5.4.1 Normal Retirement Gains

Participants sometimes retire at the age stated in the pension plan document as the **normal retirement age**, which is usually age 65.   When a participant retires, sometimes an annuity is purchased from an insurance company to cover the monthly retirement benefits. If interest rates are high, the insurance company will probably charge a premium which is lower than the actuarial liability released, and the difference will be an experience gain. If interest rates are low, the insurance company will probably charge a premium which is higher than the actuarial liability released, and the difference will be an experience loss. More often, an annuity is not purchased from an insurance company, and the monthly pension benefit is simply paid from the pension fund; at the moment of retirement, there is normally no change in actuarial liability and hence no gain or loss.

5.4.2 Early Retirement Gains

Many plans allow participants to retire earlier than the normal retirement age if certain requirements are met. These requirements might include a minimum retirement age, number of years of service, or sum of age and service. If a participant retires early, there is normally a reduction in the retirement benefits, since they will be paid out for a longer period of time. The benefits may be reduced by a certain percentage for each month or year that early retirement precedes normal retirement, although sometimes there is no reduction. For example, the plan document might specify a reduction of 4% for each year of early retirement, except that if age plus service exceeds 90 at the time of early retirement, there is no reduction.

Consider an example where the actuary assumes a retirement age of 65 and the actuarial liability at age 60 is

$$^{\exp}AL \; = \; B_{65}\, \frac{N_{65}^{(12)}}{D_{60}} - pvNC.$$

With Traditional Unit Credit, the future normal costs in the above expression will increase from age 60 to age 64 inclusive; the prospective expression is often replaced by the equivalent TUC retrospective expression

$$^{\exp}AL = B_{60} \frac{N_{65}^{(12)}}{D_{60}}.$$

If the participant decides to retire at age 60 and there is no reduction factor, then the actuarial liability will become

$$^{\text{act}}AL = B_{60} \frac{N_{60}^{(12)}}{D_{60}},$$

and the experience loss (usually substantial) will be

$$^{\text{act}}AL - {}^{\exp}AL.$$

If there is a reduction factor of 4% for each of the five years, the pension will be $.80B_{60}$, the liability will be

$$^{\text{act}}AL = .80B_{60} \frac{N_{60}^{(12)}}{D_{60}},$$

and the experience loss will be smaller. If the plan document specifies an actuarially equivalent pension, the pension will be $E \cdot B_{60}$ where

$$E \cdot B_{60} \frac{N_{60}^{(12)}}{D_{60}} = {}^{\exp}AL = B_{65} \frac{N_{65}^{(12)}}{D_{60}} - pvNC,$$

and there will be no experience loss. In such cases, an old actuarial rule of thumb says that the reduction will be roughly 6% of the accrued pension for each year of early retirement. Inflation, indexation of pensions, and late retirement could increase the 6% rule to 8% or 10%.

5.4.3 Postponed Retirement Gains

Some pension plans allow the participants to remain active past the normal retirement age if they desire and the employer agrees.

The amount of postponed pension benefit provided for in the plan document may or may not include credit for service after the normal retirement date. Credit for service may include service after the normal retirement date with an overall limit of, say, 35 years, on the theory that a pension based on 35 years is adequate.

If retirement is postponed for m years, the pension will be paid for m fewer years than normal; the accrued benefit may be increased to the actuarial equivalent, or the increase in the accrued benefit may be 0%, 3% or 6% for each year of deferral.

The final consideration is that a normal cost and contributions may or may not apply and may or may not affect the pension benefit.

As an example, consider a plan where the annual pension benefit is 2% of final average salary for each year of service, payable at BOY. (Career average salary is final average salary averaged over the entire career.) If normal retirement is at age 65, and if the actuary assumed retirement at age 65, then

$$B_{65} = .02S(65-e),$$

and at normal retirement

$$AL_{65} = B_{65} \cdot \ddot{a}_{65}.$$

If actual retirement is at age 66, and if service after normal retirement age does *not* count, then $B_{66} = .02S(65-e) = B_{65}$, and at actual retirement we have

$$AL_{66} = B_{66} \cdot \ddot{a}_{66} = B_{65} \cdot \ddot{a}_{66},$$

assuming the participant does survive to age 66. What is the expected gain to the plan as a result of the deferred retirement?

Let $B = B_{65} = B_{66}$. Intuitively the gain is $B(1+i)$, the year-end equivalent of the payment not made at age 65. To derive this result, we note that we have $B \cdot \ddot{a}_{65}(1+i)$ on hand at age 66. We need $B \cdot \ddot{a}_{66}$ if the participant has survived and we need nothing if the participant has died. Therefore, the gain is either $B[\ddot{a}_{65}(1+i) - \ddot{a}_{66}]$, with probability p_{65}, or $B[\ddot{a}_{65}(1+i) - 0]$, with probability $1 - p_{65}$. Then the expected gain is

$$^{\exp}G = B\big([\ddot{a}_{65}(1+i) - \ddot{a}_{66}]p_{65} + \ddot{a}_{65}(1+i)(1-p_{65})\big).$$

It is easy to see that this expression reduces to $B(1+i)$, as expected.

The plan may provide for actual service after age 65 and for an actuarially equivalent benefit of $E \cdot B_{66}$, where this time we have $B_{66} = .02S(66-e)$ and E is such that

$$E \cdot B_{66}\ddot{a}_{66} = B_{66} \frac{N_{65}}{D_{66}}.$$

At actual retirement we would have

$$^{\text{act}}AL = E \cdot B_{66}\ddot{a}_{66}.$$

5-7   What is the gain in the last scenario, where service after the normal retirement age counts?

5-8   What is the gain if actual retirement is at age 67?

EXAMPLE 5.19

Normal retirement benefit: $30 per month for each year of service
Actuarial cost method: Individual Level Premium
Assumed retirement age: 65
Assumed early retirements: None

Which of the following statements with respect to retirement experience are true?

I.   If the plan provides for no reduction in benefit for early retirement within 3 years of normal retirement date, a participant who retires 2 years *early* produces an actuarial loss.

II.   If the plan provides for no further benefit accrual beyond normal retirement date but benefits are actuarially equivalent for late retirement, a participant who retires *late* produces no actuarial gain.

III.   If the plan provides for continuing accrual of benefits for service beyond normal retirement date, without actuarial adjustment for late retirement, a participant who was hired at age 25 and who retires *late* produces an actuarial gain.

SOLUTION

I.   If there *were* an actuarially equivalent reduction, there would be no loss, since the plan would have the same liability as if he retired at normal retirement. Since more benefits will be paid out with a shorter period to collect contributions, there is an actuarial loss, so Statement I is *true*.

II.   Since benefits are actuarially equivalent and there is no accrual beyond normal retirement, there will not be a gain, so Statement II is *true*.

III.   This is *true*, because for an additional year, the additional year's accrual is worth only $360 N_{66}^{(12)} \div D_{65}$, which is less than the cost of the additional year's accrual with full actuarial equivalence. This latter quantity is worth about $360 \times (66 - 25) \times .06 \times N_{66}^{(12)} \div D_{65}$. (Recall the 6% rule of thumb at the end of Section 5.4.2.)   □

EXAMPLE 5.20

Normal retirement benefit: $10 per month for each year of service
Preretirement death benefit: None
Early retirement benefit: Accrued benefit reduced by 6% for each year by which the early retirement age precedes age 65
Actuarial cost method: Entry Age Normal
Preretirement terminations other than by death: None
Assumed retirement age: 60
Data for sole participant:
    Date of birth   1/1/44
    Date of hire   1/1/84
Selected commutation and annuity values:

$$D_{50} = 322 \qquad D_{60} = 151 \qquad \ddot{a}_{60}^{(12)} = 9.79$$

$$N_{40} = 8761 \qquad N_{50} = 3902 \qquad N_{60} = 1547$$

What is the actuarial liability as of 1/1/94?

SOLUTION Let 1/1/94 be time 0 and age 50. Since it is assumed that the participant will retire at age 60, the reduced benefit is

$$B_{60} = (1-.30)(10 \times 12 \times 20) = 1680.$$

To find the EAN liability, we need the normal cost at time 0, which is

$$NC_0 = B_{60} \ddot{a}_{60}^{(12)} \frac{D_{60}}{N_{40} - N_{60}} = (1680)(9.79)\left(\frac{151}{8761 - 1547}\right) = 344.$$

Retrospectively, the liability at age 50 is

$$AL_0 = NC_0 \left(\frac{N_{40} - N_{50}}{D_{50}}\right) = 344\left(\frac{8761 - 3902}{322}\right) = \$5191. \quad □$$

Note that years of service after early retirement are not counted.

EXAMPLE 5.21

Normal retirement benefit: $10 per month per year of service

Early retirement benefit: Accrued benefit, reduced $\frac{2}{3}\%$ per month for each month by which commencement precedes age 65

Actuarial cost method: Entry Age Normal

Assumed retirement age: 65

A participant who was hired on 1/1/85 retires and starts receiving his pension on 1/1/94 at age 64.

Selected commutation functions:

$$D_{64} = 110 \qquad N_{64}^{(12)} = 1110 \qquad N_{55} = 3000$$

$$D_{65} = 101 \qquad N_{65}^{(12)} = 1003 \qquad N_{65} = 1050$$

What is the gain attributable to early retirement?

SOLUTION Let 1/1/94 be time 0. We expect that the participant will retire at age 65. To calculate the expected liability we need the values of

$$pvB_{65} = (10 \times 12 \times 10)N_{65}^{(12)} \div D_{65} = 11,916$$

and

$$NC_0 = 11,916 \div \frac{N_{55} - N_{65}}{D_{65}} = 617.19.$$

Then

$$^{\exp}AL_0 = 11,916 \frac{D_{65}}{D_{64}} - 617.19 \frac{D_{64}}{D_{64}} = 10,324.$$

Since the participant actually retires at age 64, there is a reduction in his benefit. The reduction factor is $1 - \frac{2}{300}(12) = .92$. After the early retirement we have

$$^{\text{act}}AL_0 = (10 \times 12 \times 9)N_{64}^{(12)} \div D_{64} \times .92 = 10,026$$

so the gain due to early retirement is

$$10,324 - 10,026 = \$298. \qquad \square$$

EXAMPLE 5.22

Normal retirement benefit: $15 per month for each year of service
Early retirement benefit: Accrued benefit reduced by 6% for each year by
    which commencement of payments precedes age 65
Actuarial assumptions:
    Interest rate: 6%
    Preretirement deaths and terminations: None
Retirement probabilities and annuity values:

x	$q_x^{(r)}$	$\ddot{a}_x^{(12)}$
63	.50	9.85
64	.20	9.60
65	1.00	9.35

Data for sole participant:
    Date of birth   1/1/31
    Date of hire   1/1/78

What is the present value of future benefits as of 1/1/94?

SOLUTION We must take into account the number of years of service,
the reduction factor, the deferred annuity, and the probability of retirement.
The present value of the future benefits at age 63 is

$$
\begin{aligned}
pvB \; = \; & (15 \times 12 \times 16)(.88)(v^0)(9.85)(.5) \\
& + (15 \times 12 \times 17)(.94)(v^1)(9.60)(1-.5)(.2) \\
& + (15 \times 12 \times 18)(1.0)(v^2)(9.35)(1-.5)(1-.2)(1) \\
\; = \; & \$25,872.
\end{aligned}
$$

$\square$

EXAMPLE 5.23

Normal retirement benefit: $15 per month for each year of service
Early retirement benefit: Accrued benefit reduced by 6% for each of the
    first 5 years and 3% for each of the next 5 years by which commence-
    ment of payments precedes age 65
Actuarial cost method: Frozen Initial Liability
Actuarial assumptions:
    Interest rate: 8% per year
    Preretirement deaths and terminations: None
    Retirement age: 65

Data for participant Smith:

Date of birth	1/1/39
Date of hire	1/1/76
Status as of 1/1/94	Active

Original valuation results as of 1/1/94:

Present value of future benefits	$662,000
Unfunded liability	163,250
Value of assets	142,500
Normal cost per active participant	195.34
Number of active participants	150

Selected annuity values: $\ddot{a}_{55}^{(12)} = 12.33$; $\ddot{a}_{65}^{(12)} = 8.33$

After the valuation was done, it was discovered that Smith had retired on 12/31/93 and commenced receiving benefits. Another valuation was done to correct this error.

What is the increase in normal cost for 1994 as of 1/1/94 due to Smith's retirement?

| SOLUTION | Let 1/1/94 be time 0. Using FIL, the normal cost can be obtained from

$$TNC_0 \cdot \frac{\Sigma \ddot{a}}{150} = \Sigma pvB - UAL_0 - F_0.$$

Assuming retirement at age 65, Smith's value of future benefits is

$$pvB = (15 \times 12 \times 28)v^{10}(8.33) = 19,446.$$

Assuming retirement at age 55 at time 0, the value is

$$pv_0 B' = (15 \times 12 \times 18)(12.33)(.55) = 21,972$$

where the early retirement factor is $1 - 5 \times .06 - 5 \times .03 = .55$. The difference is

$$\Delta pvB = 21,972 - 19,446 = 2526.$$

Taking Smith's retirement into account,

$$TNC_0' \cdot \frac{\Sigma \ddot{a} - \ddot{a}_{\overline{10|}}}{149} = 662,000 + 2526 - 163,250 - 142,500.$$

We can find the value of $\Sigma\ddot{a}$ using the normal cost that assumes Smith's retirement at 65. We have

$$(195.34)(150)\,\frac{\Sigma\ddot{a}}{150} = 662{,}000 - 163{,}250 - 142{,}500$$

which solves for

$$\sum\ddot{a} = 1824.$$

Then $TNC_0' = 29{,}425$ and the increase in normal cost is

$$TNC_0' - TNC_0 = 29{,}425 - (195.34)(150) = \$124. \qquad \square$$

EXAMPLE 5.24

Early retirement benefit for deferred vested participants: Accrued benefit
   payable at age 65, reduced 1/15 for each of the first 5 years and 1/30
   for each of the next 5 years that retirement precedes age 65; benefits
   may commence as early as age 55

Actuarial assumptions for terminated vested participants whose benefits
   have not yet commenced:

   Interest: 6%

   Retirement age: 65

   Mortality: None prior to commencement of benefits

On 1/1/94 there are three participants, ages 56, 59 and 63. Each of them
   left employment 1/1/91 and elected to postpone commencement of the
   early retirement benefit; each elects to receive the benefits on 1/1/94.

Selected annuity values for retired employees:

Age x	$12\ddot{a}_x^{(12)}$	Age x	$12\ddot{a}_x^{(12)}$
53	144	60	130
54	142	61	128
55	140	62	126
56	138	63	124
57	136	64	122
58	134	65	120
59	132		

Which of the elections will result in an experience loss to the plan?

| **SOLUTION** | Consider a benefit of $1 of monthly income at age 65. The following table calculates the gain or loss for each participant:

Age	Expected Actuarial Liability	Reduced Benefit	Actual Early Retirement Liability	Gain or Loss
63	$120v^2 = 106.8$	$1 - \dfrac{2}{15}$	$\dfrac{13}{15} \times 124 = 107.5$	loss[*]
59	$120v^6 = 84.6$	$1 - \dfrac{5}{15} - \dfrac{1}{30}$	$\dfrac{19}{30} \times 132 = 83.6$	gain
56	$120v^9 = 71.0$	$1 - \dfrac{5}{15} - \dfrac{4}{30}$	$\dfrac{16}{30} \times 138 = 73.6$	loss

*106.8 is less than 107.5 □

| **EXAMPLE 5.25** |

Normal retirement benefit: $10 per month per year of service
Actuarial cost method: Entry Age Normal (individual basis)
Assumed retirement age: 65 (for participants not yet age 65)
Participant X attains age 65 on 12/31/94, the end of the 1994 plan year, and at that time makes an irrevocable election (as permitted under the plan) to defer retirement exactly one year, so that retirement will in fact take place (at age 66) on 12/31/95, with the amount of pension commencing at that time based on service through 12/31/95. In the 12/31/94 valuation for the 1995 plan year, the actuary therefore treats X as an active participant, with retirement date (and age) and amount of benefit as described above.

In the experience for the 1994 plan year, will this particular deferment of retirement produce a gain, a loss, or neither, or might it produce either a gain or a loss depending on the other circumstances of the case?

| **SOLUTION** | At the end of the 1994 plan year we have

$$^{\exp}AL = 120n\,\ddot{a}^{(12)}_{65} - NC \times 0$$

and

$$^{\text{act}}AL = 120(n+1)v\,p_{65}\,\ddot{a}^{(12)}_{66} - NC,$$

where n is the number of years of service if retirement occurs at age 65. The gain due to late retirement is

$$^{\text{ret}}G = {}^{\exp}AL - {}^{\text{act}}AL = 120\left[n \cdot \ddot{a}^{(12)}_{65} - (n+1)vp_{65}\ddot{a}^{(12)}_{66}\right] + NC.$$

Normally this gain would be positive, but it could be negative in unusual situations. □

5.5 Withdrawal Gains

This section discusses vesting, inflation, transfers, decrements, and gains from withdrawal. The words withdrawal and termination are synonymous. The former is used in actuarial texts such as Bowers, *et al.* [5] and Parmenter [9]; the latter is common in plan documents and descriptive material. We will use the word withdrawal and the probability symbol $q_x^{(w)}$. This decrement does not include death or disability.

5.5.1 Vesting

Suppose the pension plan document specifies an annual pension benefit of $480 per year of service with 50% vesting after three years of service and 100% vesting after six years of service. If the participant withdraws after, say, four years, the deferred pension benefit nominally will be 50% of the four-year accrual. If the plan document gives the option and the participant elects the option, the present value of the vested pension benefit may be paid out of the fund. Most U.S. plans will *only* pay the lump sum value at withdrawal if the value is less than $3500.

The participant is normally entitled to all or part of the value of the benefit at termination using the Unit Credit cost method, since this method is based on accrued pension credits. Suppose the actuarial cost method is EAN. The following table gives the necessary information including factors per dollar of deferred benefit; the actuarial basis for the factors is sometimes the same for both methods and sometimes different.

Time of Withdrawal	Accrued Benefit	Vested Benefit	Factors EAN	UC
2	$ 960	$ 0	2.0	1.0
4	1920	960	3.6	2.1
6	2880	2880	5.3	3.3

Based on the above table, we can now calculate the actuarial liability released due to withdrawal, the value of the vested benefit at withdrawal, and the gain at withdrawal (which is sometimes amortized over five years). We are assuming the service table does not include a withdrawal decrement.

Time of Withdrawal	Liability Released	Withdrawal Benefit	Difference (Gain)
2	$960 \times 2.0 = 1920$	0	$1920
4	$1920 \times 3.6 = 6912$	$960 \times 2.1 = 2016$	4896
6	$2880 \times 5.3 = 15{,}264$	$2880 \times 3.3 = 9504$	5760

In the event of termination after six years, the participant will receive an annual deferred pension of $2880, and the participant may be included in the valuation each year as a deferred vested. Alternatively, if the old and new plans allow, the withdrawal value of $9504 may be transferred to the participant's new plan. In either event, the gain at withdrawal is $5760.

There are three levels of vesting, which are (a) vesting required by statute, (b) additional vesting provided by the plan document, and (c) additional vesting in the event of plan wind-up as provided by statute.

Let us consider briefly the difficult problem of **inflation**. If the participant does not withdraw, the pension benefit may be renegotiated every three years to roughly cope with inflation before retirement and there may be partial inflation protection after retirement. If the participant does withdraw, the pension benefit may, in rare cases, be indexed each year, before and after retirement, using the same partial annual inflation factors which are used for retired lives. If the actuary makes an inflation assumption of, say, 4%, and it is the practice of the plan sponsor to index by 50% of inflation, then the actuary will consider reducing his net interest assumption for retired and deferred vested lives by 2% or, for full indexing, by 4%.

Other clauses of the plan document may increase the withdrawal benefit. For example, in the event of the participant's death before retirement, the spouse may be entitled to an immediate or deferred pension. Also, for contributory plans, the participant on withdrawal is entitled to a minimum benefit of a return of contributions with interest.

5.5.2 Gain

Section 5.4.1 shows that a *normal retirement* gain can occur if current interest rates happen to be high. Similarly, a *withdrawal* gain or loss can occur if the actuarial liability interest rate is, say, 6% and the value of the accrued benefit is computed at 7% or 5%; in many cases the withdrawal value is based on current rates of interest.

Under the TUC cost method with a vested participant, the following properties hold:

- The normal cost and actuarial liability are not affected by the value of $q_x^{(w)}$.
- Withdrawals do not cause gains.
- Early retirement benefits that are actuarially equivalent do not cause gains.
- A withdrawal gain will probably occur if the cost method is more conservative than Traditional Unit Credit (see Section 5.5.1).

The service table often does *not* include a withdrawal decrement, which means that no withdrawals are assumed. If no actual withdrawals occur, there will be no gain or loss from withdrawal; if there is an actual withdrawal between time 0 and time 1, with no vesting and no withdrawal benefit, the gain at time 1 will be the actuarial liability at time 1 for the withdrawal at time 1. If there are actual withdrawals with withdrawal benefit *WBEN*, then we add up the differences to get a gain of

$$^{\text{with}}G_1 \;=\; \sum (AL_1 - {}^i WBEN),$$

which we can call the **total actual net**.

If the service table has a withdrawal decrement, which is common for large plans, then withdrawals will be expected, and we can calculate a **total expected net** as $\sum_{A_0} q_x^{(w)}(AL_1 - {}^i WBEN)$, where the liability for every active participant is associated with a withdrawal benefit and a probability of withdrawal, and summed. We can also add up the actual liability released net of $^i WBEN$. The experience gain from withdrawals will then be the total actual net minus the total expected net, or

$$^{\text{with}}G_1 \;=\; \sum_W (AL_1 - {}^i WBEN) \;-\; \sum_{A_0} q_x^{(w)}(AL_1 - {}^i WBEN),$$

where the summations are over the actual withdrawals and the participants exposed to withdrawal, respectively.

In a large group, there are usually both actual and expected withdrawals, and *WBEN* depends on salary and duration. Recall that actual $^i WBEN$ can occur throughout the year, and accrued interest to EOY is included. The accrued interest in expected $^i WBEN$ is zero if expected withdrawals are at EOY. The situation involving *DBEN* is similar.

If the withdrawal benefit is not transferred out, then there will be a **deferred vested liability** for every such participant in every subsequent valuation until such participants become "retired" or die.

Withdrawals are also discussed in Sections 1.6.3, 5.1, and 6.6.

DISCUSSION QUESTIONS

5-9 Is there a gain when a vested participant withdraws under Traditional Unit Credit? under Projected Unit Credit? Why?

5-10 If the age at plan inception is a, the cost method is ILP, and the age at withdrawal is $a + 3$, how could the value of the accrued benefit be a lot larger than AL_3, thereby producing a large loss on withdrawal?

5-11 Does the value of AL_3 in Question 5-10 increase or decrease when we introduce probabilities of withdrawal? (See also Section 6.7.)

EXAMPLE 5.26

Normal retirement benefit: $10 per month for each year of service
Early retirement eligibility: Age 62 with 25 years of service
Early retirement benefit: Full accrued benefit, without reduction
Vesting: 100% after ten years of service; the vested benefit is either the accrued benefit deferred to age 65, or its actuarial equivalent commencing before age 65
Actuarial cost method: Unit Credit
Assumed retirement: Later of age 63 or eligibility for retirement
Net experience gain in 1993: 0

Which of the following statements regarding 1993 experience are true?

I. If an additional nonvested participant had terminated at age 40 there would have been an experience gain.

II. If an additional vested participant had terminated at age 40 there would have been an experience gain.

III. If an additional participant had retired at age 62 there would have been an experience gain.

SOLUTION

I.   *True*, because the plan would no longer be responsible for any
        retirement benefits.

II.   *True*, because $\dfrac{N_{65}^{(12)}}{D_{40}} < \dfrac{N_{63}^{(12)}}{D_{40}}$. (The vested benefit would be based on
        the actual number of years of service only and would commence at
        age 65, not age 63.)

III.   *False*, because $\dfrac{N_{62}^{(12)}}{D_{62}} > \dfrac{N_{R}^{(12)}}{D_{62}}$, where R is the later of 63 or eligibility
        for retirement.   (The participant would be eligible for early
        retirement *without* a reduction in benefit.)   □

5.6 Salary Gains

In a defined benefit plan, the normal retirement benefit is either a flat dollar
amount or an amount contingent on salary. If contingent on salary, the
normal retirement benefit is defined as a percentage of the final salary, the
final average salary, or the career average salary. Salaries are assumed to
follow a salary scale.

Assuming that salaries increase at rate s and the normal retirement
benefit is 50% of the final average salary, then the liability at age $x + 1$ is

$$^{\text{exp}}AL = (.50)(FAS)\frac{D_{65}}{D_{x+1}}\ddot{a}_{65}^{(12)} - pvNC.$$

Suppose that the actual salary increased at rate s' during the year of valuation, so that the actual actuarial liability is

$$^{\text{act}}AL' = (.50)(FAS')\frac{D_{65}}{D_{x+1}}\ddot{a}_{65}^{(12)} - pvNC',$$

where FAS' and $pvNC'$ are the projected final salary and the present value
of future normal costs, respectively, calculated using the actual salary
(increased by the rate s' during the year). The gain due to unexpected
changes in salary is then

$$^{\text{sal}}G = {}^{\text{exp}}AL - {}^{\text{act}}AL.$$

EXAMPLE 5.27

Normal retirement benefit: 50% of final salary
Actuarial cost method: Entry Age Normal
Assumed interest rate: 7.5%
Assumed salary increases: 6.0%
There are no retired participants, and no terminated participants with deferred vested benefits.
Selected valuation results:

	1/1/93	1/1/94
Present value of future benefits	$1,000,000	$1,115,566
Present value of assets	300,000	400,000
Unfunded actuarial liability	300,000	330,696
Normal cost as of 1/1	55,000	
Contribution paid at 12/31	90,000	

Each participant received a salary increase of 10% during 1993.
Experience with regard to actuarial assumptions other than salary increases and interest earnings was exactly equal to the assumed. There were no new entrants and no terminations with benefits during 1993.

What is the actuarial loss due to salary increases as of 1/1/94?

SOLUTION Let 1/1/94 be time 1. The gain due to salary increases is

$$^{sal}G = (AL_0 + NC_0)(1+i) - {}^{i}PBEN - {}^{act}AL_1$$

$$= (600,000 + 55,000)(1.075) - 730,696 = -26,571,$$

so we have a loss of $26,571.   □

Note that $^{i}PBEN$ denotes any lump sum or periodic pension benefit paid out of the plan, including interest to EOY; in this example $^{i}PBEN = 0$.

ALTERNATE SOLUTION Since

$$^{exp}UAL = (300,000 + 55,000)(1.075) - 90,000 = 291,625$$

and $^{act}UAL = 330,696$, the total loss is 39,071. The loss due to interest is

$$[300,000(1.075)+90,000] - 400,000 = 12,500.$$

Since there were no gains due to actuarial assumptions other than salary and interest, the loss from salary is

$$39,071 - 12,500 = \$26,571. \qquad \square$$

| EXAMPLE 5.28 |

Normal retirement benefit: 50% of final salary
Actuarial cost method: Aggregate
Selected valuation results as of 1/1/94:

Total present value of future benefits	$2,000,000
Present value of future benefits for retired and terminated participants	400,000
Present value of future salaries	24,000,000
Actuarial value of assets	500,000
Annual salaries	4,000,000

No participants are within one year of assumed retirement age.
After completing the valuation, it is discovered that all active participants received a 5% salary increase which had not been reported. The normal cost is then recalculated.

What is the increase in the normal cost as of 1/1/94 due to the increased salaries ?

| SOLUTION | Let 1/1/94 be time 0. Without recognizing the 5% salary increase, the normal cost under the aggregate method is

$$TNC_0 = \frac{\sum pvB_x - F_0}{\ddot{a}^s} = \frac{2,000,000 - 500,000}{24,000,000/4,000,000} = \frac{1,500,000}{6}.$$

When the actives receive a 5% increase, the normal cost becomes

$$TNC_0' = \frac{(1,600,000)(1.05) + 400,000 - 500,000}{(24 \times 1.05)/(4 \times 1.05)} = \frac{1,580,000}{6},$$

so the increase in the normal cost is

$$TNC_0' - TNC_0 = \frac{80,000}{6} = \$13,333. \qquad \square$$

EXAMPLE 5.29

Plan effective date: 1/1/93
Normal retirement benefit: 50% of final 3-year average salary
Actuarial cost method: Individual Level Premium
Actuarial assumptions:
    Interest: 7%
    Salary increases: None
    Preretirement deaths and terminations: None
    Retirement age: 65
Data for sole participant:
    Date of birth   1/1/43
    Annual salary as of 1/1/93 $25,000
    Normal cost as of 1/1/93   4,032
As of 1/1/94 the participant's annual salary increases to $50,000.

What is the normal cost as of 1/1/94?

SOLUTION Let 1/1/93 be time 0. Since the salary is not expected to increase, the normal cost is calculated at plan inception under ILP. The normal cost for each future year remains constant unless there is a change in the plan assumptions. Taking the unexpected salary increase into account, the normal cost at time 1 is

$$NC_1 = NC_0 + \Delta B \frac{D_{65}}{D_{51}} \ddot{a}_{65}^{(12)} \left(\frac{D_{51}}{N_{51} - N_{65}} \right).$$

We need the value of $\ddot{a}_{65}^{(12)}$. We also know that

$$NC_0 = 4032 = .5(25,000) \frac{D_{65}}{D_{50}} \cdot \frac{D_{50}}{N_{50} - N_{65}} \ddot{a}_{65}^{(12)} = \frac{(12,500)v^{15}\ddot{a}_{65}^{(12)}}{\ddot{a}_{\overline{15}|}}$$

from which we find

$$\ddot{a}_{65}^{(12)} = 8.673.$$

Then

$$NC_1 = 4032 + \frac{.5(25,000)v^{14}(8.673)}{\ddot{a}_{\overline{14}|}} = \$8525.$$

□

5.7 Mortality Gains

Suppose we are doing a pension valuation at time 0 where the valuation age
of each participant is x; let us consider the preretirement mortality gains
which may arise in the next year.

For most small plans the pension actuary assumes no mortality. In
most years there will be no actual deaths, and the resulting gain will be
zero. If a death occurs, the actuarial liability of AL_1 will be released and,
if there is no death benefit, a gain of AL_1 will result. If a death benefit of
^iDBEN is paid out at the time of death, the gain will be

$$^{mort}G_1 \ = \ AL_1 - {^iDBEN},$$

where the interest on $DBEN$ to EOY is at the assumed rate. If there is more
than one actual death, the right side will be a summation over all actual
deaths.

If mortality is assumed, the expected liability released is $\sum_{A_0} q_x \cdot AL_1$. If
there are no actual deaths, then $^{mort}G_1 \ = \ - \sum q_x (AL_1 - {^iDBEN})$, where the
summation is over all active lives. The death benefit itself is $DBEN$; if
deaths are assumed to occur at EOY, then the expected accrued interest is
zero. If there is one actual death, the gain is

$$^{mort}G_1 \ = \ (AL_1 - {^iDBEN}) - \sum q_x (AL_1 - {^iDBEN}).$$

If the actual death occurs at BOY, the accrued interest is for the full year.
If there is more than one actual death, the gain will be correspondingly
greater.

Example 5.33 is an example of the mortality loss when the sole retiree
survives to the end of the year.

Most pension plans have survivor benefits and due allowance must be
made for the probabilities of the participant dying and for the values of the
survivor benefits (see Example 5.35).

Mortality is also discussed in Sections 5.1.2 and 6.6.

EXAMPLE 5.30

Normal retirement benefit: $100 per month on or after age 60
There are no death benefits under the plan.
All the participants were employed at age 25

Actuarial assumptions:
Interest: 5%
Retirement: Age 65, or immediately if over age 65
Experience during 1993 for active participants age 60 and over:

Age x 1/1/93	Number of Participants 1/1/93	Deaths (all on 7/1/93)	Retirements (all on 12/31/93)	Number of Participants 12/31/93	$q_x^{(d)}$
63	8	2	1	5	.017
65	7	0	0	7	.021
67	6	0	0	6	.026
	21	2	1	18	

For all other participants, the experience during 1993 was exactly in accordance with assumptions.

Was there a gain or loss from mortality and/or retirement during 1993?

SOLUTION There is a mortality gain, since there are more deaths than expected. The actual number of deaths is 2 and the expected number of deaths is .439. Furthermore, since fewer people retired than expected, there was also a retirement gain. □

EXAMPLE 5.31

A plan has just been amended to add the option of a lump-sum settlement at normal or early retirement that is actuarially equivalent to the monthly pension that would otherwise start to be payable at that time.

Actuarial equivalence is to be on the interest and mortality assumptions used in the valuation coincident with, or next preceding, the effective date of the option. The election may be at any time prior to retirement.

Assumptions:

The option is elected by every retiring participant.

If the plan had remained on the prior basis (*i.e.*, no lump-sum option), the mortality experience would have been exactly that provided for in the mortality assumption.

What is the expected long-range effect of this amendment?

SOLUTION Since we are given the actuarial equivalent of the accrued benefits, and since the mortality assumptions are going to be respected, then there is no gain or loss due to mortality. ☐

EXAMPLE 5.32

Normal retirement benefit: $20 per month for each year of service
Preretirement death benefit: None
Actuarial cost method: Individual Entry Age Normal
Actuarial assumptions:
    Interest rate: 6%
    Preretirement terminations other than deaths: None
    Retirement age: 65
    Selected annuity value: $\ddot{a}_{65}^{(12)} = 9.35$
Participant data as of 1/1/93:

	Smith	Brown	Green
Date of birth	1/1/63	1/1/43	1/1/33
Date of hire	1/1/88	1/1/73	1/1/83

Green died during 1993.
Smith and Brown are still active participants as of 1/1/94.

Selected commutation values:

x	D_x	N_x
25	2303	37,539
30	1711	27,278
31	1613	25,567
50	509	6,723
51	477	6,214
60	260	2,870
61	241	2,610
65	178	1,745

What is the experience gain for 1993 as of 1/1/94 due to Green's death?

$\boxed{\textbf{SOLUTION}}$ Let 1/1/93 be time 0. The actual release of liability due to Green's death is AL_1, and the expected release is $q_{60} \cdot AL_1$. Thus the gain due to Green is $AL_1(1-q_{60})$. First we know that

$$NC_{50} \frac{N_{50} - N_{65}}{D_{50}} = 20 \times 12 \times 15 \times 9.35 \times \frac{D_{65}}{D_{50}},$$

from which we find

$$NC_{50} = 1203.58.$$

Next we can calculate

$$AL_{61} = 20 \times 12 \times 15 \times 9.35 \times \frac{D_{65}}{D_{61}} - NC_{50} \frac{N_{61} - N_{65}}{D_{61}} = 20,540.$$

We also need to find

$$p_{60} = 1.06 \frac{D_{61}}{D_{60}} = .98254.$$

Finally we have

$$^{\text{mort}}G_1 = (20,540)(.98254) = \$20,181. \qquad \square$$

$\boxed{\textbf{EXAMPLE 5.33}}$
Assumed interest rate: 7% per year
Age of sole retiree as of 1/1/93: 70
Retirement benefit: \$10,000 per year, payable each 1/1 for life
Status of retiree as of 1/1/94: Alive
Selected annuity value and life expectancies:

$$\ddot{a}_{70} = 7.326 \qquad e_{70} = 13.80 \qquad e_{71} = 13.25$$

What is the mortality experience loss for 1993 due to the retiree?

$\boxed{\textbf{SOLUTION}}$ Let 1/1/93 be time 0. The mortality experience loss is

$$^{\text{act}}AL_1 - {}^{\text{exp}}AL_1 = AL_1 - p_{70} \cdot AL_1.$$

To calculate p_{70}, recall that

$$e_{70} = p_{70} + {}_2p_{70} + \cdots = p_{70}(1 + p_{71} + {}_2p_{71} + \cdots) = p_{70}(1 + e_{71}),$$

so

$$p_{70} = e_{70} \div (1 + e_{71}) = .9684.$$

For the retired participant,

$$AL_0 = 10,000 \, \ddot{a}_{70} = 73,260$$

and

$$AL_1 = (73,260-10,000)(1.07) \div p_{70} = 69,897.$$

Then the mortality experience loss is

$$69,897 q_{70} = 69,897(1-.9684) = \$2209. \qquad \square$$

<hr>

EXAMPLE 5.34

Normal retirement benefit: $10 per month per year of service
Preretirement surviving spouse benefit: If a participant dies after age 55,
    the participant's spouse will receive a life pension of $5 per month for
    each year of the participant's service. This benefit is provided by the
    plan at no cost to the participant.
Actuarial assumptions:
    Interest: 6%
    Withdrawals: $q_x^{(w)} = .01$ for $x < 55$; $q_x^{(w)} = 0$ for $x \geq 55$
    Retirement: At age 65, or immediately if over age 65
    Spouses: 95% of the employees are married and husbands are four
        years older than wives
Actuarial cost method: Entry Age Normal (individual basis)
During 1994, the following events occur:

(1) Male participant Smith dies on 12/31/94 at age 64, and his wid-
    ow, who was age 60 at 12/31/94, is entitled to a spouse pension
    of $180 monthly.

(2) Female participant Jones terminates on 12/31/94 at age 45, and
    is entitled to a deferred vested pension of $170 monthly com-
    mencing at age 65.

(3) Male employee Brown, who was hired at age 59 on 12/31/87,
    1retired at age 66 on 12/31/94 with a pension of $70 monthly.

Which of the following statements about the above events are true?

I.   There was an actuarial gain from Smith's death.

II.   There was an actuarial gain from Jones' termination.

III.   There was an actuarial gain from Brown's working beyond assumed retirement age.

| SOLUTION |
I.   There was a gain from Smith's death because the liability for an accrued pension of $360 was reduced, on death, to the liability for a pension of $180 per month.

II.   There was a gain from Jones' termination because the Entry Age Normal costs up to termination were more than sufficient to fund the accrued pension benefits.

III.   There would be a gain from Brown's retirement because the Entry Age Normal costs were designed to pay a pension commencing at age 65, and the actual pension did not commence until age 66. However, Brown's service went from 6 years to 7 years, an increase of 16%; this increase would probably outweigh the first considera-tion and the statement cannot be said to be true.   □

| EXAMPLE 5.35 |
Assumed interest rate: 7%
Data for retired participant:
    Age of retiree: x
    Age of spouse: y
Annual pension benefit: $10,000 per year payable at BOY
Form of payment: Life annuity for participant with 50% continued for life of surviving spouse
Selected annuity values:

$$\ddot{a}_x = 8.157 \quad \ddot{a}_y = 10.301 \quad \ddot{a}_{x:y} = 7.281 \quad \ddot{a}_{x+1} = 7.915 \quad \ddot{a}_{y+1} = 10.059$$

What is the loss from mortality if both the retiree and spouse are alive at the end of the first year?

SOLUTION Recalling that the loss from mortality is $^{\text{act}}AL - {^{\text{exp}}AL}$, we have

$$^{\text{act}}AL_1 = 10,000 \left(\frac{1}{2}\right) \left[\ddot{a}_{x+1} + \ddot{a}_{\overline{x+1:y+1}}\right]$$

$$= 10,000 \left[\ddot{a}_{x+1} + \frac{1}{2}\ddot{a}_{y+1} - \frac{1}{2}\ddot{a}_{x+1:y+1}\right].$$

Using the relationship $\ddot{a}_{x:y} = 1 + v p_{x:y}\, \ddot{a}_{x+1:y+1}$, we can find

$$\ddot{a}_{x+1:y+1} = \frac{7.281 - 1}{(1.07)^{-1} p_x p_y}.$$

We can find p_x and p_y in a similar way. Since $\ddot{a}_x = 1 + v p_x \ddot{a}_{x+1}$ and $\ddot{a}_y = 1 + v p_y\, \ddot{a}_{y+1}$, then

$$p_x = \frac{8.157 - 1}{(1.07)^{-1}(7.915)} = .9675287,$$

$$p_y = \frac{10.301 - 1}{(1.07)^{-1}(10.059)} = .9893697,$$

and

$$\ddot{a}_{x+1:y+1} = \frac{7.281 - 1}{(1.07)^{-1}(.9675287)(.9893697)} = 7.0208567.$$

Then

$$^{\text{act}}AL_1 = 10,000\ (7.915 + 5.0295 - 3.51043) = 94,341$$

and

$$^{\text{exp}}AL_1 = p_x p_y (94341) + p_x q_y (10,000\ddot{a}_{x+1}) + q_x p_y (5000\ddot{a}_{y+1})$$

$$= 90,307 + 814 + 1616 = 92,737.$$

Then the loss is

$$94,341 - 92,737 = \$1604. \qquad \square$$

5.8 Exercises

5.1 Unfunded Liabilities and Gains
5.2 Total Experience Gains

5-1   Actuarial cost method: Entry Age Normal
        Assumed interest rate: 5%
        Valuation as of 1/1/93:
        Actuarial liability $620,000
        Assets   510,000
        Normal cost for 1993, due 1/1/93   30,000
        Actual contribution for 1993, made 6/30/93: $ 50,000
        Benefit payments for 1993, all made 6/30/93: $12,000
        Valuation as of 1/1/94:
        Actuarial liability $670,000
        Assets   560,000

        What is the actuarial gain or loss for 1993?

5-2   Actuarial cost method: Unit Credit
        Assumed interest rate: 5%
        Actuarial liability as of 1/1/93: $65,000
        Assets as of 1/1/93: $55,000
        Normal cost for 1993 due 1/1/93: $3000
        Contribution for 1993, paid 7/1/93: $5000
        Benefit payments for 1993, all paid 7/1/93: $1000
        Actuarial liability as of 1/1/94: $70,000
        Assets as of 1/1/94: $60,000

        What is the actuarial gain or loss for 1993?

5-3   Valuation assumptions:

	Preretirement	Postretirement
Mortality	None	GAM
Interest	5%	4%
$12\ddot{a}_{65}^{(12)} = 128.56$		

Valuation results (Unit Credit cost method):

	1/1/93	1/1/94
Accrued liability	$100,000	$126,000
Value of assets	96,000	120,000
Normal cost, due 1/1	20,000	24,000

Actual contributions:
    1/1/94 $24,000
    1/1/93   24,000
Benefits paid: None in either 1993 or 1994

What is the actuarial gain or loss for 1993?

5-4   Normal retirement benefit: $10 monthly per year of service
       Actuarial cost method: Unit Credit
       Assumed interest rate: 5%
       Valuation results:

	1/1/93	1/1/94
Actuarial liability	$200,000	$215,000
Actuarial value of assets	100,000	135,000
Normal cost	10,000	15,000

Contribution for 1993, paid 1/1/93: $20,000
Benefits paid 7/1/93: $5000

What is the gain or loss for 1993?

5-5   Actuarial cost method: Entry Age Normal (individual)
Assumed interest rate: 7%
Selected valuation results:

	1/1/93	1/1/94
Actuarial liability	$304,300	—
Actuarial value of assets	235,000	$275,000

Contribution for 1993, paid at 12/31/93: Normal cost plus interest
to 12/31/93 plus $21,000
Participant data as of 1/1/94:

Attained Age	Number of Participants	Annual Salary	Normal Cost as of 1/1	Present Value of Future Salary	Present Value of Future Benefits
50	1	15,500	800	250,000	45,000
55	1	18,000	1025	180,000	105,000
65	1	35,000	—	—	200,000
					350,000

What is the experience gain or loss for 1993?

5-6   Plan effective date: 1/1/93
Normal retirement benefit: 40% of final salary
Actuarial cost method: Entry Age Normal
Actuarial assumptions:
      Interest: 7%
      Salary increases: 6%
      Preretirement deaths and terminations: None
      Retirement age: 65
Selected annuity value: $12\ddot{a}_{65}^{(12)} = 115$

Data for sole plan participant:
      Date of birth   1/1/43
      Date of hire   1/1/88
      Salary for 1992 $24,000
Contribution for 1993 paid at 12/31/93: $7000
Unfunded actuarial liability as of 1/1/94: $23,000
Selected annuity factors:

$$\ddot{a}^{s}_{45:\overline{20|}} = 18.320 \qquad \ddot{a}^{s}_{45:\overline{5|}} = 4.907 \qquad \ddot{a}^{s}_{50:\overline{15|}} = 14.057$$

What is the amount of experience loss during 1993?

5.3 Investment Gains

5-7   Actuarial cost method: Entry Age Normal
       Assumed interest rate: 5%
       Valuation as of 1/1/93:
              Actuarial liability $620,000
              Assets   510,000
              Normal cost for 1993, due 1/1/93   30,000
       Actual contribution for 1993, made 6/30/93: $50,000
       Benefit payments for 1993, all made 6/30/93: $12,000
       Valuation as of 1/1/94:
              Actuarial liability   670,000
              Assets   560,000

       What are the expected investment earnings for 1993?

5-8   Actuarial cost method: Unit Credit
       Assumed interest rate: 5%
       Actuarial liability as of 1/1/93: $65,000
       Assets as of 1/1/93: $55,000
       Normal cost for 1993 due 1/1/93: $3000
       Contribution for 1993, paid 7/1/93: $5000
       Benefit payments for 1993, all paid 7/1/93: $1000
       Actuarial liability as of 1/1/94: $70,000
       Assets as of 1/1/94: $60,000

       What are the actual investment earnings for 1993?

5-9   Actuarial cost method: Entry Age Normal
       Actuarial liability, 1/1/93: $400,000
       Assets, 1/1/93: $300,000
       Normal cost for 1993, due 1/1/93: $40,000
       Contribution for 1993, paid 6/1/93: $50,000
       Benefits for 1993, all paid 7/1/93: $10,000
       Actuarial liability, 1/1/94: $500,000
       Assets, 1/1/94: $350,000
       Valuation rate of interest: 4%

       For 1993, what is the actuarial gain or loss due to interest?

5-10 Assets 1/1/93 before benefit payments then due: $50,000
Contribution for 1993 made 10/31/93: $25,000
Benefit payments for 1993: $1000 at the beginning of each month
Normal cost for 1993 due 1/1/93: $15,000
Present value 1/1/93 of all future benefits: $150,000
Assumed interest rate: 6%
Rate of return during 1993: 7%

What is the investment gain for 1993?

5-11 Assumed interest rate: 5%

Valuation results:

	1993	1994
Normal cost as of 1/1	$ 10,000	$ 12,000
Unfunded actuarial liability as of 1/1	100,000	90,000
Actuarial value of assets as of 1/1	25,000	40,000
Contribution paid at 12/31	20,000	22,000
Benefit paid at 7/1	5,000	6,000

There have been no changes of plan or assumptions.

What is the actuarial experience gain or loss for 1993 from sources other than investment?

5-12   Plan effective date: 1/1/93
Normal retirement benefit: $12 monthly per year of service
Actuarial cost method: Unit Credit
Assumed interest rate: 7%
Preretirement terminations other than by death: None
Normal cost as of 1/1/93: $1100
Actuarial liability as of 1/1/93: $7000
Contribution paid at 7/1/93: $900
Benefit payments during 1993: 0
Actuarial value of assets (market value) as of 1/1/94: $1920
Participant data as of 1/1/94 and selected commutation functions:

Attained Age x	Service of each Participant	Number of Participants	D_x	$12\ddot{a}_x^{(12)}$
35	5	7	40	
45	7	2	30	
65	0	0	5	110

What is the net experience gain or loss for 1993 from all sources other than investment?

5-13   Actuarial cost method: Unit Credit
Actuarial assumptions:
      Interest: 8%
      Retirement age: 65
Selected valuation results:

	1/1/93	1/1/94
Normal cost as of 1/1	$ 10,000	$ 11,000
Actuarial liability for actives	135,100	156,000
Actuarial liability for inactives	0	0

Actuarial value of assets as of 1/1/93: $0
Contribution for 1993: $25,000 paid at 7/1/93
Contribution for 1994: $27,500 paid at 7/1/94
No benefits were payable for 1993.
Rate of return on actuarial value of assets was 10% for 1993.

What is the noninvestment actuarial gain for 1993?

5-14   Normal retirement benefit: $20 monthly per year of service
       Actuarial cost method: Unit Credit
       Actuarial assumptions:
           Interest: 7%
           Preretirement deaths and terminations: None
           Retirement age: 65
       Data for sole participant:
           Date of birth   1/1/30
           Date of hire   1/1/88
       Unfunded actuarial liability as of 1/1/93: $2000
       Contribution for 1993: Normal cost as of 1/1 paid at 1/1/93
       Investment return for 1993: 11%
       As of 1/1/94, the assumed interest rate is changed to 8%.
       Selected annuity values: $^{7\%}\ddot{a}_{65}^{(12)} = 10$; $^{8\%}\ddot{a}_{65}^{(12)} = 9$

       What is the unfunded actuarial liability as of 1/1/94?

5-15   Normal retirement benefit: 50% of final average salary
       Actuarial cost method: Entry Age Normal
       Assumed interest rate: 5%
       Assumed deaths and terminations: None
       Valuation results:

	1/1/93	1/1/94
Actuarial liability	$ 50,000	$ 65,000
Assets	20,000	32,000
Normal cost	6,000	7,000
Contributions	10,000	12,000

Experience interest rate during 1993: 7%

What are the expected and actual unfunded actuarial liabilities as of 1/1/94?

5-16 Actuarial cost method: Frozen Initial Liability
Actuarial assumptions:
Interest: 7%
Salary increases: 5%
Preretirement deaths and terminations: None
Valuation results as of 1/1/93:

Present value of future benefits	$10,000,000
Actuarial value of assets	4,000,000
Unfunded liability	2,000,000
Annual salaries	4,000,000
Present value of future salaries	40,000,000

Contribution for 1993 paid at 12/31/93: $618,000
During the 1993 plan year all actuarial assumptions were exactly realized except that the assets earned 8%. All participants are active employees under the assumed retirement age.

What is the normal cost as of 1/1/94?

5-17 Normal retirement benefit: $15 per month for each year of service
Actuarial cost method:
Before 1993: Aggregate
After 1992: Unit Credit
Actuarial assumptions:
Interest rate: 8% per year
Preretirement deaths and terminations: None
Retirement age: 65
Valuation data for sole participant:
Date of birth   1/1/42
Date of hire   1/1/87
Selected valuation results as of 1/1/92:
Normal cost as of 1/1   898
Value of assets   1000
Contribution for 1992: Normal cost for 1992, paid on 1/1/92
There were no noninvestment experience gains or losses for 1992.
Actual rate of investment return in 1992: 5%

What is the unfunded accrued liability as of 1/1/93?

5.4 Retirement Gains

5-18 Normal retirement benefit: $25 monthly per year of service
Early retirement benefit: Accrued benefit reduced by 1/15
for each of the first 5 years preceding age 65 and 1/30 for each of
the next 5
Actuarial cost method: Unit Credit
Actuarial assumptions:
Interest: 8%
Preretirement terminations other than deaths: None
Retirement age: 65
Data for sole participant:

Date of birth	1/1/35
Date of hire	1/1/70
Date of retirement	12/31/93

Selected commutation functions:

x	D_x	$N_x^{(12)}$
58	440	4160
59	400	3740
60	365	3355
65	230	1880

What is the loss in 1993 due to the participant's early retirement?

5-19   Plan effective date: 1/1/94
       Normal retirement benefit: 1% of final salary per year of service
       Early retirement benefit: Payable immediately without reduction
       Actuarial cost method: Aggregate
       Actuarial assumptions:
           Interest rate: 7%
           Compensation increases: 7%
           Preretirement deaths and terminations: None
       Probailities of retirement:

x	$q_x^{(r)}$
62	50%
63	0
64	0
65	100

       Data for sole participant:
           Date of birth   1/1/38
           Date of hire   1/1/93
           1993 compensation $100,000
           Status as of 1/1/94   Active
       Selected annuity values: $\ddot{a}_{62}^{(12)} = 9.394$; $\ddot{a}_{65}^{(12)} = 8.736$

       What is the normal cost for 1994 as of 1/1/94?

5-20   Normal retirement benefit: $30 per month for each year of service
           up to 30 years
       Normal retirement age: 65
       Early retirement eligibility: Age 55
       Early retirement benefit:
           Less than 30 years of service:
           Accrued benefit, reduced by 6% for each year by which the
               benefit commencement date precedes the normal retirement
               date
           30 or more years of service: Accrued benefit, unreduced for
               early commencement of payments

Actuarial assumptions:
　Interest rate: 7%
　Preretirement deaths and terminations: None
　Probability of retirement at the beginning of each year:
　　Less than 30 years of service: 10%
　　30 or more years of service: 40%
　Age 65: 100%
Data for sole participant:
　Date of birth　　　　　　1/1/32
　Date of hire　　　　　　　1/1/66,
　Status as of 1/1/94　　　Active
Selected commutation functions:

x	D_x	$N_x^{(12)}$
62	3704	34,796
63	3403	31,230
64	3121	27,956
65	2857	24,956

What is the present value of future benefits as of 1/1/94?

5-21　Actuarial cost method: Unit Credit
　Actuarial assumptions:
　　Terminations other than deaths: None
　　Salary increases: None
　　Retirement age: 65
　A participant retires and starts receiving his pension at age 62. His accrued monthly benefit of $500 payable at age 65 has been reduced by .5% for each month by which commencement of payments precedes age 65.
　Selected commutation functions:

$$N_{65}^{(12)} = 300,000 \qquad D_{65} = 30,000$$

$$N_{62}^{(12)} = 400,000 \qquad D_{62} = 36,000$$

What is the actuarial loss attributable to early retirement?

5-22   Plan effective date: 1/1/87

Normal retirement benefit: $20 monthly per year of service

Normal form: Ten years certain and life

Assumed retirement age: 65

Early retirement benefit: Accrued normal benefit reduced by $\frac{5}{9}$ %
for each of the first 60 months and $\frac{5}{18}$ % for each of the next 60
months by which early retirement precedes age 65

Actuarial cost method: Entry Age Normal

Assumed interest rate: 6%

Preretirement deaths or other terminations: None

Selected annuity values: $12\ddot{a}^{(12)}_{\overline{65:10|}} = 122$; $12\ddot{a}^{(12)}_{\overline{55:10|}} = 146$

A participant who was hired at age 40 on 1/1/79 retires on 1/1/94
and starts receiving his pension immediately.

What is the amount of experience gain or loss due to this participant's early retirement?

5-23   Normal retirement benefit: $15 monthly per year of service

Early retirement benefit: Accrued benefit reduced by 2% for each
year by which commencement of payments precedes age 65

Actuarial cost method: Entry Age Normal

Actuarial assumptions:

Interest rate: 6%

Preretirement deaths and terminations: None

Retirement age: 60

Data for participant Smith:

Date of birth	1/1/35
Date of hire	1/1/73
Date of retirement	12/31/93

Selected commutation functions:

x	D_x	$N^{(12)}_x$
59	275	3019
60	260	2751
65	180	1658

What is the 1993 experience loss due to early retirement?

5-24 Normal retirement benefit: 2% of final 3-year average compensation
for each year of service
Early retirement eligibility: Age 55
Early retirement benefit: Accrued benefit, reduced by 3% for each
year by which the benefit commencement date precedes the
normal retirement date
Actuarial cost method: Projected Unit Credit
Actuarial assumptions:
Interest rate: 7% per year
Compensation increases: 5% per year
Preretirement deaths and terminations: None
Probability of retirement (assumed to occur at beginning of year):
Before 1994: 100% at age 65
After 1993: 50% at age 62, 0% at ages 63 and 64,
and 100% at age 65
Valuation data for sole participant:

Date of birth	1/1/44
Date of hire	1/1/74
1994 valuation compensation	$50,000

Selected annuity values: $\ddot{a}_{62}^{(12)} = 9.394 \quad \ddot{a}_{65}^{(12)} = 8.736$

What is the change in the accrued liability as of 1/1/94 due to the
change in the retirement age assumption?

5-25   Normal retirement benefit: $20 per month for each year of service
        Postponed retirement benefit: Actuarial equivalent of normal retire-
            ment benefit, based on postretirement valuation assumptions
        Preretirement death benefit: None
        Actuarial cost method: Unit Credit
        Actuarial assumptions:
            Interest rate: 7% per year
            Preretirement deaths and terminations: None
        Valuation data for sole participant (active as of 1/1/94):
            Date of birth   1/1/29
            Date of hire   1/1/70
        Selected probabilities of retirement (assumed to occur at beginning of
            year) and commutation functions based on postretirement valua-
            tion assumptions:

x	$q_x^{(r)}$	D_x	$N_x^{(12)}$
65	.60	94	825
66	.80	86	734
67	1.00	79	651

        What is the accrued liability as of 1/1/94?

5.5 Withdrawal Gains

5-26   Consider the following data:

Participants at 1/1/94	Liability at 12/31/94	$q_x^{(w)}$	$^i WBEN$	Status at 12/31/94
Adams	1000	.16	0	Withdrawal
Brown	2000	.14	500	Active
Cook	3000	.12	2500	Withdrawal
Douglas	4000	.10	4000	Active

What is the 1994 gain from withdrawals?

5-27   Plan effective date: 1/1/80
        Normal retirement benefit: $20 per month for each year of service
        Vesting eligibility: 100% after one year of service
        Actuarial cost method: Individual Entry Age Normal
        Actuarial assumptions:
             Interest rate: 7% per year
             Preretirement deaths and terminations: None
             Retirement age: 65
        Valuation data for participant Smith:
             Date of birth   1/1/40
             Date of hire   1/1/88
             Date of termination   12/31/92
        Selected annuity value: $\ddot{a}_{65}^{(12)} = 8.74$

        What is the experience gain or loss for 1992 due to Smith's
        termination?

5-28   Vesting: 100% after 5 years of service
        Actuarial cost method: Individual Entry Age Normal (level percent
             of compensation)
        Actuarial assumptions:
             Interest rate: 7% per year
             Compensation increases: 4% per year
             Preretirement deaths: None
             Retirement age: 65
        Valuation data for only participants (both active as of 1/1/94):

	Smith	Brown
Date of Birth	1/1/59	1/1/56
Date of Hire	1/1/94	1/1/91

        Normal cost for 1994 as of 1/1/94:
             For Smith: $17,000
             For Brown: 16,000
        Selected probabilities of termination:

x	$q_x^{(w)}$
35	.25
36	.20
37	.15
38	.10
39	.05

        What is the accrued liability as of 1/1/94?

5-29   Normal retirement benefit: $20 per month for each year of service
       Termination benefit: Accrued benefit payable at normal retirement age
       Vesting: Full and immediate
       Preretirement death benefit: None
       Actuarial cost method: Unit Credit
       Actuarial assumptions:
           Interest rate: 7% per year
           Pretermination deaths: None
           Post-termination deaths: Included in commutation functions below
           Preretirement terminations: 10% at age 50 only (assumed to occur
               at beginning of year)
           Retirement age: 65
       Valuation data for sole participant (active as of 1/1/94):
           Date of birth   1/1/54
           Date of hire   1/1/84
       Selected commutation functions using post-termination assumptions:

x	D_x
30	1262
40	632
50	311
65	94

Selected annuity value: $\ddot{a}_{65}^{(12)} = 8.7$

What is the accrued liability as of 1/1/94?

5.6 Salary Gains

5-30 Normal retirement benefit: 50% of final salary
Actuarial cost method: Aggregate
Actuarial assumptions:
  Interest: 8%
  Salary increases: 6%
  Preretirement deaths and terminations: None
Selected valuation results as of 1/1/93:

Present value of benefits for active participants	$950,000
Present value of benefits for inactive participants	0
Actuarial value of assets	500,000
Annual salaries (payable at BOY)	1,000,000
Normal cost as of 1/1	60,000

Plan experience during 1993:
  The rate of return on assets was 10%
  Salaries increased 5%
  The normal cost for 1993 was paid on 1/2/93
  No deaths, terminations, retirements, or new entrants
  No active participants within two years of assumed retirement age

What is the normal cost rate (as a percent of salaries) as of 1/1/94?

5-31 Plan effective date: 1/1/93
Normal retirement benefit: 40% of final salary
Actuarial cost method: Frozen Initial Liability
Actuarial assumptions:
  Interest: 7%
  Salary increases: 5%
  Preretirement deaths and terminations: None
  Retirement age: 65
The oldest participant on 1/1/93 was age 63.
Valuation results as of 1/1/93:

Accrued liability	$ 550,000
Present value of future salaries	4,011,000
Normal cost as of 1/1	80,000
Salaries, payable at 1/1/93	400,000

Contribution for 1993 paid on 12/31/93: $164,000
As of 1/1/94 all participants received a 10% salary increase. There
  were no deaths, terminations or new entrants in 1993.

What is the normal cost as of 1/1/94?

5-32 Effective date: 1/1/94
      Normal retirement benefit: 50% of final salary
      Normal retirement age: 60
      Actuarial cost method: Aggregate
      Actuarial assumptions:
            Interest: 6%
            Salary increases: 3%
            Retirement age: 60
      Selected annuity value: $\ddot{a}_{60}^{(12)} = 12.5$
      Data for sole participant:

Valuation Date	Age	Annual Salary	Projected Annual Benefit	$\dfrac{{}^sN_x - {}^sN_{60}}{{}^sD_x}$	$\dfrac{D_{60}}{D_x}$
1/1/94	35	50,000	50,820	17.935	.233
1/1/95	36	60,000	59,208	17.445	.247

Actuarial value of assets as of 1/1/95: $9000

What is the increase in normal cost as of 1/1/95 resulting from the salary increase in excess of that assumed?

5.7 Mortality Gains

5-33 Normal retirement benefit: 2.5% of final salary per year of service
      Preretirement death benefit: None
      Actuarial cost method: Projected Unit Credit
      Actuarial assumptions:
            Interest rate: 6%
            Compensation increases: 5%
            Preretirement terminations other than deaths: None
            Retirement age: 65
      Data for sole participant:
            Date of birth   1/1/49
            Date of hire   1/1/74
            1993 compensation $100,000
      After the valuation was done, it was discovered that the assumed
      mortality rate at age 45 was incorrectly coded as $q_{45} = .034$;
      the correct value is $q_{45} = .0034$. Another valuation was done
      to correct this error.
      Original actuarial liability as of 1/1/94: $300,000

What is the correct actuarial liability as of 1/1/94?

5-34　Data for all retirees as of 1/1/93:

	Smith	Brown
Age	60	70
Annual benefit	$54,000	$24,000
Status as of 12/31/93	Alive	Deceased

Benefits are payable as of 1/1 of each year.
All deaths in a year occur at the end of the year.
Selected probabilities of death and annuity values:

x	q_x	$\ddot{a}_x$
60	.020	9.52
61	.022	9.30
70	.040	7.28
71	.044	7.00

What is the mortality gain for 1993 due to the two retirees?

5-35　Normal retirement benefit:　$10 monthly per year of service
　　　Actuarial cost method:　Unit Credit
　　　Assumed interest rate:　6%
　　　The normal cost for a year is due at the beginning of the year.
　　　Participant data on 1/1/93:　100 participants, each attained age 40,
　　　　　each hired at age 30
　　　Selected probabilities and annuity values:

Age x	$q_x^{(d)}$	$q_x^{(w)}$	$_{65-x}|\ddot{a}_{65}^{(12)}$
39	.008	.000	2.0000
40	.010	.000	2.1371
41	.012	.000	2.2882

Three participants die between the 1/1/93 and 1/1/94 valuations.

What is the mortality gain for the plan during 1993?

5-36 Data for sole participant as of 1/1/94:
        Date of birth: 1/1/24
        Spouse's date of birth: 1/1/24
        Status: Retired
        Benefit: $6000 per year, payable annually on 1/1 for life, with
            100% continued to surviving spouse
    Selected values:

$$q_{70} = .05 \quad \ddot{a}_{70} = 8.80 \quad \ddot{a}_{71} = 8.46 \quad \ddot{a}_{70:70} = 6.11 \quad \ddot{a}_{71:71} = 5.83$$

The participant and the spouse are both alive on 1/1/95.

What is the mortality loss for 1994?

5-37 A pension benefit of $10,000 per year is payable annually for the
lifetime of a retired participant age x, with $5000 per year
payable annually to continue for the lifetime of the contingent
annuitant age y upon the death of the participant.
Assumed interest rate: 6%
Selected values:

$$
\begin{array}{llll}
\ddot{a}_x = 9.00 & \ddot{a}_{x+1} = 8.60 & \\
\ddot{a}_y = 10.00 & \ddot{a}_{y+1} = 9.80 & p_x = .9860 \\
\ddot{a}_{xy} = 8.00 & \ddot{a}_{x+1:y+1} = 7.73 & p_y = .9735
\end{array}
$$

What is the net mortality gain for the year if the contingent annuitant
dies?

5-38 Normal retirement benefit: $1000 each 1/1 until the retiree dies, then $500 to the surviving spouse (if any) each 1/1 thereafter for life
Participant data as of 1/1/93: 100 married retirees, all age 65 with spouses age 62
Deaths during 1993:
3 retirees die, leaving their spouses alive
2 spouses die, leaving the retirees alive
There were no new retirees during 1993.
Selected values:

$\ddot{a}_{62} = 9.230$ $\quad \ddot{a}_{63} = 9.024 \quad$ $\ddot{a}_{65} = 8.630 \quad$ $\ddot{a}_{66} = 8.409$
$\ddot{a}_{62:65} = 7.440 \quad \ddot{a}_{63:66} = 7.205 \quad$ $p_{62} = .985 \quad p_{65} = .980$

What is the mortality gain for 1993?

5-39 Further to Example 5.32, what are the other possibilities for actual deaths, and what is the total gain?

5-40 Normal retirement benefit: $10,000 per year, payable on 1/1
Form of payment: Upon the death of the retiree, a reduced payment of $P will be payable on 1/1 of each subsequent year to the surviving spouse.
Assumed interest rate: 7% per year
Valuation data for participant Smith:

Date of birth	1/1/23
Date of retirement	1/1/88
Spouse's date of birth	1/1/26

If Smith survives to 1/1/94, but Smith's spouse dies in 1993, the experience gain for 1993 due to mortality will be $11,300.

If Smith dies in 1993, but Smith's spouse survives to 1/1/94, the experience gain for 1993 due to mortality will be $K.

Selected annuity values:

$$\ddot{a}_{67} = 8.287 \qquad \ddot{a}_{68} = 8.061 \qquad \ddot{a}_{70} = 7.603$$

$$\ddot{a}_{71} = 7.368 \qquad \ddot{a}_{667:70} = 6.056$$

What is $K?

Chapter 6

Changes and Ancillary Benefits

Chapter 5 dealt with experience gains and losses, which arise when actual investment income, mortality, retirements, disabilities, withdrawals, and salary increases differ from the actuarial assumptions. This chapter discusses **changes in plan parameters**, including changes in the actuarial cost method, pension benefits, retirement age, and actuarial assumptions; these changes often mean a supplemental liability or an increase in the actuarial liability, or a decrease in the surplus and/or an increase in the normal cost. Assumptions must be reviewed periodically and changed if they are no longer appropriate. Chapter 6 also discusses **ancillary benefits** such as death, withdrawal, and disability benefits, and issues involving employee contributions.

6.1 Change in Cost Method

The following two examples, as well as Exercises 6-1 and 6-2, illustrate the difference in the normal cost when different actuarial cost methods are used with the same plan.

| EXAMPLE 6.1 |

Plan effective date: 1/1/94

1994 actuarial cost method: Entry Age Normal

1995 valuations (both as of 1/1/95):
  (a) Using Entry Age Normal (as used in the 1994 valuation)
  (b) Using Frozen Initial Liability (proceeding from the 1994 Entry Age Normal valuation)

Excerpts from the two 1995 valuations:

	(a) Entry Age Normal	(b) Frozen Initial Liability
Number of participants	1	1
Assets		$ 6,000
Unfunded past service liability		8,000
Present value of future benefits		30,000
Normal cost		2,400
Present value of future payroll		200,000
Actuarial experience loss in 1994	$5,000	

What is the 1995 normal cost under valuation (a), expressed as a percent of payroll?

SOLUTION Since any gain or loss is amortized through the unfunded actuarial liability under any individual method, the loss in 1994 will be included in the unfunded liability for 1995. Under EAN, we equate $pvNC$ to $pvB - AL$. Recognizing that the normal cost is $100U\%$ of salary, we find

$$U = \frac{30,000 - 8,000 - 6,000 - 5,000}{200,000},$$

which is 5.5% of payroll.   □

Note that the gross future liability is 30,000 which is partly due to the loss in 1994 (5000); part of this will be covered by the assets from 1994 (6000), part will be covered by the present value of future supplemental costs (8000), and the balance will be covered by the present value of future normal costs (5.5% of 200,000 or 11,000).

EXAMPLE 6.2

Actuarial cost method: Frozen Initial Liability
Valuation results as of 1/1/94:

Normal cost as of 1/1/94	$ 11,250
Unfunded past service liability	150,000
Actuarial value of assets	250,000
Market value of assets	300,000
Annual payroll of participants	225,000
Present value of future payroll of participants	2,500,000

If the actuarial cost method is changed to Aggregate, what is the normal cost for 1994 as of 1/1/94?

SOLUTION

Recall that there is no unfunded actuarial liability under the Aggregate method. If the actuarial cost method is changed from FIL to Aggregate, the normal cost increases so as to fund the unfunded liability over the future years. Therefore, under the Aggregate cost method, we have

$$NC = 11,250 + 150,000\,\ddot{a}^s$$

$$= 11,250 + 150,000\left(\frac{225,000}{2,500,000}\right) = \$24,750. \qquad \square$$

6.2 Change in Retirement Benefit

For individual cost methods, additional liabilities due to plan amendments which increase the normal retirement benefit are usually recognized and amortized through the supplemental liability; the normal cost will also increase. For aggregate cost methods, plan amendments are recognized in the form of a higher normal cost and, in some cases, a higher supplemental cost.

EXAMPLE 6.3

Retirement benefit:
    Before 1994: 1.00% of final salary for each year of service
    After 1993: 1.25% of final average salary per year of service
Actuarial cost method: Individual Entry Age Normal
1/1/94 valuation results for sole participant, before amendment:

Present value of future benefits	$ 4,100
Unfunded liability	800
Value of assets	1,000
Present value of future compensation	46,000
1994 compensation	4,000
Present value of accrued benefits	1,700

Find the normal cost for 1994 as of 1/1/94 after the amendment.

| SOLUTION | We need to calculate the normal cost using the original retirement benefit, which we can do at the valuation date. Starting with

$$AL \ = \ pvB - pvNC,$$

and substituting values we have

$$1000 + 800 \ = \ 4100 - NC \cdot \ddot{a}^s,$$

from which we find

$$NC \ = \ 2300 \left(\frac{4000}{46{,}000} \right) \ = \ 200.$$

Then the amended normal cost is

$$200 \left(\frac{.0125}{.01} \right) \ = \ \$250. \qquad \square$$

Note that in addition to the increase in normal cost, there will be a supplemental liability and an amortization thereof.

| EXAMPLE 6.4 |
Normal retirement benefit:
    Before 1994: $10 per month for each year of service
    After 1993: $12 per month for each year of service
Actuarial cost method: Individual Entry Age Normal
Actuarial assumptions:
    Interest rate: 7% per year
    Compensation increases: None
    Preretirement deaths and terminations: None
    Retirement age: 65
Data and valuation results for only participants as of 1/1/94:

	Smith	Brown
Date of birth	1/1/64	1/1/54
Date of hire	1/1/89	1/1/89
Status	Active	Active
Normal cost per 1000 of projected annual benefit	42.13	89.04

What is the increase in the actuarial liability as of 1/1/94 due to the amendment ?

SOLUTION We need to calculate the liability before the amendment. Since both participants have 5 years of past service, the retrospective liability at 1/1/94 is

$$AL = NC \cdot \ddot{s}_{\overline{5}|}.$$

Since the projected annual benefit is $(10)(12)(40) = 4800$ for Smith and $(10)(12)(30) = 3600$ for Brown, the total normal cost is

$$NC = 42.13(4.800) + 89.04(3.600) = 522.768,$$

and the total actuarial liability is

$$AL = 522.768(6.1532907) = 3217.$$

Since the normal retirement benefit increases by 20%, the liability also increases by 20%, so we have

$$\Delta AL = .20(3217) = \$643. \qquad \square$$

EXAMPLE 6.5
Plan effective date: 1/1/84
Normal retirement benefit:
  Effective 1/1/84: $100 per month
  Effective 1/1/94: $150 per month
Actuarial cost method: Individual Level Premium
Assumed retirement age: 65
Preretirement terminations other than by death: None
Data for sole participant:
  Date of birth   1/1/49
  Date of hire   1/1/84
Selected commutation functions:

x	D_x	N_x
35	921	12,791
45	460	5,909
65	99	904

What is the difference between the normal cost as of 1/1/94 under ILP and the normal cost as of 1/1/94 under EAN?

$\boxed{\text{SOLUTION}}$ Under ILP, the change in the normal cost due to the plan amendment is given by

$$\Delta NC\left(\frac{N_{45} - N_{65}}{D_{45}}\right) = \Delta B_{65} \frac{D_{65}}{D_{45}} \ddot{a}_{65}^{(12)},$$

leading to

$$\Delta NC = (50)(12)\left(\frac{99}{5909 - 904}\right)\left(\frac{904}{99} - \frac{11}{24}\right) = 102.93.$$

The original normal cost is

$$NC = (100)(12)\left(\frac{99}{12,791 - 904}\right)(8.673) = 86.68,$$

so the normal cost after the plan amendment is

$$NC^{ILP} = 86.68 + 102.93 = 189.61.$$

Under EAN, we simply recalculate the normal cost at the plan effective date using the new retirement benefit. Thus we have

$$NC\left(\frac{N_{35} - N_{65}}{D_{35}}\right) = (150)(12)\left(\frac{D_{65}}{D_{35}}\right)(8.673)$$

which solves for

$$NC^{EAN} = 130.02.$$

Then the difference in normal cost is

$$189.61 - 130.02 = \$59.59. \qquad \qquad \square$$

$\boxed{\textbf{EXAMPLE 6.6}}$

Normal retirement benefit:
 Before 1994: $10 per month for each year of service
 After 1993: $15 per month for each year of service
Actuarial cost method: Attained Age Normal
Actuarial assumptions:
 Interest rate: 6%
 Preretirement terminations other than deaths: None
 Retirement age: 65
 Selected annuity value: $\ddot{a}_{65}^{(12)} = 9.345$

Participant data as of 1/1/94:

	Smith	**Brown**	**Green**
Date of birth	1/1/64	1/1/54	1/1/44
Date of hire	1/1/94	1/1/84	1/1/74

Selected commutation functions:

x	D_x	N_x
30	16,721	266,509
40	9,205	136,705
50	4,968	65,680
65	1,738	17,040

What is the increase in the unfunded liability as of 1/1/94 due to the change in the normal retirement benefit?

$\boxed{\textbf{SOLUTION}}$ The benefit has increased by $5 per month, so the benefit based on past service must be increased. The benefit change for Smith is 0, the benefit change for Brown is $(5)(12)(10) = 600$, and the benefit change for Green is $(5)(12)(20) = 1200$. The present value of future benefits has increased, so the increase in unfunded liability (under the Unit Credit cost method) is

$$600\ddot{a}_{65}^{(12)}\frac{D_{65}}{D_{40}} + 1200\ddot{a}_{65}^{(12)}\frac{D_{65}}{D_{50}} = 9.345(1738)\left(\frac{600}{9205} + \frac{1200}{4968}\right) = \$4982.$$

$\square$

$\boxed{\textbf{EXAMPLE 6.7}}$
Plan effective date: 1/1/93
Normal retirement benefit: $12 per month for each year of service
Actuarial cost method: Unit Credit
Actuarial assumptions:
　　Interest: 6%
　　Preretirement deaths and terminations: None
　　Retirement age: 65
　　Selected annuity value: $\ddot{a}_{65}^{(12)} = 10$
Data for sole participant:
　　Date of birth　　1/1/48
　　Data of hire　　1/1/78

Contribution for 1993 paid at 1/1/93: $1200

Effective 1/1/94 the plan is amended to increase the normal retirement
benefit to $15 per month for each year of service. The unfunded
actuarial liability as of 1/1/94 based on the amended plan is $8100.

Find the experience gain or loss for 1993 attributable to interest.

SOLUTION   Let 1/1/93 be time 0. Recall that investment gain is given
by

$$^{inv}G \ = \ ^{act}I - {}^{exp}I.$$

We know that the value of the fund at plan inception is zero. Since $1200
is contributed at time 0, the expected interest earned during 1993 is

$$^{exp}I \ = \ 1200(.06) \ = \ 72.00.$$

Based on the amended plan we have

$$AL_1 \ = \ (15)(12)(16)(1.06)^{-19}(10) \ = \ 9518.77,$$

from which we find

$$F_1 \ = \ AL_1 - UAL_1 \ = \ 9518.77 - 8100 \ = \ 1418.77.$$

The actual interest earned on the fund is

$$^{act}I \ = \ 1418.77 - 1200 \ = \ 218.77,$$

so the interest gain is

$$^{inv}G_1 \ = \ 218.77 - 72.00 \ = \ \$146.77. \qquad \square$$

EXAMPLE 6.8

Normal retirement benefit: $15 per month per year of service
Actuarial cost method: Unit Credit
Assumed interest rate: 8%
Valuation results as of 1/1/94:

Normal cost as of 1/1	$ 500,000
Actuarial liability	10,000,000
Actuarial value of assets	2,000,000

Contribution for 1994 paid on 12/31/94: $1,000,000
Benefit payments for 1994 paid on 7/1/94: $100,000
Effective 1/1/95, the plan was amended to increase benefits from $15 to
$18 per month per year of service for all participants.
Actuarial liability as of 1/1/95: $12,000,000
There are no vested terminated participants.
There was no experience gain or loss due to investment in 1994.

What is the amount of the experience gain for 1994?

$\boxed{\textbf{SOLUTION}}$ Let 1/1/94 be time 0. The total experience gain is given by

$$^{\text{tot}}G_1 \;=\; ^{\text{exp}}UAL_1 - {}^{\text{act}}UAL_1,$$

where

$$^{\text{act}}UAL_1 \;=\; AL_1 - F_1$$

and

$$
\begin{aligned}
^{\text{exp}}UAL_1 &= (UAL_0 + NC_0)(1+i) - {}^iC \\
&= (10{,}000{,}000 - 2{,}000{,}000 + 500{,}000)(1.08) - 1{,}000{,}000 \\
&= 8{,}180{,}000,
\end{aligned}
$$

since the contribution for 1994 does not earn any interest during 1994. At
time 1, the benefit changes from $15 to $18 per month per year of service,
so we have

$$AL_1 \;=\; 12{,}000{,}000 \left(\frac{15}{18}\right) \;=\; 10{,}000{,}000.$$

The actual value of the fund at time 1 is

$$2{,}000{,}000(1.08) + 1{,}000{,}000 - 100{,}000(1.04) \;=\; 3{,}056{,}000.$$

Then the total experience gain for 1994 is

$$^{\text{tot}}G_1 \;=\; 8{,}180{,}000 - (10{,}000{,}000 - 3{,}056{,}000) \;=\; \$1{,}236{,}000. \quad \square$$

$\boxed{\textbf{EXAMPLE 6.9}}$
Normal retirement benefit: $1000 per year, payable for life
Assumed interest rate: 7%
Preretirement terminations other than by death: None
Assumed retirement age: 65
The sole participant is age 55 as of 1/1/94.

Selected values and commutation functions:

i	$\ddot{a}_{65}$	D_{55}	D_{65}
3%	11.70	1778	1149
4	10.82	1045	613
5	10.04	617	329
6	9.38	313	178
7	8.74	219	96

Effective 1/1/94 the plan is amended to provide an automatic postretirement adjustment which will increase each annual payment by 3% of the preceding payment.

What is the increase in the present value of future benefits as of 1/1/94 due to the amendment?

SOLUTION Before the amendment, the present value of future benefits, using 7% interest, is

$$pvB \; = \; 1000\frac{D_{65}}{D_{55}}\ddot{a}_{65} \; = \; 1000\left(\frac{96}{219}\right)(8.74) \; = \; 3831.23.$$

After the amendment we have

$$pvB' \; = \; 1000v^{10}\,_{10}p_{55} + 1000(1.03)\,v^{11}\,_{11}p_{55} + 1000(1.03)^2 v^{12}\,_{12}p_{55} + \cdots$$

$$= \; 1000v^{10}\,_{10}p_{55}\left[1 + \left(\frac{1.03}{1.07}\right)p_{65} + \left(\frac{1.03}{1.07}\right)^2\,_2p_{65} + \cdots\right]$$

$$= \; 1000\frac{D_{65}}{D_{55}}\left[\ddot{a}'_{65}\right],$$

where the commutation functions are based on 7% interest and $\ddot{a}'_{65}$ is based on $j = \left(\frac{1.03}{1.07}\right)^{-1} - 1 = 3.883\%$. Using linear interpolation we find

$$\ddot{a}'_{65} \; = \; .883(10.82) + (1-.883)(11.70) \; = \; 10.923.$$

Therefore

$$pvB' \; = \; 1000\left(\frac{96}{219}\right)(10.923) \; = \; 4788.16,$$

and the increase in the present value of future benefits due to the amendment is

$$\Delta pvB \ = \ 4788.16 - 3831.23 \ = \ \$956.93. \qquad \square$$

| EXAMPLE 6.10 |

Plan effective date: 1/1/88
Normal retirement benefit for each year of service:
    Before 1994: $10 per month
    After 1993: $15 per month
Preretirement death benefit: None
Actuarial cost method: Frozen Initial Liability
Actuarial assumptions:
    Interest rate: 7% per year
    Preretirement terminations other than deaths: None
    Retirement age: 65
    Selected annuity value: $\ddot{a}_{65}^{(12)} = 8.74$
Data for sole participant:
    Date of birth   1/1/39
    Date of hire   1/1/89
    Status as of 1/1/94   Active
Selected valuation results as of 1/1/94, before amendment:
    Present value of benefits $6942
    Unfunded liability   1800
    Value of assets   1000
Selected commutation functions:

x	D_x	N_x
50	94,002	1,135,407
55	64,742	727,747
65	28,570	262,659

Find the increase in normal cost for 1994 due to the amendment.

| SOLUTION | At age 55 before the amendment, we have

$$NC\left(\frac{N_{55} - N_{65}}{D_{55}}\right) = pvB - UAL - F.$$

Substituting values we have

$$NC\left(\frac{727,747 - 262,659}{64,742}\right) = 6942 - 1800 - 1000,$$

from which we find

$$NC = 576.58.$$

Like all aggregate methods, FIL is a spread gain method which recognizes gains and losses in the normal cost. At plan inception, the initial liability is the actuarial liability under EAN. At the plan amendment date, the increase in the benefit increases the unfunded liability, and we calculate thisincrease by calculating the increase in the liability under EAN. Under EAN we have

$$NC_{50}\left(\frac{1,135,407 - 262,659}{94,002}\right) = (5)(12)(15)(8.74)\left(\frac{28,570}{94,002}\right),$$

from which we find

$$NC_{50} = 257.50.$$

Next we find

$$AL_{55} = (5)(12)(15)(8.74)\left(\frac{28,570}{64,742}\right) - 257.50\ddot{a}_{55:\overline{10|}} = 1621.$$

Returning to FIL at age 55 after the amendment, we have

$$NC \cdot \ddot{a}_{55:\overline{10|}} = 6942\left(\frac{15}{10}\right) - (1800 + 1621) - 1000,$$

from which we find

$$NC = 834.08.$$

Then the increase in normal cost is

$$834 - 577 = \$257. \qquad \square$$

Note that the date of hire in this example is after the effective date; this suggests that a *former* participant was hired before the effective date and was responsible for the initial unfunded liability.

EXAMPLE 6.11

Normal retirement benefit:
    Before 1/1/94: 40% of final year's salary
    Effective 1/1/94: 50% of final year's salary
Actuarial cost method: Frozen Initial Liability
Selected valuation results, as of 1/1/94, based on the 40% benefit:
    Present value of future benefits:
        For active participants $ 1,200,000
        For retired and terminated participants   300,000
    Unfunded liability   300,000
    Actuarial value of assets   500,000
    Present value of future salaries   21,000,000
    Annual salaries   4,000,000
    Entry Age Normal actuarial liability   700,000

What is the increase in the normal cost for 1994 as of 1/1/94 due to the plan amendment?

SOLUTION This example is similar to Example 6.10. Under FIL,

$$TNC \cdot \frac{\sum pvS}{\sum S} = pvB - UAL - F.$$

Substituting values we have

$$TNC \cdot \frac{21,000,000}{4,000,000} = (1,200,000+300,000) - 300,000 - 500,000$$

which solves for $TNC = 133,333$. After the increase in retirement benefit we have

$$TNC' \cdot \frac{21,000,000}{4,000,000} = pvB' - (UAL+\Delta) - F,$$

where Δ is the increase in the unfunded liability as well as the increase in the EAN actuarial liability. Before the increase, the value of AL^{EAN} is 700,000 (400,000 for actives and 300,000 for retireds), and after the increase it is $400,000 \times \frac{50}{40} + 300,000 = 800,000$. Then the value of Δ is 100,000 and

$$TNC' \cdot \frac{21,000,000}{4,000,000} = (1,200,000 \times \frac{50}{40} + 300,000)$$

$$- (300,000+100,000) - 500,000.$$

Finally we have

$$\Delta NC \cdot \frac{21}{4} = 1,200,000 \times .25 - 100,000$$

which solves for

$$\Delta NC = \$38,095. \qquad \qquad \square$$

| EXAMPLE 6.12 |

Normal retirement benefit:

Before 1994: $50 per month for each year of service

After 1993: $54 per month for each year of service, applicable to active and inactive participants

Actuarial cost method: Attained Age Normal with FIL

Actuarial assumptions:

Interest rate: 6%

Preretirement deaths and terminations: None

Retirement age: 65

Selected valuation results:

	1/1/93 ($50 benefit)	1/1/94 ($50 benefit)
Present value of future benefits:		
Active participants	$ 840,000	$ 550,000
Inactive participants	250,000	570,000
Unfunded liability	300,000	
Actuarial value of assets	250,000	345,000
Present value of future compensation	2,340,000	2,090,000
Annual compensation	360,000	220,000
Entry Age actuarial liability for actives	690,000	410,000
Unit Credit actuarial liability for actives	600,000	320,000
Present value of years of future service	100	96
Number of actives (all under age 64)	10	8

Contribution for 1993: $88,000 paid on 12/31/93

What is the normal cost for 1994 as of 1/1/94?

$\boxed{\textbf{SOLUTION}}$ Let 1/1/93 be time 0. To calculate the new normal cost at time 1, we must first calculate the increase in the unfunded liability due to the increase in the normal retirement benefit. Since AAN (FIL) calculates its initial liability under Unit Credit, and since the benefit increase applies to all active and inactive participants, then

$$\Delta UAL = (320{,}000+570{,}000)\left(\frac{54-50}{50}\right) = 71{,}200.$$

Next we must calculate UAL_1 under the original assumptions. The general relationship $UAL_1 = (UAL_0+NC_0)(1+i) - {}^iC$ involves NC_0 under the original assumptions, so we must first calculate it under AAN (FIL). We have

$$pvNC_0 = pvB - UAL_0 - F_0,$$

or

$$NC_0(100) = (840{,}000+250{,}000) - 300{,}000 - 250{,}000,$$

which solves for

$$NC_0 = 54{,}000.$$

Now we can find

$$UAL_1 = (300{,}000+54{,}000)(1.06) - 88{,}000 = 287{,}240.$$

Finally the normal cost at time 1 is

$$NC_1 = \frac{8}{96}\left[(550{,}000+570{,}000)\left(\frac{54}{50}\right) - (287{,}240+71{,}200)-345{,}000\right]$$
$$= \$42{,}180. \qquad \qquad \square$$

Note that a slightly different answer could be found by replacing number of participants by dollars of compensation. The level dollar normal cost is used because the benefit is fixed.

$\boxed{\textbf{EXAMPLE 6.13}}$
Normal retirement benefit: \$400 per month
Normal form of benefit payment:
      Retirements before 1994: Life annuity
      Retirements after 1993: Life annuity with 10 years certain
Actuarial cost method: Entry Age Normal
Preretirement deaths or terminations: None

Selected annuity value: $\ddot{a}_{\overline{10|}}^{(12)} = 7.287$

Valuation results on 1/1/94 based on the life annuity normal form:
Present value of future benefits:

Active participants	$1,500,000
Retired participants	500,000
Actuarial value of assets	600,000
Unfunded actuarial liability	800,000
Normal cost as of 1/1	75,000

Selected commutation functions:

x	D_x	$N_x^{(12)}$
65	990	9000
75	350	2400

What is the increase in the unfunded actuarial liability as of 1/1/94 due to the change in the normal form?

$\boxed{\textbf{SOLUTION}}$ Let 1/1/94 be time 0. The liability at time 0 using the original assumptions is

$$AL_0 = UAL_0 + F_0 = 800,000 + 600,000 = 1,400,000.$$

This liability includes both active and retired participants. The liability for the retired participants is 500,000, so for active participants the liability is

$$AL_0 = 1,400,000 - 500,000 = 900,000.$$

We must assume that the plan amendment applies only to the active participants, since we are not given the current ages of the retirees. For the active participants, the liability using the new form of benefit payment can be found from the old liability as

$$AL_0' = 900,000 \left[\frac{\ddot{a}_{\overline{10|}}^{(12)} + {}_{10|}\ddot{a}_{65}^{(12)}}{\ddot{a}_{65}^{(12)}} \right]$$

$$= 900,000 \left[\frac{7.287 + 2400/990}{9000/990} \right] = 961,413.$$

The total new liability is $961,413 + 500,000 = 1,461,413$ and the new unfunded liability is

$$UAL_0' = 1,461,413 - 600,000 = 861,413.$$

Finally the increase in unfunded liability due to the change in the normal form is

$$\Delta UAL_0 = 861,413 - 800,000 = \$61,413. \qquad \square$$

| EXAMPLE 6.14 |

Normal retirement benefit:
 Before 1994: 50% of highest 3-year average compensation
 After 1993: 100% of highest 3-year average compensation
Normal form of payment:
 Retirements before 1994:
  If single, life annuity
  If married, 100% joint and survivor annuity
 Retirements after 1993: Life annuity
Actuarial cost method: Aggregate
Actuarial assumptions:
 Preretirement deaths and terminations: None
 Retirement age: 65
 Selected annuity values: $\ddot{a}_{65}^{(12)} = 10$; $\ddot{a}_{65:65}^{(12)} = 8.2$
Marital characteristics: 85% of participants are married at the time of retirement; spouses are the same age as participants
Valuation results as of 1/1/94, before amendments:

Normal cost as of 1/1	$ 94,000
Present value of future benefits for inactive participants (all became inactive before 1994)	500,000
Actuarial value of assets	730,000
Present value of future compensation	4,850,000
1994 compensation	375,000

Find the normal cost for 1994 as of 1/1/94 after the amendments.

| SOLUTION | The normal cost after the amendments is given by

$$NC\left(\frac{4,850,000}{375,000}\right) = \sum pvB' - 730,000.$$

Using the original assumptions we have

$$94,000 \left(\frac{4,850,000}{375,000} \right) \; = \; \sum pvB - 730,000$$

from which we find

$$\sum pvB \; = \; 1,945,733.$$

The value of $\sum pvB$ can be allocated between the inactive (500,000) and active $(1,945,733 - 500,000 = 1,445,733)$ participants. Suppose the highest 3-year average compensation is A. At each retirement after 1993 we would have

$$AL' \; = \; 1.00 \times A \times 10 \; = \; 10A,$$

and at each retirement before 1994 we would have

$$AL \; = \; .50A(.15)(10) + .50A(.85)(10+10-8.2) \; = \; 5.765A.$$

Then the pvB of active participants should be multiplied by $\frac{10}{5.765}$, producing

$$pvB' \; = \; 1,445,733 \left(\frac{10}{5.765} \right) \; = \; 2,507,776.$$

Finally the amended normal cost is such that

$$NC \left(\frac{4,850,000}{375,000} \right) \; = \; 2,507,776 + 500,000 - 730,000$$

from which we find

$$NC \; = \; \$176,117. \qquad \qquad \square$$

EXAMPLE 6.15

Plan benefits are paid annually, with first payment due at date of retirement. The plan provides an automatic 2% per year postretirement increase to retirees, with the first such increase one year after retirement.

Valuation interest rate: 5%

We wish to express the present value at age 65 for an initial benefit of 1, increasing as described, as a level annuity value $\ddot{a}'_{65}$ at interest rate j.

Find j. If the valuation interest rate and the automatic increase were both increased by 1%, would the annuity value be increased or decreased?

$\boxed{\textbf{SOLUTION}}$ The present value of the increasing benefit is

$$\ddot{a}'_{65} = \sum_{t=0}^{\infty} \left(\frac{1}{1.05}\right)^t {}_tp_x(1.02)^t = \sum_{t=0}^{\infty} \left(\frac{1}{1+j}\right)^t {}_tp_x,$$

where $\dfrac{1}{1+j} = \dfrac{1.02}{1.05}$, so

$$j = \frac{.03}{1.02} = .0294.$$

An increase of 1% would lower j slightly from .0294 to .0291, so the annuity value would increase. Note that the net rate of interest for valuing the annuity approximates a gross interest rate minus an inflation rate. As another example, if expected interest and inflation rates were 14% and 10.5%, respectively, a net valuation rate of 3.5% would not be unreasonable. $\qquad\square$

6.3 Change in Retirement Age

The definition of the normal retirement age in a pension plan may include a specified age and a minimum number of years of service. The actuary may make the assumption that all participants will retire at the normal retirement age, or more than one retirement age may be assumed in which case a probability of retirement must be assigned to each. The following examples show the change in the normal cost when the normal retirement age or assumed retirement age is changed.

$\boxed{\textbf{EXAMPLE 6.16}}$

Plan effective date: 1/1/90
Normal retirement date under original plan: The later of age 65 and 10 years of participation
Normal retirement date under plan as amended on 1/1/95: Age 65
Normal retirement benefit: $500 per month
Actuarial cost method: Aggregate
Normal cost for participants assumed to retire on the valuation date: None
Assumed interest rate: 5%
Assumed retirement: Normal retirement date
Deaths or other terminations prior to assumed retirement: None
Participant data as of 1/1/95: 2 participants age 40 and 65, who commenced participation on 1/1/90

Valuation results as of 1/1/95 before plan amendment:
  Present value of future benefits: $56,893
  Actuarial value of assets: $20,000
Selected annuity values: $12\,\ddot{a}_{65}^{(12)} = 120;\quad 12\,\ddot{a}_{70}^{(12)} = 100$

What is the change in the normal cost for 1995 payable 1/1/95 as a result of the change in normal retirement date?

$\boxed{\text{SOLUTION}}$ The normal cost under the Aggregate method is given by

$$NC = \frac{pvB - F}{\sum pvS} \sum S.$$

We are given pvB under the old assumptions, but we can also calculate it as

$$pvB = 500(120)(1.05)^{-25} + 500(100)(1.05)^{-5} = 56,893.$$

Let the annual salary for each participant be $1. Then $\Sigma S = n = 2$, and

$$pvS = 1 \cdot \ddot{a}_{\overline{25}|} + 1 \cdot \ddot{a}_{\overline{5}|} = 14.799 + 4.546 = 19.345.$$

The total normal cost under the old assumptions is

$$NC = \frac{56,893 - 20,000}{19.345} (2) = 3814,$$

and the total normal cost under the new assumptions is

$$NC' = \frac{500(120)(1.05)^{-25} + 500(120) - 20,000}{14.799} (1) = 3900.$$

The increase in normal cost due to the amendment is

$$3900 - 3814 = \$86. \qquad \square$$

$\boxed{\textbf{EXAMPLE 6.17}}$
Normal retirement benefit: $10 per month for each year of service
Actuarial cost method: Frozen Initial Liability
Actuarial assumptions:
  Interest: 6%
  Preretirement deaths and terminations: None
  Retirement age: Normal retirement age

Date of birth of sole participant: 1/1/44

The plan is amended effective 1/1/94 to change the normal retirement age from 65 to 62, and to increase the benefit rate for all years of service from $10 to $12.

Valuation results as of 1/1/94, based on $10 benefit rate:

	Assumed Retirement Age	
	65	62
Present value of future benefits	$15,000	$18,400
Unfunded liability	6,150	—
Actuarial value of assets	5,000	5,000
Actuarial liability under EAN	13,100	16,350

What is the normal cost for 1994 as of 1/1/94?

$\boxed{\text{SOLUTION}}$ Under FIL,

$$NC \cdot \ddot{a}_{\overline{n}|} = pvB - UAL - F.$$

After the two amendments,

$$NC \cdot \ddot{a}_{\overline{12}|} = 18,400 \times \frac{12}{10} - (UAL + \Delta) - F,$$

where

$$\Delta = \Delta UAL = \Delta AL^{EAN} = 16,350 \times \frac{12}{10} - 13,100 = 6520.$$

Then

$$NC \cdot \ddot{a}_{\overline{12}|} = 18,400 \times \frac{12}{10} - (6150 + 6520) - 5000,$$

from which we find

$$NC = \$496.24. \qquad \square$$

6.4 Change in Interest Assumption

Section 5.2 dealt with the concept of investment gain, defined as the excess of actual investment income over expected investment income.   This section examines the assumed interest rate, considerations in changing the assumed interest rate, and examples of the consequences of changing the rate, including the effect on the early retirement benefit and on the benefits under certain optional forms of payment.
    Investment income includes the following items:

- Bond coupons, bank interest and mortgage interest.
- Amortization of premium or discount, where bonds are purchased above or below face value.
- Dividends on shares of stock.
- Realized capital gains and losses or, where amortized, a portion
  thereof.
- All or part or none of unrealized capital gains and losses; where
  the market values of assets are used, investment income includes
  all of the unrealized capital gains and losses.

The interest assumption is closely related to the first two items above with respect to existing assets and, to a lesser degree, to the other items, and to expected investment income from future assets.   If assets are growing steadily, an approximate relationship between investment income, assets, and the estimated earned rate of interest is

$$ i \approx \frac{I}{\frac{1}{2}(F_0 + F_1 - I)} , $$

where I is the investment income, and F_0 and F_1 are the asset values at BOY and EOY, including any accrued interest.
    Investment income is a broader concept than interest income, and it is often riskier and more volatile.   We seek a risk free "interest assumption" for the future, although an "investment assumption" might also make sense.
    The interest assumption is the most important assumption in pension mathematics.   The following important concepts are associated with the interest assumption.
    Yield Curves.   The yield on long-term bonds is usually higher than on short-term bonds.   Sometimes the yield curve is fairly flat, and in times of uncertainty the yield on short-term bonds can be higher.   The pension business is normally very long term.

Realistically Conservative. Because future interest rates are uncertain, a little conservatism is justified; the more the uncertainty, the more the conservatism. It should also be kept in mind that employers will not be thrilled with several consecutive investment losses. On the other hand, regulators aim at realistic computations, and the accounting profession does not approve of undue conservatism.

Risk and Reward. Corporate bonds usually yield more than government bonds, and the extra yield may more than compensate for the risk of default. The interest assumption is a low-risk concept, and the investment income is normally net of capital losses due to default.

Taxation. In pension funds there is normally very little taxation of investment income; where applicable, the interest assumption and the investment income would be net of investment income taxation.

Matching. If long-term liabilities are matched with long-term assets, the risk will be lessened; on the other hand, a mismatch will generate enormous risk. If short-term assets are purchased this year in anticipation of switching to higher yielding long-term assets next year, the long-term reward may be great.

Change in Yield Rates. If yield rates become 2% higher next year, the market value of long-term bonds will be much lower and there will be a large investment loss. However, if the interest assumption for the liability value is increased by 2% there will be a large gain; if there is good matching, the net gain or loss will be small. If yield rates decrease, the reverse is true.

If the gains and losses are amortized and if yield rates go up and down, the employer contributions as a percentage of payroll may be fairly steady even in the common situation where the interest assumption is not changed.

DISCUSSION QUESTIONS

6-1   The interest assumption and the current yield rate are both 7%. Generate a simple asset scenario to show the investment loss after two years if the yield rate suddenly jumps to 9%.

6-2   Generate a simple scenario to show the possible loss described in the first sentence of the above paragraph entitled Matching.

6-3   Generate a simple scenario to show the possible gain described in the second sentence of the same paragraph.

6-4   Assets are invested in government bonds and valued at market, and
       the yield curve is flat.
       (a) The bond yield is 8% and the interest assumption is 6% for, say,
           five consecutive years.   Would you say that the interest
           assumption of 6% is conservative in relation to the experience
           rate? Would you say that the expected rate is 6% or 8%? Is
           there a gain from interest each year even though the investment
           income is exactly what is expected?
       (b) After the five-year period, the interest assumption is (finally)
           changed to 8% and the (frivolous) bond yields then change to
           7%. Is there a gain or loss in the sixth year? Do you think that
           the contribution is likely to decrease?
       (c) At the beginning of the seventh year there is a reorganization.
           The unfunded liability is eliminated by using the gain in the sixth
           year, the assets are matched to the liabilities by seeking similar
           durations, and the interest assumption is changed to 7%. Will
           the total gain from subsequent interest rate variations be close to
           zero? Why?

EXAMPLE 6.18

Postretirement joint and survivor (J & S) pensions, with full benefits to the
survivor, are the actuarial equivalent of the single life pension otherwise
payable. The amount of the J & S pension is determined by multiplying the
J & S factor by the amount of the single life pension.   Early retirement
pensions are the actuarial equivalent of the accrued (deferred) single life
retirement pension otherwise payable. The amount of the early retirement
pension is determined by multiplying the early retirement factor by the
amount of the accrued normal retirement pension. The normal retirement
age is 65.

Which of the following statements are true concerning the effect of
changing the interest assumption from 6% to 7%?

I.   The early retirement factor, E, is less than 1.00.

II.   The early retirement factor decreases if the interest rate increases.

III.   The J & S factor, $E_{J\&S}$, is less than 1.00.

IV.   The J & S factor for a male participant with a younger wife increases
       if the interest rate increases.

SOLUTION To obtain insight into the above statements, we make a simple model where $q_x^m = q_x^f = .10$, for $x = 63,64,65,66$, and $q_x = 1$ for all other x. Let the annual accrued pension be $1, and let $i = 0$ (for simplicity). This will give an indication but not a proof.

I.   For simplicity, let the early retirement age be 63. The equation of value at age 63 is

$$E(1+.9+.9^2+.9^3) = 1(1+.9)(.9^2),$$

which solves for $E = .4475$, which shows that I is true. A smaller benefit is payable for a longer time.

II.   If the interest rate increases from 0% to 10%, then

$$E\left[1 + 1\left(\frac{.9}{1.10}\right) + 1\left(\frac{.9}{1.10}\right)^2 + 1\left(\frac{.9}{1.10}\right)^3\right] = 1\left(\frac{.9}{1.10}\right)^2 + 1\left(\frac{.9}{1.10}\right)^3,$$

which solves for $E = .40099$, so II is also true. The deferred annuity is discounted more than the annuity-due.

III. Let the male be age 65 and the wife age 63. Using 0% interest, we equate the present value of the J & S option to the present value of the life option as

$$E_{J\&S}\left\{1 + [.9^2+2(.9)(.1)] + .9^2 + .9^3\right\} = 1 + .9,$$

which solves for $E_{J\&S} = .538$, so III is also true. A smaller benefit is payable for a longer time. (As the age of the wife increases, $E_{J\&S}$ increases and approaches 1.)

IV.   Using 10% interest we have

$$E_{J\&S}\left\{1+\frac{1}{1.10}[.9^2+2(.9)(.10)]+\left(\frac{.9}{1.10}\right)^2+\left(\frac{.9}{1.10}\right)^3\right\} = 1 + \left(\frac{.9}{1.10}\right),$$

leading to $E_{J\&S} = .583$. IV is also true, since the factor increased.

□

EXAMPLE 6.19

A pension plan provides reduction factors for early retirement benefits and conversion factors for optional benefits based on actuarial equivalence. The following changes in actuarial assumptions are contemplated:

Interest: From 7% to 8%

Mortality: From GA-71 Table to 1983 GAM Table

Which of the following statements are true?

I.   The change in interest rate alone would decrease benefits at early retirement and increase contingent-annuitant benefits at normal retirement.

II. The change in mortality table alone would decrease benefits at early retirement and increase contingent-annuitant benefits.

III. The change in mortality table alone would increase or decrease benefits payable for a period certain and life, depending on the duration of the certain period.

SOLUTION Let the accrued benefit at age 62, payable at age 65, be B_{62}. Then $pv_{62}B_{62} = B(N_{65}/N_{62})$. Let E be the early retirement reduction factor defined by

$$B_{62} \cdot \frac{N_{65}}{D_{62}} = E \cdot B_{62} \cdot \frac{N_{62}}{D_{62}} \; .$$

This equation solves for

$$E = \frac{N_{65}}{N_{62}} = \frac{N_{63}}{N_{62}} \cdot \frac{N_{64}}{N_{63}} \cdot \frac{N_{65}}{N_{64}} \; .$$

Note the identity

$$\frac{N_{x+1}}{N_x} = \frac{N_{x+1}}{N_{x+1} + D_x} = \frac{1}{1 + a_x^{-1}} \; .$$

Then as i goes up, a_x goes down, a_x^{-1} goes up, $1 + a_x^{-1}$ goes up, $[1 + a_x^{-1}]^{-1}$ goes down, E goes down, and early retirement benefits go down. Next let $pv_x B_x = B_x \cdot a_x = E_{J\&S} \cdot B_x(a_x + a_y - a_{xy})$, where $E_{J\&S}$ is a 100% J & S reduction factor. Then

$$E_{J\&S} = \frac{a_x}{a_x + a_y - a_{xy}} = \left[1 + \frac{a_y - a_{xy}}{a_x}\right]^{-1}.$$

As i goes up, a_x goes down, $\dfrac{a_y - a_{xy}}{a_x}$ goes down, because $a_{y|x}$ is more sensitive to interest than is a_x, $E_{J\&S}$ goes up, and $E_{J\&S} \cdot B_x$ goes *up* for 100% J & S. Therefore I is *true*.

The 1983 q_x values are lower. As the q's go down, a_x goes up, $[1 + a_x^{-1}]^{-1}$ goes up, $E_{J\&S}$ goes *up*, and therefore II is *false*.

(As the q's go down, a_x goes up, $\dfrac{a_y - a_{xy}}{a_x}$ goes down because $a_{y|x}$ is less sensitive to mortality than is a_x, $E_{J\&S}$ goes up, and $E_{J\&S} \cdot B_x$ goes up.) Let

$$pv_x B_x = B_x \cdot a_x = E_{C\&L} \cdot B_x \cdot a_{\overline{x:n|}}$$

so that

$$E_{C\&L} = \frac{a_x}{a_{\overline{x:n|}}} = \frac{a_{\overline{x:n|}} + {}_n|a_x}{a_{\overline{n|}} + {}_n|a_x}.$$

As the q's go down, $E_{C\&L}$ goes up and approaches 1.00. Therefore III is *false*. $\square$

EXAMPLE 6.20

Plan effective date: 1/1/93
Normal retirement benefit: 50% of final year's compensation
Actuarial cost method: Individual Level Premium
Actuarial assumptions:
    Interest rate:
        Before 1994: 8%
        After 1993: 6%
    Compensation increases: None
    Preretirement deaths and terminations: None
    Retirement age: 65

Data for sole participant:

Date of birth	1/1/58
Date of participation	1/1/93
1993 compensation	$24,000
1994 compensation	28,800

Selected values for $\ddot{a}_{65}^{(12)}$:

Before 1994	8.1958
After 1993	9.3452

What is the increase in the actuarial liability as of 1/1/94 due to the change in the actuarial assumptions?

SOLUTION Let 1/1/93 be time 0, 1/1/94 be time 1. At time 0 we have

$$B = .50 \times 24,000 = 12,000$$

so that

$$NC_0 = \frac{pv_0 B}{\ddot{a}_{\overline{30|}}} = (12,000)(8.1958)(1.08)^{-30} \div \ddot{a}_{\overline{30|}} = 803.86$$

and

$$AL_1 = (803.86)(1.08) = 868.$$

Solution (1) (using 6% from effective date):
We have

$$NC_0 = (12,000)(9.3452)(1.06)^{-30} \div \ddot{a}_{\overline{30|}} = 1338.19$$

and

$$AL_1^{(1)} = (1338.19)(1.06) = 1418,$$

so

$$\Delta AL = AL_1^{(1)} - AL_1 = 550.$$

Solution (2) (using 6% from time 1):
We have the old policy (with $AL_1 = 868$) and an *additional* policy with

$$NC_1^{(2)} = \frac{pvB_1^{6\%} - AL_1^{8\%}}{\ddot{a}_{\overline{29|}\,6\%}},$$

and

$$AL_1^{(2)} = 0,$$

since time 1 is duration 0 for the additional policy. Then

$$\Delta AL = \left(AL_1^{(2)} + AL_1\right) - AL_1 = 0.$$

Solution (3) (larger additional policy using 6% and new salary):
This time we have

$$AL_1^{(3)} = 0,$$

so

$$\Delta AL = \left(AL_1^{(3)} + AL_1\right) - AL_1 = 0. \qquad \square$$

Note the interesting nature of Solution (3). (Do you agree with it?) Under ILP, a change at 1/1/94 does not change the liability at 1/1/94. Note also that this example is a *valuation* problem, involving a change in the interest assumption; the other three examples in this section are problems in actuarial equivalence, where a change in the interest assumption is being considered.

6.5 Change in Salary Increase Assumption

Salary (also called compensation) is discussed in Sections 1.3.3, 2.2, 3.2, 5.5, and 8.3. This section discusses the salary scale assumption and its interaction with the interest rate assumption; it also gives examples of the effects of changes in actual and expected salaries.

The **interest rate assumption** will include, explicitly or implicitly, a cost of-living component (often about 3.5% per year) and a real rate of return component (often about 3% per year). The **salary scale assumption** will include, explicitly or implicitly, components for cost of living, productivity, and merit. The cost-of-living component will normally be the same in both assumptions, but sometimes the price index assumption will differ from the wage index assumption. The productivity component is often .5% or zero. The merit component may grade from 10% of salary at the young ages to zero at the old ages, or an average of, say, 1% may be used for all ages. If the plan benefits are integrated with Social Security benefits, the Social Security wage base will be indexed in a consistent manner.

Pension funding is a very long-term business, and a decrease in the interest assumption of 1% often increases the normal cost by about 24%. However, it is important to know whether this decrease in the interest assumption came from the cost-of-living component or from the pure interest component. If the cost-of-living component is 1% less, the salary scale assumption should be 1% less and the 24% increase in the normal cost would be substantially reduced. Furthermore, if pension benefits are indexed, and if the cost-of-living assumption for pensioners is reduced from, say, 3.5% per year to, say, 2.5% per year, there might be very little or no net increase in normal cost. Similarly, a decrease in the interest assumption will mean a substantial increase in the actuarial liability, but there will often be a partial offset due to a change in the salary assumption and there may be a further offset due to reduced pensioner liability. It is also important to note that there will be an increase in the market value of bonds if there is a decrease in interest rates.

The actual real rate of return on stocks and bonds (excluding the cost-of-living component) and the actuary's assumed real rate of return often exhibit little correlation in the recent past, but rational assumptions for the future must nevertheless be made.

EXAMPLE 6.21

Plan effective date: 1/1/1994
Normal retirement benefit: The lesser of 50% of final annual salary, or
    $50,000 per year
Actuarial cost method: Aggregate (level percent of salary)
Actuarial assumptions:
    Interest: 6%
    Retirement age: 65
    Salary increase: 4%
Data for sole participant as of 1/1/94
    Age: 45
    Annual salary: $80,000
This participant will be the sole participant until he retires.
The experience will be exactly the same as the actuarial assumptions.
The actuary considers the following two methods:
    Method 1: Using the 4% salary increase assumption without limit, and imposing a $50,000 limit on annual benefits where necessary
    Method 2: Making the assumption that no covered salary will exceed $100,000

Which of the following statements are true?

I.   The 1994 normal cost will be the same under either method.

II. The 1994 normal cost will be larger under Method 2.

III. If Method 1 is adopted, the percentage increase in the dollar amount of normal cost in each year prior to the participant's retirement will be at least as great as if Method 2 had been adopted.

$\boxed{\textbf{SOLUTION}}$ The normal cost under Method 1 is $\dfrac{50,000 \, _{20|}\ddot{a}_{45}}{\ddot{a}^{s}_{\overline{20|}}}$, where

$$\ddot{a}^{s}_{\overline{20|}} = 1 + \left(\frac{1.04}{1.06}\right) + \cdots + \left(\frac{1.04}{1.06}\right)^{19}.$$

The Method 2 normal cost has a reduced denominator. The Method 1 normal cost is smaller, but it always grows by 4%. The Method 2 normal cost is larger, but it grows by 4% for n years and then it is level. Therefore Statements II and III are correct. $\qquad\square$

$\boxed{\textbf{EXAMPLE 6.22}}$

Normal retirement benefit: 1% of final salary per year of service
Actuarial cost method: Frozen Initial Liability
As of 1/1/94, the assumed interest rate is changed from 5% to 7%, and the salary increase assumption is changed from 3% to 6%. The unfunded liability is adjusted as of 1/1/94 to reflect these changes.
Selected valuation results as of 1/1/94:

	Old Assumptions	New Assumptions
Present value of future benefit	$ 6,148,750	$ 7,146,000
Present value of future salaries	37,250,000	39,100,000
Unfunded liability	750,000	
Actuarial value of assets	3,350,000	3,350,000
Normal cost as of 1/1	132,000	
Entry Age Normal accrued liability	4,175,000	4,875,000

Find the normal cost as of 1/1/94 based on the new assumptions.

SOLUTION   Using the old assumptions we have

$$NC \cdot \frac{pvS}{S} = pvB - F - UAL,$$

or

$$132,000 \left(\frac{37,250,000}{S} \right) = 6,148,750 - 3,350,000 - 750,000$$

from which we find

$$S = 2,400,000.$$

Since the liability under EAN increased when the new assumptions were introduced, the unfunded liability increased to

$$UAL = 750,000 + (4,875,000 - 4,175,000) = 1,450,000.$$

The new normal cost under FIL is

$$NC = \frac{7,146,000 - 3,350,000 - 1,450,000}{39,100,000}(2,400,000) = \$144,000.$$

□

Note that the interest rate, the unfunded liability, and the normal cost all increased; is this normal?

EXAMPLE 6.23

Plan effective date: 1/1/89
Normal retirement benefit:
   Before 1994: 30% of final year's compensation
   After 1993: 40% of final year's compensation
Actuarial cost method: Frozen Initial Liability
Actuarial assumptions:
   Interest rate: 7%
   Compensation increases: 5%
   Preretirement deaths and terminations: None
   Retirement age: 65
Selected valuation results as of 1/1/93:

Normal cost as of 1/1	$ 25,000
Present value of future benefits	700,000
Unfunded liability	275,000
Present value of future compensation	5,675,000
1993 compensation	500,000

Contribution for 1993: $50,000 paid on 12/31/93

As of 1/1/93, there were no inactive participants and no active participants
over age 63. There were no new participants, deaths, terminations, or
retirements during 1993. There are no new participants on 1/1/94.
All participants received a 10% salary increase from 1993 to 1994.
Selected valuation results as of 1/1/94, after amendment:

Value of assets: $250,000

Accrued liability under Entry Age Normal: $550,000

What is the normal cost for 1994 as of 1/1/94?

SOLUTION Let 1/1/93 be time 0. In this question there is a change in
compensation (which increases the value of the benefits), a benefit
improvement (which increases pvB and the unfunded liability), and an asset
gain (which decreases the new normal cost). Under FIL we have

$$NC_1 \cdot \ddot{a}^s = pv_1 B - UAL_1 - F_1.$$

We know that ΣpvS has decreased by the 1993 compensation, that it has
increased with interest, and that the participants received a 10% instead of
a 5% increase in compensation from 1993 to 1994. Thus we have

$$\sum pv_1 S = (5{,}675{,}000 - 500{,}000)(1.07)\left(\frac{1.10}{1.05}\right) = 5{,}801{,}000.$$

The present value of future benefits at time 0 is 700,000. Allowing for
interest, the increase in the benefit, and the increase in compensation,

$$\sum pv_1 B = 700{,}000(1.07)\left(\frac{.40}{.30}\right)\left(\frac{1.10}{1.05}\right) = 1{,}046{,}000.$$

The unfunded actuarial liability at time 1 is given by

$$UAL_1 = (UAL_0 + NC_0)(1+i) - {}^i C$$

$$= (275{,}000 + 25{,}000)(1.07) - 50{,}000 = 271{,}000.$$

Since it also increases by $550{,}000\left(\frac{.4 - .3}{.4}\right) = 137{,}500$, its actual value is

$$UAL_1 = 271{,}000 + 137{,}500 = 408{,}500.$$

We also have $F_1 = 250{,}000$ and $\Sigma S_1 = 500{,}000(1.10) = 550{,}000$. Then
the normal cost at time 1 is

$$NC_1 = (1{,}046{,}000 - 408{,}500 - 250{,}000)\left(\frac{550{,}000}{5{,}801{,}000}\right) = \$36{,}740. \qquad \square$$

6.6 Changes in Decrement Assumptions

Withdrawal and mortality gains are discussed in Sections 5.4 and 5.6. This section deals with the effect on the liability of introducing, deleting, or changing the probabilities of withdrawal and death, $q_x^{(w)}$ and $q_x^{(d)}$, and the withdrawal and death benefits, *WBEN* and *DBEN*.

6.6.1 Mortality Rates

Some pension plans formerly used the male mortality rates from the 1951 Group Annuity Mortality Table (Ga-51). Instead of using a female table to obtain the mortality rate for a female of a certain age, they used the rate for a male 5 years younger; this reflects the fact that women have lower death rates and, in turn, live longer. These tables may be used with a projection scale so that the mortality rates in later years are reduced to reflect the declining death rates over time. In 1971, new tables were introduced (1971 GAM) with both male and female rates, but most pension plans used only the male table and set back the female ages 6 years. These were followed by the 1983 GAM tables and the unisex UP-84 table. The UP-84 table was based on the experience of groups which were 80% male and 20% female. Where required, actuaries use unisex tables with reasonable male/female proportions or with a reasonable age setback.

Three recently constructed mortality tables are the UP-94, GAR-94, and GAM-94. These are the Uninsured Pensioner Mortality, Group Annuity Reserving, and Group Annuity Mortality tables, respectively.[1]

Actuaries anticipate lower mortality from pensioners than from the general population, and they may use a projection scale to provide for the long-term safety of the pension plan. Instead of a projection scale, actuaries sometimes use a one-year age setback for each ten years of projection; for example, if the male 1983 GAM table is used for a valuation in 1993, the setback could be one year for males and seven years for females.[2]

6.6.2 Withdrawal Rates

The withdrawal rate $q_x^{(w)}$ at most ages is much larger than the other decrements, and $q_{[x]+k}^{(w)}$ is high for small k and decreases as k increases. The

---

[1] For more on the development of these tables, see *TSA* XLVII (1995).

[2] For more on the development of the 1983 GAM tables, see *TSA* XXV (1983).

actuary can use published tables for low, medium, or high withdrawal rates or, for large groups, a table can be constructed.

After age 50, $q_x^{(w)}$ is often assumed to be zero and, for simplicity, select and ultimate rates often are not used. Withdrawal assumptions are not appropriate for fully insured plans and, in the event of withdrawal, all or most of the net liability released is usually credited to the plan sponsor in accordance with the plan document. The reason for assuming withdrawals with a trusteed plan and not assuming withdrawals with a fully insured plan can be seen by considering a year in which there are no withdrawals. With the trusteed plan the cost is discounted for withdrawals, and there will be a loss which will be offset by a gain in a year of heavy withdrawals. With the fully insured plan the cost is guaranteed and hence there will be no gain or loss; in a year of heavy withdrawals there will be a large refund credited, but again no gain or loss.

In the event of **plan termination**, most jurisdictions require full vesting and no subsequent withdrawals would be assumed in a wind-up valuation.

6.6.3 Disability Rates

Actuaries use the symbol $q_x^{(i)}$ for the probability of becoming disabled and remaining disabled for the elimination period (usually three or six months), with due consideration for the definition of disability in the pension plan document.

EXAMPLE 6.24

Plan effective date: 1/1/92
Normal retirement benefit: $50 per month for each year of service
Actuarial cost method: Aggregate
Assumed absolute rates of decrement: $q_{25}^{\prime(d)} = .02$; $q_{25}^{\prime(w)} = .20$
The sole plan participant is age 25 as of 1/1/94 and will not be eligible for vesting until after age 26. There are no preretirement death or severance benefits.
Selected valuation results as of 1/1/94:

Present value of future benefits	$20,000
Actuarial value of assets	2,000
Normal cost as of 1/1	1,080

The absolute rate of decrement for withdrawal at age 25 is changed to $q_{25}^{\prime(w)} = .30$, with all other assumptions remaining the same. The normal cost is then recalculated.

What is the recalculated normal cost?

$\boxed{\text{SOLUTION}}$ Under the Aggregate method we have

$$NC \cdot \ddot{a}^s = pvB - F.$$

Using the old assumptions we find

$$\ddot{a}^s = \frac{20,000 - 2,000}{1,080} = 16.67.$$

The present value of future benefits under the old assumptions is

$$B_r \, v^{r-25} \, p_{25}^{(\tau)} \, {}_{r-26}p_{26}^{(\tau)} \, \ddot{a}_r^{(12)} = 20,000.$$

We know that $p_{25}^{(\tau)}$ will change under the new assumptions. Before the change we have

$$p_{25}^{(\tau)} = \left(1 - q_{25}^{\prime(d)}\right)\left(1 - q_{25}^{\prime(w)}\right) = (1 - .02)(1 - .20) = .784,$$

and after the change we have

$$p_{25}^{(\tau)} = (1 - .02)(1 - .30) = .686.$$

Using the new assumption, pvB becomes $20,000\left(\frac{.686}{.784}\right) = 17,500.$ Next recall that

$$\ddot{a}^s = 1 + \left(\frac{1+s}{1+i}\right)p_{25}^{(\tau)} + \left(\frac{1+s}{1+i}\right)^2 p_{25}^{(\tau)} p_{26}^{(\tau)} + \cdots.$$

Then the salary-based annuity under the new assumption is

$$\ddot{a}^s = (16.67 - 1)\left(\frac{.686}{.784}\right) + 1 = 14.71,$$

and the recalculated normal cost is

$$NC = \frac{17,500 - 2,000}{14.71} = \$1054. \qquad \square$$

EXAMPLE 6.25

Plan effective date: 1/1/93
Actuarial cost method: Entry Age Normal
Assumed mortality basis: 1983 Group Annuity Mortality (GAM)
Participant data as of 1/1/93:

Attained Age x	q_x	Number of Participants
49	.004	1000
50	.005	2000
51	.006	1000

Which of the following statements are true?

I. If 21 participants die during 1993, this must cause a gain.

II. If, effective 1/1/94, the assumed mortality basis is changed to 1983 GAM projected to 1992, this must cause a decrease in actuarial liability.

III. If, effective 1/1/94, a withdrawal assumption is introduced, this must cause a decrease in actuarial liability.

SOLUTION

I. If 21 participants die, this may cause a loss. For example, suppose $AL_{49} = 300$, $AL_{50} = 400$, and $AL_{51} = 500$. Then the expected release is

$$1000 \, q_{49}(300) + 2000 q_{50}(400) + 1000 q_{51}(500) \; = \; 8200.$$

The actual release (if the 21 deaths are age 49) is $21(300) = 6300$. Then the loss is $8200 - 6300 = 1900$, so I is *false*.

II. $\ddot{a}_{65}^{(12)}$ will increase and the liability will probably increase, so II is *false*.

III. Recall that $AL = pvB - pvNC$. The introduction of a withdrawal assumption will decrease both pvB and $pvNC$. The net effect will *probably* be a decrease, but *may* be an increase, so III is *false*. □

EXAMPLE 6.26

Early retirement benefit: Actuarial equivalent of accrued normal benefit
Postponed retirement benefit: Normal benefit actuarially increased
The basis of actuarial equivalence was changed as of 1/1/95 as follows:

    Before change: 1971 GAM and 6% interest
    After change: 1983 GAM and 6% interest

Which of the following statements are true?

I.   The change decreases early retirement benefits.

II.   The change increases postponed retirement benefits.

(For the purpose of this question disregard the legal requirements prohibiting the reduction of accrued benefits.)

SOLUTION Assuming early retirement at age x, the equation of value is

$$B_x \ddot{a}_x^{(12)} = B_{65} \frac{D_{65}}{D_x} \ddot{a}_{65}^{(12)} .$$

The early retirement adjustment factor at age x is

$$\frac{N_{65}^{(12)}}{N_x^{(12)}} = \frac{N_{65}^{(12)}}{N_{64}^{(12)}} \cdot \frac{N_{64}^{(12)}}{N_{63}^{(12)}} \cdots \frac{N_{x+1}^{(12)}}{N_x^{(12)}} .$$

Recall that for any x,

$$\frac{N_{x+1}}{N_x} = \frac{N_x - D_x}{N_x} = 1 - \frac{1}{\ddot{a}_x} .$$

Then as q_x decreases, p_x increases, $\ddot{a}_x$ increases, $\frac{1}{\ddot{a}_x}$ decreases, and $1 - \frac{1}{\ddot{a}_x}$ increases, so statement I is *false*. Conversely, as q_x decreases, $\frac{N_x}{N_{x+1}}$ decreases, so statement II is also *false*.   □

EXAMPLE 6.27

Normal retirement benefit: $20 per month for each year of service
Vesting: 100% after 10 years of service
Actuarial cost method: Unit Credit
Assumed interest rate: 7%
Assumed retirement age: 65

The service table is a double-decrement table based on separate single decrement mortality and withdrawal tables, as follows (ℓ's are from single-decrement tables):

Age x	$\ell_x^{\prime(d)}$	$\ell_x^{\prime(w)}$	$\ddot{a}_x^{(12)}$
30	1000	1000	—
65	900	400	9

Data on sole participant as of 1/1/94: Age 30 with 10 years of past service

What is the portion of the actuarial liability as of 1/1/94 which is attributable to benefits for vested terminations before age 65?

$\boxed{\text{SOLUTION}}$ The participant is vested and will receive a pension upon survival to age 65 (with probability .90). At 1/1/94, discounting for interest and mortality, we have

$$AL = (20 \times 12 \times 10)\left(v^{35}\,\ddot{a}_{65}^{(12)}\right)(.90) = 1821.$$

We can divide the liability into the portion for retirements (who do not terminate) and the portion for vested terminations (who terminate). The latter portion is

$$1821\left(1 - \frac{400}{1000}\right) = \$1092. \qquad \square$$

$\boxed{\textbf{EXAMPLE 6.28}}$
Plan effective date: 1/1/91
Eligibility: 3 years of service
Vesting: 100% upon entry into plan
Benefit formula: $10 per month for each year of service
Early retirement: Age 55, with accrued benefit reduced to the actuarially equivalent benefit, based on mortality and interest assumptions currently used for the valuation
Actuarial cost method: Unit Credit
All plan participants are between age 30 and age 50
The actuary does not expect that gains or losses from one assumption will offset gains or losses from other assumptions.

Which of the following statements are true?

I.   Since the trust fund will not accumulate a significant amount of assets for a number of years, the selection of the interest assumption is relatively unimportant.

II.   The actuary may reasonably use an age 65 retirement as-sumption even though he expects the average age at retirement to be 62.

III.   The actuary may reasonably assume no withdrawals.

> **SOLUTION**   Interest is always important; statement I is *false*. Statement II is *true*; ages 65 and 62 are equivalent under Unit Credit. (Note that there would be a gain on retirement at age 62 under EAN.) Statement III is *true*, since there is no gain on termination. (There would be a gain on termination under EAN or with partial vesting.)   □

EXAMPLE 6.29

Vesting schedule: 100% after 10 years
Amended vesting schedule: 100% after 8 years, effective 1/1/94
Normal retirement benefit: $10 per month per year of service
Actuarial cost method: Entry Age Normal
Assumed retirement age: 65
All terminations are assumed to occur at the beginning of the year.
Data for sole plan participant as of 1/1/94:

Age	Age at Hire	$D_{50}^{(\tau)}$	$^{a}M_{58}^{(w)}$	$^{a}M_{59}^{(w)}$	$^{a}M_{60}^{(w)}$
50	50	250	45	40	38

$$^{a}M_{x}^{(w)} = \sum_{t=x}^{64} \ell_{t}^{(\tau)} \, v^{t} \, q_{t}^{(w)} \,_{65-t}|\ddot{a}_{t}^{(12)} \qquad \ddot{a}_{65}^{(12)} = 10$$

The commutation functions, $\ell_{x}^{(\tau)}$ and $q_{x}^{(w)}$ are from the active service table; annuity values are based on mortality and interest only.

What is the increase in the present value of future benefits as of 1/1/94 resulting from the change in the vesting schedule?

SOLUTION The cost of new vesting at ages 58 and 59 is

$$10 \times 12 \times 8 \times \frac{{}^{a}C_{58}^{(w)}}{D_{50}^{(\tau)}} + 10 \times 12 \times 9 \times \frac{{}^{a}C_{59}^{(w)}}{D_{50}^{(\tau)}}$$

$$= 960 \left(\frac{{}^{a}M_{58}^{(w)} - {}^{a}M_{59}^{(w)}}{D_{50}^{(\tau)}} \right) + 1080 \left(\frac{{}^{a}M_{59}^{(w)} - {}^{a}M_{60}^{(w)}}{D_{50}^{(\tau)}} \right)$$

$$= 960 \left(\frac{5}{250} \right) + 1080 \left(\frac{2}{250} \right) = \$28. \qquad \square$$

6.7 Ancillary Benefits

The main purpose of a pension plan is to provide monthly pension benefits, but most pension plans also have **additional benefits** such as death, disability, and withdrawal benefits, in accordance with the plan document.

The death benefits may be quite different before and after retirement, and may be greater if there is a spouse and if there are employee contributions. The disability monthly benefit usually ceases at the earliest of death, recovery, or retirement. The withdrawal benefit depends on the vesting; sometimes the plan pays a deferred monthly pension and sometimes a lump sum at termination.

In this section we develop the present values of future pension, death before retirement, withdrawal, and disability benefits, based on a multiple decrement service table with these three decrements only. These values will be useful in determining the cost of changing the probabilities and in computing the total actuarial liability. The formulae will be based on a benefit payable annually in advance and a retirement age of r, but they can easily be modified to a benefit payable monthly and a multiple retirement age assumption.

The present value of the *projected* pension benefit is

$$pv_{x}B_{r} = B_{r} \cdot v^{r-x} \,_{r-x}p_{x}^{(\tau)} \cdot \ddot{a}_{r},$$

where B_{r} is the projected pension benefit and the valuation age is x. The present value of the *accrued* pension benefit is

$$pv_{x}B_{x} = B_{x} \cdot v^{r-x} \,_{r-x}p_{x}^{(\tau)} \cdot \ddot{a}_{r},$$

where B_{x} is the accrued pension benefit. If we assume deaths at EOY and if the preretirement death benefit just before age $x + k$ is the value of the deferred accrued pension, then the present value at age x of the death benefit is

$$pv_x DBEN = \sum_{k=1}^{r-x} \frac{d_{x+k-1}^{(d)}}{\ell_x^{(\tau)}} \cdot B_{x+k} \frac{N_r}{D_{x+k}} v^k.$$

If we assume withdrawals at EOY and if the withdrawal benefit just before age $x + k$ is the deferred accrued pension, then the present value at age x is

$$pv_x WBEN = \sum_{k=1}^{r-x} \frac{d_{x+k-1}^{(w)}}{\ell_x^{(\tau)}} \cdot B_{x+k} \frac{N_r}{D_{x+k}} v^k.$$

If the disability benefit is an annuity-due for life of the accured pension benefit, the present value of the disability benefit is

$$\sum_{k=1}^{r-x} \frac{d_{x+k-1}^{(i)}}{\ell_x^{(\tau)}} \cdot B_{x+k-1/2} \frac{N_{x+k}}{D_{x+k}} v^k,$$

assuming disabilities at midyear with an elimination period of six months.

In practice, there are many variations from the above illustrations in ancillary benefits. The commutation functions would normally be used on one decrement.

The normal cost for each ancillary benefit may be computed in accordance with the philosophy of the actuarial cost method. For example, for the withdrawal benefit under EAN, the normal cost is such that at entry age

$$NC \cdot \ddot{a}_{\overline{e:r-e|}} = \sum_{k=1}^{r-e} \frac{d_{e+k-1}^{(w)}}{\ell_e^{(\tau)}} \cdot B_{e+k} \frac{N_r}{D_{e+k}} v^k.$$

Alternatively, whether or not the cost method for pension benefits is Unit Credit, the normal cost for ancillary benefits can be computed under the Unit Credit method. For example the normal cost at age x for the withdrawal benefit is

$$q_x^{(w)} \cdot B_{x+1} \cdot \ddot{a}_r \cdot v^{r-x} {}_{r-x-1}p_{x+1}.$$

EXAMPLE 6.30

Employee contributions: Previously required; discontinued as of 12/31/93
Death or termination benefit: Employee contributions plus interest at 5% are returned at the end of the year of death or termination

Assumed interest rate: 7%
Assumed retirement age: 65
Decrements other than deaths are assumed to occur at EOY.
Data for sole participant as of 1/1/94:
    Attained age: 40
    Accumulated employee contributions plus interest: $1000
Selected functions:

x	$\ell_x^{\prime(d)}$ (mortality only)	$\ell_x^{(\tau)}$ (all decrements)
39	1093	855
40	1091	842
41	1088	830

What is the present value, as of 1/1/94, of the return of employee contributions with interest for all decrements other than death which occur during 1994?

SOLUTION The probability of not dying during the year is $\frac{1088}{1091}$, and the probability of withdrawing at EOY is

$$\frac{1}{842}\left[(842)\left(\frac{1088}{1091}\right) - 830\right] = .011502.$$

Then the present value is

$$\frac{.011502(1000)(1.05)}{1.07} = 11.29. \qquad \square$$

Note that since withdrawals occur EOY, then $q_x^{(d)} = q_x^{\prime(d)}$, so

$$q_{40}^{(w)} = q_{40}^{(\tau)} - q_{40}^{(d)} = \frac{12}{842} - \frac{3}{1091} = .011502.$$

6.8 Employee Contributions

Most defined contribution plans have employer and employee contributions. These plans are sometimes called **money purchase, profit sharing**, or, in the United States, **401(k) plans**. Normally, within reasonable limits, the employer contributions are deductible in arriving at employer taxable income and the employee contributions are deductible in arriving at employee taxable income.

Many defined benefit plans in Canada have employer and employee contributions which are deductible as discussed in the previous paragraph. In the United States, very few defined benefit plans are contributory (with employee contributions) because, while the employer contributions are deductible, the employee contributions are not.

Reasons for contributory plans include (a) lower employer costs, (b) the accumulation of larger pension and withdrawal benefits, and (c) a greater interest in, and appreciation of, the pension plan by its participants. In order to increase future benefits, participants may be allowed to voluntarily contribute amounts in excess of the contributions required. Employee contributions complicate the administration of the plan and may decrease the actual number of employees that elect to participate in the plan.

Recall that the employer's annual cost consists of the normal cost and the supplemental cost for the year. If there is also a contribution being made by the employee, then the employer's annual cost will be smaller.

Employee is a narrower term than participant, but we will use it in this section because participants who are not employees generally belong to noncontributory plans. Employee contributions may be level dollar, level percent, or a graded percent of compensation.

The new concepts in this section include the following:

- The employer normal cost, NC, is smaller by part, but not all, of the employee contributions.
- In the event of withdrawal or death before retirement, the employee or beneficiary is entitled to a minimum benefit of all employee contributions plus interest. We will call this the **refund benefit**, *RBEN*.
- If a refund benefit is payable t years after an employee contribution, denoted by C^{ee}, the benefit is $C^{ee}(1+j)^t$, and the value of the benefit at the date of contribution is

$$C^{ee}(1+j)^t \cdot (1+i)^{-t} = C^{ee},$$

  under the simplifying assumption that the accumulation and valuation rates of interest are the same. We will make this assumption, as do most actuaries.

- In computing the value of the refund benefit, we should consider the *past* contributions accumulated with interest to the date of valuation, AC, combined with the probabilities of withdrawal and death before retirement, and the *future* contributions combined with the probabilities of withdrawal and death after the future contributions but before retirement.

- The death benefit after retirement is often a life annuity with a five-year certain period, or a life annuity with a refund at death of the excess, if any, of the employee contributions with interest at the accumulation rate to the date of retirement less the annuity payments received.

- We assume that C^{ee} is received at EOY with BOY value $v \cdot C^{ee}$; if C^{ee} is received at BOY or at midyear, an adjustment can easily be made.

6.8.1 Unit Credit with Employee Contributions

B_x is the pension benefit accrued to age x, and the pension plan liability for the employee's accrued pension is $B_x \dfrac{D_r}{D_x} \ddot{a}_r^{(12)}$. If AC_x is the value at age x of the employee's contributions before age x with interest to age x, then the liability at age x for the refund in the event of death or withdrawal before retirement is

$$AC_x \left[(1+j)\frac{d_x}{\ell_x}(1+i)^{-1} + (1+j)^2 \frac{d_{x+1}}{\ell_x}(1+i)^{-2} + \cdots \right] = AC_x \frac{\ell_x - \ell_r}{\ell_x}.$$

The total liability is

$$AL_x = B_x \frac{D_r}{D_x} \ddot{a}_r^{(12)} + AC_x \frac{\ell_x - \ell_r}{\ell_x},$$

and the service table is often double decrement.

The normal cost at age x for the pension benefit accruing in the year commencing at age x is $b_x \dfrac{D_r}{D_x} \ddot{a}_r^{(12)}$.

For the year commencing at age x, the employee contribution is C^{ee} with value at age x of $v \cdot C^{ee}$, and the normal cost for the refund benefit associated with this contribution is

$$v \cdot C^{ee} \left[(1+j)\frac{d_x}{\ell_x}(1+i)^{-1} + \cdots \right] = v \cdot C^{ee} \frac{\ell_x - \ell_r}{\ell_x}.$$

Putting the employer normal cost, NC_x, with the other three items, we have

$$NC_x + v \cdot C^{ee} = b_x \frac{D_r}{D_x} \ddot{a}_r^{(12)} + v \cdot C^{ee} \frac{\ell_x - \ell_r}{\ell_x}.$$

The employer normal cost is the cost of the pension and refund benefits, *less* the employee contribution, which is

$$NC_x = b_x \frac{D_r}{D_x} \ddot{a}_r^{(12)} - v \cdot C^{ee} \frac{\ell_r}{\ell_x}.$$

6.8.2 Entry Age Normal

At entry age, assuming no salary increases, the normal cost is such that

$$NC \cdot \ddot{a}_{e:\overline{r-e}|} + v \cdot C^{ee} \cdot \ddot{a}_{e:\overline{r-e}|} = B_r \frac{D_r}{D_e} \ddot{a}_r^{(12)} + pvRBEN.$$

At age $e+1, e+2, \ldots$, the refund benefit is $C^{ee} \cdot s_{\overline{1}|}, C^{ee} \cdot s_{\overline{2}|}, \ldots$, so

$$pvRBEN = \sum_{z=e}^{r-1} \frac{C_z}{D_e} C^{ee} \cdot s_{\overline{z-e+1}|}$$

$$= v \cdot C^{ee} \cdot \ddot{a}_{e:\overline{r-e}|} - C^{ee} \cdot s_{\overline{r-e}|} \frac{D_r}{D_e}.$$

Substituting this expression for *pvRBEN* into the normal cost equation, and multiplying both sides by $\frac{D_e}{D_r}$ we obtain

$$NC \cdot \ddot{s}_{e:\overline{r-e}|} = B_r \cdot \ddot{a}_r^{(12)} - C^{ee} \cdot s_{\overline{r-e}|},$$

and we note the similarity to the Chapter 3 equation

$$NC \cdot \ddot{s}_{e:\overline{r-e}|} = B_r \cdot \ddot{a}_r^{(12)}.$$

The value of the pension at retirement, in excess of any contributions accumulated with interest, will be provided by the accumulated normal costs.

The first equation in this section can be modified for more complicated plans. For example, the refund benefit in the case of death before retirement could be a lump sum, or the accumulated contributions if greater, and the refund benefit in the case of withdrawal could be the deferred accrued pension if vested, or the accumulated contributions if not vested.

EXAMPLE 6.31

Age at entry: 30
Annual salary: $30,000
Normal retirement benefit: 2% of salary per year of service
Employee contributions: 5% of salary
Refund benefit: Accumulated employee contributions
Actuarial Assumptions:

Interest: 5%

Combined decrement rate: $q_x^{(d)} + q_x^{(w)} = .01$

Combined discount factor: $v' = v \cdot p_x^{(\tau)} = \frac{.99}{1.05} = .94285$

Selected annuity value: $\ddot{a}_{65}^{(12)} = 10$

Salary increase: None
Retirement age: 65

Calculate and compare the value of the non-contributory normal costs (^{non}NC), the contributory employer normal costs (^{ce}NC), and the total contributory costs ($^{ce}NC + v \cdot C^{ee}$), under each of UC and EAN. Give some thought to the advantages of each method.

SOLUTION

Unit Credit age 30:

$^{non}NC = 30,000 \times .02 \times 10 \times (.94285)^{35}$ $\qquad = \quad 768$

$^{ce}NC = 768 - 30,000 \times .05 \times (1.05)^{-1} \times (.99)^{-35}$ $\qquad = \quad -237$

$^{ce}NC + v \cdot C^{ee} = -237 + 1500 \times (1.05)^{-1}$ $\qquad = \quad 1192$

Unit Credit age 50:

$^{non}NC = 30,000 \times .02 \times 10 \times (.94285)^{15}$ $\qquad = \quad 2482$

$^{ce}NC = 2482 - 30,000 \times .05 \times (1.05)^{-1} \times (.99)^{15}$ $\qquad = \quad 1253$

$^{ce}NC + v \cdot C^{ee} = 1253 + 1500(1.05)^{-1}$ $\qquad = \quad 2682$

Entry Age Normal:

$^{non}NC = 30,000 \times .02 \times 35 \times 10 \div \ddot{s}_{\overline{35}|.06061}$ $\qquad = \quad 1758$

$^{ce}NC = 1758 - 1500 \times s_{\overline{35}|.05} \div \ddot{s}_{\overline{35}|.06061}$ $\qquad = \quad 624$

$^{ce}NC + v \cdot C^{ee} = 624 + 1500 \times (1.05)^{-1}$ $\qquad = \quad 2053$

□

Moving now from the normal cost to the actuarial liability, we find the total pension plan liability at age x to be

$$B_r \frac{D_r}{D_x} - NC \frac{N_x - N_r}{D_x} + AC_x \frac{\ell_x - \ell_r}{\ell_x} - C^{ee} \cdot s_{\overline{r-x}|} \frac{D_r}{D_x},$$

where the first and second terms give the liability for pensions, and the third and fourth terms give the liability for contributions. The third term is the contributions before age x accumulated to the valuation date multiplied by the probability of dying or withdrawing before retirement; the interest and discount between valuation and payout cancel out, leaving us with the value of the withdrawal benefit with respect to prevaluation contributions. The fourth term consists of the postvaluation contributions accumulated with interest to retirement and discounted for interest and mortality to the valuation date, utilizing the same simplification as with the normal cost.

It should be noted that there is a difference between the pension plan balance sheet and the employer balance sheet. The liability included in the former is for pensions (and can be called the employer liability) and for the refund portion of the contributions (which is additional liability to the employees). Similarly, the pension fund assets include the accumulated contributions for each active employee and the balance of assets (primarily for pensions).

6.8.3 Aggregate

The normal cost is such that, at the date of valuation,

$$NC \cdot \sum \ddot{a}^s + \sum pvC = \sum pvB + \sum pvRBEN - F.$$

The first term on the right side represents pension benefits accruing before and after the date of valuation; included would be active and retired employees. The second term represents the return of contributions with interest, in the event of death or withdrawal before retirement, which were made before and after the date of valuation. The third term recognizes funds on hand at the date of valuation. The second term on the left side recognizes the expected value of employee contributions after the valuation date.

Let the contribution at age z be C_z^{ee} at EOY. Then

$$pvC = \sum_{z=x}^{r-1} v \cdot C_z^{ee} \cdot \frac{D_z}{D_x},$$

$$pvB = B_r \cdot \ddot{a}_r^{(12)} \cdot \frac{D_r}{D_x},$$

and

$$pvRBEN = \sum_{z=x}^{r-1} AC_z \cdot \frac{C_z}{D_x}.$$

It would not be very difficult for a computer to handle the summations for each employee and for all employees. We could then solve for the normal cost.

In the rare cases where there are additional voluntary employee contributions, they are handled as in a defined contribution plan and are not part of the actuarial cost method.

| EXAMPLE 6.32 |

Rate of employee contribution: 1.5% of compensation
Death benefit: Refund of employee contributions, with interest
Actuarial cost method: Aggregate
Valuation results as of 1/1/94:

Present value of future retirement benefits	$1,500,000
Present value of future death benefits	30,000
1994 employee contributions	15,000
Actuarial value of assets	400,000
Accumulated employee contributions with interest (included in assets)	60,000
Present value of future compensation	8,000,000
Annual compensation	1,000,000

What is the employer's normal cost for 1994 as of 1/1/94?

| SOLUTION | Let 1/1/94 be time 0. First we develop the values of

$$\ddot{a}^s = \frac{8,000,000}{1,000,000} = 8$$

and

$$pvC^{ee} = 15,000(8) = 120,000.$$

Assume the interest rate for employee contributions and the valuation interest rate are the same, or, alternatively, assume $i = 0$. Let p be the probability of survival until retirement; since the present value of future death benefits is 30,000 and $i = 0$, we have

$$(120{,}000+60{,}000)(1-p) = 30{,}000$$

from which we find $p = \frac{5}{6}$. In other words, $\frac{5}{6}$ of C^{ee} will help to buy pensions and $\frac{1}{6}$ of C^{ee} will be returned with interest at death.

The present value of all future employer normal costs plus the present value of a portion of all future employee contributions equals the present value of the future retirement benefits minus the present value of the fund. Thus we have

$$\left(NC_0+15{,}000 \times \frac{5}{6}\right)8 = 1{,}500{,}000 - \left(400{,}000-60{,}000 \times \frac{1}{6}\right)$$

which solves for

$$NC_0 = \$126{,}250. \qquad \qquad \square$$

EXAMPLE 6.33

Actuarial cost method: Aggregate
Selected valuation results as of 1/1/94:

Present value of all future benefits	$10,850,000
Present value of future death and termination benefits due to accumulated and future employee contributions (included above)	850,000
Present value of future employee contributions	2,000,000
Value of assets, including $1,200,000 of accumulated employee contributions	4,800,000
Present value of future compensation	50,600,000
Annual compensation	3,500,000

What is the increase in the employer's normal cost for 1994 as of 1/1/94 if future employee contributions were discontinued and all accumulated employee contributions were refunded to participants as of 12/31/93?

SOLUTION

Let 1/1/94 be time 0. With employee contributions we have

$$NC_0 \frac{\sum pvS_x}{\sum S_x} = pvB - F_0 - pvC^{ee},$$

or

$$NC_0 \left(\frac{50,600}{3500} \right) = 10,850,000 - 4,800,000 - 2,000,000$$

from which we find

$$NC_0 = 280,138.$$

Without employee contributions we have

$$NC_0 \left(\frac{50,600}{3500} \right) = (10,850,000 - 850,000) - (4,800,000 - 1,200,000) - 0,$$

which solves for

$$NC_0 = 442,688.$$

The increase in the employer's normal cost is therefore

$$442,688 - 280,138 = \$162,550. \qquad \square$$

| **EXAMPLE 6.34** |

Actuarial cost method: Aggregate with contributions
Present value of benefits (excluding any benefits provided by voluntary employee contributions) as of 1/1/94:

Retirement	$ 500,000
Return of accumulated and future mandatory employee contributions at death or non-vested termination	10,000
Vesting	40,000
Actuarial value of total assets as of 12/31/93	100,000
Accumulated mandatory employee contributions, included in total assets	15,000
Accumulated voluntary employee contributions, included in total assets	10,000
Annual compensation of employees	300,000
Present value of future compensation	2,400,000

1994 employee contributions, assumed made 1/1/94:

Mandatory	$1500
Voluntary	1100

What is the employer normal cost for 1994 as of 1/1/94?

| **SOLUTION** | Let 1/1/94 be time 0. First we calculate

$$\ddot{a}_0^s = \frac{2,400,000}{300,000} = 8.$$

Let *TNC* denote the total normal cost. Then we have

pvB for pensions and refunds: $500{,}000 + 10{,}000 + 40{,}000 = 550{,}000$

   F (excluding voluntary): $100{,}000 - 10{,}000 = 90{,}000$

   $TNC \cdot \ddot{a}_0^s = pvB - F$: $550{,}000 - 90{,}000 = 460{,}000$

from which we find
$$TNC = 57{,}500.$$
Finally the employer normal cost is
$$57{,}500 - 1{,}500 = \$56{,}000. \qquad \square$$

EXAMPLE 6.35

Employee contributions: 2% of compensation, paid at BOY
Actuarial cost method: Frozen Initial Liability
Assumed interest rate: 6%
Valuation results as of 1/1/94:

Present value of future benefits (including refunds of employee contributions)	$ 2,600,000
Actuarial value of assets	650,000
Unfunded liability	300,000
Present value of future compensation	12,500,000
Annual compensation	1,000,000

What is the employer's normal cost for 1994 as of 12/31/94?

SOLUTION Let 1/1/94 be time 0. The total normal cost under FIL is
such that
$$TNC \cdot \ddot{a}^s = \sum pvB - UAL_0 - F_0 ,$$
or
$$TNC \left(\frac{12{,}500}{1000} \right) = 2{,}600{,}000 - 300{,}000 - 650{,}000$$
which solves for
$$TNC = 132{,}000.$$
The employee contributions at time 0 are
$$C_0^{ee} = .02 \times 1{,}000{,}000 = 20{,}000.$$

The employer's normal cost at time 0 is

$$NC_0 = 132,000 - 20,000 = 112,000$$

so at time 1 it is

$$NC_1 = 112,000 \times 1.06 = \$118,720. \qquad \square$$

6.9 Exercises

6.1 Change in Cost Method

6-1   Actuarial cost method:
        Before 1993: Unit Credit
        After 1992: Frozen Initial Liability
    Assumed interest rate: 6%
    Assumed compensation increases: 5% per year
    Selected valuation results:

	1/1/93	1/1/94
Present value of future benefit	$ 11,000,000	$ 12,000,000
Actuarial value of assets	3,000,000	4,000,000
Present value of future compensation	112,500,000	115,000,000
Annual compensation	16,500,000	—
Accured liability under UC	4,325,000	5,000,000
Accrued liability under EAN	6,500,000	7,600,000

Contribution for 1993: $1,000,000 paid on 12/31/93.

What is the normal cost as a percentage of compensation for 1994 as of 1/1/94?

6-2   Normal retirement benefit: $25 monthly per year of service
    Actuarial cost method:
        Before 1994: Unit Credit
        After 1993: Aggregate
    Actuarial assumptions:
        Interest: 6%
        Preretirement deaths and terminations: None
        Retirement age: 65

Data for sole participant:
Date of birth   1/1/46
Date of hire   1/1/84
Valuation results as of 1/1/93:
Actuarial value of assets: $6300
Unfunded actuarial liability: $2500
Contribution for 1993: $1250 paid on 12/31/93
There were no noninvestment experience gains or losses during
1993. The rate of return on the actuarial value of assets during
1993 was 10%.

What is the normal cost for 1994 as of 1/1/94?

6.2 Change in Retirement Benefit

6-3   Plan effective date: 1/1/84
Normal retirement benefit: $500 per month
Actuarial cost method: ILP, with changes due to plan amendments
funded from attained age
Actuarial assumptions:
Interest: 8%
Preretirement terminations other than deaths: None
Retirement age: 65
Participant data as of 1/1/94 and selected commutation functions:

Age at hire	Attained Age x	Number of Employees	D_x	$N_x - N_{65}$	$N_x^{(12)}$
—	25	0	265	3390	3355
25	35	1	125	1455	1485
25	45	2	55	570	630
—	55	0	25	170	245
—	65	0	10	0	80

Effective 1/1/94, the plan is amended to increase the normal retirement benefit to $550 per month.

What is the increase, due to the amendment, in the normal cost for
1994 as of 1/1/94?

6-4   Plan effective date: 1/1/87
       Normal retirement benefit: $10 per month for each year of service;
           increased by plan amendment effective 1/1/92 to $15 per month
           for each year of service
       Actuarial cost method: ILP, with benefit increases from plan amend-
           ments funded through the normal cost rather than through
           adjustment of the actuarial liability.
       Actuarial assumptions:
           Interest: 7%
           Preretirement mortality and turnover: None
           Selected annuity value: $12 \, \ddot{a}_{65}^{(12)} = 100$
       Data for sole participant:
           Date of birth   1/1/42
           Date of hire   1/1/82
           Date of death   1/2/94
           Death benefit paid 1/2/94 $4000

       What is the mortality gain for 1994 as of 12/31/94?

6-5   Plan effective date: 1/1/93
       Normal retirement benefit for each year of service:
           Effective 1/1/93: $10 per month
           Effective 1/1/94: $15 per month
       Actuarial cost method: Attained Age Normal
       Actuarial assumptions:
           Interest: 7%
           Preretirement deaths and terminations: None
           Retirement age: 65
           Selected annuity value: $12 \, \ddot{a}_{65}^{(12)} = 100$
       Participant data as of 1/1/94:

	Smith	Brown
Date of birth	1/1/48	1/1/58
Date of hire	1/1/88	1/1/83

       Valuation results as of 1/1/94, based on the $10 benefit:
           Unfunded liability $2500
           Actuarial value of assets   1100

       Find the present value of future normal costs as of 1/1/94.

6-6   Plan effective date: 1/1/90
       Normal retirement benefit: $100 per month
       Assumed retirement age: 65
       Preretirement terminations other than by death: None
       As of 1/1/95, there is one participant age 45, hired 1/1/90.
       Effective 1/1/95 the plan is amended to increase the normal
          retirement benefit to $150 per month.

   (a) Using the Entry Age Normal cost method, find an expression in
       commutation functions for the increase in accrued liability as of
       1/1/95 resulting from the amendment.

   (b) Using the Individual Level Premium cost method, find an
       expression in commutation functions for the increase in the
       normal cost resulting from the amendment.

6-7   Normal retirement benefit: $100 per month.
       Optional retirement benefit: $75 per month payable for life; upon
          participant's death, $75 per month is continued for the life of
          the surviving spouse (if any)
       All participants are male.
       Actuarial cost method: Aggregate
       Actuarial assumptions:
          Percent eligible to elect option: 80%
          Percent of eligibles who elect: 25%
          Age of spouse: 3 years younger than participant
          Retirement age: 65
       Selected annuity values:

$$\ddot{a}_{65m}^{(12)} = 10.0 \qquad \ddot{a}_{62f}^{(12)} = 12.0 \qquad \ddot{a}_{65m:62f}^{(12)} = 8.7$$

       Valuation results as of 1/1/95:
          Actuarial value of assets $50,000
          Present value of future normal costs   50,000
          Normal cost as of 1/1/95   5,000
       There are no retired or terminated vested participants.
       An amendment is proposed effective 1/1/95 to increase the optional
          retirement benefit to $90 for both the participant and surviving
          spouse. The actuary expects that this will double the frequency
          of election of the option.

       What is the estimated normal cost for 1995, payable 1/1/95, if the
       amendment is adopted?

6-8   Normal retirement benefit:
        Before 1993: 40% of final 5-year average compensation
        After 1992: 50% of final 3-year average compensation
    Normal form of payment:
        Before 1993:   Life annuity
        After 1992:   Fully subsidized 100% joint and survivor annu-
        ity for married participants; life annuity for unmarried
        participants
    Actuarial cost method: Entry Age Normal (level dollar)
    Actuarial assumptions:
        Interest rate: 7% per year
        Compensation increases: 3% per year
        Preretirement deaths and terminations: None
        Retirement age: 65
        Marital characteristics: 80% married; spouse same age as
        participant
    Valuation data for each of the plan's 100 participants as of 1/1/93:
        Date of birth   1/1/53
        Date of hire   1/1/80
        1993 compensation $40,000
    Selected annuity values: $\ddot{a}_{65}^{(12)} = 8.736$ $\ddot{a}_{\overline{65:65}}^{(12)} = 10.576$

What is the increase in the accrued liability as of 1/1/93 due to the changes in plan provisions?

6.3 Change in Retirement Age

6-9   Normal retirement benefit: $100 per month
    Postponed retirement benefit: $100 per month
    Actuarial cost method: Entry Age Normal
    Assumed retirement age: 65
    Preretirement terminations other than by death: None
    All participants have the same entry age and are younger than 65.
    Normal cost: $800 per active participant
    Selected commutation functions:

x	D_x	$N_x^{(12)}$
65	100	1200
66	95	1103

If the assumed retirement age is changed to age 66, what is the new normal cost per active participant?

6-10   Normal retirement age:
          Before 1994: 65
          After 1993: 64
        Normal retirement benefit: $20 monthly per year of service
        Actuarial cost method: Aggregate
        Actuarial assumptions:
          Interest rate: 8%
          Preretirement deaths and terminations: None
          Retirement age: Normal retirement age
        Data for sole participant:
          Date of birth: 1/1/39
          Date of hire: 1/1/69
        Actuarial value of assets as of 1/1/94: $10,000
        Selected annuity values: $\ddot{a}_{64}^{(12)} = 8.35$; $\ddot{a}_{65}^{(12)} = 8.14$

        What is the increase in the normal cost for 1994 as of 1/1/94 due to
        the change in the normal retirement age?

6-11   Normal retirement benefit: $20 monthly per year of service
        Early retirement benefit:
          Before 1994: Accrued benefit reduced by 6% for each
                year preceding age 65
          After 1993: Unreduced accrued benefit, plus a monthly
                supplement payable to 65 of $6.67 per month for each
                year of service
        Actuarial cost method: Projected Unit Credit
        Actuarial assumptions:
          Interest: 8%
          Preretirement terminations other than deaths: None
          Retirement age:
                Before 1994: 65
                After 1993: 60
        Data for sole participant as of 1/1/94:
          Date of birth   1/1/44
          Date of hire   1/1 /74
        Selected commutation functions:

$$D_{50} = 202 \qquad D_{55} = 133 \qquad D_{60} = 86 \qquad D_{65} = 54$$

$$N_{50}^{(12)} = 2162 \qquad N_{55}^{(12)} = 1330 \qquad N_{60}^{(12)} = 787 \qquad N_{65}^{(12)} = 440$$

        What is the combined increase in the actuarial liability as of 1/1/94
        due to the plan amendment and assumption change?

6-12 Normal retirement benefit: $25 monthly per year of service
Early retirement benefit: Accrued benefit reduced by $\frac{1}{15}$ for each
year by which commencement of payments precedes age 65
Actuarial cost method: Unit Credit
Actuarial assumptions:
Interest rate: 6%
Preretirement deaths and terminations: None
Retirement:
Before 1994: 100% retire at age 65
After 1993: 40% retire at age 62; 60% at age 65
Data for sole participant:
Date of birth   1/1/32
Date of hire   1/1/84
Selected annuity values: $\ddot{a}_{62}^{(12)} = 10.10$; $\ddot{a}_{65}^{(12)} = 9.35$

What is the increase in the actuarial liability as of 1/1/94 due to the
change in the assumed retirement age?

6.4 Change in Interest Assumption

6-13 A pension plan provides reduction factors for early retirement
benefits and conversion factors for a contingent annuitant option
based on actuarial equivalence. Which of the following statements
are true?

I.   A uniform percentage reduction in the assumed rates of mortality will increase both early retirement benefits and contingent
annuitant benefits.

II. An increase in the interest rate alone will decrease early
retirement benefits.

III. An increase in the interest rate alone will increase contingent
annuitant benefits.

6-14   Early retirement age: 55
       Basis for conversion between annuity forms: Actuarial equivalence
       The following changes in the assumptions for actuarial equivalence
          are being considered:
       Interest: Increase from 5% to 8%
       Mortality: Change from 1983 GAM (Males) to 1983
                   GAM (Males) set back three years
       Which of the following statements regarding a participant age 40 are
       true?

   I.   If only the mortality assumption is changed, early retirement
        benefits in the normal form will increase.

   II. If only the interest assumption is changed, early retirement
        benefits in the normal form will increase.

   III. If only the mortality assumption is˙ changed, normal re-
        tirement benefits in the life-with-ten-years-certain optional form
        will increase.

6-15   Normal retirement benefit:
           Effective 1/1/93: $15 per month for each year of service
           Effective 1/1/94: $18 per month for each year of service
       Actuarial cost method: Entry Age Normal
       Actuarial assumptions:
           Interest rate:
               Before 1994:   7% per year
               After 1993:   6% per year
           Preretirement deaths and terminations: None
           Retirement age: 65
       Valuation data for sole participant (active as of 1/1/94):
           Date of birth   1/1/53
           Date of hire   1/1/80
       Selected annuity values:

	6%	7%
$12\ddot{a}^{(12)}_{656}$	112.14	104.83

As of 1/1/94, the increase in the accrued liability due to the change in the assumed interest rate is determined before the increase in the accrued liability due to the plan amendment.

What is the absolute value of the difference between (a) the increase in the accrued liability as of 1/1/94 due to the change in the assumed interest rate, and (b) the increase in the accrued liability due to the plan amendment?

6.5 Change in Salary Increase Assumption

6-16   Actuarial cost method: Entry Age Normal (individual basis)
Normal retirement benefit: 50% of average monthly compensation in the 60 months preceding retirement, minus 50% of the employee's Social Security benefit
Assumed retirement age: 65
Assumed mortality table: 1983 GAM
Preretirement terminations other than by death: None
Data for plan participant Smith as of 1/1/94:

Monthly compensation	$2000
Age	45
Years of service	5

Under which set of assumptions shown below will the 1994 normal cost for Smith be greatest?

	(A)	(B)	(C)	(D)	(E)
Interest	5%	5%	5%	6%	6%
Annual Compensation Increase	5%	5%	6%	6%	7%
Annual Increase in Maximum Taxable Wages under social Security	5%	6%	6%	6%	7%

6-17   Normal retirement benefit:
Before 1995: 40% of final 3-year average compensation
After 1994: 50% of final 3-year average compensation
Actuarial cost method: Aggregate
Actuarial assumptions:
Interest rate: 7%
Compensation increases: 5%
Preretirement deaths and terminations: None
Retirement age: 65

Valuation results as of 1/1/94:

Present value of future benefits:

Active participants	$ 800,000
Inactive participants	0
Value of assets	300,000
Present value of future compensation	11,250,000
1994 compensation	900,000

As of 1/1/94, all participants were under age 64.

Contribution for 1994: Normal cost for 1994 paid on 1/1/94

There were no experience gains or losses due to new participants, deaths, terminations, or retirements during 1994.

There were no new participants as of 1/1/95.

All active participants received an 8% salary increase for 1995.

Normal cost for 1995 as of 1/1/95: 60,000

What is the value of assets as of 12/31/94?

6.6 Changes in Decrement Assumptions

6-18   Normal retirement benefit: $10 per month for each year of service prior to age 65

Early or late retirement benefit: Actuarial equivalent of accrued benefit based on mortality and interest assumptions which are (coincidentally) the same as those used for valuation

Vesting: 100% immediately

Actuarial cost method: Unit Credit

As of 1/1/94 no participants are eligible for early or normal retirement.

Which of the following statements with respect to the 1/1/94 valuation of the plan are true?

I.   The choice of withdrawal assumption will have no effect on the valuation results.

II.   The choice of assumed retirement age will have no effect on the valuation results.

III. If the plan is amended to provide full accrued benefits upon early retirement after age 62, and an assumed retirement age of 65 is used in the valuation, retirements prior to age 65 will be a source of experience loss.

6-19 Normal retirement benefit: $10 monthly per year of service
Early retirement benefit: None
Actuarial cost method: Entry Age Normal
Two valuations (X and Y) are performed using identical assumptions, except that valuation X uses a withdrawal assumption and valuation Y does not. There are active participants at ages at which withdrawals are assumed.

Which of the following statements are true?

I.   The present value of accrued benefits which are vested on the valuation date is the same in valuation X as in valuation Y.

II. The actuarial liability in valuation X may be greater than that in valuation Y.

III. The actuarial liability in valuation X may be less than that in valuation Y.

6-20 The plan provides that the early retirement benefit is the actuarial equivalent of the accrued normal retirement benefit, based on the interest and mortality assumptions used in the valuation of the plan.
Proportion of female employees: 20%
The mortality assumption used in all previous valuations was the 1983 Group Annuity Table (males), without projection and with a 5-year age setback for females.
The mortality assumption to be used for the current valuation is the 1983 Group Annuity Table (males), without projection and with no age setback for females.
Actuarial valuation method: Aggregate

Which of the following statements about the effect of the change in the mortality assumption are true?

I.   The present value of normal retirement benefits will decrease.

II. The early retirement benefits for females will decrease.

6.7 Ancillary Benefits

6-21 Normal retirement benefit: $20 monthly per year of service
Early retirement benefit: Accrued benefit reduced by 5% for each
      year by which commencement of payments precedes age 65
Preretirement death benefit: 50% of early retirement benefit
      payable monthly to the participant's spouse for life
Actuarial assumptions:
      Interest rate: 6%
      Preretirement mortality: 2% at the end of each year
      Preretirement terminations other than death: None
      Retirement age: 65
Marital characteristics: 90% of participants are married at the time
      of death; spouses are the same age as parti cipants
Data for sole participant:
      Date of birth   1/1/31
      Date of hire   1/1/64
Selected annuity values: $\ddot{a}_{63}^{(12)} = 9.85$; $\ddot{a}_{64}^{(12)} = 9.60$; $\ddot{a}_{65}^{(12)} = 9.35$

What is the present value of preretirement death benefits as of
1/1/94?

6-22 Normal retirement benefit: 10 per month for each year of service
Preretirement death benefit: Lump sum equal to 100 times the pro-
      jected monthly normal retirement benefit, payable at the end
      of the year of death
Actuarial cost method: Unit Credit for retirement benefits; term cost
      for preretirement death benefits
Actuarial assumptions:
      Interest rate: 7% per year
      Preretirement terminations other than deaths: None
      Retirement age: 65
Selected commutation functions:

x	D_x	N_x
44	4885	63,045
45	4548	58,163
46	4236	53,615
64	1054	9,926
65	965	8,872
66	881	7,907

Data for sole participant:
    Date of birth   1/1/47
    Date of hire   1/1/72

What is the total normal cost for 1992 as of 1/1/92?

6.8 Employee Contributions

6-23   Type of plan: Contributory
    Accrued benefit: $50 per month for each year of service
    Preretirement death and termination benefit: Refund of employee
        contributions with 6% interest (no vesting)
    Actuarial cost method: Unit Credit
    Assumed interest rate: 6%
    Data for sole participant as of 1/1/94:
        Date of birth   1/1/54
        Date of hire   1/1/89
    Employee contributions:

Accumulated with interest to 12/31/93	$2500
Expected to be contributed for 1994 at 12/31/94	475
Rate of interest credited	6%

Selected annuity value: $\ddot{a}_{65}^{(12)} = 10$

Selected commutation functions:

x	D_x	C_x	M_x
35	2522	174	1226
36	2205	149	1052
40	1314	80	576
41	1160	68	496
64	127	2	45
65	118	1	43

What are the actuarial liability and the employer normal cost as of 1/1/94?

6-24   Type of plan:

        Before 1993: Contributory

        After 1992: Noncontributory

     Preretirement death or termination benefits: Employee contributions with interest accumulated at 6%, returned at the end of the year of death or termination

     Assumed interest rate: 6%

     Valuation data for sole participant:

Date of birth	1/1/32
Accumulated employee contributions with interest as of 12/31/92	$15,000

     Retirements occur at the beginning of the year.

     Selected service table values:

x	$\ell_x^{(\tau)}$	$q_x^{(r)}$
61	1000	0.0
62	950	0.5
63	465	0.2
64	360	0.2
65	278	1.0

What is the total normal cost for 1/1/92?

6-25 Type of plan: Contributory

Employee contributions: 1.5% of annual compensation

Actuarial cost method: Aggregate

Employee contributions are assumed to be paid on 1/1 of each year.

Selected valuation results as of 1/1/93:

Present value of future benefits:

Retirement benefits	$2,000,000
Refunds of employee contributions upon death or termination	70,000
Other death and termination benefits	200,000
Value of total assets	500,000
Accumulated employee contributions included in total assets	80,000
Present value of future compensation	7,000,000
Annual compensation	1,000,000

What is the employer's normal cost for 1993 as of 1/1/93?

Chapter 7

Options and Assets

7.1 Retirement Options

The first section of this chapter discusses (a) early retirement options and (b) late retirement options. The topic of optional forms of the pension benefit is covered in Section 7.2.

The concept of **actuarial equivalence** is to be found in all the chapters (*e.g.*, present value of benefits equals present value of normal costs) and especially in this chapter; for example, we might ask what optional joint and survivorship pension benefit would be equivalent to the normal form of pension benefit with no gain or loss to the plan.

Participants are eligible to receive the full amount of their accrued benefit upon reaching the **normal retirement age**, usually age 65. The normal form of the retirement benefit is usually a single life annuity, sometimes with a period certain, payable monthly, with the first payment on the first day of the month after the participant has reached the normal retirement age. (It is convenient when the last salary is on the last day of the month in which the participant reaches retirement age.)

The plan may allow a participant to start receiving benefits early or late, or the plan may allow the participant to choose other forms of the retirement benefit as long as the actuarial present values of the optional form and of the normal form are equivalent. This stipulation ensures that the pension plan will not be responsible for a greater benefit than the one which has been funded. However, this calculation may be complex and the actuarial equivalence is often abandoned in favor of a simpler or more generous approach which normally has a measurable cost.

7.1.1 Early Retirement Option

If a participant has reached the age of early retirement eligibility and has completed the minimum service requirement, he may elect to retire at an age that is earlier than the normal retirement age; that is, he may elect the **early retirement option**. Since the benefit is being paid from an earlier age, we can understand that, in order for the actuarial present values of future benefits under early retirement and normal retirement to be equivalent, the benefit accrued until age of early retirement must be *reduced*. However, some plans provide for partial reduction only, and some plans provide the full accrued benefit if retirement occurs on or after age 62, or if the total of age plus service exceeds some number such as 85. Note that many forces may be at work when dealing with early retirement: fewer contributions, less investment income, longer benefit period, antiselection, state of health, love of work, loss of salary, and possibly non-pension assets.

Omitting the intangible forces, the early retirement benefit is calculated by equating the actuarial present values of the early retirement benefits and the normal retirement benefits. If the normal retirement age is r and a participant chooses to retire early at age x, then his yearly benefit, B, payable monthly, can be determined from

$$B \cdot \ddot{a}_x^{(12)} = B_x \frac{D_r}{D_x} \ddot{a}_r^{(12)},$$

where B_x is the benefit payable from normal retirement, based on the participant's service and salary at age x.

DISCUSSION QUESTION

7-1   What is the loss to a 2%-of-salary plan if a participant elects a non-reduced pension at age x?

EXAMPLE 7.1

The plan is a defined benefit plan covering 3 male participants.

Assume that on early retirement under the plan, the participant becomes entitled to a monthly benefit, commencing immediately, in an amount actuarially equivalent (calculated so as not to produce actuarial gain or loss) to the benefit accrued up to the time of early retirement.

Valuation assumptions:

	Preretirement	**Postretirement**[*]
Mortality	None	GAM
Interest	5%	4%

[*]Assume annuities are purchased at the time of actual retirement; annuity purchase rates are on the basis indicated for the postretirement period.

If y is the early retirement age, r is the normal retirement age, and B_y is the annual benefit (payable monthly starting at r) accrued to the date of early retirement, give an expression for the annual amount of the early retirement benefit?

$\boxed{\text{SOLUTION}}$ Let $E \cdot B_y$ denote the annual amount of the early retirement benefit, where E is the early retirement factor as in Example 6-19. Equating the actuarial present values of the future benefits under early and normal retirement, we have

$$E \cdot B_y \cdot \ddot{a}_y^{(12)} = B_y \frac{D_r}{D_y} \ddot{a}_r^{(12)},$$

where $E \cdot B_y$ and B_y are annual benefits, and the annuities are based on the postretirement interest rate of 4%. Since there is no preretirement mortality, the above equation reduces to

$$E \cdot B_y \cdot \ddot{a}_y^{(12)} = B_y (1.05)^{-(r-y)} \cdot \ddot{a}_r^{(12)},$$

and the expression for the annual early retirement benefit is

$$E \cdot B_y = B_y \left(\frac{1}{1.05} \right)^{r-y} \frac{\ddot{a}_r^{(12)}}{\ddot{a}_y^{(12)}}. \qquad \square$$

$\boxed{\textbf{EXAMPLE 7.2}}$

Plan effective date: 1/1/94

Normal retirement benefit: $10 per month for each year of service

Early retirement benefit (retirement at or after age 60): Actuarial equivalent of accrued benefit, based on valuation assumptions

Actuarial assumptions for valuation:

Mortality: 1971 GAM

Retirement: 65

Withdrawals: None

1994 experience: One participant retires at age 62 on 12/31/94 and one terminates fully vested at age 43 on 12/31/94. All other experience is exactly according to the actuarial assumptions.

What is the experience gain or loss during 1994 under each of the Entry Age Normal and Unit Credit cost methods?

> **SOLUTION** We can analyze the situation for each participant under each cost method as follows:

(1) The one who retires early:
    Entry Age:
        The participant receives the actuarial equivalent of the *accrued benefit*. Since the method has funded for more than the accrued benefit, there will be a gain on withdrawal.
    Unit Credit:
        The method has funded for exactly the accrued benefit, thus producing no gain or loss.
(2) The one who withdrew:
    The same situation as for person (1) prevails.

Thus the Entry Age Normal method produces a gain, but the Unit Credit method is not influenced by these two movements. Note that, in general, a gain or loss will result if a participant in a plan that uses a cost method other than Unit Credit retires early.   □

There are different ways of reducing the benefit when the early retirement option is chosen. A method for a level percentage plan would be to reduce the accrued benefit by a certain percentage for each month that early retirement precedes the normal retirement age. For a flat dollar plan, the flat dollar paid per month could be reduced. Another method would be to reduce the amount of the benefit upon reaching the age where Social Security payments begin, usually age 62. This results in a level amount of income during the participant's entire retirement, so this option is sometimes referred to as the **level income option**. The reduced amount before age r and the increased amount after age r would give a level income, when Social Security is included, and would be actuarially equivalent to the non-adjusted benefit. In other words, the value of the early retirement benefit is equated to the value of the level income payments less the value of the Social Security benefit.

EXAMPLE 7.3

Early retirement eligibility: Age 55

Early retirement benefit: Accrued benefit reduced $\frac{5}{12}\%$ per month for the first 60 months, and $\frac{3}{12}\%$ for each additional month, by which benefit commencement precedes age 65

A level income option is available at early retirement under which the pension reduces at age 62 by the amount of the estimated Social Security benefit. The level-income pension is actuarially equivalent to the normal pension, where the actuarial equivalence is based on the plan's early retirement factors. Smith retires at age 58 with an accrued benefit of $450 per month, and elects the level income option. Smith's Social Security benefit commencing at age 62 is estimated at $300 per month.

What is Smith's monthly benefit at age 58?

SOLUTION Since the actuarial equivalence is based on the plan's early retirement, we equate the actuarial present values of the level income option and the early retirement option. For retirement at age 58 the reduction is $60(\frac{5}{12}) + 24(\frac{3}{12}) = 31\%$, and for retirement at age 62 the reduction is $36(\frac{5}{12}) = 15\%$. Therefore, replacing $12\ddot{a}_x^{(12)}$ by a_x for notational convenience, we have

$$B_{58} \cdot a_{58:\overline{4}|} + (B_{58}-300)\frac{D_{62}}{D_{58}} a_{62} = 450(1-.31)a_{58}.$$

From the actuarial reduction, we notice that

$$(1-.31)a_{58} = (1-.15)\frac{D_{62}}{D_{58}} a_{62},$$

or $\frac{D_{62}}{D_{58}} \cdot \frac{a_{62}}{a_{58}} = \frac{.69}{.85}$. Replacing $a_{58:\overline{4}|}$ by $a_{58} - \frac{D_{62}}{D_{58}} a_{62}$ and dividing by a_{58}, we have

$$B_{58}\left[1 - \frac{D_{62}}{D_{58}} \cdot \frac{a_{62}}{a_{58}}\right] + (B_{58}-300)\frac{D_{62}}{D_{58}} \cdot \frac{a_{62}}{a_{58}} = 310.50,$$

or

$$B_{58}\left[1 - \frac{.69}{.85} + \frac{.69}{.85}\right] = 310.50 + 300\left(\frac{.69}{.85}\right).$$

Then Smith's monthly benefit at age 58 is

$$B_{58} = \$554. \qquad \square$$

7.1.2 Deferred Retirement Option

A participant may elect **late retirement**; that is, he may choose to retire at an age that is later than the normal retirement age. Some plans allow participants to remain active until age 70, and service beyond age 70 is with the consent of the employer. The benefit payable upon actual retirement may or may not give credit for service and salary increases beyond the normal retirement age. For example, the benefit payable from the late retirement age may just be the benefit that would otherwise have been payable from the normal retirement age if the participant had retired at that time. The benefit may also be determined using the formula for the normal retirement benefit, taking the service and the salary increases since normal retirement age into consideration. Finally, the present value of the future benefits may be actuarially equivalent to the present value of the future benefits payable under normal retirement.

EXAMPLE 7.4

Normal retirement age: 62
Normal retirement benefit: $10 per month for each year of service
Late retirement benefit: $10 per month for each year of service
Actuarial cost method: Unit Credit
Actuarial assumptions:
> Interest: 7%
> Preretirement deaths and terminations: None

Selected probabilities of retirement and annuity values:

x	$q_x^{(r)}$	$\ddot{a}_x^{(12)}$
60 or less	0.0	—
61	0.0	10.8
62	0.0	10.6
63	0.2	10.4
64	0.5	10.2
65	1.0	10.0

Retirements are assumed to occur at the beginning of the year.
Data for sole participant as of 1/1/94:
> Date of birth   1/1/34
> Date of hire   1/1/74

What is the actuarial liability as of 1/1/94?

⬚ **SOLUTION** ⬚ The Unit Credit liability is the present value of the pension benefit that has accrued so far, so it is based on the number of past years of service. Since retirement may occur at the beginning of three different years, we must take the probability of retirement into account, being careful to discount the annuity back to 1/1/94. The actuarial liability at that time is

$$(10 \times 12 \times 20) \left[v^3 \, \ddot{a}_{63}^{(12)} \, q_{63}^{(r)} + v^4 \, \ddot{a}_{64}^{(12)} \, p_{63}^{(\tau)} \, q_{64}^{(r)} + v^5 \, \ddot{a}_{65}^{(12)} p_{63}^{(\tau)} \, p_{64}^{(\tau)} \, q_{65}^{(r)} \right]$$

$$= 2400 \left[(1.07)^{-3} (10.4)(.2) + (1.07)^{-4} (10.2)(1-.2)(.5) \right.$$

$$\left. + (1.07)^{-5} (10)(1-.2)(1-.5)(1) \right] = \$18,390. \qquad \square$$

7.2 Optional Forms of Benefit

The normal form of the retirement benefit is sometimes a life annuity payable from the normal retirement age. This annuity provides the retiree with a monthly benefit which ceases upon his death. The plan may allow the participant, prior to retirement, to choose another form of the retirement benefit. This optional form should have an actuarial present value of future benefits equivalent to that under the normal form of the retirement benefit. This equivalence is used to determine the amount of the monthly benefit payable under the optional form. E, usually with a subscript, is used to denote the factor that the amount of the benefit in the normal form must be multiplied by in order to obtain the amount of the benefit in the optional form. Note that E is usually less than 1.00.

There are many different forms of a retirement benefit from which the participant may choose. A few of the most common options will be presented in this section. The optional form of payment usually provides protection for the participant's spouse (and children) in the event that the participant dies first.

Some plans offer a 10-year certain and life annuity. The benefit will be paid for 10 years if the participant dies within 10 years of retirement, or it will be paid until the participant dies if death occurs after 10 years of retirement. This option ensures the spouse (or another named beneficiary) of 10 years of income even if the participant has died. Using the equivalence principle, the benefit payable under the 10-year certain and life option, $E_{C\&L} \cdot B_{65}$, can be found from

$$E_{C\&L} \cdot B_{65} \left(\ddot{a}_{\overline{10|}}^{(12)} + {}_{10|} \ddot{a}_{65}^{(12)} \right) = B_{65} \cdot \ddot{a}_{65}^{(12)},$$

assuming retirement occurs at age 65 and the normal form is a life annuity.

DISCUSSION QUESTION

7-2 Give a scenario where E would exceed 1.00.

EXAMPLE 7.5

Early retirement benefit: Actuarial equivalent of pension payable at normal
retirement age 65

Optional form of pension: Life annuity with 120 months certain, on an actuarially equivalent basis

E_x is the factor by which the amount of pension in the normal form commencing at age 65 must be multiplied in order to obtain the amount
of pension in the optional form commencing at age x.

Find an expression for E_{55}.

SOLUTION The benefit under the optional form, $E_{55} \cdot B_{65}$, is paid from
age 55. Equating the actuarial present values of the future benefits under
the optional and the normal forms gives us

$$E_{55} \cdot B_{65} \left[\ddot{a}^{(12)}_{\overline{10}|} + {}_{10|}\ddot{a}^{(12)}_{55} \right] = B_{65} \frac{D_{65}}{D_{55}} \ddot{a}^{(12)}_{65},$$

so

$$E_{55} = \left[\frac{\ddot{a}^{(12)}_{65} \frac{D_{65}}{D_{55}}}{\ddot{a}^{(12)}_{\overline{10}|} + {}_{10|}\ddot{a}^{(12)}_{55}} \right],$$

or

$$E_{55} = \left[\frac{N^{(12)}_{65}}{D_{55} \cdot \ddot{a}^{(12)}_{\overline{10}|} + N^{(12)}_{65}} \right]. \qquad \square$$

Another common choice is the 100% joint and survivor payment
option. In this case the benefit is payable for the entire life-time of the participant and the spouse, ceasing upon the death of the last survivor. The
equivalence principle gives us

$$E_{J\&S} \cdot B_{65} \cdot \ddot{a}^{(12)}_{\overline{65:y}} = B_{65} \cdot \ddot{a}^{(12)}_{65},$$

where y is the age of the spouse. Recall that $\ddot{a}_{x:y}$ denotes a joint annuity
where payments cease upon the first death, and recall the relationship

$$\ddot{a}_{\overline{x:y}} = \ddot{a}_x + \ddot{a}_y - \ddot{a}_{x:y}.$$

There is also a joint and survivor option where the participant receives 100% of the benefit while alive, but the spouse receives only 50% of the benefit after the participant's death. The equivalence relationship becomes

$$E_{J\&50\%} \cdot B_{65} \cdot {}^{50\%}\ddot{a}_{\overline{65:y}}^{(12)} = B_{65} \cdot \ddot{a}_{65}^{(12)},$$

where

$${}^{50\%}\ddot{a}_{\overline{65:y}}^{(12)} = \frac{1}{2}\left(\ddot{a}_{65}^{(12)} + \ddot{a}_{\overline{65:y}}^{(12)}\right) = \ddot{a}_{65}^{(12)} + \frac{1}{2}\ddot{a}_y - \frac{1}{2}\ddot{a}_{\overline{65:y}}^{(12)}.$$

EXAMPLE 7.6

Normal retirement benefit: $1000 per month
Basis for early retirement or optional form conversion: Actuarial equivalence
Data for sole participant:

Date of birth	1/1/39
Date of retirement	1/1/94
Spouse's date of birth	1/1/42

Form of payment elected: Monthly benefit for life, with 50% continuing to the surviving spouse for life
Selected commutation functions:

x	N_x	$N_{x:x-3}$	x	N_x	$N_{x:x-3}$
51	377	3234	61	147	1106
52	345	2935	62	132	978
53	316	2659	63	119	862
54	289	2403	64	106	757
55	263	2168	65	95	661
56	240	1951	66	85	575

What is the spouse's monthly benefit if the participant dies first?

SOLUTION For notational simplicity, let $12\ddot{a}_x^{(12)}$ be denoted by a_x. The present value at age 55 of the normal pension is

$$1000\,\frac{D_{65}}{D_{55}}\,a_{65} = 12{,}000\,\frac{N_{65}^{(12)}}{D_{55}}.$$

If B is the spouse's monthly benefit, then the present value at age 55 of the optional pension is

$$2B \cdot \frac{1}{2} [a_{55} + a_{\overline{55:52}}] = B [2a_{55} + a_{52} - a_{55:52}]$$

$$= 12B \left[2 \frac{N_{55}^{(12)}}{D_{55}} + \frac{N_{52}^{(12)}}{D_{52}} - \frac{N_{55:52}^{(12)}}{D_{55:52}} \right].$$

Recall that $N_x^{(12)} \approx N_x - \frac{11}{24}D_x$ and $N_x = \sum_{k=0}^{\infty} D_{x+k}$. Then we have the values

$$N_{52}^{(12)} = 345 - \frac{11}{24}(345 - 3126) = 331.71,$$

$$N_{55}^{(12)} = 263 - \frac{11}{24}(263 - 240) = 252.46,$$

$$N_{65}^{(12)} = 95 - \frac{11}{24}(95 - 85) = 90.42,$$

and

$$N_{55:52}^{(12)} = 2168 - \frac{11}{24}(2168 - 1951) = 2068.54.$$

Solving for B we find

$$B = \frac{1000(90.42)/23}{2(252.46/23 + 331.71/29 - 2068.54/217)} = \$164.77. \qquad \square$$

EXAMPLE 7.7

Normal retirement benefit: $2500 per year, payable 1/1 each year

Normal form of payment: Life annuity payable to the retiree

For married participants, the plan provides for the following two optional forms of payment which are actuarially equivalent to the normal form of payment.

Option A: Annuity payable for the life of the retiree, with surviving spouse, after retiree's death, receiving 50% of the amount payable during their joint lifetime

Option B: Annuity payable during the joint life of the retiree and the spouse, with the survivor, after the first death, receiving 50% of the amount payable during their joint lifetime

Data for sole participant:

Date of birth   1/1/29

Date of retirement   1/1/94

Spouse's date of birth   1/1/32

Present value of future benefits as of 12/31/93: $26,000

Initial annual benefit under Option B: $2376

Selected annuity value: $\ddot{a}_{65:62} = 9.42$

What is the initial annual benefit under Option A?

| SOLUTION | The actuarial present value of future benefits under Option A, Option B, and the normal form are all equivalent. They are, respectively,

$$pvB_A = B_A \cdot \frac{1}{2}\left(\ddot{a}_{65} + \ddot{a}_{\overline{65:62}}\right),$$

$$pvB_B = (2376)\left(\frac{1}{2}\right)(\ddot{a}_{65} + \ddot{a}_{62}),$$

and

$$pvB_N = 2500\ddot{a}_{65}.$$

We know that the present value of future benefit is 26,000 so we can find

$$\ddot{a}_{65} = \frac{26,000}{2500} = 10.4$$

and

$$\frac{1}{2}(\ddot{a}_{65} + \ddot{a}_{62}) = 10.943.$$

Using the relationship $\ddot{a}_{\overline{65:62}} + \ddot{a}_{65:62} = \ddot{a}_{65} + \ddot{a}_{62}$, we have

$$pvB_A = B_A\left(\ddot{a}_{65} + \frac{1}{2}\ddot{a}_{62} - \frac{1}{2}\ddot{a}_{65:62}\right)$$

$$= B_A\left(10.943 + \frac{10.4}{2} - \frac{9.42}{2}\right) = 11.433B_A,$$

from which we find

$$B_A = \frac{26,000}{11,433} = \$2274. \qquad \square$$

EXAMPLE 7.8

Normal form of benefits: Straight life annuity
Mortality assumption: Unisex table subject to Gompertz' law
Age of participant at retirement: 65
Age of spouse at participant's retirement: 58
Gompertz adjustment for 7-year age difference: 4 years added to older life

The plan provides an option for an actuarially equivalent benefit on a joint
and survivor basis, with 120 months certain, as follows:

(1) The reduced initial monthly amount B is paid to the retired
participant for life.

(2) Upon death of the participant *after* having received at least
120 monthly payments, the surviving spouse receives monthly payments of $.75B$ for life.

(3) Upon the death of the participant *before* having received at
least 120 monthly payments, monthly payments of B will be
paid for the rest of the 120 month period to the spouse (if
alive) otherwise to the beneficiary, and then monthly
payments of $.75B$ will be continued to the spouse for life.

Find an expression for the factor to be multiplied by the amount of the
monthly pension on the normal form in order to find the initial monthly
amount B?

SOLUTION If the optional form were a 75% joint and survivor annuity,
then the equation of value would be

$$12B_{65} \cdot \ddot{a}_{65}^{(12)} = 12B_{J\&S}\left(.25\ddot{a}_{65}^{(12)} + .75\ddot{a}_{\overline{65:58}}^{(12)}\right)$$

$$= 12B_{J\&S}\left(\ddot{a}_{65}^{(12)} + .75\ddot{a}_{58}^{(12)} - .75\ddot{a}_{\overline{65:58}}^{(12)}\right).$$

Adjusting this to account for the payment of B for 10 years certain, we
obtain

$$B_{65} \cdot \ddot{a}_{65}^{(12)} = B\left(\ddot{a}_{\overline{10|}}^{(12)} + .25 \,_{10|}\ddot{a}_{65}^{(12)} + .75 \,_{10|}\ddot{a}_{\overline{65:58}}^{(12)}\right)$$

$$= B\left[\ddot{a}_{\overline{10|}}^{(12)} + \,_{10|}\ddot{a}_{65}^{(12)} + .75\left(\,_{10|}\ddot{a}_{58}^{(12)} - \,_{10|}\ddot{a}_{\overline{65:58}}^{(12)}\right)\right],$$

and solving for B we have

$$B = B_{65} \frac{\dfrac{N_{65}^{(12)}}{D_{65}}}{\ddot{a}_{\overline{10|}}^{(12)} + \dfrac{N_{75}^{(12)}}{D_{65}} + .75\dfrac{N_{68}^{(12)}}{D_{58}} - .75\dfrac{N_{79}^{(12)}}{D_{69}}} \cdot$$

□

Note that $_{10|}\ddot{a}_{65:58}^{(12)} = \dfrac{N_{75:68}^{(12)}}{D_{65:58}}$. Then Gompertz' law enables this joint annuity to be written in the form of a single life annuity by adding 4 years to the oldest age, giving us $\dfrac{N_{79}^{(12)}}{D_{69}}$.

| **EXAMPLE 7.9** |

Normal retirement benefit: $600 per month for life, with $300 per month
  continuing to the surviving spouse
Preretirement death benefit: None
Actuarial assumptions:
    Interest rate: 6%
    Preretirement terminations other than deaths: None
    Retirement age: 65
Data for sole participant:
    Date of birth   1/1/34
    Spouse's date of birth   1/1/29
Selected probability and annuity values (based on a unisex mortality table
  and 6% interest):

$$_{10}p_{60} = .80 \qquad 12\ddot{a}_{60}^{(12)} = 127 \qquad 12\ddot{a}_{60:65}^{(12)} = 94$$

$$_{5}p_{65} = .87 \qquad 12\ddot{a}_{65}^{(12)} = 112 \qquad 12\ddot{a}_{65:70}^{(12)} = 79$$

$$12\ddot{a}_{70}^{(12)} = 97$$

What is the present value of the normal retirement benefit as of 1/1/94?

| SOLUTION | Assuming retirement at age 65, there are 2 cases to be considered:

(1) The spouse dies before the participant reaches 65, so the participant receives a life annuity at retirement.

(2) The spouse is alive when the participant reaches 65, so the participant receives a 50% joint and survivor annuity. The case where the participant dies before reaching age 65 is not

considered since there is no preretirement death benefit. Then
the present value of future benefits at age 65 is

$$7200 \left[v^5 \, {}_5p_{60} \, {}_5p_{65} \, {}^{50\%}\ddot{a}^{(12)}_{65:70} + v^5 \, {}_5p_{60} \, (1 - {}_5p_{65})\ddot{a}^{(12)}_{65} \right]$$

$$= 7200 \left[v^5 \, {}_{10}p_{60} \left(\ddot{a}^{(12)}_{65} + .5\ddot{a}^{(12)}_{70} - .5\ddot{a}^{(12)}_{65:70} \right) + v^5 ({}_5p_{60} - {}_{10}p_{60})\ddot{a}^{(12)}_{65} \right]$$

$$= 43,401 + 6003 = \$49,404. \qquad \qquad \square$$

EXAMPLE 7.10

Optional form of benefit: Joint and 100% survivor annuity, actuarially
    equivalent to the normal form on valuation assumptions
Actuarial cost method: Aggregate
Assumed spouse's age: Same as participant's age
Assumed percent of normal pensions that will be paid under the joint-and-
    survivor form: 80
Assumed retirement age: 65
Valuation results as of 1/1/94:

Present value of future benefits for active participants	$ 960,000
Present value of future benefits for retired participants	700,000
Actuarial value of assets	800,000
Present value of future salaries	12,000,000
Annual salaries	1,500,000

Selected annuity values: $\ddot{a}^{(12)}_{65} = 10$; $\ddot{a}^{(12)}_{65:65} = 13$

After the above results were obtained, the plan was amended effective
    1/1/94 to provide, for participants retiring after that date, a uniform
    10% reduction rather than an actuarially equivalent reduction for the
    optional form. The 1/1/94 normal cost was then recalculated.

What is the recalculated normal cost for 1994 as of 1/1/94?

SOLUTION
Before the plan was amended, the benefit under the optional form was $E_{J\&S} \cdot B_{65}$, where

$$E_{J\&S} \cdot B_{65} \cdot \ddot{a}^{(12)}_{65:65} = B_{65} \cdot \ddot{a}^{(12)}_{65},$$

so $E_{J\&S} = \frac{10}{13}$. After the amendment the benefit is $E_{J\&S} = .90$, so the benefit improvement factor is

$$(.20)(1) + (.80)(.90) \div \left(\frac{10}{13}\right) = 1.136.$$

Under the Aggregate method we have $pvB - F = TNC \cdot \ddot{a}^s$, leading to

$$700{,}000 + 960{,}000(1.136) - 800{,}000 = TNC \cdot \frac{12{,}000{,}000}{1{,}500{,}000},$$

from which we find

$$TNC = \$123{,}820. \qquad \square$$

EXAMPLE 7.11

Normal retirement benefit: 50% of final year's compensation
Normal form of payment:
    Retirements before 1994: Life annuity
    Retirements after 1993:
        Single retirees: Life annuity
        Married retirees: Joint and 50% survivor annuity
Actuarial cost method: Aggregate
Retirement age: 65
Marital characteristics: 85% of participants are married at the time of retirement; spouses are the same age as participants
Valuation results as of 1/1/94, before change in normal form:

Normal cost as of 1/1	$ 85,000
Present value of future benefits for retired participants	400,000
Actuarial value of assets	600,000
Present value of future compensation	4,200,000
Annual compensation	350,000

Selected unisex annuity values: $\ddot{a}_{65}^{(12)} = 9.90$; $\ddot{a}_{65:65}^{(12)} = 7.82$

What is the normal cost for 1994 as of 1/1/94?

SOLUTION Under the Aggregate cost method, before the change in the normal form of payment we have

$$TNC \frac{\sum pvS}{\sum S} = \sum pvB - F,$$

where $\sum pvB$ is for retired and active participants. Letting $\sum pvB'$ denote the present value of future benefits for active participants, we have

$$85,000 \left(\frac{4,200,000}{350,000} \right) = (400,000 + \sum pvB') - 600,000$$

so

$$\sum pvB' = 1,220,000.$$

After the change in the normal form of payment,

$$\sum pvB' = 1,220,000(.15) + 1,220,000(.85) \frac{^{50\%}\ddot{a}^{(12)}_{\overline{65:65}}}{\ddot{a}^{(12)}_{65}},$$

where

$$^{50\%}\ddot{a}^{(12)}_{\overline{65:65}} = 9.9 + \frac{1}{2}(9.9) - \frac{1}{2}(7.82) = 10.94.$$

Then $\sum pvB' = 1,328,937$ and we can find the revised normal cost as

$$TNC = [(400,000+1,328,937) - 600,000] \left(\frac{350,000}{4,200,000} \right) = \$94,078. \quad \square$$

| EXAMPLE 7.12 |

Smith, age 60, is entitled to a pension payable under either Option A or Option B, which are actuarially equivalent.

          Option A: A life annuity-due paying $(B+500)$ per month for two years and B per month thereafter

          Option B: A life annuity-due paying 500 per month as long as Smith and his spouse (also age 60) are both alive, reducing at the first death to $(500-.50 \times B)$

Selected commutation functions and annuity values:

$$D_{60} = 147.8 \qquad\qquad D_{62} = 125.3$$

$$\ddot{a}^{(12)}_{60} = 9.8 \qquad\qquad \ddot{a}^{(12)}_{62} = 9.4 \qquad\qquad \ddot{a}^{(12)}_{60:60} = 8.1$$

What is B?

| SOLUTION | Let $12\ddot{a}^{(12)}_{x} = a_x$ for notational simplicity. The present value of Option A is

$$(B+500)a_{60:\overline{2}|} + B \frac{D_{62}}{D_{60}} a_{62} = (B+500)a_{60} - 500\frac{D_{62}}{D_{60}} a_{62}.$$

The present value of Option B is

$$2\left(500-\frac{B}{2}\right)a_{60} + (B-500)a_{60:60},$$

which gives $2\left(500-\frac{B}{2}\right) + (B-500)$ per year until the first death and $500-\frac{B}{2}$ thereafter until the second death. Equating, we have

$$(B+500)(9.8) - 500\left(\frac{125.3}{147.8}\right)(9.4) = (1000-B)(9.8) + (B-500)(8.1),$$

which solves for
$$B = \$420.39. \qquad \square$$

7.3 Assets

This section discusses asset issues, including dollar-weighted rates of return, time-weighted rates of return, and side funds.

Pension fund assets are what a pension fund owns. In order to understand a pension fund balance sheet and pension fund surplus, it is necessary to understand how the invested assets are valued.

Three ways of determining the value of **stock shares** are cost, market value, and actuarial value. Cost has the merit of simplicity but it becomes increasingly out of date. The chief disadvantage of market value is volatility. Actuarial values are market values with dampened volatility; one example of an actuarial value is $AV_t = AV_{t-1} + .20(MV_t - AV_{t-1})$ where MV_t is the market value of each asset at time t and AV_0 is the cost at the time of purchase, which is time 0. Another example is cost plus one-third of the sum of the unrealized capital gains in the last three years.

Three ways of determining the value of **bonds** are market value, amortized value, and actuarial value, which is a variation of the first two ways.

In addition to the actuarial value of invested assets, F, occasionally there are noninvested assets, such as bond coupons due but not received and other amounts owing.

EXAMPLE 7.13

Actuarial cost method: Unit Credit
Assumed interest rate: 7%

Valuation results:

	1/1/93	1/1/94
Normal cost as of 1/1	6,000	7,500
Actuarial liability	70,000	75,000
Actuarial value of assets	45,000	

Contribution for 1993 paid at 12/31/93: $9000
Net experience gain for 1993: $4500
Benefits paid at 7/1/93: $2000

What is the actuarial value of assets as of 1/1/94?

$\boxed{\text{SOLUTION}}$ Let 1/1/93 be time 0. Recall that the total experience gain is defined as $^{\text{exp}}UAL_1 - {}^{\text{act}}UAL_1$. Then we have

$$^{\text{tot}}G_1 = (UAL_0 + NC_0)(1+i) - {}^iC - UAL_1,$$

or

$$4500 = (25,000 + 6,000)(1.07) - 9,000 - (75,000 - F_1),$$

from which we find

$$F_1 = \$55,330. \qquad \square$$

Note that benefits paid do not affect gain because, normally, actual benefits equal expected benefits.

$\boxed{\text{EXAMPLE 7.14}}$
A master trust contains the assets for Plans A, B, and C. Total investment income each year is allocated to each plan in proportion to expected interest, using simple interest. Trust values and transactions for 1993:

	Plan A	Plan B	Plan C
Value of asssets as of 1/1/93	100,000	60,000	0
Contributions for 1993:			
3/31/93	20,000	40,000	100,000
6/30/93	20,000	0	0
9/30/93	20,000	40,000	0
12/31/93	20,000	0	200,000
Benefit payments for 1993:			
6/30/93	10,000	15,000	0
12/31/93	10,000	0	5,000

Total investment income for 1993: $100,000

What is the value of assets for Plan C as of 1/1/94?

$\boxed{\textbf{SOLUTION}}$ Let I be the interest earned on $1000 during one quarter.
The investment income for Plans A, B, and C, respectively, is

$$[(100 \times 4) + (20 \times 3) + (20 - 10)2 + 20]I \;=\; 500I,$$

$$[(60 \times 4) + (40 \times 3) - (15 \times 2) + 40]I \;=\; 370I,$$

and

$$(100 \times 3)I \;=\; 300I.$$

The total investment income for 1993 is $100,000 so we have

$$500I + 370I + 300I \;=\; 100{,}000$$

from which we find

$$I \;=\; 85.47.$$

Then the value of the assets for Plan C at 1/1/94 is

$$100{,}000 + 300(85.47) + 200{,}000 - 5{,}000 \;=\; \$320{,}641. \qquad \square$$

| EXAMPLE 7.15 |

A pension plan provides that any assets not needed to provide accrued
    benefits following plan termination are to be returned to the employer.
Plan vesting provision: 100% vested after 10 years service or upon earlier
    plan termination
Market value of assets at plan termination: $57,500
Participant data as of plan termination:

	Smith	Brown	Green
Age at entry	40	35	30
Age at plan termination	70	50	35
Accrued monthly benfit at termination	$400	$300	$150

Annuities will be purchased using annuity premiums based on the following
    commutation functions and annuity values without loading:

Age x	D_x	$12\ddot{a}_x^{(12)}$
30	23.0	
35	18.0	
40	14.0	
50	8.8	
65	3.3	100
70	2.5	90

What is the amount available to be returned to the employer?

| SOLUTION | Following plan termination, the employer receives the
excess of the assets over the amount of the accrued benefits. Assets are
valued at $57,500 and the present value of the accrued benefit can be
calculated using the participants' actuarial liabiliities, producing

$$AL = (400 \times 90) + \left(300 \times 100 \times \frac{3.3}{8.8}\right) + \left(150 \times 100 \times \frac{3.3}{18}\right) = 50,000.$$

Then the refund is

$$F - AL = \$7500. \qquad \square$$

7.3.1 Dollar-Weighted Rate of Return

Suppose we are given two values of the pension fund assets at different times and the transactions (contributions deposited and benefits withdrawn) that occur between the two dates. We can estimate the rate of return, i, earned on the fund throughout this time period by setting up the equation of value illustrated in the following examples. The rate estimated in this manner is called the **dollar-weighted rate of return.**

EXAMPLE 7.16

Market value of assets:

As of 1/1/94	$1,000,000
As of 6/30/94	1,025,000
As of 9/30/94	1,550,000
As of 12/31/94	1,500,000
Employer contribution at 7/1/94	500,000
Disbursement at 10/1/94	100,000

Using the approximation $(1+i)^t = 1 + t \cdot i$ for $t < 1$, what is the dollar-weighted rate of investment return for these assets for 1994?

SOLUTION The equation of value (in thousands) is

$$1000(1+i) + 500\left(1+\frac{1}{2}i\right) - 100\left(1+\frac{1}{4}i\right) = 1500,$$

from which we find

$$i = .0816. \qquad \square$$

Note that intermediate fund values are *not* used in this method.

EXAMPLE 7.17

Value of fund at 12/31/93: $65,000
Benefit payments: $1000 per month starting 1/1/94
Plan contributions: $5000 on each of 1/1/94, 4/1/94, 7/1/94, and 10/1/94
Amount withdrawn to pay plan expenses: $2000 on 7/1/94
Normal cost as of 1/1/94: $12,000
Assumed interest rate: 6%
Value of fund at 12/31/94: $80,000

What is the dollar-weighted rate of return for 1994?

SOLUTION The equation of value (in thousands) is

$$80 = 65(1+i) + 5\left[4+i\left(\frac{4}{4}+\frac{3}{4}+\frac{2}{4}+\frac{1}{4}\right)\right]$$
$$- 1\left[12 + i\left(\frac{12}{12}+\frac{11}{12}+\cdots+\frac{1}{12}\right)\right] - 2\left(1+\frac{1}{2}i\right),$$

which reduces to

$$80 = 65 + 65i + 20 + 5i\left(\frac{10}{4}\right) - 12 - i\left(\frac{78}{12}\right) - 2 - 2i\left(\frac{1}{2}\right),$$

from which we find

$$i = .1285. \qquad \square$$

EXAMPLE 7.18

The actuarial value of assets is determined as the average of book value and market value. You are given the following values:

	Book Value	Market Value
Value as of 1/1/94	1,000,000	800,000
Contribution paid at 7/1/94	100,000	100,000
Interest and dividends	100,000	100,000
Realized gains (losses)	(50,000)	(50,000)
Unrealized gains (losses)	N/A	100,000
Value as of 12/31/94	1,150,000	1,050,000

What is the dollar-weighted rate of return on the actuarial value of assets during 1994?

SOLUTION The actuarial value of the assets at 12/31/94 is

$$\frac{1,150,000 + 1,050,000}{2} = 1,100,000.$$

The equation of value is

$$\frac{1,000,000 + 800,000}{2}(1+i) + 100,000\left(1+\frac{i}{2}\right) = 1,100,000$$

which solves for

$$i = .1053. \qquad \square$$

Note that the actuarial value of assets in this question does not involve gains or losses.

7.3.2 Time-Weighted Rate of Return

In order to calculate the **time-weighted rate of return** on a pension fund, we must know the value of the fund at the beginning and at the end of each time interval, and the deposits and withdrawals made on the fund at the end of each time interval.

If the amount of the fund just before time t is F_t, and C_{t-1} is the contribution made at time $t-1$, then the rate of return for that interval is defined by

$$1 + i_t = \frac{F_t}{F_{t-1} + C_{t-1}}.$$

Note that t refers to the time of a transaction and that the different times between transactions may not be the same length. Note also that C_{t-1} may be positive or negative. Values of $1 + i_t$ must be calculated every time a deposit or a withdrawal is made.

Then the time-weighted rate of return is i, defined by

$$(1+i)^k = (1+i_1)(1+i_2) \cdots (1+i_n),$$

where the total time interval is k years and the number of transactions made during these k years is n.

EXAMPLE 7.19

Plan effective date: 1/1/93
Summary of fund activity for the period 1/1/93 to 1/1/95:

Date	Contributions	Benefits	Fund Balance (Market Value) After Transaction
1/1/93	$1000	—	$1000
7/1/93	500	—	1525
4/1/94	—	$1000	550
7/1/94	2000	—	2575
1/1/95	—	2500	0

What is the time-weighted annual rate of return for the period 1/1/93 to 1/1/95?

SOLUTION   We need the fund balance just before each transaction:

Date	Fund Balance Just Before Transaction
1/1/93	0
7/1/93	1025
4/1/94	1550
7/1/94	575
1/1/95	2500

Then the time-weighted annual rate of return is obtained from

$$(1+i)^2 = \frac{1025}{0+1000} \times \frac{1550}{1025+500} \times \frac{575}{1550-1000} \times \frac{2500}{575+2000},$$

which leads to
$$i = .0283. \qquad \square$$

Note that there is a multiplication term for each *time interval* in this method, and a *dollar weight* for each equation-of-value term in the dollar-weighted method.

EXAMPLE 7.20

All of a plan's assets are invested in the XYZ Mutual Fund.
As of 1/1/94, the assets consisted entirely of 10,000 shares of XYZ Mutual Fund, with a market value of $100,000.
On 7/1/94, the annual contribution of $24,000 was made, which purchased an additional 3000 shares of XYZ Mutual Fund. No other transactions occurred during the year.
As of 12/31/94, the assets consisted entirely of 13,000 shares of XYZ Mutual Fund, with a market value of $136,500.
The actuary is valuing the assets of the plan on a market value basis, and is using a 6% valuation interest rate.

Which of the following statements are true?

I.   There was a gain from investments for the year.

II.   The size of the annual contribution did not affect the time-weighted rate of return.

III.   The dollar-weighted rate of return exceeded the time-weighted rate of return for the year.

SOLUTION First we find the share values at each date, which are needed to find the fund balances:

At 1/1/94 there are 10,000 shares at \$10/share.

At 7/1/94 there is a contribution of 3000 shares at \$8/share, so the fund balance is 80,000 just before the contribution, and 104,000 just after it.

At 12/31/94 there are 13,000 shares at \$10.50/share.

The equation of value used to calculate the dollar-weighted rate of return is

$$100,000(1+i) + 24,000\left(1+\frac{1}{2}i\right) = 136,500$$

leading to a dollar-weighted rate of .11161. For the time-weighted rate we have

$$1+i = \frac{80,000}{100,000} \times \frac{136,500}{104,000},$$

leading to a time-weighted rate of .05. Using a 6% valuation rate, the expected year-end fund is

$$F_1 = 100,000 \times 1.06 + 24,000 \times 1.03 = \$130,720.$$

Then we see that Statement I is *true*, since the actual fund of 136,500 exceeds the expected fund of 130,720. Statement II is also *true*, as can be seen by recalculating the time-weighted rate using a contribution of greater or less than 24,000. It is easy to see that Statement III is *true*, since .11161 > .05. □

7.3.3 Side Funds

Some pension plans provide for monthly pension benefits from the normal retirement age along with a preretirement death benefit. A life insurance policy accumulates cash values and provides for the death benefit. These cash values will not normally accumulate to the full amount needed at retirement to pay for the future benefits, which have a present value of $pv_r B_r$ at that time. The balance needed will be accumulated at interest in a **side fund**. If 65 is the normal retirement age, then

$$pv_{65}B_{65} = CV_{65} + SF_{65},$$

where CV_{65} is the cash value at age 65 and SF_{65} is the amount in the side fund at age 65. The employer contribution is normally the premium for the insurance plus the normal cost for the side fund.

The normal cost is such that

$$NC \cdot \ddot{s}_{\overline{r-a}|} = SF_r = pv_r B_r - CV_r.$$

This formula may be added to the Summary of Cost Methods in Section 4.6.
Side funds are less important today than they were in the 1970's.

EXAMPLE 7.21

Plan effective date: 1/1/94
Normal retirement benefit: $500 per month
Preretirement death benefit: 100 times the monthly normal retirement
benefit (provided by individual insurance policies)
Actuarial cost method: Individual Level Premium
Actuarial assumptions for side fund:
   Interest: 6%
   Preretirement mortality and withdrawal: None
   Retirement age: 65
   Selected annuity value: $\ddot{a}_{65}^{(12)} = 10$
Participant data as of 1/1/94:

	Smith	Brown
Attained age	45	59
Age at hire	25	40
Cash value of insurance at age 65	$25,000	$12,000

What is the normal cost for the side fund for 1994 as of 1/1/94?

SOLUTION Since the normal costs paid into the side fund will accumulate to SF_{65} at age 65, then

$$NC \cdot \ddot{s} = SF_{65}.$$

Normal costs are paid for 20 years for Smith and 6 years for Brown. We
must calculate SF_{65} for each individual. For Smith we have

$$SF_{65} = pv_{65}B_{65} - CV_{65} = (500)(12)(10) - 25,000 = 35,000$$

and for Brown we have

$$SF_{65} = (500)(12)(10) - 12,000 = 48,000.$$

The total normal cost for the side fund is

$$NC = \frac{35,000}{\ddot{s}_{\overline{20}|}} + \frac{48,000}{\ddot{s}_{\overline{6}|}} = \$7389. \qquad \square$$

EXAMPLE 7.22

A plan is split-funded with insurance policies and a side fund. The guaranteed cash values of the insurance policies at retirement are used to provide a portion of the retirement benefits at a conversion rate of $1200 per $10 of monthly pension. The remainder of the retirement benefit is provided through the side fund. The amount of whole life insurance purchased is 60 times the expected monthly pension benefit.

Actuarial cost method: Individual Level Premium
Actuarial assumptions for the side fund:

Interest: 6%
Salary scale: None
Mortality and other decrements prior to age 65: None
Selected annuity value: $12\ddot{a}_{65}^{(12)} = \$120$

An insurable female participant enters the plan on 1/1/94 at age 39 with an expected benefit of $200 per month. The cash value of her insurance policy at age 65 is $550 per $1000 of insurance.

What is the normal cost for 1994 as of 1/1/94 for the side fund for this participant?

SOLUTION The ILP normal cost is

$$NC = (pv_{65}B_{65} - CV_{65})(1.06)^{-26} \div \ddot{a}_{\overline{26}|}$$
$$= (200 \times 120 - 6600) \div \ddot{s}_{\overline{26}|} = \$276.66. \qquad \square$$

EXAMPLE 7.23

Plan effective date: 1/1/93
Actuarial cost method: Individual Level Premium (split-funded); the total normal cost is equal to the side-fund normal cost plus life insurance premiums
Normal retirement benefit: 60% of final salary
Death benefit: 50 times the projected monthly normal retirement benefit, provided by whole life insurance
Actuarial assumptions for the side fund:

Interest: 8%
Salary increases: None
Preretirement deaths and terminations: None
Retirement age: 65
Selected annuity value: $12\ddot{a}_{65}^{(12)} = 100$

Data for sole participant:

Date of birth	1/1/58
1/1/93 monthly salary	$3000
1/1/94 monthly salary	$3300

Insurance policy data:

Issue Age	Premium per $1000	Cash Value at 65 per $1000
35	$30	$500
36	32	450

What is the excess of the total normal cost for 1994 as of 1/1/94 over the total normal cost for 1993 as of 1/1/93?

SOLUTION Let 1/1/93 be time 0. The change in the monthly normal retirement benefit is

$$\Delta B_{65} = (3300-3000)(.60) = 180,$$

and the change in the death benefit is

$$180 \times 50 = 9000.$$

The cash value at age 65 is

$$CV_{65} = 450 \times 9 = 4050,$$

and

$$pv_{65}B_{65} - CV_{65} = 180 \times 100 - 4050 = 13,950.$$

Under ILP,

$$\Delta NC_1 \cdot \ddot{s}_{\overline{29}|} = 13,950$$

so that

$$\Delta NC_1 = 124.24.$$

Then the total normal cost is

$$NC_1 = 124.24 + 32 \times 9 = \$412.24. \qquad \square$$

EXAMPLE 7.24

Normal retirement benefit: 50% of final salary

Actuarial cost method: Aggregate with normal costs determined as level
   dollar amount, split-funded

Actuarial assumptions for the side fund:

   Interest: 6%

   Salary increases: 4%

   Preretirement deaths and terminations: None

   Retirement age: 65

   Selected annuity value: $\ddot{a}_{65}^{(12)} = 10$

Data for sole participant as of 1/1/94:

Date of birth	1/1/59
Annual salary for 1993	$50,000

Life insurance policy data:

Annual premium	$ 3,250
Current cash value	10,000
Guaranteed cash value at age 65	110,000

Actuarial value of assets (not including cash value) as of 1/1/94: $20,000

What is the side-fund normal cost for 1994 as of 1/1/94?

SOLUTION The benefit at 65 is

$$B_{65} = (.5)(50,000)(1.04)^{29} = 77,966.$$

Subtracting the guaranteed cash value at age 65 from the present value of
future benefits at age 65, we obtain

$$pv_{65}B_{65} - CV_{65} = 77,966(10) - 110,000 = 669,663.$$

Since the assets of 20,000 do not include the insurance cash value, the
normal cost at 1/1/94 is

$$NC \cdot \ddot{a}_{\overline{30|}} = (669,663)(1.06)^{-30} - 20,000 = \$6620. \qquad \square$$

To check the result, note that the value in the side fund after 30 years is
$20,000(1.06)^{30} + 6620\ddot{s}_{\overline{30|}}$. Adding in the cash value of 110,000 we have
the correct amount to purchase the required pension.

7.4 Exercises

7.1 Retirement Options

7-1   Early retirement eligibility: Age 55
       Early retirement benefit: Accrued benefit actuarially reduced
       The plan offers a "level income" option to participants who retire
         before age 65, under which the pension payable at early
         retirement is larger than the normal amount, but reduces at
         age 65 by the estimated Social Security benefit commencing at
         age 65. The optional form is actuarially equivalent to the
         normal form.
       Smith retires at age 60.
       Smith's accrued normal retirement benefit: $500 per month
       Smith's estimated Social Security benefit at age 65: $400 per month
       Selected commutation functions:

Age x	D_x	$N_x^{(12)}$
55	1600	23,000
60	1300	16,000
65	1000	10,000

       What is the monthly benefit from age 60 to age 65 to Smith under
       the "level income" option?

7-2   Normal retirement benefit: 50% of average compensation deter-
         mined by using the 5 consecutive year period prior to normal
         retirement date that provides the highest average
       Postponed retirement benefit: The actuarial equivalent of the benefit
         that would have been payable had the participant retired at
         normal retirement date, with no provision for any interim
         death benefit
       Selected actuarial factors:

Age x	D_x	$12\ddot{a}_x^{(12)}$
65	1200	110
66	1100	105
67	1000	100

Participant Smith was born 1/1/31, was hired on 1/1/80, and postponed retirement until 1/1/98.

Smith's compensation history is as follows:

Year	Compensation
1980 -1984	Under $4,000
1985 -1989	Under 10,000
1990	12,400
1991	12,600
1992	15,000
1993	11,400
1994	10,400
1995	10,000
1996	16,200
1997	11,800

What is Smith's monthly retirement benefit on 1/1/98?

7.2 Optional Forms of Benefit

7-3   An employee age x is entitled to a monthly life annuity of $100 commencing immediately. He elects to take his benefit as a reduced annuity payable for his life, with 75% of the reduced annuity payable after his death to his spouse age y.

Selected commutation functions:

$$N_x^{(12)} = 1,000,000 \qquad D_x = 104,000$$

$$N_y^{(12)} = 1,100,000 \qquad D_y = 110,000$$

$$N_{xy}^{(12)} = 800,000 \qquad D_{xy} = 92,000$$

Find the monthly benefit to which the employee is entitled.

7-4   There are two joint and survivor options under a plan, provided on
      an actuarial equivalent basis:
      100% option: Pension is paid for life of employee; upon employee's
            death, if there is a surviving spouse, 100% of amount paid to
            employee is paid for the life of the spouse
      50% option: Pension is paid for life of employee; upon employee's
            death, if there is a surviving spouse, 50% of amount paid to
            employee is paid for the life of the spouse
      The "factor" is multiplied by the amount of the employee's pension
            on a single life annuity basis to determine the amount of
            pension under the joint and survivor option prior to the em-
            ployee's death.

      If the factor for the 100% option is .6 for a particular employee and
      spouse, what is the factor for the 50% option?

7-5   Normal retirement benefit: 1000 per month
      Normal form of payment: Life annuity with 5 years certain

      Actuarially equivalent optional forms of payment:

          Option A: The initial monthly benefit is payable for 5 years
      certain and the remaining lifetime of the participant, with 50% of
      the initial monthly benefit payable for the surviving beneficiary's
      lifetime following the participant's death.   However, there is no
      reduction in the benefit paid to the surviving beneficiary until the
      end of the 5-year certain period.

          Option B: Same as Option A, except the percentage continu-
      ing to the surviving beneficiary is 75%.

      Initial monthly benefit under Option A: 840

      What is the initial monthly benefit under Option B?

7.3 Assets

7-6   Actuarial cost method: Entry Age Normal
Assumed interest rate: 6%
Unfunded actuarial liability as of 1/1/93: $60,000
1993 contribution: Normal cost plus $4000, paid at 1/1/93
There were no experience gains or losses in 1993.

Data as of 1/1/94:

Attained Age	Number of Partic- ipants	Annual Salary	Normal Cost as of 1/1	Present Value of Future Salaries	Present Value of Future Benefits
45	1	$14,000	$700	$225,000	$ 40,000
65	1	25,000	—	—	140,000

What is the actuarial value of assets as of 1/1/94?

7-7   Asset data for 1994:

	Date	Amount
Market values of fund:	1/01/94	$50,000
	3/31/94	50,515
	6/30/94	46,705
	9/30/94	48,136
	1/01/95	63,651
Benefits paid:	4/01/94	5,200
	12/31/94	10,100
Contributions received:	10/01/94	20,000
	12/31/94	2,700

What is the dollar-weighted rate of return for 1994?

7-8   On 1/1/94, plan assets consist of common stocks with a market
       value of $1,911,000.
       Transactions during 1994:
           On 3/31/94 a contribution of $120,000 is made. Immediately
               after this contribution is made, the market value of the assets
               is $2,222,000.
           On 9/30/94, a lump sum distribution of $4000 is made. Immed-
               iately after this distribution is made, the market value of the
               assets is $2,107,000.
       On 12/31/94, the assets have a market value of $2,194,000.
       Use the approximation $(1+i)^t = 1 + ti$, for $0 < t < 1$.

       What was the plan's dollar-weighted and time-weighted rate of
       investment return for 1994?

7-9   Asset data for 1993:

	Fund A	Fund B
Value 1/1/93	$1000	$1000
Value 3/1/93	1100	1100
Contribution 7/1/93	0	1000
Value 7/1/93 (including above contribution)	990	1990
Value 1/1/94	1089	2189

       There were no disbursements from either fund. Which of the
       following statements regarding the rate of return for 1993 are true?

       I.   For Fund A, the time-weighted rate of return is equal to the
            dollar-weighted rate of return.

       II. The time-weighted rates of return for Fund A and Fund B are
            equal.

       III. For Fund B, the dollar-weighted rate of return exceeds the time-
            weighted rate of return.

7-10 Plan effective date: 1/1/94
      Funding medium: Individual life insurance policies with side fund
      Amount of life insurance: 75 times the expected monthly pension
      Actuarial cost method: Individual Level Premium
      The side fund normal cost is determined separately for benefits not
          provided by cash values of insurance policies at age 65.
      Normal retirement benefit: 40% of final average salary
      Actuarial assumptions for side fund:
          Interest: 6%
          Preretirement mortality and terminations: None
          Salary increases: None
          Retirement age: 65
          Selected annuity value: $12\ddot{a}_{65}^{(12)} = 110$
      Data as of 1/1/94 for sole participant:
          Date of birth   1/1/53
          Date of hire   1/1/93
          1994 annual compensation $54,000
      Cash value at age 65 per $1000 of insurance: $350

      Find the 1994 normal cost for the side fund as of 1/1/94.

7-11 Normal retirement benefit: $1000 per month
      Preretirement death benefit: 100 times normal retirement benefit
          (provided by individual ordinary life policies)
      Actuarial cost method: Aggregate (split-funded)
      Actuarial assumptions for the side fund:
          Interest: 7%
          Preretirement deaths and terminations: None
          Retirement age: 65
          Selected annuity value: $\ddot{a}_{65}^{(12)} = 10$
      Participant data as of 1/1/94:

	Attained Age	Cash Value of Insurance at Age 65
Smith	30	$40,000
Brown	40	30,000

      Actuarial value of side-fund assets as of 1/1/94: $5000

      What is the side-fund normal cost for 1994 as of 1/1/94?

7-12 An actuary is currently valuing several pension plans (each covering 2 to 10 participants) using assumptions which do not include a salary scale. The actuary is considering retaining the same assumptions except that a salary scale will be added; future normal costs will be calculated under the Aggregate cost method as a level percentage of the future anticipated payroll to the normal retirement date.

Which of the following statements concerning the effect of this proposed change are true?

I. The percentage increase in plan normal costs as a result of the salary scale will be greater for an "excess only" plan (*e.g.*, a benefit of $k\%$ of aggregate monthly compensation in excess of $500) than if the benefit under the plan were $k\%$ of the average monthly compensation.

II. One plan is being split-funded with life insurance policies; the guaranteed cash values of the policies at normal retirement are being used to provide a portion of the participant's benefit, with the remaining benefit being funded through the side fund. (When the salary scale is added, there will be no assumption as to purchases of additional life insurance policies.)   The percentage increase in the side fund normal cost for this split-funded plan will be greater than if this plan were not split-funded.

III. Certain plans provide that the 5-year average monthly compensation used to determine benefits will be calculated excluding compensation within the 5-year period immediately preceding the normal retirement date.   It is possible that the normal cost for some of these plans will be lower with a salary scale than without a salary scale.

7-13   Plan effective date: 1/1/94
       Funding medium: Individual life insurance policies with side fund
       The plan provides insurance coverage of $1000 for each $10 of ex-
           pected monthly retirement income.
       Actuarial cost method: Individual Level Premium, with side fund
           normal cost determined separately for benefits not provided by
           cash values of insurance policies at age 65
       Actuarial assumptions for side fund:
           Interest: 5%
           Turnover: None
           Preretirement mortality: None
           Salary increases: None
           Retirement age: 65
           Selected annuity value: $12\,\ddot{a}_{65}^{(12)} = 100$
       Insurance and participant data as of 1/1/94:

	Smith	Brown
Insurance coverage	$35,000	$40,000
Cash value of policy at age 65	15,000	18,000
Policy premium due 1/1/94	580	970
Age on 1/1/94	30	40
Age at hire	25	25

       What is the side-fund normal cost for 1994 as of 1/1/94?

7-14   Plan effective date: 1/1/93
       Actuarial cost method: Individual Aggregate with side fund
       Actuarial assumptions:
           Interest rate: 6%
           Compensation increases: None
           Preretirement deaths and terminations: None
           Retirement age: 65
       Preretirement death benefit: 100 times the monthly projected retire-
           ment benefit, provided by a whole life insurance policy

Data and valuation results for sole participants as of 1/1/94:

	Smith	Brown
Age	60	57
Monthly projected retirement benefit	$ 500	$ 200
Present value of retirement benefits	41,900	14,072
Allocated assets	7,500	0
Annual premium as of 1/1	3,000	1,000
Cash value of policy at age 65 per $1000 of insurance	200	250

Find the 1994 normal cost plus premiums as of 1/1/94.

7-15   Normal retirement benefit: 40 per month for each year of service
        Preretirement death benefit: Lump sum equal to 50 times the
            monthly projected normal retirement benefit; provided by a
            whole life insurance policy
        Actuarial cost method: Aggregate, split-funded with life insurance
        Actuarial assumptions:
            Interest rate: 7% per year
            Preretirement deaths and terminations: None
            Retirement age: 65
        Data for sole participant:
            Date of birth   1/1/52
            Date of hire   1/1/87
        Cash value at age 65 per 1000 of life insurance: 200
        Annual premium as of 1/1/92: 800
        Value of assets in side fund as of 1/1/92: 5000
        Selected annuity value: $\ddot{a}_{65}^{(12)} = 8.74$

What is the normal cost for the side fund for 1992 as of 1/1/92?

Chapter 8

Observations

8.1 Comparison of Methods

8.1.1 Traditional Unit Credit

Compared to other methods, Traditional Unit Credit has the lowest normal costs at the low ages, because of discounting for interest (v^{r-x}) and mortality ($_{r-x}p_x$) for many years, and the highest normal costs at the high ages because there is discounting for interest and mortality for just a few years. The discounting is clearly seen in the expression

$$NC_x = .02 \times S_x \times v^{r-x} \,_{r-x}p_x \cdot \ddot{a}_r^{(12)}$$

for a 2% plan. As a percentage of salary, the age 60 normal cost can be more than 100 times the age 30 normal cost. If we allow for modest inflation, the dollar normal cost at age 60 (in 30 years) can be expected to be 300 times the normal cost at age 30.

For a young work force, the funding is comparatively low under this method, and it should be realized that the method does not take into account the cost of future accruals or even the total cost of past accruals when the benefits are based on future salary. When the benefits are based on future salary, it is not appropriate to calculate a normal cost without a salary scale assumption. For an older work force, the normal cost is high, and, in an economic recession, if young union workers are laid off, the normal cost can increase considerably as a percentage of payroll. If older middle managers are laid off, the normal cost will decrease. For an average work force in average economic times, the normal cost as a percentage of payroll will increase very slowly each year as the age distribution matures. The actuary should consider including the future expected trend in normal costs in the valuation report.

The actuarial liability is lower than under other methods. This can be seen retrospectively, because the normal costs at the low ages are low, and prospectively, because the normal costs at the high ages are high:

AL = accumulation of past normal costs (net of benefits)

= pv of benefits accrued before and after valuation, minus pv of future normal costs (where the normal costs increase each year as age increases)

The withdrawal benefit for vested participants under all actuarial cost methods is usually equal to the TUC actuarial liability, which, in turn, is equal to the present value of the accrued benefit. However, the withdrawal benefit could be larger if (a) the plan is contributory, (b) a lower interest rate is used, or (c) an inflation assumption is used in calculating the withdrawal benefit.

We can treat the withdrawal of vested participants as a decrement and obtain the normal cost for the retirement benefit, or we can obtain the normal cost for the retirement and withdrawal benefits by not using the withdrawal decrement.

As an historical note, recall that two expressions for the normal cost are

$$NC_x = b_x \cdot v^t \cdot {_tp_x} \cdot \ddot{a}_r^{(12)}$$

and

$$NC_x = \Delta B_x \cdot v^t \cdot {_tp_x} \cdot \ddot{a}_r^{(12)}.$$

If the first expression is used, a supplemental liability is required when there is an experience loss; this is consistent with other cost methods as discussed in Section 3.6. If the second expression is used, NC_x is larger and *includes* the experience loss; this is an older form of Unit Credit which does not meet the requirements of ERISA.

DISCUSSION QUESTION

8-1   What are the arguments for and against using the Unit Credit method for a flat benefit plan, where the benefit is, say, $30 per month for each year of service subject to renegotiation every third year? (Note that the increase usually applies to service before and after the renegotiation date, and sometimes to retirees.)

8.1.2 Projected Unit Credit

For example, for a final salary 2% plan,

$$NC_x = .02 \times S_x \times (1.05)^{64-x} \times v^{r-x}{}_{r-x}p_x \cdot a_r^{(12)}.$$

This method utilizes a salary scale assumption, which means that the pension benefit accrued in most years, the normal cost in most years, and the actuarial liability in all years are larger than under the traditional unit credit method. The ratio of the age 60 normal cost to the age 30 normal cost might be around 300 with a zero salary scale, 30 with a low salary scale, and 3 with a high salary scale. Similarly, the higher the salary scale the higher the actuarial liability. It is important to use carefully considered and consistent assumptions for salary, inflation, and interest. (See also Sections 8.3.5, 8.3.7, and 8.3.10.)

| DISCUSSION QUESTIONS |

8-2 If $NC_{30} > NC_{60}$, is the salary scale too high between the ages of 30 and 60?

8-3 Is it better to express contributions in dollars or as a percentage of salary?

8-4 For a final salary plan with one member at each age, would the total normal cost be higher under Traditional Unit Credit or Projected Unit Credit? Would the answer change if the plan were career average?

The following questions are helpful in understanding the differences between the Traditional and Projected Unit Credit methods. For simplicity, assume a benefit of 2% of *current* salary for each year of service, with $e = 30$, $\ddot{a}_{65}^{(12)} = 10$, $i = 0$, and no expected mortality.

8-5 Under Traditional Unit Credit:

(a) At time 0, if $S_{50} = 10,000$, what are AL_{50} and NC_{50}?

(b) At time 1 we learn that $S_{51} = 10,500$; what are AL_{51} and NC_{51}?

(c) What is the experience loss due to salary; in other words, what amount of AL_{51} is due to the extra salary?

(d) At time 2 we learn that the actual S_{52} is 10,700; what is AL_{52}? What is the experience loss due to salary which is included in AL_{52}?

8-6   Under Projected Unit Credit using final salary with $s = .02$:

(a) Calculate AL_{50}, NC_{50}, AL_{51}, NC_{51}, and AL_{52}.

(b) What is the experience loss due to higher-than-expected salary which emerges at time 1 and time 2? Are these losses included in, or in addition to, AL_{51} and AL_{52}?

8.1.3 Modified Unit Credit

The Traditional Unit Credit and Projected Unit Credit methods divide the total pension benefit by the years of participation so that the benefit accruing each year is $b = \dfrac{B}{r - e}$ if actual salary equals expected salary.

Modified Unit Credit methods can employ a salary scale and an accrual each year which is a percentage of salary. For example, suppose the pension benefit is 2% of final salary for, say, 35 years of service and a 5% salary scale is used. Let $b_x = K \cdot S_x$ and note that $B = .70S_{64}$. Then $K(S_{30}+S_{31}+ \cdots) = .70S_{64}$, or

$$K = \frac{.70S_{64}}{S_{30} + S_{31} + \cdots}.$$

Then

$$NC_{30} = K \cdot S_{30} \times v^{35} \, {}_{35}p_{30} \cdot \ddot{a}_{65}^{(12)},$$

$$NC_{31} = K \cdot S_{31} \times v^{34} \, {}_{34}p_{31} \cdot \ddot{a}_{65}^{(12)},$$

and so on. Modified Unit Credit is not a standard cost method; for this reason it was not discussed in Chapter 2.

DISCUSSION QUESTIONS

8-7   (a) Write expressions for each of NC_{30}, NC_{31}, and NC_{32} for each of the three methods above, where salaries increase by 5% each year.

(b) Are these normal costs level or increasing?

8-8   Revise the three expressions for NC_{32} developed in Question 8-7(a) in the cases where (a) the actual salaries are $S_{31} = 1.06S_{30}$ and $S_{32} = 1.07S_{31}$, and (b) the future expected salaries are are given by the relationship $S_{x+1} = $ actual $S_x \times 1.05$.

8.1.4 Entry Age Normal

With the level dollar method, the cost of the projected benefit is spread as a level dollar cost over the working years. (Note that the "projected" benefit is the accrued benefit for all years of service, whereas "Projected" Unit Credit is Unit Credit with a salary scale.)

With the level percentage method, the cost of the projected benefit is spread as a level percent of pay over the working years which, compared to the level dollar method, would equate to lower dollar normal cost in the early years and higher in the later years. More employees in practice are covered under level percentage than under level dollar.

If a salary scale is not used with a final pay plan, the normal costs are lower but experience losses emerge.

If a mortality decrement is not used, normal costs are higher but experience gains emerge in the event of death before retirement, assuming that the death benefit is less than the actuarial liability.

If a withdrawal decrement is not used, normal costs are higher but experience gains emerge in the event of withdrawal, assuming that the withdrawal benefit is less than the actuarial liability.

The actuarial liabilities under Entry Age Normal and Unit Credit are compared in the following figure.

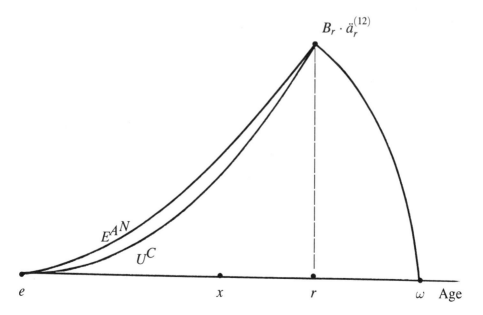

DISCUSSION QUESTIONS

8-9   Assuming no salary scale, show that the level dollar EAN actuarial
       liability is always greater than the UC actuarial liability.

8-10   When is the UC normal cost greater than the EAN normal cost?

8-11   Would the above graph need to be substantially modified to allow for
       (a) a salary scale? (b) level percent EAN instead of level dollar
       EAN?

8-12   In a plan with an accrued benefit of 2% of career average pay, what
       is the gain on vested withdrawal if the cost method is Traditional
       Unit Credit?

8-13   Referring to the above graph and Questions 8-11(b) and 8-12, what
       is the gain if the cost method is (a) level dollar EAN? (b) level
       percent EAN?

8-14   If there is one member at each age, is the total normal cost higher
       under Entry Age level dollar or level percentage?

8-15   Assuming inflation of, say, 5% per year for many years, explain
       why costs as a level percent of pay can make more sense than level
       dollar costs.

8.1.5 Individual Level Premium

This method spreads the cost of the pension benefit, usually in level dollars, from the age at inception to the age at retirement. Additional pension
benefits involve additional normal costs. Sometimes the costs (premiums)
are guaranteed and the actuarial bases and actuarial liabilities are suitably
conservative.
    Spreading the cost as a level percent of pay is not usually done with
this method. If there is a large salary increase near retirement, there will
be a large increase in normal cost until retirement; with EAN there would
be a smaller increase in supplemental cost for a longer period.

8.1.6 Individual Attained Age Normal

This method is not commonly used, and was not discussed in Chapter 3
(although it had been included in the first edition of this text). Individual
AAN starts off with an initial unfunded liability for past service computed

under the Unit Credit Cost Method (and hence smaller than EAN). The following properties apply to IAAN:

- $UAL_a = B_a \cdot \dfrac{D_r}{D_a} \cdot \ddot{a}_r^{(12)}$

- The amortization of UAL_a is over the period to retirement (unless otherwise stated).

- The normal cost is such that, at age a,

$$NC^{\text{IAAN}} \cdot \ddot{a}_{a:\overline{r-a|}} = pv_a(B_r - B_a).$$

- $AL_x = pv_x(B_r - B_a) - pv_x NC^{\text{IAAN}}.$

DISCUSSION QUESTIONS

8-16   Compare and contrast level dollar EAN, IAAN, and ILP.

8-17   Which of the following characteristics affect plan cost: age, sex, service, salary, active participants, terminated participants, disabled participants, retired participants, and beneficiaries?

8.1.7 Individual Aggregate

Recall that this method is characterized by

$$pvNC = pvB - F^P,$$

where NC is the normal cost for a participant, and F^P is the portion of the fund allocated to the participant. At the inception of the plan, some of the individual normal costs can be very high because (a) there is normally no supplemental liability, (b) some of the participants may be near retirement age, and (c) the fund is small or zero.

Individual Aggregate is widely used for small plans, and can be more appropriate than Aggregate when there are a few older and a few younger participants.

This individual cost method is similar to most aggregate cost methods in that the larger the fund, the smaller the normal cost. It is dissimilar from the other aggregate cost methods in that the prime aggregate concept, ΣpvB, is missing.

8.1.8 Aggregate

This cost method is characterized by

$$TNC \cdot \ddot{a}^s = \sum pvB - F.$$

The Aggregate cost method has no supplemental liability and no supplemental cost; the future normal costs and the existing fund provide for all the pension benefits. At the inception of the plan the normal cost tends to be high because (a) there is no supplemental liability, (b) some of the participants may be near normal retirement age, and (c) the fund is small or zero. The normal cost tends to decrease as a percentage of payroll until the participants at the inception of the plan gradually cease to be active. The excess of contributions this year over normal cost (after allowing for interest) will increase the fund and hence will decrease future normal costs.

If the average age is low, gains/losses will be spread over many years. If the average age is high, gains/losses will be spread over the few years remaining until retirement. However, in most cases, the Aggregate method is very sound and very simple.

In the event of an early vested termination or retirement with considerable service before the inception of the plan, the value of the benefit may exceed the assets of the plan. If the cash payout is imminent the employer may need to make supplemental contributions, but if the cash payout is sufficiently deferred there may be no cash crisis.

DISCUSSION QUESTIONS

8-18 Prepare balance sheets for ILP and Aggregate given the following data:

pvB (active)	=	$200,000
pvB (retired)	=	100,000
UAL (ILP)	=	50,000

8-19 Aggregate normal cost is usually higher than EAN normal cost. Construct a scenario where the reverse is true.

8.1.9 Frozen Initial Liability

This cost method is summarized by the equation

$$TNC \cdot \ddot{a}^s = \sum pvB - F - FIL.$$

This method has a normal cost which is lower than the Aggregate normal cost initially but identical to the Aggregate normal cost ultimately (when the frozen initial liability disappears).

If the initial unfunded liability is calculated using Unit Credit, the normal costs will be higher than if the initial liability is calculated using Entry Age Normal. The Unit Credit version is sometimes called **Frozen-Attained-Age**, or Attained Age Normal with FIL, or just AAN, and the more common Entry Age version is sometimes called **Frozen-Entry-Age** or just Frozen Initial Liability.

Note that the methods of Sections 3.4 and 4.3 are both sometimes called Attained Age Normal. The aggregate form is more common than the individual form.

Historically, the initial unfunded liability was amortized after n years, and the unamortized balances each year were developed and "frozen" at the effective date. Today the unamortized balance is also reduced each time there is an excess contribution.

DISCUSSION QUESTIONS

8-20 Will excess interest and mortality gains decrease the normal cost or the frozen initial liability?

8-21 If the contribution exceeds the annual cost, will the excess contribution decrease next year's normal cost, the unfunded actuarial liability, or both? Would your answer be the same for the Aggregate method?

8-22 What are the reasons for the difference between Aggregate and FIL normal costs in, say, year seven?

8.1.10 Plan Termination Cost Method

The **Plan Termination cost method** contemplates the termination of all plan participants on the valuation date. The plan is then responsible for all benefits accruing from service prior to the valuation date. This liability is called the **plan termination liability**.

For retired participants, the plan termination liability is the present value of the future benefits. For active participants, it is the present value of the accrued benefits, so that

$$AL_x = B_x \times \frac{D_r}{D_x} \cdot \ddot{a}_r^{(12)}.$$

To calculate the present value of the deferred benefit, we must discount $\ddot{a}_r^{(12)}$ with interest and mortality only. The accrued benefit will be paid at the normal retirement age regardless of whether or not decrements other than death occur between valuation and normal retirement. For example, if an employee becomes disabled sometime between valuation and normal retirement, he will not receive any disability benefits since the plan has already been terminated, and will only begin receiving benefits at normal retirement age. Furthermore, this method does not take account of future withdrawals or salary adjustments. Early retirement is occasionally allowed in cases of long service. If a final five year average benefit is terminated, the accrued benefit is based on the final five year average compensation at termination. There is no normal cost after the valuation date because the plan is paid up.

When a pension plan terminates, annuities may be purchased from an insurance company to cover all benefits for active and non-active participants. If the amount in the plan fund is equal to the insurance company single premium, then the plan will be able to exactly meet the cost of all future benefit payouts. If the premium is greater than the fund, then the employer must cover the shortfall, make a claim on the guarantee fund, or reduce the benefits. If there is a surplus, it may be used in some cases, in whole or in part, to partially index the benefits for inflation after retirement only, or both before and after retirement.

The earlier cost methods are associated with ongoing actuarial work. Wherever the possibility of plan termination arises, however, the cost method of this section must be contemplated.

DISCUSSION QUESTIONS

8-23   Compare and contrast the Plan Termination cost method with Unit Credit. Would the interest assumption be the same for both valuations?

8-24   Show the relationships among the cost method, the normal cost, the supplemental cost, the contributions, and the pension legislation.

8-25   Is the actuarial work with the aggregate methods simpler or more complicated than with the individual methods? Why?

8-26   What are the pros and cons of using a method with a supplemental liability?

8.1.11 Aggregate Entry Age Normal

The normal cost for all active participants is such that

$$TNC \cdot \frac{\sum \dfrac{{}^s N_e - {}^s N_r}{{}^s D_e} \cdot S_e}{\sum S_e} = \sum pv_e B.$$

The $\sum pvB$ term is included with this cost method as it is with all aggregate cost methods. The pvB for retired participants and the value of the fund do not affect the normal cost.

The same normal cost is used for all entry ages, and is comparatively low because the pension costs are spread over the entire working lifetimes. A supplemental liability based on past service is calculated at plan inception.

8.1.12 Employee Contributions

If employee contributions are not deductible in computing employee taxable income, they are generally considered to be unattractive; however, this unattractiveness is more than offset by the absence of tax on the interest earned on the accumulated contributions over a long period of time (see Section 8.4.2 on Tax Assistance).

Contributory plans are much more complicated to administer, but employer normal costs are lower (see Example 6.31). Employee contributions are deductible under the Canadian Income Tax Act, and, consequently, contributory plans are more common in Canada than in the United States.

In many cases, employees making contributions have more interest in the plan, in their future pensions, and in their preretirement benefits. Sometimes the withdrawal benefits are quite small in noncontributory plans.

8.1.13 Employer Contributions

Employer contributions (with all cost methods) are usually equal to the annual cost, with an allowance for interest, but they may be higher or lower. Low employer cash flow might suggest lower contributions (this year), whereas a desire for lower income taxes (this year) might suggest higher employer contributions. The contribution limits are contained in the pension legislation. The Funding Standard Account under ERISA is a demonstration of the limits.

8.2 Alternatives

8.2.1 Choice of Method

The following factors affect the choice of the actuarial cost method:

(1)   Age and salary distribution
(2)   Anticipated growth of the work force
(3)   Withdrawal rates
(4)   Career average or final average benefits
(5)   Level dollar or level percentage of payroll cost
(6)   Desire for tax deductions
(7)   Need for cash in the business
(8)   Availability of cash for the pension plan
(9)   Past service liability at inception of plan
(10) Pension expense in the employer income statement
(11) Participant security
(12) Number of participants
(13) Early retirement options

For example, a new business with above average prospects might wish to have low initial costs because of a greater ability to pay later. A large business might prefer the predictability of EAN (level percent) to the greater unpredictability of projected unit credit.

An old business with a high past service liability at the inception of a new pension plan might find the aggregate method too expensive, and might prefer the spreading of greater past service costs under EAN or FIL (EAN) to the spreading of lesser past service costs under FIL (AAN).

One way to compare costs would be to work out the normal cost and supplemental cost at inception and at five-year intervals assuming no new entrants (the closed group approach), or assuming new entrants (open group), or both.

A business with good profits and good cash flow might prefer higher early funding, whereas a business with a current need for cash and high future anticipated profits might prefer lower early funding. A small business would be unlikely to choose the Aggregate or FIL methods; a large business would hardly choose the Individual Aggregate method.

8.2.2 Actuarial Valuations

Actuarial valuations of pension plans are performed every year or two years or three years in the United States and Canada for the following reasons:

(1) To compute the normal cost and actuarial liability
(2) To compute the minimum, maximum, and recommended contributions for the next three years
(3) To compute the expense for each year for accounting purposes
(4) To comply with pension legislation
(5) To provide information to plan participants and share-holders
(6) To compute assets, liabilities and surplus in a manner appropriate to the circumstances, in connection with a contemplated wind-up, sale, or merger

8.2.3 Alternative Liabilities

For the same age, compensation, and service, there are differences in the bases for (a) the ongoing actuarial liability, (b) the value of the withdrawal benefit, and (c) the plan termination liability. The differences are related to the following factors.

Interest rate. Item (a) is based on a long-term assumption, with a small weight given to current rates of interest; items (b) and (c) give a larger weight to current rates of interest.

Inflation. This may be fully included in the salary scale assumption before retirement, and there may be a partial allowance for inflation after retirement for item (a). For items (b) and (c), there are usually no allowances for future inflation or salary increases.

Vesting. Item (a) may involve a probability of vesting; item (b) may in some cases involve no vesting and hence no withdrawal benefit; item (c) will be based on full vesting where required by legislation.

Cost method. Items (b) and (c) are usually based on the accrued benefit and the Traditional Unit Credit cost method. The general equation

$$TAL_x = \sum pvB - pvNC$$

is true for all actuarial cost methods, and the term $\sum pvB$ has the same value for all cost methods. Then if the normal cost is larger for one cost method than for another, the liability will consequently be smaller.

Funding. Item (b) may be reduced to the extent that funds are not available.   Item (c) may reflect the guarantees of the Pension Benefits Guarantee Corporation.

DISCUSSION QUESTION

8-27   Are future rates of withdrawal and mortality used in items (a), (b), and (c)?

8.2.4 Small and Large Plans

The examples in this text are based on a small number of plan participants. For large plans, computers are normally used. Software is available which applies the methods of this text to each and every participant. In order to be user friendly, the software may display a specimen plan on the screen which can then be tailored to the desired specifications. For example, the software may start with a retirement age of 65 which can be amended to a desired age of 62; the software may start with a table of withdrawal rates which can be replaced by alternative tables.   The valuation will be performed for the entire plan and for each participant, or for every twentieth participant, and the results can be checked by the methods of this text. The power of the computer means that alternative valuations can be produced to show the effect of using a different retirement age or withdrawal table or of making a change in any other factor.

Software is also available to provide great assistance in the administration of pension plans. Accrued and projected pension benefits, death and withdrawal benefits, accumulated employee contributions, and employee statements can be produced every year or more often.

8.2.5 Closed and Open Groups

Most pension valuations are performed on a closed group of participants, meaning those who are actually participating on the valuation date. To get a better idea about future cash flows, the actuary can make assumptions with regard to future new entrants and perform an open-group valuation at the end of, say, five, ten and fifteen years from the current valuation date.

Closed-group valuations are usually based on ongoing assumptions, but are sometimes based on the plan termination assumptions discussed in previous sections. Open-group valuations and plan termination valuations must always be clearly labeled to avoid confusion.

8.3 Concepts

In this section we will summarize and comment on many of the fundamental concepts encountered earlier in the text.

8.3.1 Pension Benefit

The pension benefit at retirement age in a defined benefit plan should be a suitable percentage of the final average preretirement salary. For example, a defined benefit of 70% of salary (including Social Security) is generally considered to be adequate and appropriate. This retirement benefit should accrue over the working lifetime.

The pension benefit in a defined contribution plan may turn out to be much larger, about the same, or much smaller than in a defined benefit plan if the investment experience is good, average, or poor, respectively. (See also Section 8.3.2.)

8.3.2 Inflation

Full (or at least partial) protection against the erosion of the purchasing power of the pension after retirement is very desirable for the participant. Provision for indexation is often made in the interest rate assumption. For example, if the plan provides indexation equal to or usually equal to the increase in the consumer price index, the actuary might use an interest rate net of inflation of 3% or 3.5%. For partial indexation, the actuary might use 4% or 5%. For no indexation, the actuary might use 6% or 7%.

A few plans also provide inflation protection in the after-termination, pre-retirement period.

8.3.3 Final Average Salary

Compared to a pension based on career average salary, a pension based on final average salary provides a much better link with preretirement income, and the allowance for inflation before retirement is much more complete. For example, if the CPI at age 60 is three times the CPI at age 35, the salary at age 60 can be expected to be roughly three times the salary at age 35, plus an appropriate amount for 25 years of merit increases. A pension based on final average salary would include an allowance for almost all of the preretirement inflation, whereas a pension based on career average salary would not include an allowance for a considerable proportion of the preretirement inflation.

8.3.4 Salary Scale

In many pension situations, a salary scale is necessary; it should be kept in mind that a simple scale (such as 5%) may possibly be too low for reasonable merit increases at the young ages, too high for reasonable merit increases at the older ages, and not responsive enough to changes in inflation.

8.3.5 Percent of Salary

Compared to level dollar, pension cost developed as a level percent of salary is a sounder concept.

8.3.6 Vesting

In defined contribution plans, vesting refers to the employer contributions. For example, a participant terminating with 60% vesting is entitled to 60% of the employer contributions with interest.

Participants also receive their own contributions with interest, and normally vesting is 100% at retirement.

In defined benefit plans, vesting refers to the defined benefit. For example, if the defined benefit is 2% of final average salary for each year of service, a participant terminating with 60% vesting is entitled to 60% of the accrued pension. The pension starting at the normal retirement date could be $.02S \times n \times .60$, where S is the final average salary at termination and n is the number of years from entry to termination. In many cases, the participant would be entitled to the deferred vested pension, the value at termination of the deferred vested pension, or, if contributory, the accumulated participant contributions, at the terminating participant's option.

The proportion of the defined benefit which is vested is spelled out in the plan document. The proportion of the defined benefit which is funded (on a cost method such as EAN) may be more than the value of proportion vested. If there is advance funding and if the actual terminations exceed the expected terminations, there will be an experience gain from terminations.

In some jurisdictions, full vesting is required after two years of service. In some plans, there is full or partial indexing for inflation after retirement; in a few plans, the deferred vested pension is indexed for inflation from termination to retirement.

8.3.7 Assumptions

Actual experience will not duplicate the actuarial assumptions, so gains or losses will arise and will normally be spread over future years subject to government regulations. The amount of, and the amortization of, *liability* gains/losses are quite different under the various cost methods. The amount of *asset* gain/loss is not so different under the various methods.

Many actuaries feel that actuarial assumptions should stand independently of the actuarial cost method. In other words, the long-term scenario should be set first, and then the pace of the funding should be selected.

Actuaries often use *best estimates* of mortality, interest, turnover, and salary. However, actuaries cannot foresee the future and a great deal of variability can be expected. If future experience should be worse than expected, participant security may be impaired, losses will be more common than gains, and erosion of the purchasing power of pensions will be harder to handle. For these reasons, plan sponsors often prefer realistically conservative assumptions. (See also Section 6.4.)

The actuarial cost method and the actuarial assumptions should be discussed and agreed with the plan sponsor. The experience gain or loss should be analyzed each year and the assumptions should be reviewed and changed if necessary.

8.3.8 Surplus

Surplus in a pension fund can (a) offset experience losses, (b) provide participant security, (c) fund early retirement windows, and (d) facilitate partial indexation or contribution holidays. The ownership of surplus should be part of the plan document. Surplus arises from good experience, but it can be greatly affected by actuarial assumptions and changes in actuarial assumptions.

8.3.9 Not Guaranteed

The premiums for traditional non-participating insurance products are guaranteed; if experience is good the insurer profits, and if experience is bad the insurer loses. Normal costs based on realistically conservative assumptions are often of a magnitude comparable to premiums, but they are *not* guaranteed. If experience is good the plan sponsor will normally gain through smaller subsequent costs; if experience is bad the subsequent costs will be larger.

8.3.10 Projected Benefit

Spreading the cost of the entire projected benefit (based on all years of service) over the entire working lifetime may be sounder than the accrued benefit approach which funds the past accruals without consideration of future accruals. Keep in mind, however, the effects of experience gains and losses.

8.3.11 New Entrants

If a participant enters the plan between time 0 and time 1 and receives pension credit for, say, six months of service, then AL_1 will quantify the EOY cost. This cost will be partially offset, or more than offset, by plan contributions. For example, if $AL_1 = .02S$, where S is the new entrant salary, and if the contributions for half a year are $.05S$, then the new entrant gain will be $.03S$. This gain or loss will be recognized immediately under a method such as Projected Unit Credit, but under, say, the Aggregate method the gain or loss will be spread in the usual manner. Because of starting salaries at starting ages, losses from new entrants are usually small and not estimated in advance but, of course, they could be if the actuary so desired.

8.3.12 Active and Retired Participants

Participants enter the plan, grow older, retire and die. A pension plan is dynamic and ever-changing.

Using individual cost methods, there is a normal cost for each active participant but no normal cost for retired participants. The actuarial liability for each participant increases and reaches a maximum at retirement; it then decreases to zero at death. The actuarial liability for the plan is the sum of the actuarial liabilities for all active and retired participants.

Using aggregate cost methods, there is a normal cost for the plan as a whole, which is based on the excess of pvB for active and retired participants at the valuation date over the assets on hand for the benefit of active and retired participants.

For individual and aggregate cost methods, we must consider supplemental liabilities which arise and eventually run off to zero. The normal cost must be recalculated almost every year as conditions change. We must include terminated vested participants who are still part of the plan, and we must exclude terminated participants who are no longer part of the plan.

8.3.13 Early Retirement

An employee, say, age 58 may elect to retire seven years early, and may or may not be replaced by a new entrant. There will be a net salary savings and a net change in productivity. If the pension plan provides an early retirement subsidy or a Social Security bridge, a liability will be created upon early retirement which may require amortization. To the extent that the age 58 employee is not receiving salary *increases* and if the new entrant *is* receiving salary increases, then the early retirement will trigger seven unexpected salary increases (with smaller effects even beyond the seven years). Finally, early retirment participants will experience a drop in total income until age 65 and probably beyond.

8.3.14 Trusteed and Insured Plans

Pension fund assets are carefully protected in order to ensure participant security and to meet taxation and regulatory requirements. In some pension plans, the normal cost and actuarial liability are guaranteed by a life insurance company to provide the promised benefits; these are called **fully insured plans**. Some pension plans have limited insurance company guarantees. Some pension plans place retired life assets (but not active life assets) with insurance companies on a fully guaranteed basis, but most pension fund assets, by far, are trusteed without benefit guarantees. This means that if experience is worse than expected the unfunded liability must be made up, usually by the employer; if experience is better than expected, the surplus, if any, can be used in any manner specified in the plan document. Most of the actuarial cost methods are not suitable for fully insured plans.

8.3.15 Funding

The funding of the defined benefit in private pension plans should be spread over the working years (while the pension plan is operating). The reasons for this are that (a) the funds built up before retirement provide security for the participant, (b) the annual cost of the pension should be related to the annual productivity of the working participant, (c) the cost before retirement is discounted for interest and is usually acceptable, whereas a postretirement cost is sometimes unmanageable, and (d) preretirement funding is usually tax effective.

What happens if there are *ad hoc* cost-of-living increases in the monthly pension benefit and if, for highly salaried participants, the monthly pension benefit is such that the annual cost is not deductible? Sometimes there is inadequate funding, but the reasons for funding in the previous paragraph should be contemplated. Another example of little or no funding is mentioned in Section 8.4.1.

8.3.16 Cost Methods

The various cost methods have a considerable effect on the *incidence* of cost but not on the ultimate cost. Employer contributions are influenced by (a) the cost method used in the actuarial valuation, (b) the availability of employer funds, (c) deductibility for tax purposes, and (d) the desire for participant security.

Standard pension terminology refers to **spread gain cost methods** as those which automatically spread the actuarial gain or loss through the calculation of the normal cost. For example, with FIL and Aggregate,

$$NC_0 \cdot \ddot{a} = pvB - UAL_0 - F_0.$$

If the value of the average annuity is 15, then NC_0 will be $10 lower if there is an implicit gain of $150 at time 0 than if there is no gain or loss at time 0. The implicit gain is spread over the future working lifetimes of the participants. **Immediate gain cost methods** are those which recognize the explicit gain or loss through a comparison of the actual and expected unfunded actuarial liabilities (*e.g.*, EAN and PUC), and which amortize the gain or loss as a portion of the supplemental cost.

8.3.17 Expensing vs. Funding

The comments in several of the previous sections refer to the funding of a pension plan.

The accounting profession in the U.S. and Canada, in the interest of comparability between different businesses and between different years in the same business, requires the use of the Projected Unit Credit cost method by the actuary for the purpose of calculating the **pension plan expense** for inclusion in the employer's statement of revenue and expense. In the U.S., this matter is dealt with in a Statement of Financial Accounting Standards (SFAS 87), which was promulgated by the Financial Accounting Standards Board.

The accounting profession decided to standardize on the Projected Unit Credit method because it was felt that the amounts of annual pension accrual under this method best corresponded to those calculated from the plan document and from a traditional accounting viewpoint.

If the annual contribution based on the funding method is higher (lower) than the annual expense based on of the expensing method, an asset (liability) will develop on the balance sheet of the employer based on the accumulated difference.

8.3.18 Financial Reporting

Financial reporting means full and accurate disclosure of all significant matters, and this concept is receiving a great deal of attention in all areas of actuarial science including life, health, casualty, and pensions.

In pensions, salary assumptions are now more realistic, market values and asset matching are receiving more attention, gains and losses by source are being disclosed, and more valuations are being performed annually. Market values, and hence realized and unrealized capital gains and losses, and rates of return are also receiving more attention.

DISCUSSION QUESTIONS

8-28 Is the theory of pension funding and pension expensing appropriate for other postretirement benefits such as life insurance or health insurance? Why?

8-29 Is the computation of experience gains and losses by source, as discussed in Chapter 5, equally important in the actuarial areas of policyholder dividends, individual life and health, and group life and health?

8-30 Is the computation of the cost of benefit changes and policy options, as discussed in Chapters 6 and 7, important in other actuarial areas?

8.4 Government Aspects

Governments have a major involvement with pension plans in many ways. In this section we consider the following topics:

(1) Social pension plans
(2) Tax assistance for private pension funds
(3) Protection of private pension plan members
(4) Public service pension plans

8.4.1 Social Pension Plans

Social plans are sponsored by the governments and provide a floor of protection for almost everyone on a mandatory basis. (The establishment of a private pension plan is voluntary and the benefits are in addition to, or integrated with, social plans.) There is a transfer of funds each year to provide the legal entitlements of the beneficiaries of the social plans, and the funds come in large part from payroll taxes and income taxes. While funds are on hand for the benefits required to be paid in the next several months, there is often very little advance funding. As the population ages, the number of beneficiaries increases rapidly while the number of workers increases more slowly or possibly decreases. When the cost per worker is increasing rapidly, the funding method, the level of benefits, and the retirement age must be reconsidered. For example, slow increases in the retirement age may lead to fewer beneficiaries, more workers, and a lower cost per worker. In the United States, Germany, Norway, Sweden, and Denmark, the retirement age for social security is being increased to above age 65.

If the payroll tax in the future will be higher than today, it may be far-sighted to increase the payroll tax today and to lower the future tax to an actuarially equivalent long-term level. This means putting money aside today for the future. It is tempting to spend this money on increased benefits instead of putting it aside, but it is important to realize that this would compound the future problem.

To understand why the cost of private pension plans on a funded basis is less than the ultimate cost of social plans on a pay-as-you-go basis, let us consider the benefit in one typical year. Consider a benefit entitlement of $1000 at age 75. Using pay-as-you-go, the cost is the same $1000, with little or no discounting for interest. If the funding is in a typical working year, say at age 45, the cost is $1000(1+i)^{-30} = \$308$, using 4% interest. Generalizing, we can say that a cost of $308 in each working year may purchase a benefit of roughly $1000 in each retirement year, whereas the pay-as-you-go cost may be three times as high. Whereas the private plan enjoys the discounting, it is almost impossible to set up a social plan on a fully funded basis, and it is even more difficult to switch from pay-as-you-go to fully funded.

Canadian Social Plans. Old Age Security provides about $400 per month (in 1995) to those over age 65, and the amount is increased four times per year in accordance with the Consumer Price Index. For those earning

$55,000 per year, a small amount of the OAS benefit is "clawed back" and the clawback grades linearly to 100% for those earning over $80,000 per year. Many years ago OAS commenced at age 70, and perhaps in many years this age will again be approached. The funding is from general revenue.

The Canada Pension Plan provides 25% of final average indexed earnings up to the Average Industrial Wage, which was about $2700 per month in 1993. The resulting payroll cost was 2.5% for employers and 2.5% for employees in 1993, but increasing each year and probably doubling by 2016. Benefits normally start at age 65 but can start up to five years earlier or later with a reduction or increase of 6% per year. Under age 65, retirement is required in order to commence CPP, but reemployment is permitted. Full CPI increases are given each January. As well as pension benefits, the CPP provides survivor, disability, and small death benefits. The Quebec Pension Plan is very similar and replaces the CPP in Quebec.

CPP, QPP and net OAS benefits are taxable income. In 1996, the maximum combined benefit was about $1122 from age 65, and the cost was roughly equivalent to 8% of payroll.

Provincial health plans cover all Canadian residents. The funding is from general revenue and payroll taxes.

OASDI. The Old-Age, Survivors, and Disability Insurance program had its genesis in 1935. The benefit is 90% of the first portion, 32% of the second portion, and 15% of the balance of the worker's average indexed monthly earnings. Full, or almost full, CPI increases are given each January. In January 1990, the average monthly benefit for retired workers was $566 and the maximum benefit for a worker retiring at age 65 was $975. The normal retirement age is 65 before the year 2000 and will increase to age 67 for years after 2021. A delayed retirement credit is available to workers retiring between normal retirement age and age 70, and an early retire-ment debit is applied to workers retiring between normal retirement age and age 62; for example, the debit from age 67 to age 62 will be 30%.

There is an earnings test under age 70. Up to half of Social Security benefits are taxable income. The payroll cost in 1993 for OASDI was 6.20% of earnings not in excess of $57,600 for a worker and the same amount for the employer. In addition to retirement benefits, there are also survivor and disability benefits under the plan. Medicare and Medicaid provide benefits to the elderly and the needy, respectively.

8.4.2 Tax Assistance

Section 8.4.1 described the various social programs sponsored by governments in both the U.S. and Canada. These plans are funded on a pay-as-you-go basis with contributions/taxes paid by wage earners and transferred to the retired population.

Governments also encourage voluntary, funded retirement programs. The *primary* encouragement consists of tax sheltering the investment earnings of qualified pension funds in the U.S. and registered pension funds in Canada. Such plans have accumulated large pools of assets and have become a major factor on investment markets in the U.S. and Canada. For example, over 100 pension funds in North America have assets of over one billion dollars. The *secondary* encouragement consists of the deductibility (within limits) of qualified/registered contributions. However, these contributions and the investment earnings thereon are taxable at payout. Allowing for the time value of money, we can see the offset. The *tertiary* encouragement occurs when the tax rate at payout is lower. There is an offset, however, when the rate at payout is higher.

The following two examples are designed to show that the primary encouragement is huge, whereas the secondary and tertiary encouragements are comparatively trivial. The assumptions for the examples are as follows:

Before-tax Earned Income:	$1000
Tax Rate at Payout (TRAP):	31% for Example 8.1; 41% for 8.2
Tax Rate before Payout:	36%
Interest Earned:	9% before tax (5.76% after tax)
Inflation:	5%
Time from Contribution to Payout:	30 years
After-tax Payout:	Both tax-assisted and non-tax-assisted

Note that 30 years represents the duration from a typical contribution age, such as 45, to an average retiree age, such as 75.

EXAMPLE 8.1

Based on a TRAP of 31%, find both the tax-assisted and non-tax-assisted payouts, and analyze the tax loss to the government.

SOLUTION   The tax-assisted payout is

$$1000 \times (1.09)^{30} \times .69 = 9154.70,$$

compared to the non-tax-assisted payout of

$$1000 \times .64 \times (1.0576)^{30} = 3434.18.$$

The government foregoes tax of $9154.70 - 3434.18 = \$5720.52$. This represents 62% of the tax-assisted payout. We can divide the "encouragement" of $5720.52 at payout into its three components:

PRIMARY: $1000 \times .64\left[(1.09)^{30} - (1.0576)^{30}\right] = \quad \$5057.13$

SECONDARY: $1000 \times .36\left[(1.09)^{30} - (1.09)^{30}\right] = \quad 0.00$

TERTIARY: $1000 \times (1.09)^{30} \times (.36 - .31) = \quad \underline{663.38}$

$\phantom{TERTIARY: 1000 \times (1.09)^{30} \times} \$5720.51$

□

EXAMPLE 8.2

Repeat Example 8.1 using a TRAP of 41%.

| **SOLUTION** | This time the tax-assisted payout is $7827.93. The non-tax-assisted payout is still $3434.18. The government foregoes tax of $4393.75, which is 56% of the tax-assisted payout. Recognizing the time value of money to payout, we analyze the savings in its three components:

PRIMARY: $1000 \times .64\left[(1.09)^{30} - (1.0576)^{30}\right] = \quad \$5057.13$

SECONDARY: $1000 \times .36\left[(1.09)^{30} - (1.09)^{30}\right] = \quad 0.00$

TERTIARY: $1000 \times (1.09)^{30} \times (.36 - .41) = \quad \underline{-663.38}$

$\phantom{TERTIARY: 1000 \times (1.09)^{30} \times} \$4393.75$

We are not surprised to find a negative tertiary component in this case, because people who make substantial provision for retirement tend to develop in the direction of higher taxes. The total of the secondary and tertiary components, in either example, is very small.   □

We can draw the following conclusions from Examples 8.1 and 8.2, using the 30-year duration from contribution to payout:

- The tax-assisted result is usually more than twice the non-tax-assisted result.

- The government foregoes tax of over 50% of the tax-assisted payout.

- The deductibility of the contribution is roughly counterbalanced by the taxability of the payout. This allows for the time value of money. However, note the delay in the receipt of tax on the contribution by the Treasury, and the delay in the payment of tax from the time the income is earned to the time of benefit receipt.

We conclude this section with some comments on inflation, taxes, investment income, short durations, and variations.

Inflation.   In Examples 8.1 and 8.2, we started with $1000 before tax. After 30 years of 5% inflation and a TRAP of either 31% or 41%, we ended with an after-tax result.   We can translate our inflated after-tax investment and the tax foregone to non-inflated dollars by dividing by $(1.05)^{30}$. A summary of our results is given in the following table:

	Results after 30 Years		
	Investment	**Tax Foregone**	**Tax Foregone (% of Investment)**
Non-tax-assisted	$3434		
Tax-assisted	7827	$4394	56%
	Results in Non-inflated Dollars		
Non-tax-assisted	$ 795		
Tax-assisted	1811	$1016	56%

Taxes.   The government foregoes taxes while the taxpayer saves taxes in the same amount. If no taxes were foregone, there would be much less investment. The tax assistance encourages saving with a positive impact on the economy. In addition, it encourages people to save for retirement, which makes them less dependent on the government when they retire. It has been suggested that governments could generate additional tax revenue by taxing the investment income which is currently accumulating tax free. A large tax would defeat the purpose of encouraging savings, but a small excise tax would still encourage retirement savings. The after-tax result (compared with the non-tax-assisted result) would be very attractive.

Investment Income. In these examples, we considered investment income to be interest. Non-interest investment income is often taxed at a lower rate, and would decrease the difference between the tax-assisted and the non-tax-assisted results. Other non-tax-assisted examples can easily be constructed.

Short Durations. Many qualified/registered investments are cashed out after a few years. The government objective of encouraging pensions is usually not achieved in such cases. But tax is still foregone if the wage earner is in a lower tax bracket in the year of cashout.

Variations. The assumptions of Examples 8.1 and 8.2 can be modified to cope with any desired situation. For example, using a TRAP of 31% and an excise tax of 7% of the interest earned net of inflation, we have the following results:

Interest earned net of inflation: $.09 - .05 = .04$
Interest earned net of excise tax: $.09 - .07(.04) = .0872$
Non-tax-assisted result: $1000 \times .64 \times (1.0576)^{30} = 3434$
Tax-assisted result: $1000(1.09)^{30} \times .64 = 8491$
Result with excise tax: $1000(1.0872)^{30} \times .64 = 7861$

	Result after 30 years	Net Rate of Interest Earned after Excise Tax, Income Tax on Interest, and Inflation
Non-tax-assisted	$3434	$.0576 - .05 = .0076$
Tax-assisted	8491	$.0900 - .05 = .0400$
Net of Excise Tax	7861	$.0872 - .05 = .0372$

The following numerical results can be observed:

- The accumulated excise tax in this example is $8491 - 7861$, or $630 per original investment of $1000.

- The tax assistance with no excise tax amounts to $.0900 - .0576$, or 3.24% of assets each year.

- The tax assistance net of excise tax amounts to $.0872 - .0576$, or 2..96% of assets each year.

The following opinions can then be stated:

- The non-tax-assisted result is unacceptably low because of the tax on the inflationary growth.

- The difference between the tax-assisted and the non-tax-assisted results is unacceptably high.

- A low rate of excise tax provides tax revenue and gives a result much closer to the tax-assisted result than to the non-tax-assisted result. (See Aitken [1].)

8.4.3 Regulation and Protection

The tax assistance discussed in the previous section cannot be unlimited. There are limits on funding, contributions, eligible salary, and benefits provided. The regulations are to be found in the Employee Retirement Income Security Act and in various sections of the Internal Revenue Code of the U.S., and in the Income Tax Act of Canada.

In addition to the limits on tax assistance, there are regulations for the protection of participants dealing with minimum contributions, minimum funding, minimum vesting, annual reporting, triennial actuarial valuations, and trusteeship of pension funds. In the U.S., the protection of participants is to be found in ERISA, the regulations put out by the Department of Labor, and the rules and regulations put out by IRS. In the event of bankruptcy or the wind-up of the pension plan, the pension benefits within limits are guaranteed by the Pension Benefits Guarantee Corporation. Federal regulation of retirement plans preempts state regulation. In Canada, each province has a Pension Benefits Act which is administered by a Pension Commission. There is a federal Pension Benefits Standards Act for the benefit of participants in federally regulated industries such as communications and banking. Pension guarantees are included only in the Ontario Act. Premiums to support the Guarantee Fund are based on the number of participants and the size of the unfunded liability.

For the pension funds, a trust agreement or an insurance contract is necessary. There are reasonable investment restrictions; for example, in Canada 80% of the funds (on a cost basis) must be Canadian and not more than 20% may be foreign. In both countries, a cost certificate, an actuarial valuation report, and a plan document are required; the latter must describe who can participate, benefit accrual, vesting, and many other items. Any item viewed as discriminatory under the Charter of Rights in the U.S. or Section 15 of the Canadian Constitution could result in a loss of qualification or registration status. Some discrimination by age is allowed; employees under the minimum age are not required to join the plan to avoid excessive administration costs, and pensions are required to commence by a maximum age to prevent undue loss of taxation revenue.

There are minimum vesting requirements. In Canada, most provinces require 100% vesting after two years. The United States provides a choice for new plans of (a) 100% vesting after five years, or (b) 20% vesting after two years grading linearly to 100% vesting after six years.

In both countries, (a) participants must receive a summary of the plan provisions, (b) annual reports must be filed which provide information on contributions and contributors, and (c) cost certificates must be filed for defined benefit plans to control underfunding and overfunding.

It is necessary to be aware of the regulations to resolve problems in the following areas:

(1) Allowable cost methods
(2) Amortization periods for supplemental liabilities
(3) Contributions issues
    (a) Minimum contributions required
    (b) Deductible limits
(4) Benefit issues
    (a) Maximum allowed
    (b) Integration with Social Security
    (c) Split of benefits on marriage dissolution
(5) Discrimination issues
    (a) Defined contribution plans
    (b) Contributions for older ages
    (c) Defined benefit plans
(6) Actuarial assumptions (in the U.S.)
    (a) Interest rate
    (b) Salary scale
    (c) Loading
    (d) Mortality
(7) Asset issues
    (a) Actuarial value of assets
    (b) Investment rules
    (c) Interest assumptions
    (d) Interest credits

(8)   Plan document issues, including communication with partici-
      pants
(9)   Plan termination issues
      (a)   Pension benefit guarantees
      (b)   Pension benefit guarantee premiums
      (c)   Wind-up benefits
      (d)   Distribution of surplus on wind-up
(10) Penalties

This section discusses the triple role of government in pension matters
in the United States and Canada only.   Pensions are important in other
countries as well; for example, pension assets in the United Kingdom
exceed six hundred billion dollars.   Plan administrators have complex
duties and fiduciary responsibilities.   Accountants have an important role
concerning the effect of pensions on the balance sheet and income
statement of the plan sponsor.   More and more questions are being directed
to lawyers, including the treatment of pensions in marriage dissolution and
pension surplus in the event of pension plan wind-up.   Last but not least is
the need for expert investment management.   Pension actuaries have an
interactive role with many audiences.

8.4.4 Public Service Pension Plans

A very important actuarial principle is that of **equity**.   It is easy to think of
hundreds of examples of equity and inequity.   Most actuarial solutions to
actuarial problems keep inequity to a minimum.
      In the matter of compensation, we submit that less inequity would be
desirable in the private and in the public sectors.   If we compare the public
sector with the private sector, we should expect to find rough equity in
salaries, pensions, and other benefits.
      We confine our attention here to defined benefit pension plans.   The
following areas are considered:

(1)   The defined benefit
(2)   Indexing
(3)   Survivorship benefits
(4)   Early retirement benefits
(5)   Participation
(6)   Scope of coverage

There is a great deal of variation in the public sector, but even more in the private sector. Comparing the two sectors, it appears that public pensions are more generous in all of the above areas. A brief discussion of each area follows.

The Defined Benefit. In the private sector, the defined benefit is often 2% of salary for each year of service. But often the unit is less than 2%, say 1 3/4% or 1 1/2%. The unit is almost never more than 2%. Salary is defined in the plan document to mean final average salary in many cases, and career average salary in many cases. Many employers have defined benefit plans, many have defined contribution plans, and many have no pension plans at all.

In the public sector, final average salary defined benefit plans are very common, and career average plans are not common. Defined contribution pension plans and the absence of pension plans are not common. Service with different employers in the public service areas is often additive for pension benefit purposes. The 2% unit is very common, and smaller units are uncommon. Elected officials sometimes enjoy a unit which is much larger than 2%, such as 5% of final average salary for the first 15 years of service. The cost of such a plan can be as much as 30% of current salary. Inequity results when approval and implementation of pension plans are not at arm's length.

Indexing. The indexing of pension benefits each year, using the Consumer Price Index, is designed to avoid the loss of purchasing power. Full, or nearly full, indexing is common in the public sector and much less common in the private sector. Private sector employers do not like to make a commitment in the pension plan document to unknown costs. *Ad hoc* pension increases are common. Often they counteract about half of the erosion from inflation.

Survivorship Benefits. These benefits are common in the public sector. For example, half of the defined benefit is payable to the spouse if the participant dies first. If each partner has an adequate pension, the survivorship feature is excessive and the cost may amount to roughly 1% of payroll. In the private sector, survivorship benefits are available, but often there is an actuarial reduction in the defined benefit. For example, instead of receiving 100% of the defined benefit, the participant can elect to receive 90% of the defined benefit and the spouse will then receive half of the 90% of the defined benefit if the participant dies first.

Early Retirement Benefits.   These benefits are common in the private sector.   But for each year of early retirement, there is an extra year of pension, and hence there is a reduction in the (otherwise deferred) pension benefit.   In some social plans and in many private plans, the reduction is 6% for each year of early retirement.   With a 6% reduction, the gain or loss to the pension plan is very small.   Many private plans have a 4% reduction.   This means that there is a fair-sized loss to the plan for each early retirement.   A smaller reduction may be used when downsizing is necessary.

Many public plans have no reduction, subject to age and service requirements.   For example, the pension plan Act may allow retirement with no reduction when age and service add up to ninety.   The early retirement cost can be measured by the number of pension dollars paid out before age 65 (for which no work is done).   Or the cost can be measured by calculating the percentage of payroll required to provide the benefit. This may work out to be roughly 1% of payroll.

Participation.   The participation rate is often 100% of employees in the public sector.   In the private sector, participation is 100% in many defined benefit plans, less than 100% in many defined contribution plans, and, of course, many employers have no plans at all.   The average, very roughly, in the private sector might be 50% participation.

Scope of Coverage.   Public sector plan coverage is very broad in some cases.   For example, health and hospital workers and teachers and judges are included in some jurisdictions, but not in others.

Equity between sectors and actuarial cost have often received insufficient attention.

Answers to Text Exercises

Chapter 2

2-1   78,000

2-2   (a) 33,125   (b) 3,047,490   (c) 3,180,000   (d) 3,312,510

2-3   (a)   (b) 6720

	Smith	Brown	Jones	Green
NC_0	100	680	0	0
AL_0	0	6120	2200	13,400

2-4   405,339

2-5   2912

2-6   1071

2-7   6269

Chapter 3

3-1 $4200 \dfrac{N_{55}^{(12)}}{N_{20} - N_{55}} + 2400 \dfrac{N_{60}^{(12)}}{N_{40} - N_{60}} + 1800 \dfrac{N_{65}^{(12)}}{N_{50} - N_{65}}$

3-2   II and III

3-3   75,790

3-4   29,385

3-5   I and II

3-6   597

3-7   2108

3-8   3699

3-9   5985

3-10   54,196

3-11   9995

3-12   2520

3-13   6362

3-14   9432

3-15   14,498

3-16   177

3-17   48,006

3-18   38,378

3-19   47,849

Chapter 4

4-1   4130

4-2   897

4-3   12,281

4-4   3805

4-5   1322; 0

4-6   4100

4-7   1515

4-8   19,056

4-9   3324

4-10   5650

4-11   2676;   15,000;   0

4-12   (38,793)

4-13   11,392

4-14   91,333

4-15   15,551

4-16   11,391

4-17   Unit Credit, Entry Age Normal, same, same

4-18   15,167

4-19   680

4-20   64,764

4-21   8400

4-22   11,446,713

4-23   159

4-24   26,970

4-25   3955

4-26   922

4-27   2300

4-28   3571

Chapter 5

5-1   Loss of 14,250

5-2   Loss of 1475

5-3   Loss of 6000

5-4   Gain of 14,500

5-5   Gain of 1304

5-6   2644

5-7   26,450

5-8   1000

5-9   Loss of 2966.67

5-10   476.67

5-11   Gain of 6625

5-12   Loss of 188

5-13   708

5-14   260

5-15   27,300;   33,000

5-16   415,639

5-17   1021

5-18   8796

5-19   10,208

5-20   79,659

5-21   4667

5-22   Gain of 3979

5-23   1762

5-24   2123

5-25   51,060

5-26   1070

5-27   1992

5-28   78,440

5-29   3783

5-30   5.76%

5-31   91,489

5-32   1485

5-33   309,503

5-34   151,236

5-35   6041

5-36   1688

5-37   9400

5-38   5153

5-39   Yes; 0

5-40   36,598

Chapter 6

6-1   3.992%

6-2   1783

6-3   201

6-4   3576

6-5   13,600

6-6   (a) $600\dfrac{N_{65}^{(12)}}{D_{45}} \cdot \dfrac{N_{40} - N_{45}}{N_{40} - N_{65}}$ (b) $600\dfrac{N_{65}^{(12)}}{N_{45} - N_{65}}$

6-7   5793

6-8   1,575,341

6-9   696.89

6-10   580

6-11   10,996

6-12   275

6-13   All

6-14   I and III

6-15   98

6-16   (C)

6-17   397,860

6-18   All

6-19   All

6-20   Both

6-21   1140

6-22   350

6-23   4230;   366

6-24   1230

6-25   1230

6-26   237,857

Chapter 7

7-1   562.50

7-2   679.80

7-3   90.77

7-4   .75

7-5   778

7-6   109,390

7-7   12.23%

7-8   8.35%;   8.81%

7-9   All

7-10   2799

7-11   1450

7-12   II only

7-13   649.89

7-14   11,692

7-15   1281

Bibliography

1. Aitken, W.H., "The Taxation of Pensions," *PCIA*, XXII (1990), No. 3, 288.

2. Anderson, A.W., *Pension Mathematics for Actuaries* (Second Edition). Winsted: ACTEX Publications, Inc., 1992.

3. Berin, B.N., *The Fundamentals of Pension Mathematics*. Schaumburg: Society of Actuaries, 1989.

4. Bleakney, T.P. and J.D. Pacelli, *Benefit Design in Public Employee Retirement Systems*. Chicago: Government Finance Officers Association, 1994.

5. Bowers, N.R., *et al.*, *Actuarial Mathematics*. Schaumburg: Society of Actuaries, 1986.

6. Jordan, C.W., *Life Contingencies* (Second Edition). Schaumburg: Society of Actuaries, 1967.

7. McGill, D.M. and D.S. Grubbs, *Fundamentals of Private Pensions* (Sixth Edition). Homewood: Richard D. Irwin, Inc., 1989.

8. Mercer Bulletin, William M. Mercer Company, Toronto, ON, Canada, September 1993.

9. Parmenter, M.M., *Theory of Interest and Life Contingencies, with Pension Applications: A Problem-Solving Approach* (Revised Edition). Winsted: ACTEX Publications, Inc., 1990.

10. Winklevoss, H.E., *Pension Mathematics with Numerical Illustrations* (Second Edition). Philadelphia: University of Pennsylvania Press, 1993.

Index of Notation

This index lists all symbols specific to this text, and identifies the page on which each symbol first appears and is defined. The symbols are alphabetical by principal letter. Note that standard actuarial symbols, such as ℓ_x, p_x, q_x, d_x, D_x, N_x, $\ddot{a}_x$, $\ddot{a}_{\overline{n|}}$, and so on, are not included in this index.

Subject Index